Austin-Healey 3000

Road Test Portfolio

Compiled by
R M Clarke

ISBN 9781783180394

BROOKLANDS BOOKS LTD.
P.O. BOX 146, COBHAM,
SURREY, KT11 1LG. UK
sales@brooklands-books.com

www.brooklandsbooks.com

AH3RP

4T5/2333

ROAD TEST SERIES

Abarth Road Test Portfolio 1950-1971
AC Cars 1904-2011
AC Ace Aceca Road Test Portfolio 1953-1962
AC & Cobra 1962-2011
Alfa Romeo A Brooklands Portfolio 1920-1940
Alfa Romeo Giulietta Gold Portfolio 1954-1965
Alfa Romeo Giulia Berlina Lim. Edit. Extra 1962-76
Alfa Romeo Giulia Coupes Lim. Edit. Ultra 1973-76
Alfa Romeo Alfasud 1972-1984
Alfa Romeo Spider Ultimate Portfolio 1966-1994
Alfa Romeo Spider & GTV Perf. Port. 1995-2005
Allard Limited Edition Ultra
Alpine Renault Ultimate Portfolio 1958-1995
Alvis Gold Portfolio 1919-1967
AMC Rambler Limited Edition Extra 1956-1969
AMX & Javelin Gold Portfolio 1968-1974
Armstrong Siddeley Gold Portfolio 1945-1960
Aston Martin Gold Portfolio 1921-1947
Aston Martin Ultimate Portfolio 1948-1968
Aston Martin Ultimate Portfolio 1968-1980
Aston Martin Ultimate Portfolio 1981-1993
Aston Martin Ultimate Portfolio 1994-2006
Auburn Cord Duesenberg - A Brooklands Portfolio
Audi Quattro Gold Portfolio 1980-1991
Audi TT Performance Portfolio 1998-2006
Austin Seven & Ten Road Test Portfolio
Austin-Healey 100 & 100/6 Gold Port. 1952-1959
Austin-Healey 3000 Road Test Portfolio
Bentley & Rolls-Royce Portfolio 1990-2002
BMW 6 & 8 Cyl. Cars Limited Edition 1935-1960
BMW 700 Limited Edition 1959-1965
BMW 2002 Ultimate Portfolio 1968-1976
BMW 6 Cylinder Coupes & Saloons Gold P. 1969-1976
BMW 316, 318, 320 (4 cyl.) Gold Port. 1975-1990
BMW 320, 323, 325 (6 cyl.) Gold Port. 1977-1990
BMW 3 Series Gold Portfolio 1991-1997
BMW M3 Ultimate Portfolio 1986-2006
BMW M5 Gold Portfolio 1980-2003
BMW 5 Series Gold Portfolio 1988-1995
BMW 6 Series Ultimate Portfolio 1976-1989
BMW 7 Series Performance Portfolio 1977-1986
BMW 7 Series Performance Portfolio 1986-1993
BMW 8 Series Performance Portfolio
BMW X5 Limited Edition Extra 1999-2006
BMW Alpina Performance Portfolio 1967-1987
BMW Alpina Performance Portfolio 1988-1998
BMW Z3, M Coupe & M Roadster Gold Port. 1996-02
Bond Cars 1949-1974 Road Test Portfolio
Borgward Isabella Limited Edition
Bristol Cars Portfolio HARD COVER
Bugatti Type 10 to Type 40 Road Test Portfolio
Bugatti Type 41 to Type 55 Road Test Portfolio
Bugatti Type 57 to Type 251 Road Test Portfolio
Bugatti Type 10 to Type 251 Road Test Portfolio
Buick Performance Portfolio 1947-1962
Buick Riviera Performance Portfolio 1963-1978
Cadillac Performance Portfolio 1948-1958
Cadillac Performance Portfolio 1959-1966
Cadillac Eldorado Performance Portfolio 1967-1978
Cadillac Allante Limited Edition Extra
Caterham Seven Road Test Portfolio 1974-1999
Caterham Seven Road Test Portfolio 2000-2010
Checker Automobiles Road Test Portfolio
Impala & SS Muscle Portfolio 1958-1972
Corvair Performance Portfolio 1959-1969
Chevy II & Nova SS Gold Portfolio 1962-1974
Chevelle & SS Gold Portfolio 1964-1972
Camaro Muscle Portfolio 1967-1973
Blazer & Jimmy Limited Edition Extra 1969-1982
Blazer & Jimmy Limited Edition Extra 1983-1994
Camaro Performance Portfolio 1993-2000
Chevrolet Caprice Road Test Portfolio 1965-1990
Chevrolet Corvette Gold Portfolio 1953-1962
Chevrolet Corvette Sting Ray Gold Port. 1963-1967
Chevrolet Corvette Gold Portfolio 1968-1977
Chrysler Imperial Gold Portfolio 1951-1975
Citroen Traction Avant Limited Edition Premier
Citroen 2CV Ultimate Portfolio 1948-1990
Citroen DS & ID 1955-1975
Citroen DS & ID Gold Portfolio 1955-1975
Citroen CX Road Test Portfolio
Shelby Cobra Gold Portfolio 1962-1969
Damlier SP250 Dart & V-8 2.5 litre 250 RTP 1959-69
Datsun Roadsters Performance Portfolio 1960-71
Datsun 240Z & 260Z Road Test Portfolio
Datsun 280Z & 280ZX Road Test Portfolio
Delahaye Road Test Portfolio
Delage Road Test Portfolio
DeLorean Gold Portfolio 1977-1995
De Soto Limited Edition 1952-1960
Dodge Limited Edition 1949-1959
Dodge Dart Limited Edition Extra 1960-1976
Dodge Muscle Portfolio 1964-1971
Charger Muscle Portfolio 1966-1974
Elfin Sports and Racing Cars
Elva Sports Racers Road Test Portfolio
ERA Gold Portfolio 1934-1994
Facel Vega Limited Edition Extra 1954-1964
Ferrari Road Cars 1946-1956 Road Test Portfolio
Ferrari Dino Limited Edition Extra 1965-1974
Ferrari 308 & Mondial Ultimate Portfolio 1975-85
Ferrari 328 348 Mondial Ultimate Portfolio 1986-94
Ferrari F355 & 360 Gold Portfolio 1995-2004
Fiat 500 1936-1972 Road Test Portfolio
Fiat Dino Road Test Portfolio
Fiat 124 Spider Performance Portfolio 1966-1985
Fiat Abarth 1972-1987 Road Test Portfolio
Fiat X1/9 Gold Portfolio 1973-1989
Fiat Barchetta Road Test Portfolio
Ford Zephyr, Zodiac, Executive Mk. III & IV 1962-1971
High Performance Capris Gold Portfolio 1969-1987
Capri Muscle Portfolio 1974-1987
High Performance Fiestas 1979-1991
Ford Escort RS & Mexico Limited Edition 1970-1979
High Performance Escorts 1980-1985
High Performance Escorts 1985-1990

www.brooklandsbooks.com

Ford Thunderbird Performance Portfolio 1955-1957
Ford Thunderbird Performance Portfolio 1958-1963
Ford Thunderbird Performance Portfolio 1964-1976
Ford Fairlane Performance Portfolio 1955-1970
Ford Ranchero Muscle Portfolio 1957-1979
Falcon Performance Portfolio 1960-1970
Ford GT40 & GT Ultimate Portfolio 1964-2006
Ford Torino Performance Portfolio 1968-1974
Ford Bronco 4x4 Performance Portfolio 1966-1977
Shelby Mustang Ultimate Portfolio 1965-1970
Mustang Muscle Portfolio 1967-1973
High Performance Mustang IIs 1974-1978
Mustang 5.0L Muscle Portfolio 1982-1993
Ginetta Cars Limited Edition Ultra 1958-2007
Goggomobil Limited Edition
Hispano-Suiza Road Test Portfolio
Honda - Acura NSX Ultimate Portfolio 1989-2005
Honda CRX 1983-1987
Honda S2000 Performance Portfolio 1999-2008
Hudson Performance Portfolio 1946-1957
International Scout Gold Portfolio 1961-1980
Isetta Gold Portfolio 1953-1964
ISO & Bizzarrini Limited Edition Ultra 1962-1974
Jaguar Mk 7, 8, 10 & 420 Road Test Portfolio
Jaguar Mk 1 & Mk 2 1955-1969 Road Test Portfolio
Jaguar E-Type Ultimate Portfolio 1961-1975
Jaguar XJ6 Series I & II Gold Portfolio 1968-1979
Jaguar XJ6 Series III Perf. Portfolio 1979-1986
Jaguar XJ-S V12 Ultimate Portfolio 1988-1996
Jaguar XK8 & XKR Performance Portfolio 1996-2005
Jeep CJ-5 Limited Edition 1960-1975
Jeep CJ-5 & CJ-7 4x4 Perf. Portfolio 1976-1986
Jeep J-Series Pickups 1970-1982
Jeepster & Commando Limited Edition 1967-1973
Jeep Cherokee & Comanche Pickups P. P. 1984-91
Jeep Wrangler 4x4 Performance Portfolio 1987-99
Jeep Cherokee & Grand Cherokee 4x4 P. P. 1992-98
Jensen Road Test Portfolio 1934-1965
Jensen Interceptor Ultimate Portfolio 1966-1992
Jensen - Healey Road Test Portfolio 1972-1976
Jowett Road Test Portfolio
Kaiser - Frazer Limited Edition 1946-1955
Lagonda Gold Portfolio 1919-1964
Lancia Fulvia Gold Portfolio 1963-1976
Lancia Montecarlo & Scorpion 1975-1982 RTP
Lancia Stratos Limited Edition Extra
Lancia Delta & integrale Ultimate Portfolio
Land Rover Series I, II & IIA Gold Portfolio 1948-71
Land Rover 90 110 Defender Gold Portfolio 1983-94
Land Rover Discovery Perf. Port. 1989-2000
Lamborghini Performance Portfolio 1964-1976
Lamborghini Performance Portfolio 1977-1989
Lamborghini Gold Portfolio 1990-2004
Lincoln Gold Portfolio 1949-1960
Lincoln Continental Performance Portfolio 1961-1969
Lola Sports Racing Cars Lim. Ed. Premier 1958-1985
Lotus Sports Racers Portfolio - covering 1951-1965
Lotus Seven Gold Portfolio 1957-1973
Lotus Elite Limited Edition 1957-1964
Lotus Elan Ultimate Portfolio 1962-1974
Lotus Cortina Road Test Portfolio
Lotus Elite & Exlat Road Test Portfolio 1984-1972
Lotus Excel Road Test Portfolio
Lotus Europa Gold Portfolio 1966-1975
Lotus Elise & Exige Gold Portfolio 1995-2005
Marcos Coupés & Spyders Gold Portfolio 1960-1997
Maserati Cars Performance Portfolio 1957-1970
Maserati Cars Performance Portfolio 1971-1982
Maserati Cars Performance Portfolio 1982-1998
Maserati Cars Ultimate Portfolio 1999-2007
Matra Road Test Portfolio
Mazda Miata MX-5 Performance Portfolio 1989-1997
Mazda Miata MX-5 Performance Portfolio 1998-2005
Mazda Miata MX-5 Takes On The Competition
McLaren F1 • GTR • LM Sportscar Perf. Portfolio
Mercedes-Benz 1925-1939 - A Portfolio
Mercedes 190SL 300SL 300SLR - A Portfolio
Mercedes S & 600 Limited Edition Extra 1965-1972
Mercedes S Class Limited Edition Extra 1980-1991
Mercedes 230SL 250SL 280SL Ultimate Port. 1963-71
Mercedes-Benz SLs & SLCs Ultimate Port. 1971-1989
Mercedes SLs Performance Portfolio 1989-1994
Mercedes E-Class W124 Road Test Portfolio 1986-1995
Mercedes G-Wagen Gold Portfolio 1981-2005
Mercedes AMG Gold Portfolio 1983-1999
Mercedes AMG Ultimate Portfolio 2000-2006
Mercury Gold Portfolio 1947-1966
Mercury Comet & Cyclone Lim. Edit. Extra 1960-1975
Messerschmitt Gold Portfolio 1954-1964
MG Gold Portfolio 1929-1939
MG TD & TF Gold Portfolio 1949-1955
MG Y Type & Magnette Road Test Portfolio
MGA & Twin Cam Gold Portfolio 1955-1962
MG Midget Road Test Portfolio 1961-1979
MGB Roadsters 1962-1980
MGB MGC & V8 Gold Portfolio 1962-1980
MGC & MGB GT V8 Limited Edition
MGF & TF Performance Portfolio 1995-2005
Mini Gold Portfolio 1959-1969
Mini Gold Portfolio 1969-1980
Mini Gold Portfolio 1981-1997
High Performance Minis Gold Portfolio 1960-1973
Mini Cooper Gold Portfolio 1961-1971
Mini Moke Ultimate Portfolio 1964-1994
Mini Performance Portfolio 2001-2006
Starion & Conquest Performance Portfolio 1982-1990
Mitsubishi 3000GT & Dodge Stealth P.P. 1990-1999

Morgan Three-Wheelers Ultimate Portfolio 1909-52
Morgan Four-Wheelers Ultimate Portfolio 1936-67
Morgan Ultimate Portfolio 1968-1990
Morgan Ultimate Portfolio 1991-2009
Morris Minor MM & Series II Road Test Portfolio
Morris Minor 1000 Road Test Portfolio
Nash Limited Edition Extra 1949-1957
Nash-Austin Metropolitan Gold Portfolio 1954-1962
Nissan 350Z Road Test Portfolio
Nissan Skyline GT-R Ultimate Portfolio 1969-2010
Noble Sports Cars Road Test Portfolio
NSU Ro80 Limited Edition
Oldsmobile 1948-1963 Limited Edition Premier
Cutlass & 4-4-2 Muscle Portfolio 1964-1974
Opel GT Ultimate Portfolio 1968-1973
Packard Automobiles 1920-1958 - A Portfolio
Pantera Ultimate Portfolio 1970-1995
Panther Gold Portfolio 1972-1990
Plymouth Limited Edition 1950-1960
Plymouth Fury Limited Edition Extra 1956-1976
Barracuda Muscle Portfolio 1964-1974
Plymouth Muscle Portfolio 1964-1971
Pontiac 1946-1963 Limited Edition Premier
High Performance Firebirds 1982-1988
Firebird & Trans Am Performance Portfolio 1993-00
Pontiac Fiero Performance Portfolio 1984-1988
Porsche Sports Racing Cars UP 1952-1968
Porsche 917 • 935 • 956 • 962 Gold Portfolio
Porsche 365 Ultimate Portfolio 1952-1965
Porsche 911 1965-1969
Porsche 911 SC & Turbo Gold Portfolio 1978-1983
Porsche 911 Ultimate Portfolio 1990-1997
Porsche 911 Takes On The Competition 1990-1997
Porsche 911 Ultimate Portfolio 1998-2004
Porsche 912 Limited Edition Extra 1965-1976
Porsche 914 Ultimate Portfolio
Porsche 924 Gold Portfolio 1975-1988
Porsche 928 Gold Portfolio 1977-1995
Porsche 928 Takes On The Competition
Porsche 944 Ultimate Portfolio
Porsche 968 Limited Edition Extra
Porsche Boxster Ultimate Portfolio 1996-2004
Railton & Brough Superior Gold Portfolio 1933-1950
Range Rover Gold Portfolio 1970-1985
Range Rover Gold Portfolio 1985-1995
Range Rover Performance Portfolio 1995-2001
Range Rover Takes on the Competition
Riley RM Series Pathfinder 2.6 A Brooklands Port.
Rolls-Royce Silver Clould & Bentley S Ultimate Port.
Rolls-Royce Silver Shadow Ultimate Port. 1965-80
Rover P4 1949-1959
Rover P6 1963-1977
Rover 2000 & 2200 1963-1977
Studebaker Ultimate Portfolio 1946-1966
Studebaker Hawks & Larks Lim. Edit. Premier 1956-66
Avanti Limited Edition Extra 1962-1991
Subaru Impreza Turbo Limited Edition Extra 1994-00
Subaru Impreza WRX Performance Port. 2001-2005
Sunbeam Alpine Limited Edition Extra 1959-1968
Suzuki SJ Gold Portfolio 1971-1997
Vitara, Sidekick & Geo Tracker Perf. Port. 1988-1997
Tatra Cars Road Test Portfolio
Toyota Land Cruiser Gold Portfolio 1956-1987
Toyota Land Cruiser 1988-1997
Toyota Supra Performance Portfolio 1982-1998
Toyota MR2 Road Test Portfolio 1984-1989
Toyota MR2 Road Test Portfolio 1990-1999
Toyota MR2 Road Test Portfolio 2000-2007
Toyota MR2 Takes On The Competition
Triumph TR2 & TR3 Road Test Portfolio
Triumph TR4, TR5 & TR250 Road Test Portfolio
Triumph TR6 Road Test Portfolio
Triumph Herald 1959-1971
Triumph Vitesse 1962-1971
Triumph 2000, 2.5, 2500 1963-1977
Triumph GT6 Gold Portfolio 1966-1974
Triumph Spitfire Road Test Portfolio
Triumph Stag Road Test Portfolio
TVR Limited Edition Ultra 1958-1985
TVR Performance Portfolio 1986-1994
TVR Performance Portfolio 2000-2005
VW Beetle Gold Portfolio 1935-1967
VW Beetle Gold Portfolio 1968-1991
VW Bus Camper Van Perf. Portfolio 1954-1967
VW Bus Camper Van Perf. Portfolio 1979-1991
VW Karmann Ghia Gold Portfolio 1955-1974
VW Golf GTI Limited Edition Extra 1976-1991
VW Golf Cabriolet 1979-2002 Road Test Portfolio
VW Corrado Limited Edition Premier 1989-1995
Volvo PV444 & PV544 Perf. Portfolio 1945-1965
Volvo 120 Amazon Ultimate Portfolio
Volvo 1800 Ultimate Portfolio 1960-1973
Volvo 140 & 160 Series Gold Portfolio 1966-1975
Forty Years of Selling Volvo
Westfield Performance Portfolio 1982-2004

MILITARY VEHICLES

Complete WW2 Military Jeep Manual
Dodge WW2 Military Portfolio 1940-1945
German Military Equipment WW2
Hail To The Jeep
Combat Land Rover Portfolio No. 1
Land Rover Military Portfolio
Off Road Jeeps Civilian & Military 1944-1971
US Military Vehicles 1941-1945
Standard Military Motor Vehicles-TM9-2800 (WW2)
VW Kubelwagen Military Portfolio 1940-1990
WW2 Allied Vehicles Military Portfolio 1939-1945
WW2 Jeep Military Portfolio 1941-1945

RACING & THE LAND SPEED RECORD

The Land Speed Record 1898-1919
The Land Speed Record 1920-1929
The Land Speed Record 1930-1939
The Land Speed Record 1940-1962
Can-Am Racing 1966-1969
Can-Am Racing 1970-1974
The Carrera Panamericana Mexico - 1950-1954
Le Mans - The Bentley & Alfa Years - 1923-1939
Le Mans - The Jaguar Years - 1949-1957
Le Mans - The Ferrari Years - 1958-1965
Le Mans - The Ford & Matra Years - 1966-1974
Le Mans - The Porsche Years - 1975-1982
Le Mans - The Porsche & Jaguar Years - 1983-91
Le Mans - The Porsche & Peugeot Years - 1992-99
Mille Miglia - The Alfa & Ferrari Years - 1927-1951
Mille Miglia - The Ferrari & Mercedes Years - 1952-57
Targa Florio - The Porsche & Ferrari Years - 1955-64
Targa Florio - The Porsche Years - 1965-1973
Brabham Ralt Honda The Ron Tauranac

RESTORATION & GUIDE SERIES

BMW 2002 - A Comprehensive Guide
BMW 02 Restoration Guide
BMW E30 - 3 Series Restoration Bible
BMW E36 - 3 Series Restoration Tips & Techniques
BMW - 5 & 6 Series Restoration Tips & Techniques
Classic Camaro Restoration
Engine Swapping Tips & Techniques
Ferrari Life Buyer's Portfolio
Land Rover Restoration Portfolio
PC on Land Rover Series I Restoration
Lotus Elan Restoration Guide
Lotus Twin Cam Engines
MG T Series Restoration Guide
MGA Restoration Guide
PC on MGB Restoration
Mustang Restoration Tips & Techniques
Practical Gas Flow
Range Rover - The First Fifty
Restoring Sprites & Midgets an Enthusiast's Guide
Solex Carburettors Tuning Tips and Techniques
SU Carburetters Tuning Tips & Techniques
The Great Classic Muscle Cars Compared
Weber Carburettors Tuning Tips and Techniques

ROAD & TRACK SERIES

Road & Track on Aston Martin 1962-1990
Road & Track on Austin Healey 1953-1970
Road & Track on BMW Cars 1966-1974
R & T BMW Z3, M Coupe & M Roadster Port. 96-02
R & T Camaro & Firebird Portfolio 1993-2002
Road & Track on Corvette 1968-1982
Road & Track on Corvette 1982-1986
Road & Track on Corvette 1986-1990
Road & Track Corvette Portfolio 1997-2002
Road & Track Dodge Viper Portfolio 1992-2002
Road & Track on Ferrari 1975-1981
Road & Track on Ferrari 1984-1988
Road & Track Ferrari V-12 Portfolio 1992-2002
Road & Track Ferrari F355 360 F430 Portfolio 95-06
Road & Track on Jaguar 1950-1960
Road & Track on Jaguar 1961-1968
Road & Track on Jaguar 1968-1974
R & T Jaguar XJ-S - XK8 - XKR Portfolio 1975-2003
Road & Track MX-5 Miata Portfolio 1989-2002
Road & Track on Mercedes 1952-1962
R & T Mercedes SL - SLK - CLK Portfolio 1990-2003
Road & Track on MG Sports Cars 1949-1961
Road & Track on MG Sports Cars 1962-1980
Road & Track Mustang Portfolio 1994-2002
Road & Track Nissan 300ZX & 350Z Portfolio 1984-03
Road & Track on Porsche 1951-1967
Road & Track on Porsche 1975-1978
Road & Track on Porsche 1979-1982
Road & Track Porsche 928 Portfolio 1977-1994
Road & Track Porsche 911 Portfolio 1990-1997
R & T on Rolls Royce & Bentley 1950-1965
Road & Track on Volkswagen 1951-1968
Road & Track on Volkswagen 1968-1978
Road & Track on Volvo 1957-1974
Road & Track on Volvo 1977-1994
Road & Track - Best of PS
Road & Track - Peter Egan Side Glances 1983-1992
Road & Track - Peter Egan Side Glances 1992-1997
Road & Track - Peter Egan Side Glances 1998-2002
Road & Track - Peter Egan Side Glances 2002-2006

CAR AND DRIVER SERIES

Car and Driver on BMW 1957-1977
Car and Driver on Ferrari 1955-1962
Car and Driver on Ferrari 1963-1975
Car and Driver on Porsche 1955-1962
Car and Driver on Porsche 1963-1970
Car and Driver on Porsche 1970-1976
Car and Driver on Porsche 1977-1981
Car and Driver on Porsche 1982-1986
Car and Driver on Volvo 1955-1976

HOT ROD 'ENGINE' SERIES

Chevy 265 & 283
Chevy 302 & 327
Chevy 348 & 409
Chevy 396 & 427
Chevy 454 thru 512
Chevy Monster Big Blocks
Chrysler Hemi
Chrysler 273, 318, 340 & 360
Chrysler 361, 383, 400, 413, 426 & 440
Ford 289, 302, Boss 302 & 351W
Ford 351C & Boss 351
Ford Small Block
Ford Big Block

MOTORCYCLES

To see our range of over 70 titles visit www.brooklands-books.com

Contents

Acknowledgements

Regular readers of Brooklands books will know that our Road Test Portfolios and other road test volumes make available printed material which has become hard to find. In putting these books together, we depend on the generosity and understanding of those who originally published the material, and for the present volume, our sincere thanks go to the owners of *Autocar, Autosport, Car and Driver, Cars and Car Conversions, Classic & Sports Car, Classic Car, Motor, Motor Life, Motor Trend, Practical Classics, Road & Track, Safety Fast, Sporting Motorist, Sports Car Graphic* and *Sports Car World*. Our thanks also go to the Austin-Healey Club for their support and to Bob Kemp for providing us with photos for the front and back cover of this book. For information on the Club, please contact them via their website - www.austinhealeyclub.com

R.M. Clarke

By the time the Austin-Healey 3000 appeared in July 1959, the Big Healey was a familiar sight on British and North American roads. The new models were hard to distinguish from their forebears by a cursory visual examination, but they incorporated one very significant improvement. This was a big-bore 2912cc version of the BMC six-cylinder engine. Not only was this more powerful than its 2638cc predecessor, but it was also more torquey. The result was that the Healey 3000 was faster through the gears and had a higher top speed than all of its standard-production forebears.

In 1962, the triple-carburettor Mk. II version appeared, offering even more power but no real performance improvements from an engine that proved difficult to keep in tune. So the Mk. II convertible - with a proper soft top and 2+2 seating - reverted to twin carburettors, and the final Mk.III models introduced in 1964 looked to other means for their power increase.

In their final years, the works Healeys became respected rally machines. The 3000, durable as it was, could not last forever: production came to an end late in 1967, largely because of the cost of modifying the car to meet safety and exhaust emissions regulations due to be introduced in the USA during 1968.

A big Healey still has undeniable charisma, and these classic British sports cars of the 1960s are today much prized by enthusiasts all over the world.

James Taylor

Austin Healey 3000 with 2.9-litre Engine

DESIGNED by Donald Healey, the larger Austin Healey sports car has enjoyed continuous success since its introduction in 1952. First models were fitted with a four-cylinder, 2.6-litre Austin engine; four years later, the B.M.C. C-series six-cylinder unit was substituted, the car then being designated the 100-Six.

Towards the end of 1957 a new cylinder head, having separate ports and fed by a separate, light-alloy inlet manifold was introduced, and the improved gas flow increased power output from 102 b.h.p. at 4,600 r.p.m. to 117 b.h.p. at 4,750 r.p.m. The C-series B.M.C. engine has now been increased in capacity from 2,639 to 2,912 c.c. by enlarging the bores, and the net power output goes up to 124 b.h.p. at 4,600 r.p.m. This increase in engine capacity will be welcomed by competition-minded owners since the make will now be able to compete on more favourable terms in the international class D for cars having an engine swept volume up to 3,000 c.c.

A new casting has been designed for the combined cylinder block and crankcase; the cylinder bores have been increased from 79.4 to 83.36 mm, while the crankshaft stroke remains unchanged at 89 mm. To accommodate this increase in bore size the coolant passages between numbers 1 and 2, 3 and 4 and 5 and 6 cylinders are siamesed. At the same time the crankcase has been stiffened at the flywheel end by the addition of external webs. Flat-topped pistons are fitted, and the compression ratio is raised from 8.5 to 1 to 9.0 to 1.

In addition to these changes, the C-series engines have been improved in detail since our last description, published on 29 November, 1957. Among modifications which have occurred at intervals since that date have been alterations to the crankshaft damper, elimination of a reduced diameter section of the inlet valve stems, and the use of a gear-type oil pump in place of the previous rotor-type.

Main differences between the engine as used in the Austin Healey 3000 and those for other six-cylinder B.M.C. models are the six-port cylinder head, used in conjunction with separate inlet manifold, and semi-downdraught HD6 S.U. carburettors.

A thermostatically controlled auxiliary carburettor for cold starting is fitted; polythene hose is used for sections of the fuel pipe line, and an S.U. electric pump feeds the carburettors from a 12-gallon tank.

To cope with the extra torque from the new engine, stronger transmission gears are fitted, as well as a new 10in diameter single-plate Borg and Beck clutch which has a friction area of 78 sq in, compared with 66 sq in of the previous 9in-diameter unit.

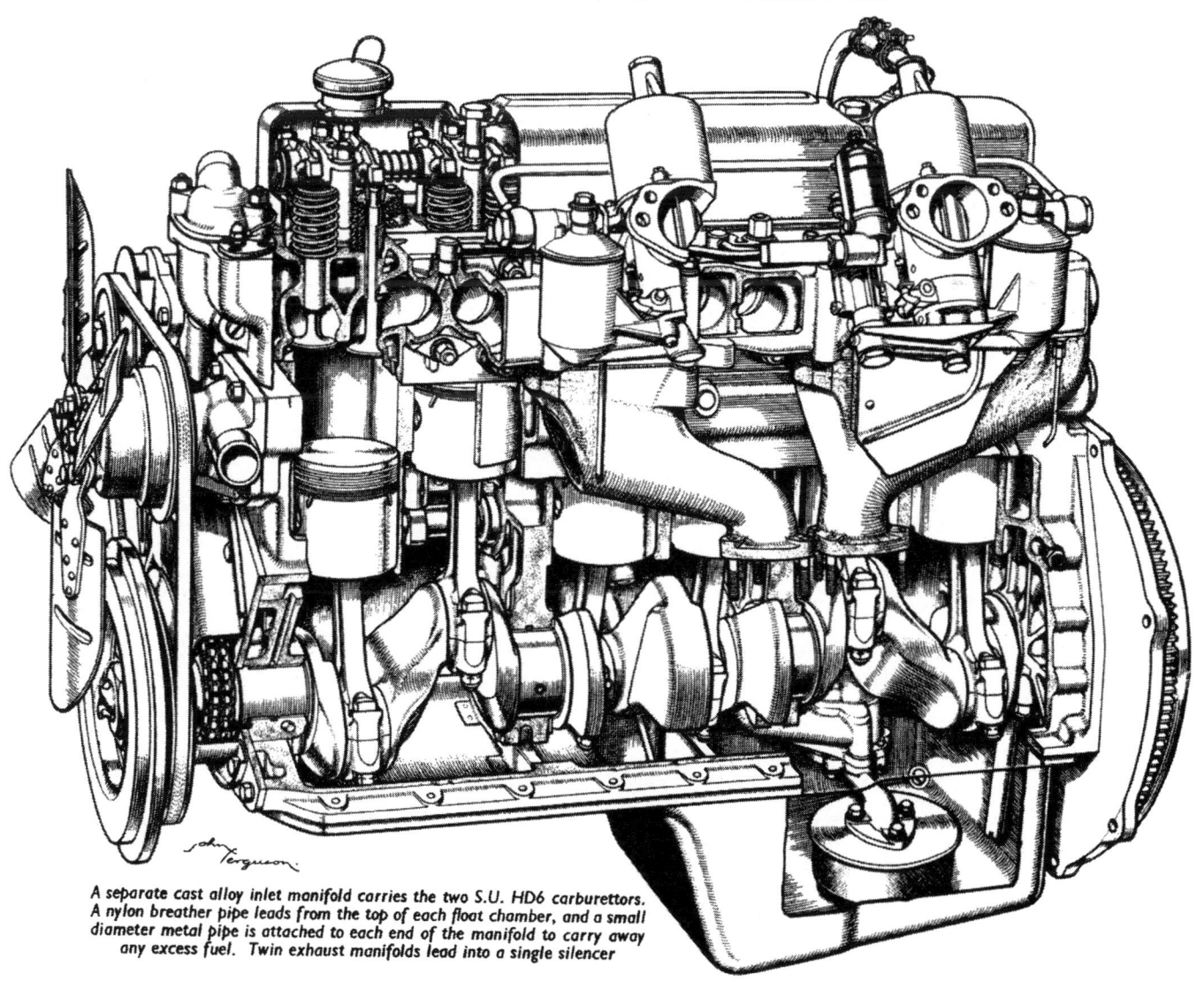

Net performance curves for the new engine compared with those for the previous one

A separate cast alloy inlet manifold carries the two S.U. HD6 carburettors. A nylon breather pipe leads from the top of each float chamber, and a small diameter metal pipe is attached to each end of the manifold to carry away any excess fuel. Twin exhaust manifolds lead into a single silencer

5

AUSTIN-HEALEY 3000
and M.G. A 1600

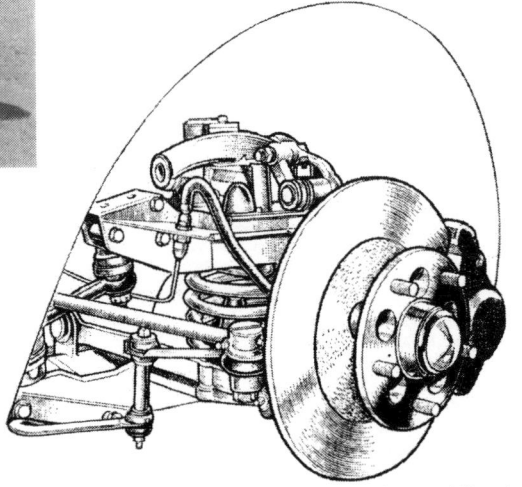

Left: In its latest form the Austin-Healey is externally unchanged and, apart from nameplates and new rear light/flasher plinths the M.G. A 1600 (*below, left*) also retains the appearance of its forerunner. Disc front brakes are now standard on both cars, the type shown below being as fitted on the Healey. The flange allows bolt-on wheels to be used: centre-lock wire wheels are an extra.

Also increased in engine size and fitted in this instance with Lockheed disc front brakes, the M.G. MGA is now of 1,588 c.c. In outward appearance the two models, open and coupé, are very similar to the 1500 versions they supersede, only minor differences being visible in the form of reshaped rear wing plinths and of sliding side screens.

The 'B' series engine now gives 78 b.h.p. compared with the previous 72 by virtue of its enlarged cylinder bore, the excellent four-speed gearbox and 4.3 rear axle ratio being retained unaltered. Disc front brakes are combined with improved linings for the drums at the rear. With seven new colour schemes available and a host of extras which include almost everything except overdrive, the M.G. can be either a fully equipped fast, two-seat, touring car or a comfortable and usable competition vehicle. That the added features of the latest model are not coupled with any price increase makes it even more desirable than before.

CONTINUOUSLY developed over the seven years of its existence, the main alteration during this period being the introduction of the six-cylinder engine in place of the four-cylinder version, the latest Austin-Healey now has an enlarged engine, improved braking and a suitably strengthened gearbox and clutch.

The six-port head, standardized on this model a short while ago, is now fitted to a new cylinder block of greater bore which increases engine capacity from 2,639 to 2,912 c.c., this coupled with a slightly raised compression ratio giving a power increase of 7 b.h.p. and improving torque from 149 to 175 lb. ft. To transmit this a 10-in. diameter clutch is fitted in place of the previous 9-in. one, the gear cluster is strengthened and the ratios slightly respaced. Rear axle ratios vary according to whether or not the optional overdrive (now of slightly smaller step-up ratio) is fitted, but are raised to take advantage of the improved torque.

A system of Girling disc brakes at the front and drums at the rear is now standardized to cope with the improved performance.

Although detail refinements such as the introduction of a battery master switch in the lockable boot have also been made, the layout of seats, instruments, and the body shape have not changed. The 3000 is available with soft or hard top and in two or occasional four-seat form.

AUSTIN-HEALEY 3000 SPECIFICATION

ENGINE.—Dimensions: Cylinders, 6; bore, 83.3 mm.; stroke, 89; cubic capacity, 2,912 c.c.; piston area, 50.7 sq. in.; valves, overhead (push-rod); compression ratio, 9.03 : 1. **Performance:** Max. b.h.p., 124 (130 gross) at 4,600 r.p.m.; b.h.p. per sq. in. piston area, 2.45. **Details:** Carburetters, twin S.U.HD6; ignition control, centrifugal and vacuum; fuel tank capacity, 12 gal.; cooling system capacity, 20 pints; oil filter, full flow.

TRANSMISSION.—Clutch, 10 in. s.d.p.; overall gear ratios: with overdrive, O/D top, 3.214; top, 3.91 (s/m); O/D 3rd, 4.207; 3rd, 5.118 (s/m); 2nd, 8.026 (s/m); 1st, 11.456; reverse, 14.78; without overdrive, top, 3.545 (s/m); 3rd, 4.64 (s/m); 2nd, 7.378 (s/m); 1st, 10.387; reverse, 13.4; prop. shaft, Hardy Spicer, open; final drive, hypoid.

CHASSIS DETAILS.—Brakes: Girling hydraulic, disc front, drum rear; disc diameter, 11¼ in.; drum internal diameter, 11 in. **Suspension:** Front, independent (coil spring, wishbone and anti-roll bar); rear, semi-elliptic and Panhard rod; dampers, Armstrong lever type; wheel type, disc or wire; tyre size, 5.90-15 Road Speed.

DIMENSIONS.—Wheelbase, 7 ft. 8 in.; track: front 4 ft. 0¾ in., rear 4 ft. 2 in.; overall length, 13 ft. 1½ in.; overall width, 5 ft. 0½ in.; overall height (hood up), 4 ft. 2 in.; ground clearance, 4½ in.; turning circle, 35 ft.

PERFORMANCE DATA.—Top gear m.p.h. per 1,000 r.p.m.— 20.9; O/D top, 23.1; direct (o/d ratios), 18.94.

PRICE.—(2-seater) £824 0s. 0d., plus £344 9s. 2d. purchase tax, total £1,168 9s. 2d.

M.G. A 1600 SPECIFICATION

ENGINE.—Dimensions: Cylinders, 4; bore, 75.39 mm.; stroke, 88.9 mm.; cubic capacity, 1,588 c.c.; piston area, 27.53 sq. in.; valves, overhead (push-rod); compression ratio, 8.3 : 1. **Performance:** Max. b.h.p., 78 (gross) at 5,500 r.p.m.; b.h.p. per sq. in. piston area, 2.83. **Details:** Carburetters, twin S.U.H4; ignition control, centrifugal and vacuum; fuel tank capacity, 10 gal.; cooling system capacity, 10 pints; oil filter, full flow.

TRANSMISSION.—Clutch, 8 in. s.d.p.; overall gear ratios: top, 4.3 (s/m); 3rd, 5.908 (s/m); 2nd, 9.52 (s/m); 1st, 15.652, reverse, 20.468; prop. shaft, Hardy Spicer, open; final drive, hypoid.

CHASSIS DETAILS. — Brakes: Lockheed hydraulic, disc front, drum rear; disc diameter, 11 in.; drum internal diameter, 10 in. **Suspension:** Front, independent (coil spring and wishbone); rear, semi-elliptic; dampers, Armstrong lever type; wheel type, disc or wire; tyre size, 5.60-15.

DIMENSIONS.—Wheelbase, 7 ft. 10 in.; track, front 3 ft. 11½ in., rear 4 ft. 0¾ in.; overall length, 13 ft. 8 in.; overall width, 4 ft. 9¼ in.; overall height, 4 ft. 2 in.; ground clearance, 6 in.; turning circle, 28 ft.

PERFORMANCE DATA.—Top gear m.p.h. per 1,000 r.p.m., 17.

PRICE.—£663 0s. 0d., plus £277 7s. 6d. purchase tax, total £940 7s. 6d.

ROAD TEST AUSTIN-HEALEY 3-LITER

On a jag in a Healey

ALL OF ROAD & TRACK's previous road tests of Austin-Healeys—there have been five, not counting this one or the Sprite, since 1954—have been performed in California under practically identical conditions. In the case of the new 3000 model a slight obstacle presented itself. This obstacle was some 2800 miles of road between New York (where the only two 3000's in the country happened to be at the end of May) and California, where the test crew waited with anxious eyes on the deadline for this issue.

Quickly our small but enthusiastic New York staff, consisting of Harvey B. Janes, Eastern Editor, and David E. Davis, Jr., Eastern Advertising Manager, offered a solution. They would drive one of the new cars nonstop from New York to the Road & Track offices in California. Thus we would have our test car in plenty of time and they would be firmly established as heroes, having set all sorts of new coast-to-coast driving records.

They got underway in the early evening on a Monday and, with the aid of a package of innocent-looking but highly potent pep pills, pulled up at the Road & Track

Stock except for its Lucas road lights, the 3-liter looks much better after a bath, even in Los Angeles water.

Here it is as it arrived at the Road & Track office, with a weary Dave Davis and Eastern Editor Harvey Janes.

With the hardtop, a comfortable all-weather town car . . .

And for traveling, better endowed than some sports cars.

offices a little over 57 hours later, full of praise for the car and for their own powers of endurance. When we informed them that a certain French economy sedan had covered the same distance in roughly 54 hours, they were only mildly impressed. The drivers of this French car, they told us, had cheated; they had not stopped to eat along the way. Of the total elapsed time of 57 hours in the Healey, at least three and a half hours had been consumed in various restaurants along the route. In addition, they had been forced to drive through a wild rainstorm and flood in Ohio and had wasted nearly an hour in a bootleg sports car garage just outside of St. Louis trying to replace a silly little rubber grommet that had fallen off the throttle linkage and into a sealed compartment under the instrument panel. In view of all this, our drivers steadfastly and with glassy eyes claimed the following coast-to-coast records: fastest trip in an English car; fastest in an Austin-Healey; fastest in a 3-liter car; fastest in a four-seater roadster with detachable hardtop; fastest by a bearded and mustachioed two-man crew. We might add that it was also the longest distance ever covered in the course of a Road & Track road test.

With the first part of our program successfully completed, we proceeded with the actual performance testing without so much as changing the oil or greasing the car.

When the Healey left New York, it had just under 500 miles on the odometer. We had hoped to be able to complete our tests in California without tuning the engine in any way; by the time the car arrived it was so well broken in and running so beautifully—in spite of having been driven hard—that this was entirely feasible.

The speedometer proved to be extremely accurate, which helped our heroes keep up a good on-the-road average. During the acceleration runs it seemed that the gearbox, still somewhat stiff, might be adversely affecting the car's performance; but when we checked the times against those on the 100-6 last year they proved to be just about right in view of the changes that have been incorporated in the new car. The engine of the 3000 is nothing more or less than a bored-out version of the 100-6 powerplant. Displacement is now 2912 cubic centimeters, or roughly 10% larger than before.

On the other hand the rear-axle ratio has been changed from 4.1 to 3.9, which would figure to knock about 5% off the performance all along the line. This leaves a net improvement of 5%. In other words, the increase in engine displacement has more than made up for the change in axle ratio. Acceleration, pulling power on hills, etc., are therefore improved about 5% over last year's car.

On long grades the car pulls beautifully in top overdrive.

The cockpit is the neat and practical one of other models.

It looks the same, but it isn't: see text and performance data.

PHOTOGRAPHY: POOLE

8

During our top-speed runs we found that if the 3000 is held in 4th gear until about 100 miles per hour, it will fairly leap ahead when overdrive is engaged, and acceleration will continue smoothly and steadily up to better than 112 mph. All of our drivers agreed that in the matter of performance and smoothness the latest Austin-Healey was pleasantly similar to the original XK-120 Jaguar.

Previously, in all our tests on Austin-Healeys, we experienced considerable difficulty in getting the true ultimate top speed. The older models will over-rev in 4th, but when overdrive is engaged at about 100 mph, the car fails to respond. In other words, it takes several miles to obtain terminal velocity. The new car, with the larger engine and closer-ratio overdrive, still has lots of punch at 100 mph and accelerates from that speed to an indicated 120 mph in just over a mile. Tapley readings, for example, are almost exactly 5% better in each gear, as expected, but in overdrive the readings averaged 10% better. The 100-6 used a .778 overdrive ratio with a 4.10 rear axle; the 3000 employs a .820 overdrive ratio which, with the new 3.90 rear axle, gives the same over-all ratio as before in this gear. Here's how the production models compare:

		3000	MM	100-6	100-4
Time,	0-40	5.2	5.2	6.1	6.2
	0-60	9.8	10.4	12.2	11.7
	0-80	17.5	19.2	22.5	20.8
ss ¼		17.1	17.4	18.2	18.1
Top speed		112.5	109.0	105.0	102.0

For the performance tests we adhered to the red line on the tachometer (5200 revolutions per minute). Yet the 6-cylinder engine is very smooth, and it will run well past 5500 rpm with no complaint and no audible sign of valve clatter setting in. The indirect gears are quiet except for 1st, which growls a little. If you get tired of this, it's perfectly possible to forget it and use 2nd gear for starting up. The gearbox was still rather stiff and shifts were hard to make, a feature rather typical of British sports cars for the first few thousand miles. Obviously the gearbox hadn't been used much in the course of the cross-country run.

Handling characteristics are extremely friendly once you get used to the automobile. The steering is quite sensitive to throttle opening—too little produces oversteer, especially on fast bends that have been entered a bit too quickly. Adding more throttle will give fairly constant understeer all the way up to the breakaway point. From there, too much throttle will produce oversteer again, although this can be used to advantage to flick the tail out in tight corners.

Considering the softness of the suspension the ride is surprisingly firm at lower speeds, but above 60 mph it smoothes out considerably and the adhesion seems actually improved, even on rough surfaces. The Dunlop RS-4 tires give excellent traction and on the cross-country trip proved themselves, happily, to be far better on wet roads than previous Dunlops. The 3000 has disc brakes in the front and finned drums in the rear. There is no booster for these brakes, and at speeds below 30 mph the pedal pressure required to stop the car within a comfortable distance is noticeably greater than with the all-drum brake system on the 100-6. At the equivalent of racing speeds the braking is smooth and powerful, with a minimum of nose dive. Even when slight fade is finally produced, after several panic stops from 100 mph, recovery is extremely quick.

The best way to describe the new Austin-Healey 3000 is to say that it is a real enthusiasts' sports car: fun to drive, with lots of performance and good handling and braking characteristics. It could have better cockpit ventilation and seating position, and we still wish that the manufacturer would return to the cleaner styling of the older 4-cylinder cars, but these are only minor grievances. Dollar for dollar this is still one of the top sports cars on the market.

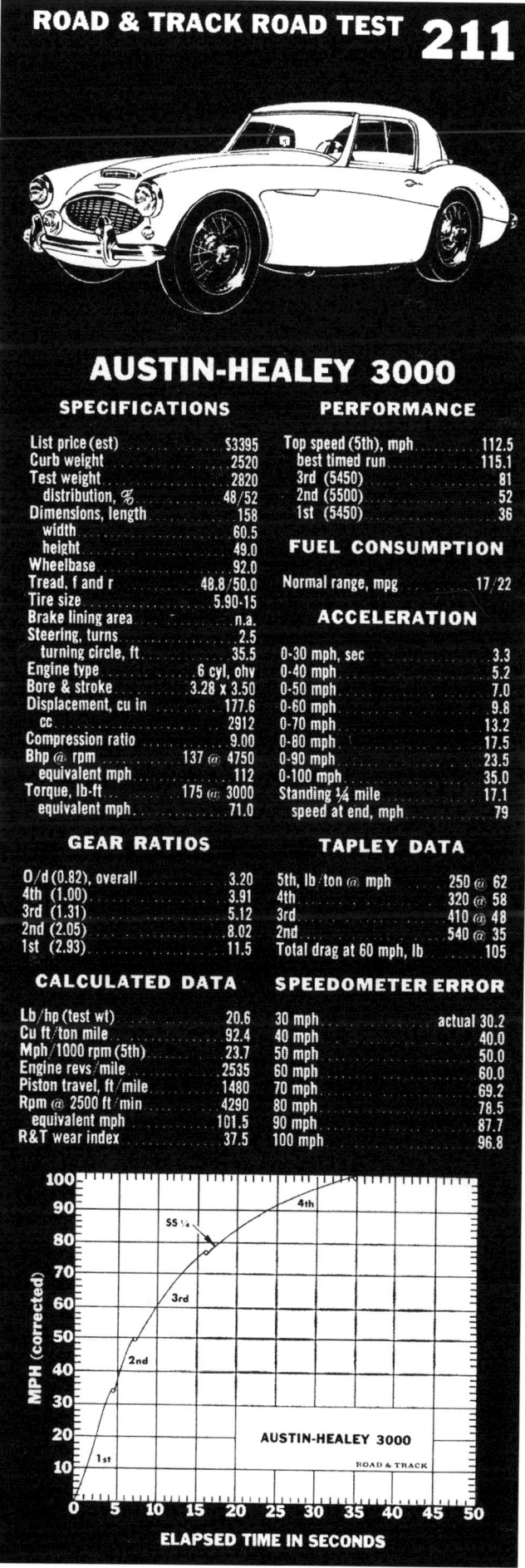

AUSTIN-HEALEY 3000

SPECIFICATIONS

List price (est)	$3395
Curb weight	2520
Test weight	2820
distribution, %	48/52
Dimensions, length	158
width	60.5
height	49.0
Wheelbase	92.0
Tread, f and r	48.8/50.0
Tire size	5.90-15
Brake lining area	n.a.
Steering, turns	2.5
turning circle, ft	35.5
Engine type	6 cyl, ohv
Bore & stroke	3.28 x 3.50
Displacement, cu in	177.6
cc	2912
Compression ratio	9.00
Bhp @ rpm	137 @ 4750
equivalent mph	112
Torque, lb-ft	175 @ 3000
equivalent mph	71.0

PERFORMANCE

Top speed (5th), mph	112.5
best timed run	115.1
3rd (5450)	81
2nd (5500)	52
1st (5450)	36

FUEL CONSUMPTION

Normal range, mpg	17/22

ACCELERATION

0-30 mph, sec	3.3
0-40 mph	5.2
0-50 mph	7.0
0-60 mph	9.8
0-70 mph	13.2
0-80 mph	17.5
0-90 mph	23.5
0-100 mph	35.0
Standing ¼ mile	17.1
speed at end, mph	79

GEAR RATIOS

O/d (0.82), overall	3.20
4th (1.00)	3.91
3rd (1.31)	5.12
2nd (2.05)	8.02
1st (2.93)	11.5

TAPLEY DATA

5th, lb/ton @ mph	250 @ 62
4th	320 @ 58
3rd	410 @ 48
2nd	540 @ 35
Total drag at 60 mph, lb	105

CALCULATED DATA

Lb/hp (test wt)	20.6
Cu ft/ton mile	92.4
Mph/1000 rpm (5th)	23.7
Engine revs/mile	2535
Piston travel, ft/mile	1480
Rpm @ 2500 ft/min	4290
equivalent mph	101.5
R&T wear index	37.5

SPEEDOMETER ERROR

30 mph	actual 30.2
40 mph	40.0
50 mph	50.0
60 mph	60.0
70 mph	69.2
80 mph	78.5
90 mph	87.7
100 mph	96.8

AUSTIN-HEALEY 3000

ROAD & TRACK

ELAPSED TIME IN SECONDS

Bigger Brother for Austin-Healey

New 130-hp model boasts 3-liter engine,
front disc brakes, optional hard top

Hard top gives new 3-liter Healey a brutish look, but it still keeps refined profile. Entry, however, requires some squirming. All changes to engine are internal—bore has been increased to 3.28 in. Girling 11¼-in. discs at front brake extra speed.

by Len Griffing

SINCE ITS INCEPTION the Austin-Healey—first the 100-4, later the 100-6—has held a comfortable niche between the bigger Jaguar and the smaller MG. Its popularity is easy to understand. Its body lines are handsome, and the engine—even in absolutely factory tune—develops enough suds to get off briskly from a stoplight with stockers from Detroit. Handling, though not flashing in true stock condition, is fair, and very responsive to minor modification. All the elements are there, including a Panhard rod at the rear and a stabilizer bar at the front.

But, of course, times change. The Plymouth Fury and the Pontiac Bonneville not only dragged away from stock 100-6'ers, but did it ignominiously. It was no contest. Something had to be done.

Fast the in-line six might not have been, but durable and sturdy it most assuredly was. The hundred-plus-a-few horses extracted from its 2639cc did not represent fabulous output, so why not take out a few more? But how to go about it?

To begin, the stroke/bore ratio was 1.12:1 (3.50 in. x 3.125 in.). There seemed to be only one way to go. Besides, the modern trend is toward shorter strokes—shorter, that is, in relation to the bore. The cylinder was opened up to 3.282 in., giving a new stroke/bore ratio of 1.064:1.

The result is a new displacement of 2912cc (171.7 cu. in.), and a new power rating of 130 hp, peaking at 4750 rpm. Compression ratio is now 9.03 to 1.

To accommodate the new power, higher rear end gears are fitted, which give higher mph at equal rpm. Without the Laycock de Normanville overdrive unit, standard gearing is 3.55, producing 20.9 mph/1000 in top gear. If ordered with overdrive, a lower 3.91 gearing is standard. Coupled with the .822:1 speed step-up, overdrive top produces 23.1 mph/1000 rpm. This is a net reduction of 10.6 per cent over the smaller-engined car. Transmission ratios also have been altered in the new model.

Because of the added displacement, the torque factor is substantial. It's no problem to pull a hill at 1000 rpm in fourth over-

ACCELERATION

0-45	7.0 secs.
0-60	12.6
¼-mile	18.8 & 75 mph

PASSING SPEEDS

30-50	6.4
45-60	5.5
50-80	13.4

drive. And the engine really doesn't appear to be working, even though we certainly don't recommend this kind of lugging.

As a companion to the bigger engine, a 10-inch clutch replaces the nine-inch disc, and 11¼-inch disc brakes are fitted to the front wheels (which do most of the stopping), while 11-inch x 2½-inch drums are retained at the rear. As to stopping power, well, you just can't fade a disc brake. Fade is caused by friction heat expanding the friction-producing components away from each other. A disc brake expands the friction pads into the disc; the hotter they get the better they work.

In the appearance department, a new glass-reinforced resin roof is available. This roof is identical to the roofs installed on the cars at Sebring (a touring car must have a roof), except that the finish and the appointments are lush. It stands as an example of what can be done if someone puts his mind to making a luxury accessory for a luxury car. Roof interior is finished in a leather-like perforated material, padded at the front end for safety and appointment value. It looks good, though on the pilot models fit was a bit vague around the edges.

Test car was equipped with Dunlop R-4 tires, an excellent choice. Weight, with full tank of gasoline, was 2580 lbs. Suspension seemed a bit soft, but it was a road machine. Besides, anybody knows how little you have to do to make a street Austin-Healey handle like a race car.

The Autocar
ROAD TEST
1739
Austin-Healey 3000

The latest Austin-Healey can be recognized by the type number on the radiator grille and a glimpse of the disc brakes through the wheel spokes

IN general appearance the larger Austin-Healey has changed but little, since its successful Earls Court debut in 1952. Most of the changes made have been mechanical, and particularly in respect of the power unit. Three years ago the original 2.6-litre four-cylinder engine was replaced by a six-cylinder, and this has now been developed to its present size of 2.9 litres. Girling brakes again deal successfully with the higher speed capabilities of the latest model, and now 11in diameter discs at the front enable faster average speeds to be maintained without the bogey of brake fade to worry the driver.

These cars always have had a capacity for covering long distances in an effortlesss manner. Improved acceleration, particularly above 70 m.p.h., and appreciable increases in maximum speeds have resulted from the use of the larger engine. Compared with the last Road Test of a six-cylinder Austin-Healey which was fitted with a 4.1 to 1 axle ratio—than the 3000 is 3.9 to 1—there is a cut of 4.9sec in the time from 0 to 100 m.p.h. Acceleration in the gears pays more generous dividends from the 50-70 m.p.h. range and upwards; over that range, in overdrive third, top and overdrive top, there are reductions of 0.7, 0.6 and 1.3sec on the last model's times. As the engine speed rises the times are cut further, and in the same gears between 70-90 m.p.h. the times come down by 1.1, 1.0 and 3.2sec. In the 80-100 m.p.h. range in top gear and overdrive top improvements of 4.1 and 3.4sec are recorded.

A noteworthy achievement is the gain in maximum speeds. In overdrive top there is an increase of 5 m.p.h. to 116 m.p.h., while in normal top the speed has gone up from 100 m.p.h., recorded by the 100-Six in May 1958, to no less than 110 m.p.h. for the new 3000 model. These figures are a good indication that the 2.9-litre engine is well able to deal with the extra weight and higher final drive gearing of the latest Austin-Healey.

None of the low-speed characteristics of the engine has been lost, and it pulls well on a light throttle; in town traffic the car can be driven quite comfortably in overdrive third and top gears, when low engine speeds are accompanied by an unobtrusive exhaust note. Most starts from rest can be made in second gear, even when fully loaded, and first is required only on gradients to get the car rolling.

Well-mannered as the car is when hemmed in by brick and concrete canyons, it makes a driver impatient to be outside city limits where the full performance can be savoured. Cruising speeds are entirely dependent upon road conditions, and on a Continental motorway 100 m.p.h. can be main-

tained without any mechanical distress. If time is a factor on a cross-country route, the engine responds willingly to every demand from the driver and it can be taken up to the normal limit mark for engine speed of 5,200 r.p.m. time after time without protest. Above 3,000 r.p.m. there is a fair amount of intake roar and fan noise.

The new engine has a compression ratio of 9.03 to 1, compared with the previous 8.25 to 1, and it does not take kindly to the premium grade petrol available on the Continent. Pinking when pulling at low engine speed, and excessive running on when the engine was switched off were evident during the testing abroad. The engine operated satisfactorily on British premium fuel, although care was needed to avoid pinking when pulling hard in top gear; many owners will prefer to use super premium grade. The fuel tank holds only 12 gallons and so refuelling stops are fairly frequent.

One of the optional extras fitted to the test car was a Laycock-de Normanville overdrive operating on third and top gears. This works with the efficiency and silence one has come to expect of the unit, and it is a valuable adjunct to the normal transmission. Its use keeps engine speed down, not only assisting economical fuel consumption but minimizing use of a revolution range where the exhaust note may become tiring to the occupants of the car. A control switch is placed on the right of the facia where it is quickly reached. Changes into and out of overdrive are snatch-free and immediate, and

Accessibility of all units likely to require routine attention is good. A single reservoir feeds fluid to the brake and clutch operating cylinders. A gauze air filter is fitted to each carburettor

Both sidescreens are secured to the doors by strong wing nuts: the screens are a good fit, and the windscreen pillars cause a minimum of obstruction

Austin-Healey 3000 . . .

the whole of the transmission unit stands up well to full throttle test requirements. A larger clutch has been fitted to deal with the extra power of the 2.9-litre engine, and the gear teeth have been strengthened.

Clutch operation is light and there is a smooth take-up, with no slip evident during standing start acceleration tests. There is no doubt that the times taken for these tests, up to 70 m.p.h. at least, could have been improved upon if the gear change had not been so stiff, and if the rear wheels had maintained contact with the ground on initial take-off. As soon as the clutch was fully home and power applied, each time a test start was made, it was difficult to avoid axle hop.

The new gear ratios are well suited to the performance of the engine and car. Third and top, with their overdrive ratios, are pleasantly close, but not too much so, and acceleration in second and third is of the " kick-in-the-back " variety, care being necessary on wet roads to avoid wheel spin with full throttle.

Little difference has been made to the steering or suspension of the car by the extra weight compared with that of the previous model. The greater percentage is still on the rear axle and the car handles well. On wet roads, with the Dunlop Road Speed tyres inflated to 20 lb front and 23 lb rear, the back of the car is apt to swing when cornering. Steering characteristics in all normal circumstances are neutral; self-centring action is adequate without being forceful. In general the car is directionally stable providing a guiding hand rather than a firm grip is kept on the steering wheel; there is no sign of instability at maximum speed. On bad road surfaces there was some kick-back reaction at the steering wheel.

Tyre pressures are quite critical and the car handles best, two-up, with 23 lb sq in front and 26 lb rear—an increase of 3 lb on the makers' recommendation. For the high speed runs on an *autoroute* these pressures were increased by a further 6 lb front and rear.

The suspension is well damped, and firm enough to ensure that the car does not roll when cornering fast. Continental pavé can be uncomfortable if the tyre pressures are set only a few pounds above the lowest recommended. Ground clearance is limited, and "colonial" sections of road must be tackled with caution.

It was said of the drum brakes fitted to the last Austin-Healey tested that they proved entirely suitable. This may be repeated for the front disc, rear drum equipment of the 3000 model. The total test mileage amounted to over 1,500 miles, and at all times the brakes were excellent. On several occasions when they were applied very hard at speeds in

excess of 100 m.p.h. they retarded the car safely and surely.

For maximum results pedal pressures are rather high; normal check braking, however, is well within the capability of a woman driver. Servo assistance is not fitted, and providing the pedal pressures do not increase with use and wear it would not be necessary. The hand brake is efficient and the lever, between the driving seat and propeller shaft tunnel on right-hand drive cars, is easy to operate.

A number of points criticized on earlier models remain unchanged and, therefore, appear perhaps even more prominent and undesirable in a car which is basically very good. Driver comfort, for example, is marred by lack of room around the pedals; it is difficult to clear the throttle pedal when braking. The seat adjustment, pedal travel and steering wheel position suit a long-legged driver but not one of smaller stature who, in order to reach the pedals, must sit much too close to the wheel. The seat back rests, which tip forward to give access to the rear cockpit, are well raked and comfortable, but are not laterally stable. The seat cushions become " thin " after more than a 100-mile drive, and a tall driver lacks support under the thighs.

Most of the test driving was done with the hard top in position, and the performance figures were taken with the car so equipped. It is certainly a very desirable, if somewhat expensive piece of equipment; in some ways it improves the appearance of a car which is good-looking without it; it provides a warm, snug interior at night, and proved to be watertight. It is light in weight and is easily fitted to or removed from the car; there are four securing points.

The conventional folding hood, which is standard equipment, provides almost equally good protection, at the cost of more wind noise when driving fast. In order to make it neat and well fitting, no more material has been used than was necessary, and erection during a sudden rainstorm proved to be neither quick nor simple to an admittedly inexperienced crew. The same sliding Perspex side screens are used in conjunction with either hard top or hood; they are strong and well made, and fit well in the door apertures. There is no means of locking the car, and if it is left unattended for any length of time, valuables must be removed or locked in the boot.

Visibility in all directions from the driving compartment is good, the screen pillars are commendably thin, the top of each wing can be seen, and head room with hard top or hood erected is not stinted for driver or passenger. It is not really practicable for an adult to sit in the rear cockpit of the closed car, as even a child is not comfortable in this position, with its restrictions on height and leg room.

In comparison with photographs of the Austin-Healey 100 road tested by *The Autocar* in September 1953, there is very little difference to be seen in the layouts of the original production car and the latest version—another indication that the general design was satisfactory from the start. Leathercloth covers the facia, and the instruments are grouped in pairs on each side of the steering column. At night the panel lighting is sufficiently bright without causing dazzle, although there is no rheostat control. Recessed in the lower centre of the panel are the heater and demister controls.

In rain the screen of the closed car fogs up quickly, but the blower fan deals effectively with this without a great deal of noise. Self-parking screen wipers work well, and are helped by a simple form of screen washer. The water container for this is located in a hole in the shelf below the facia, where it not only occupies valuable space but is awkward to replace after filling. There is a strong grab handle in front of the passenger seat, and an ashtray sunk into the top of the propeller shaft tunnel has a sensible lid to prevent ash being blown about the car. Tucked away underneath the left side of the facia is the choke control. The bonnet release is even more elusive, to the right of the steering column behind the panel.

Powerful head lamps are essential for a fast car, and the 3000 is well equipped. There is a foot-operated dip switch which is easy to reach. Flashing direction indicators are combined with the parking and brake lights so that they are white and red, a system which does not find favour in many

European countries where amber coloured flashers are preferred.

Luggage accommodation is very limited, as the spare wheel and the battery take up a large proportion of the space in the locker. Normally, with the car used as a two-seater the space behind the front seats can be used for stowage. When the optional extra rear seats are not fitted two 6-volt batteries are placed forward of the rear axle beneath the floor and the spare wheel fits into a recess, leaving more room for luggage. A battery master switch is a useful item of standard equipment; it is in the right-hand corner of the luggage locker and provides a measure of security when the car is left unattended.

Roadside wheel changing involves the use of an old-fashioned screw-type jack, whose tedious operation would be annoying on a wet dark night. Every 1,000 miles 14 chassis points require grease gun lubrication, in addition to the checking of various oil levels.

The latest Austin-Healey maintains the reputation of a good quality, fast sports-touring car which its predecessors established; its original styling has not dated and the new performance will make it even more competitive.

AUSTIN-HEALEY 3000

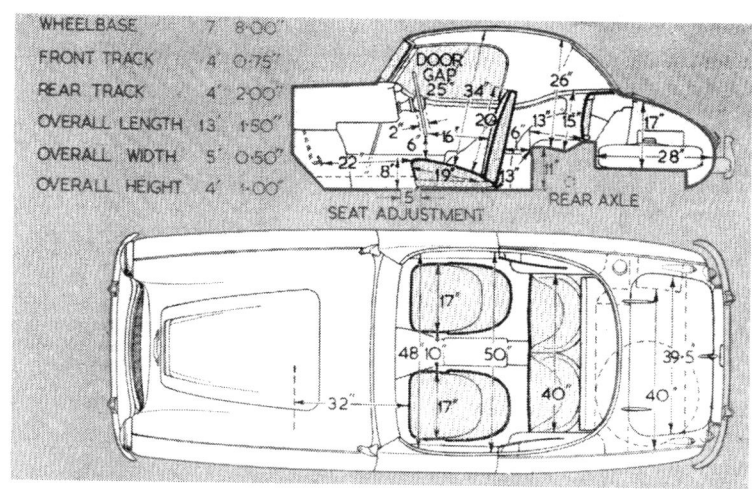

WHEELBASE	7' 8·00"
FRONT TRACK	4' 0·75"
REAR TRACK	4' 2·00"
OVERALL LENGTH	13' 1·50"
OVERALL WIDTH	5' 0·50"
OVERALL HEIGHT	4' 1·00"

Scale ¼in to 1ft. Driving seat in central position. Cushions uncompressed.

DATA

PRICE (basic), with four-seater body, **£829.**
British purchase tax, **£346 10s 10d.**
Total (in Great Britain), **£1,175 10s 10d.**
Extras (with tax): Radio £34 Heater £21 19s 2d, Overdrive £66 8s 2d, Wire wheels £35 8s 4d, Hard top £85.

ENGINE: Capacity, 2,912 c.c. (177.7 cu. in).
Number of cylinders: 6 in line.
Bore and stroke: 83.36 × 88.9 mm (3.3 × 3.5in).
Valve gear: overhead, pushrods and rockers.
Compression ratio: 9.03 to 1.
B.H.P. nett 124 at 4,600 r.p.m. (B.H.P. per ton laden 97.4).
Torque: 175 lb ft at 3,000 r.p.m.
M.P.H. per 1,000 r.p.m. in top gear, 18.94.
M.P.H. per 1,000 r.p.m. in O/D top, 23.1.

WEIGHT: (with 5 gals fuel), 22.5 cwt (2,513 lb).
Weight distribution (per cent): F, 47.3; R, 52.7.
Laden as tested: 25.5 cwt (2,849 lb).
Lb per c.c. (laden): 0.97

BRAKES: Type: Girling, disc front, drum rear.
Method of operation: hydraulic.
Drum dimensions: R, 11in diameter; 2.25in. wide.
Disc diameter: F, 11.25in;
Swept area: F, 228 sq in; R, 155.5 sq in. (301.5 sq in per ton laden).

TYRES: 5.90×15in Dunlop Road Speed.
Pressures (lb sq in): F, 25; R,23 (normal); F, 20; R, 26 (with full load).

TANK CAPACITY: 12 Imperial gallons.
Oil sump, 12 pints.
Cooling system, 20 pints.

DIMENSIONS: Wheelbase: 7ft 8in.
Track: F, 4ft 0.75in; R, 4ft 2in.
Length (overall): 13ft 1.5in.
Width: 5ft 0.5in.
Height: 4ft 2in with hood up.
Ground clearance: 4.5in.
Frontal area: 16.7 sq ft (approximately).

ELECTRICAL SYSTEM: 12-volt; 5/ ampère-hour battery.
Head lights: Double dip; 50-40 watt bulbs.

SUSPENSION: Front, independent coil springs, wishbones and stabilizing bar. Rear, half-elliptic leaf springs and Panhard rod.

PERFORMANCE

ACCELERATION (mean):

Speed Range, Gear Ratios and Time in sec.

M.p.h.				3.21 to 1*	3.91 to 1	4.2 to 1*	5.12 to 1	8.03 to 1	11.45 to 1
10—30	..	..	..	—	—	—	5.4	3.6	2.8
20—40	..	..	..	9.0	6.8	6.5	5.1	3.5	—
30—50	..	..	..	9.0	6.8	6.5	5.2	—	—
40—60	..	..	..	9.0	7.1	6.6	5.6	—	—
50—70	..	..	..	9.5	7.3	7.0	6.1	—	—
60—80	..	..	..	10.3	8.4	8.2	—	—	—
70—90	..	..	..	13.0	10.4	9.9	—	—	—
80—100	..	..	..	16.7	13.9	—	—	—	—

*Overdrive.

From rest through gears to:

30 m.p.h.	..	3.5 sec.
40	..	5.6
50	..	8.0
60	..	11.4
70	..	14.3
80	..	18.9
90	..	24.8
100	..	32.8

Standing quarter mile, 17.9 sec.

MAXIMUM SPEEDS ON GEARS:

Gear			m.p.h.	k.p.h.
O.D.	..	(mean)	114.0	183.3
		(best)	116.0	186.5
Top	..	(mean)	108.0	173.6
		(best)	110.0	177.0
O/D 3rd	..	..	98.0	157.7
3rd	..	..	78.0	125.5
2nd	..	..	49.0	78.8
1st	..	..	34.0	54.7

TRACTIVE EFFORT (by Tapley meter):

			Pull (lb per ton)	Equivalent Gradient
O.D.	..	..	240	1 in 9.3
Top	..	..	316	1 in 7.0
O/D 3rd	..	..	325	1 in 6.8
3rd	..	..	424	1 in 5.2
2nd	..	..	625	1 in 3.6

SPEEDOMETER: Accurate.

BRAKES (at 30 m.p.h. in neutral):

Pedal load in lb	Retardation	Equivalent stopping distance in ft
25	0.22g	135
50	0.38g	79
75	0.60g	50
100	0.76g	39
120	0.90g	33.6

FUEL CONSUMPTION (at constant speeds):

Speed	Direct Top	O.D. Top.
30 m.p.h.	30.5 m.p.g.	35.4 m.p.g
40	27.5 „	33.0 „
50	23.2 „	29.8 „
60	21.0 „	25.0 „
70	19.6 „	22.4 „
80	18.3 „	20.5 „
90	16.6 „	18.6 „
100	—	16.4 „

Overall fuel consumption for 1,200 miles, 20.0 m.p.g. (14.12 litres per 100 km).
Approximate normal range 17—25 m.p.g. (16.6—11.3 litres per 100 km.)
Fuel: Premium grade.

TEST CONDITIONS: Weather: dry, cloudy. 10-20 m.p.h. wind. Air temperature, 65-70 deg. F.

STEERING: Turning circle:
Between kerbs, 33ft 11in R.H.; 36ft 11in L.H.
Between walls: 35ft 2in R.H.; 38ft L.H.
Turns of steering wheel from lock to lock, 3¼.

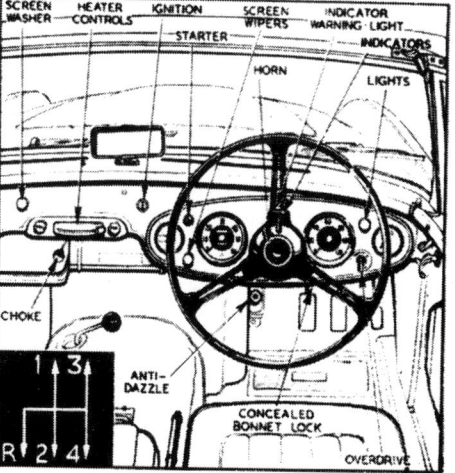

► "I don't know how the man does it. Every time he makes a change it's a winner and this one is the best of the lot."

This was an executive of a huge imported car firm talking. The reference was to Donald Healey and his Austin-Healeys. The allusion to winning was not made to races but to public acceptance of the product although in truth he could have said the same thing in that context.

When it comes to designing a car that will have people standing in line to buy, Mr. Healey ranks with the great men of the day — the likes of the Porsches, father and son — and very few others.

The reasons for this, at least as far as the American market is concerned, are far from complex. Each version from the BN-1 to the newest BN-7, subject of this test, has been a *sports* car in every sense of the word. Second, they have from the beginning been priced within reason; in fact it's hard to see how one can buy more car for the money. Finally, Healey has used his knowledge of the American likes and dislikes to full advantage. We Americans, he knows, are used to sheer, solid torque and a wide power range in our cars, giving gobs of acceleration off the mark or away from a stoplight. Every Austin-Healey built has, for its displacement, been a draggin' fool, especially the later six-cylinder versions. The final American preference is for a car that will cruise effortlessly at fairly high and steady average speeds over superhighways and freeways. Healey offers an overdrive to provide this aspect and the proof of the thinking is shown by the fact that by far the largest slice of the A-H pie sold in the U.S. is overdrive equipped.

The latest Austin-Healey embodies all of these factors and carries them to a new high. There are 26 more pounds/feet of torque and 15 more horses, the figures being 149 lbs/ft at 3000 rpm and 130 bhp at 4750 rpm respectively. This has been accomplished by the simple expedient of increasing the bore to 3.282 inches which brings the displacement out to 171 cubic inches or 2912 cc and as an added bonus also ups the compression ratio to 9.03 to 1 since the same head is used. The stroke remains the same at 3.5 inches

This is the major change and it can be felt in the seat of the pants by those familiar with earlier models. The main effect is that low rpm performance is increased tremendously. The new A-H 3000 can be lugged from a standstill in second gear with no effort and will muddle through five mile-an-hour traffic all day in that gear without protest. Ten miles an hour is no particular strain in third and fourth gear can be used for anything from a shade under 20 mph to top speed. Another effect is that rapid acceleration is done in that tremendous rush-without-clamor that marks the American V8, the only noises being a low booming exhaust note and an unobjectionable buzz from the gearbox in the two lower gears. Torque is such that on a really rapid take-off there is a chirp from the rear tires every time a gear is changed except into fourth.

For a sports car, the revs are not high. This is not a "winding" type of engine, being red-lined at 5200 rpm, but it doesn't

ROAD TEST AUSTIN HEALEY 3000

U.S. Importer ....Hambro Autotomotive Corp.
27 W. 57th St., New York 22, N. Y.

PERFORMANCE

ACCELERATION:

From zero to	seconds
30 mph	3.4
40 mph	5.3
50 mph	7.3
60 mph	10.9
70 mph	14.2
80 mph	19.2
Standing ¼ mile	17.8
Speed at end of quarter	78 mph

SPEED RANGES IN GEARS: (5300 rpm max)

I	7-38
II	10-54
III	16-85
IV	21-top

SPEEDOMETER CORRECTION:

Indicated Speed	Timed Speed
30	28
40	39
50	49
60	60
70	70
80	80

SPECIFICATIONS

POWER UNIT:

BN7 engine	Water-cooled, in-line Six
Valve Operation	Pushrod ohv
Bore & Stroke	3.282x3.50 in (83.36x89 mm)
Stroke/Bore Ratio	1.07/1
Displacement	171.7 cu in (2912 cc)
Compression Ratio	9.03/1
Carburetion by	Two SU H.D. 6
Max. Power	130 gross bhp @ 4750 rpm (124 net @ 4600)
Max. Torque	175 lbs-ft @ 3000 rpm

DRIVE TRAIN:

Transmission ratios		overall ratio
I	2.93	(10.38)
II	2.05	(7.27)
III	1.31	(4.64)
IV	1.00	(3.54)
Final drive ratio	3.54	(3.91)
		with 0.822 O.D.

Axle torque taken by leaf springs

RATING FACTORS:

Specific Power Output (net)	0.72 bhp/cu in
Power to Weight Ratio (as tested)	22.1 lbs/hp
Piston speed @ 60 mph	1675 ft/min
Speed @ 1000 rpm in top gear	20.9 mph

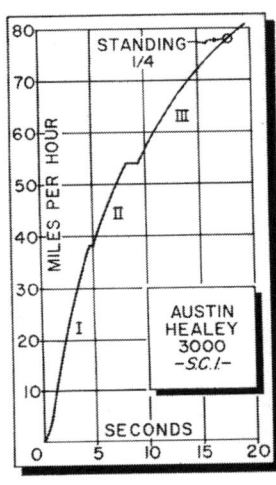

STANDING 1/4

III

II

I

MILES PER HOUR

AUSTIN
HEALEY
3000
—S.C.I—

SECONDS

14

Above: Top is erected by first plugging bows into place then fastening fabric to windshield.
Below: Sticker on speedo indicates overdrive model.

Above: Engine looks exactly like previous six-cylinder but has more punch.

Left: The three liter stays flat in the corners, really storms out.

need to wind. It builds car speed through sheer *push*. This steam-engine-like torque is coupled to high enough gear ratios so that the Healey 3000 engine is loafing where others are buzzing their hearts out. An engine that doesn't need to be twisted to high rotational speeds doesn't tend to wear which may give a clue as to why there are so many early BN-1 and BN-4 units in everday use. It also shows why the Healey is one of those cars that can be race-prepared at home, driven to the track, raced and then, barring accidents, driven home again. Under normal use the damn' things just don't wear out. The bodies may rattle after a few years and a few haybales and the plastic trim may peel off in time but they keep running like the tractors their engine characteristics resemble.

To take advantage of the added power there are a host of other minor changes, some apparent and some not so noticeable. The first and most noticeable change is a switch to Girling disc (segment type) brakes on the front wheels. The back wheels retain the 11 by 2¼ inch drums. Stopping power is, though quite smooth, of the *right now* variety. Not nearly as much pedal pressure is required as with the racing-option full disc set-up nor, for that matter, as with the earlier drums. No matter how we pounded it we could not induce fade or more than a tiny fraction of pedal loss. This tiny loss could probably be traceable to lining wear in the rear drum brakes which were kept working overtime to keep up with the discs. Stops were almost as powerful as with the full Dunlop racing disc layout on the Sebring Healey.

Another change, which will probably be noticed only by those familiar with the BN-cars, is found in the gearbox. Low gear has been raised to 2.93 to 1 as opposed to 3.076 in the earlier box. Second has been *dropped* in ratio to 2.053 as opposed to 1.913 and third has been raised to 1.309, replacing the former 1.333. The effect is a

bit disconcerting at first to a BN-6 driver due to the close spacing of first and second gears and the wide jump into third. We fail to see the reason for increasing this spread unless it is to produce that second gear lugging ability mentioned earlier. It's nice to have but it was also nice to be able to wind it up in second in the older versions. It's sort of a personal choice and not an easy one.

The overdrive unit, too, has been changed. It's less radical now with a 0.822 step-up instead of the 0.778 ratio used formerly. This has the favorable result that the engine can now peak in OD, formerly virtually impossible. Also the step up or down is not nearly as violent as in former models. The rear end ratio in non-OD cars is 3.545 instead of the 3.91 to 1 gears used before. The latter ratio is used in the AH 3000 when equipped with overdrive, replacing the 4.1 to 1 unit used earlier.

Another apparent change doesn't show up in the specification but can be felt. Exactly *what* was done is hard to place but the handling of the car is even better than before. Healeys are noted for their handling qualities — it takes a pretty major goof to make one come loose — but the new one has much of the feel of the competition prepared version but without the rock-hard feel of the race car. It shares with the competition car the feeling that you couldn't turn it over with a derrick. Spin it out, yes, Turn it over, no.

It is hard to truly judge the handling characteristics of the new Healey but from a few hurried laps around the course at Lime Rock Park with ordinary tires, it would seem to be a mildly final oversteering car. For a while, of course, one must turn *in* to the corner. Then for a noticeable period, long or short depending on the radius and speed of the bend, the car can be held in its drift with the wheels pointed dead ahead, steering done by throttle. Finally and fairly gently, more and more reverse lock must be ap-

plied, particularly if the corner is fairly tight. In this respect it resembles the competition BN-6 with which this writer has had some personal experience in overcooking on a corner — twice to be exact. In each case the end result was that the car went off to the inside with the tail leading the way. This fits the classic, if oversimplified, description of oversteer which holds that if the car goes through the fence nose first you're understeering; if it goes out tail first, you have oversteered.

The final piece of improvement may seem relatively minor to all but other Healey owners. This one involves the top. Personally and collectively the staff of SCI has cursed the top used on the BN-6 which takes two strong men and a very agile boy to put up. The bows were stiff and almost impervious to coaxing and the front bow almost impossible to fasten. Once fastened it became a matter of dislocating fingers and thumbs to fasten the back curtain down. The new top has removable bows that can be unfolded first and then stuck into a pair of sockets and a front bow that will attach to the windshield frame without hammering. The back of the top now fits and can be fastened reasonably easily. True, it's still not a one-handed operation and it still takes time but one man *can* do the job without breaking a finger in the process. For those who still don't want to struggle we can only suggest the hard-top. In fact we'll suggest it anyway since it's far and away the best looking and best engineered fiberglas top in the industry. Used in conjunction with the Healey aluminum rimmed side curtains it makes the car as weather tight as any roadster can possibly become — and some coupes too for that matter.

Summing up: The new Austin Healey 3000 is a comfortable car, a fast car and a very quick car. Above all it is an eminently safe car. Even more important it's a good *sports* car.

A TYPICAL British sports car, the Austin-Healey 3000 retains its position as one of the most attractive-looking machines in its class.

fitted to the test car, and this has a rather smaller step-up ratio than before. A short open Hardy Spicer propeller shaft conveys the drive to the hypoid axle.

The body is a very handsome open two-seater of the individual shape which we have come to associate with the larger Austin-Healey. The body fitted to the test car had the optional two children's seats which actually render it an occasional four-seater in effect. This model has a fair-sized luggage boot, but it is largely occupied with the spare wheel, tools and battery. A very neat hard top with excellent lines was fitted to the test car, and the sidescreens had sliding panels for signalling and ventilation.

The driving position is comfortable, though the adjustable steering wheel is rather close to the driver even in its most forward position. The seats give good support to the back, and if the cushions are not particularly soft, this is an advantage for a fast sports car. It is necessary to criticize the pedals rather strongly, for the clutch and brake are

JOHN BOLSTER TESTS THE
THE AUSTIN-HEALEY 3000
A Genuine 115 m.p.h. Machine of Impeccable Manners

Way back in 1952, when AUTOSPORT was quite a pup and I had a little more hair than I have now, I was the first journalist ever to drive an Austin-Healey. Belgium was the country where my secret tests were conducted, and subsequently, in 1956, I tried the six-cylinder version of the car around Europe in general and the Nürburgring in particular. Now, a bigger six-cylinder engine and disc brakes have come along, and so once again I have been enjoying some Austin-Healey motoring.

The new 3000 can be described as a typical British sports car with an exceptionally large and powerful engine. A conventional box-section frame has independent front suspension by wishbones and helical springs. There is an anti-roll torsion bar, and the steering is by a cam and peg type box. Behind, the hypoid rear axle is on semi-elliptic springs with a Panhard rod for lateral location. The Girling hydraulic brakes have 11¼ ins. discs in front aad 11 ins. drums at the rear. The 5.90-15 ins. Road Speed tyres may be on disc or wire wheels to choice.

The big six-cylinder engine has a cast iron block and head, the latter having six inlet ports. Carburation is by twin SU HD6 instruments, and there is a dual exhaust system. The crankshaft runs on four main bearings and the chain driven camshaft operates the valves by pushrods and rockers. The exhaust valves are in KE965 steel, and the solid-skirt aluminium pistons are tin

plated. The capacity of this nearly square unit is 3 litres, and it develops 130 b.h.p. at 4,750 r.p.m. on a compression ratio of just over 9 to 1.

Compared with previous Austin-Healeys, a larger clutch has had to be fitted to take the formidable torque of the engine, and the four-speed gearbox has wider pinions. The optional Laycock-de Normanville overdrive was

much too close together. The gear lever is also badly placed for a right-hand drive car, and tends to be stiff in action, but the synchromesh on the upper three speeds is excellent.

On moving off, one is at once impressed by the sheer power of the big engine, and this feeling persists after hundreds of miles of driving. The Austin-Healey 3000 is a wonderfully

DRIVING POSITION is comfortable, but clutch and brake pedals are rather too close together and the gear lever is badly placed for right-hand drive.

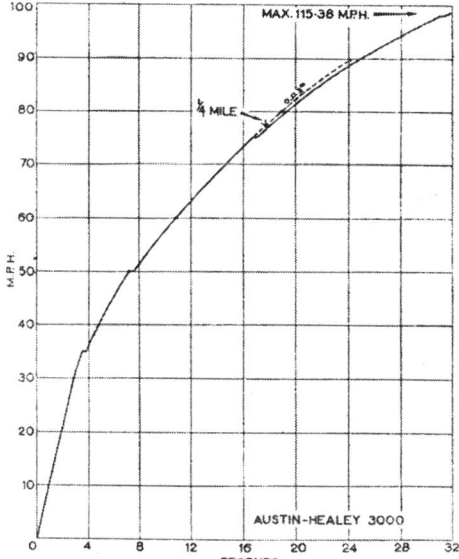

ACCELERATION GRAPH

effortless car, and even if it is driven mostly on top gear it will fly past all the usual opposition. If the lower gears are used, real kick-in-the-back acceleration is available. Tried against other genuine 100 m.p.h. sports cars, the 3000 simply leaves them standing, its acceleration being really fierce.

In the past, I have sometimes criticized B.M.C. engines for their lack of "bottom end" performance. The designers have now found the trick, and this new big six has all the torque in the world almost down to zero revs. It does tend to pink, and runs on when the ignition is switched off, which makes one hope that an aluminium head may later be offered as an extra. It is a power unit which joins in the fun when hard driving is afoot, and though it is fairly audible inside the small car, it never becomes rough however hard it is driven.

The ride is quite soft, and the urge of the engine enables the sharper curves to

DISTINCTIVE FLASHES on the front and rear of the car distinguish it from the successful 2.6-litre machine.

be slid under power when the cops are looking the other way. Driven as a fast touring car, this Austin-Healey is very controllable, and cruising at considerable speeds is all the more enjoyable because there is always more power available under the right foot. On a racing circuit, rather firmer suspension would be appreciated. The car remains controllable during fast cornering, but there is some pattering of the front wheels when racing techniques are employed. Similarly, the back axle can be made to hop during violent acceleration. It would be fair to say that the present suspension set-up is ideal for 90 per cent. of customers, but the remainder would applaud a little stiffening up here and there.

The brakes are powerful and do not fade. They do require a somewhat

heavy right foot, but the ability to stop is always there if one really presses. The clutch is also a little heavier than some, but one forgives all because it really grips at once and never slips or becomes fierce—even during the rigours of acceleration testing. The gears are commendably quiet, and can be snatched through really quickly when the rather unusual movement of the lever has been mastered.

Both for high speed work and touring the overdrive is a splendid device. On a winding road, third and overdrive third are the gears to use, and instantaneous up and down changes may be made without recourse to the gear lever. For fast cruising, one uses the overdrive top, flicking down to the direct drive for curves or overtaking. The ratios of the gearbox, rear axle and overdrive allow the potent engine to give of its best under all conditions.

The general finish of the car is pleasing and the appearance wholly delightful. The bonnet is rather full of engine, but normal maintenance is not unduly difficult. In spite of its impressive length of bonnet, the machine feels quite small and compact to drive and park. It has impeccable manners in traffic, and is a perfectly practical shopping car. When driven flat out, the big engine consumes a modicum of petrol, but at fast cruising speeds a praiseworthy 20 m.p.g. may be expected.

The Austin-Healey 3000 is a genuine 115 m.p.h. car which will yet appeal to many drivers who never exceed "eighty". It gives a wonderful feeling of reserve power which is perhaps one of motoring's greatest enjoyments. A touch of the pedal sends it flying uphill, and one never seems to be overdriving it. In spite of its great performance, the car employs no unusual components, and there is nothing to worry the most remote country garage. For the driver who enjoys horsepower and who finds the smaller sports cars a little too "gear-happy", this 3-litre speed model is just the job.

SPECIFICATION AND PERFORMANCE DATA

Car Tested: Austin-Healey 3000 occasional 4-seater. Price £1,175 10s. 10d. (including P.T.). Extras on test car: Hard top, £85; overdrive, £66 8s. 2d.; wire wheels, £35 8s. 4d.; heater, £21 19s. 2d.; radio, £34 (all including P.T.).

Engine: Six-cylinders 83.36 mm. x 88.9 mm. (2,912 c.c.). Pushrod operated overhead valves. 9.03 to 1 compression ratio. 130 b.h.p. at 4,750 r.p.m. Twin SU HD6 carburetters. Lucas coil and distributor.

Transmission: Borg and Beck 10 ins. clutch. Four-speed gearbox with synchromesh on upper three gears with central gear lever, ratios 3.214 o/d., 3.91, 4.207 o/d., 5.118, 8.026, and 11.456 to 1. Laycock-de Normanville overdrive. Open Hardy Spicer propeller shaft. Hypoid rear axle.

Chassis: Box-section pressed-steel frame. Independent front suspension by wishbones and helical springs with anti-roll torsion bar. Cam and peg steering gear. Rigid rear axle on semi-elliptic

springs with Panhard rod. Piston-type dampers. Girling hydraulic brakes with 11¼ ins. discs in front, 11 ins. drums behind. Knock-on wire wheels fitted 5.90-15 ins. Road Speed tyres.

Equipment: 12-volt lighting and starting. Speedometer, rev. counter, oil pressure, water temperature and fuel gauges. Windscreen washer. Flashing indicators. Extra: Heater, radio.

Dimensions: Wheelbase, 7 ft. 8 ins. Track, front 4 ft. 0¾ in., rear 4 ft. 2 ins. Overall length, 13 ft. 1½ ins. Width, 5 ft. 0½ in. Turning circle, 34 ft. Weight, 22½ cwt.

Performance: Maximum speed, 115.38 m.p.h. Speeds in gears, direct top 98 m.p.h., overdrive 3rd 90 m.p.h., 3rd 75 m.p.h., 2nd 50 m.p.h., 1st 35 m.p.h. Standing quarter-mile 17.6 secs. Acceleration: 0-30 m.p.h., 2.8 secs.; 0-50 m.p.h., 7.2 secs.; 0-60 m.p.h., 10.8 secs.; 0-80 m.p.h., 19.2 secs.; 0-100 m.p.h., 36 secs.

Fuel Consumption: 20 m.p.g.

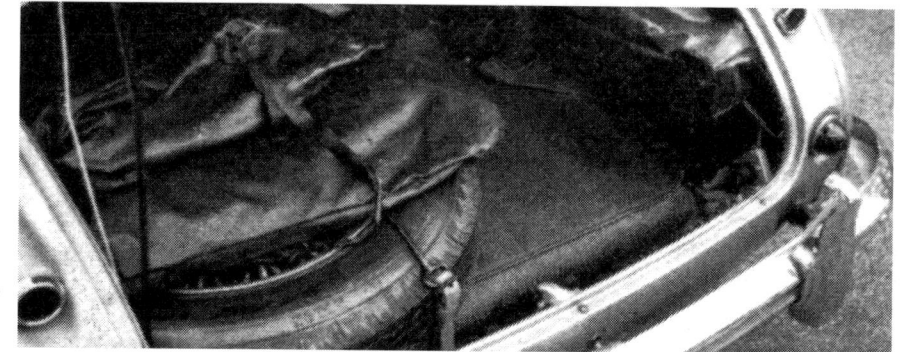

BOOT is of sufficient size for practical touring, though it contains battery, spare wheel and tools.

COMPACT and shapely, the Austin-Healey has a comparatively lazy engine which has now been tuned to realize its full potential.

will ever exceed 120 m.p.h., but above that speed he would be well advised to exercise some caution. The machine is short and has a rather conventional chassis, which becomes a little lively at the top end even in this improved form. Bumps or gusts of wind tend to deflect the car somewhat, but under suitable conditions it is safe to attain 125 m.p.h.

The Ruddspeed Austin-Healey is a car that will appeal to many because of the glorious sensation of sheer power that it gives. I was able to pass some very expensive speed models, particularly up hills, where this car really shines. There is some increase in the noise over the standard model, but the deep, powerful note is generally rather pleasing.

THE Austin-Healey 3000 is a good-looking sports car capable of well over 100 m.p.h. which combines exceptional flexibility with real acceleration. At its price, it is almost unbeatable as a practical high-performance sports-touring car. Yet, the temptation to develop that relatively lazy 3-litre, 6-cylinder engine is strong, and Rudds of Worthing have now made it possible to turn the big Healey into a real fire-eating monster.

The first essential is to modify the cylinder head, and the ports are opened up, valve seats modified, combustion chambers matched and polished, and the compression ratio is raised to 9.7 to 1. This work costs £25 including fitting charge. For another £25, Rudds will fit a special camshaft, and a triple inlet manifold plus a third S.U. carburetter can be installed for £39.

This work really allows the hefty power unit to realize its full potential, and in the compact and well-shaped sports two-seater, the performance cannot help being immense. However, such an engine is far too powerful for the roadholding afforded by the standard chassis, and a great deal of work has been carried out in rendering the performance usable.

The front shock absorbers and springs must be replaced by competition-type equipment, at a price of £25. New rear springs are £12, and a servo is fitted to the disc brakes at £19 10s. All these prices include fitting, and in certain instances an allowance is made for returned equipment. In addition, the test car had Michelin X tyres of 6.40-15 ins. size, for which a small body modification was required to give adequate clearance.

On the road, the performance is really fierce. Unfortunately, the Austin-Healey gearbox has a slow change from second to third which cannot be hurried. In spite of this considerable disadvantage, the following somewhat startling figures were recorded. Standing quarter-mile 16.8 secs.; 0-30 m.p.h., 2.8 secs.; 0-50 m.p.h., 5.8 secs.; 0-60 m.p.h., 9.4 secs.; 0-80 m.p.h., 14.8 secs.; 0-100 m.p.h., 21.6 secs. Driven hard, the fuel consumption is 17 m.p.g., which is not unreasonable for a 3-litre car. In spite of its high compression ratio, the engine pinks less than the standard power unit.

IMMENSE performance has been achieved by these Rudd modifications but the power gained by this very potent engine must be matched by improved roadholding.

JOHN BOLSTER TRIES

THE RUDDSPEED AUSTIN-HEALEY 3000

A Good Looking Car of Really Fierce Performance

The maximum speed is 125 m.p.h. with hood and sidescreens in position. The hood stands up to this great velocity remarkably well, but the sidescreens tend to bulge outwards. The work on the suspension eliminates the flap and patter of the front wheels, and the rear axle does not bounce during acceleration. The ride is firm but by no means unpleasantly so.

It is unlikely that the average owner

After prolonged slow-speed work in traffic, the engine tended to run unevenly, but cleared itself at once when the open road was reached. Starting was always instantaneous and the top gear flexibility was surprisingly good. As a practical sports-touring car for everyday use, yet with a capacity to flash past the "hundred" at the drop of a hat, this good-looking two-seater must represent exceptional value for money.

A Healey for Hurrying

Ruddspeed conversion makes a fast sports car phenomenally potent

WHEN the Austin-Healey was changed from a four- into a six-cylinder machine many enthusiasts were not entirely happy with the resultant performance. Since then the six-port head has rendered an improvement and the engine size has been increased to three litres from the original 2.6. In this form the car is now really fast enough to meet the needs of most drivers, but for those who are suitably experienced and wish to turn their Healey into something quite remarkable, or possibly to use it in competitions, Rudds of Worthing offer for well under £200 a conversion which not merely improves but rather transforms an already good sports car.

Far from being merely an engine conversion, the whole car has been modified, including the brakes and suspension, so that not only is performance increased but also it is made if anything more usable, some caution however being necessary on wet roads. It must be remembered, however, that the car is still comparatively cheap and so the general feeling of control is not the same as that of a highly expensive specialist-built machine. This results in the Healey being somewhat tiring to drive over long distances, but this is largely due to the fact that with the rev. counter at 3,000 r.p.m. and the speedometer needle at about 80 m.p.h., one feels that the car is waffling along so slowly that one really ought to get a move on and so a very few seconds later is travelling at over 100 m.p.h., at which speed a certain amount of concentration becomes desirable. Also tiring is the exhaust noise, which was sufficient to make the police look decidedly interested even if they did not essay a chase. However for everyday use the standard exhaust system can be used, presumably with some loss of power.

Our last road test of a standard Austin-Healey Six covered the smaller-engined version, so figures are not accurately comparative. Nevertheless, a Maximile speed which has risen from 103.9 m.p.h. to 113.1 m.p.h. mean, and acceleration which has enabled the Ruddspeed car to better standing quarter and 0-100 m.p.h. times by 2.0 and 11.9 seconds respectively, cannot to any great extent be due to an extra 273 c.c. of engine. Overall fuel consumption has, however, dropped by some 5 m.p.g. as might be expected when the additional carburetter is considered, although steady speed consumptions are not greatly different and at some speeds actually better.

For all the performance the car does not suffer unduly from temperament, starting being of the first time variety without

the need of any choke after a night in the open. Driving can be done almost exclusively in direct top with commendable smoothness if desired, whilst starts can be made in second gear without protest. Slight pinking could, however, be provoked even on 100 octane petrol on occasion, and after hard driving there was a tendency to run on.

Not every owner would, one feels, wish to convert his Healey to give the exceptional standard of performance offered by the Rudd conversion, but for those who wish to own a car which will reduce any road to a series of curves, all the straights having mysteriously disappeared and all other cars having stopped, this is a way in which such a vehicle can be acquired without enormous expense.

PERFORMANCE DATA: RUDDSPEED AUSTIN-HEALEY 3000

WEATHER

Dry with light wind (temperature 40°–44°F.: Barometer 29.4 in. Hg.).

"Maximile" Speed. (Timed quarter mile after one mile accelerating from rest.)

Mean of four opposite runs	..	..	..	113.1 m.p.h.
Best one-way time equals ..	..	..	..	113.9 m.p.h.

FUEL CONSUMPTION

Overdrive top m.p.g.	Direct top m.p.g.	
29½	26½	At constant 30 m.p.h. on level.
30	26½	At constant 40 m.p.h. on level.
27	24	At constant 60 m.p.h. on level.
23½	21	At constant 80 m.p.h. on level.
17½		At constant 100 m.p.h. on level.

Overall fuel consumption for 926 miles, 60.65 gallons, equals 15.3 m.p.g.

ACCELERATION TIMES (from standstill)

0–30 m.p.h.	..	..	3.1 sec.	0–70 m.p.h.	.. .. 11.4 sec.
0–40 m.p.h.	..	..	4.7 sec.	0–80 m.p.h.	.. .. 14.3 sec.
0–50 m.p.h.	..	..	6.4 sec.	0–90 m.p.h.	.. .. 18.2 sec.
0–60 m.p.h.	..	..	8.8 sec.	0–100 m.p.h.	.. .. 24.47 sec.

Standing quarter mile: 16.2 sec.

Acceleration times on upper ratios

	O/D top gear sec.	Direct top gear sec.	Direct third gear sec.
10–30 m.p.h.	8.8 ..	7.1 ..	5.3
20–40 m.p.h.	9.3 ..	7.4 ..	5.3
30–50 m.p.h.	9.5 ..	7.0 ..	4.9
40–60 m.p.h.	9.2 ..	7.0 ..	4.3
50–70 m.p.h.	9.5 ..	6.6 ..	4.6
60–80 m.p.h.	9.7 ..	6.3 ..	—
70–90 m.p.h.	9.8 ..	7.3 ..	—
80–100 m.p.h.	13.0 ..	10.1 ..	

Brakes from 30 m.p.h.

0.93 g retardation (equivalent to 32½ ft. stopping distance) with 70 lb. pedal pressure.
0.80 g retardation (equivalent to 37½ ft. stopping distance) with 50 lb. pedal pressure.
0.49 g retardation (equivalent to 61½ ft. stopping distance) with 25 lb. pedal pressure.

Mighty powerhouse. Three carburetters at once distinguish the engine compartment of this tuned Austin-Healey, but a specially modified cylinder head, different camshaft and special exhaust system also help to raise the power output.

RUDDSPEED AUSTIN-HEALEY 3000 MODIFICATIONS

	£	s.	d.
Modified cylinder head 9.7/1 compression ratio	25	0	0
Special camshaft	25	0	0
Triple inlet manifolds and two extra S.U. carburetters ..	39	0	0
Large bore exhaust system with chromed tail pipes ..	14	0	0
Stronger front springs and competition shock absorbers	25	0	0
Modified rear springs	12	0	0
Brakes modified to servo assistance	19	10	0
Michelin X 640×15 tyres on exchange for new tyres ..	15	0	0
(including modifying body to give wheel clearance)			
Oil temperature gauge and ammeter	12	10	0
Extension pedals (for short drivers)	1	0	0
Gear lever extension with wooden knob	1	15	0
Total	**189**	**15**	**0**
Allowances when a new car is modified:			
For shock absorbers and springs	7	10	0
For camshaft	2	0	0
For cylinder head and manifold	2	0	0

All charges include fitting.
Suppliers: K. N. Rudd (Engineers), Ltd., 41, High Street, Worthing.

Make: Austin-Healey   Type: 3000 Hardtop (B.T.7.) With overdrive
Makers: The Austin Motor Co., Ltd., Longbridge, Birmingham
Test Data

World copyright reserved ; no unauthorized reproduction in whole or in part.

CONDITIONS : Weather : Dry, wind 5-15 m.p.h. (Temperature 70°-75°F., Barometer 29.7 in. Hg.) Surface : Dry tarmacadam. Fuel : 100 octane pump petrol.

INSTRUMENTS
Speedometer at 30 m.p.h.	19% fast
Speedometer at 60 m.p.h.	10% fast
Speedometer at 90 m.p.h.	9% fast
Distance recorder	2% slow

WEIGHT
Kerb weight (unladen, but with oil, coolant and fuel for approx. 50 miles) .. 22 cwt.
Front/rear distribution of kerb weight 50/50
Weight laden as tested.. .. 25¾ cwt.

MAXIMUM SPEEDS
Flying Mile
Mean of six opposite runs .. .. 115.0 m.p.h.
Best one-way time equals .. .. 116.9 m.p.h.
"Maximile" Speed. (Timed quarter mile after one mile accelerating from rest.)
Mean of opposite runs .. .. 107.1 m.p.h.
Best one-way time equals .. .. 108.4 m.p.h.
Speed in gears
Max. speed in Direct Top gear .. 98 m.p.h.
Max. speed in Overdrive 3rd gear .. 92 m.p.h.
Max. speed in 3rd gear .. .. 75 m.p.h.
Max. speed in 2nd gear .. .. 48 m.p.h.
Max. speed in 1st gear .. .. 33 m.p.h.

FUEL CONSUMPTION
(Overdrive top gear)
35½ m.p.g. at constant 30 m.p.h. on level.
35 m.p.g. at constant 40 m.p.h. on level.
32 m.p.g. at constant 50 m.p.h. on level.
29 m.p.g. at constant 60 m.p.h. on level.
23½ m.p.g. at constant 70 m.p.h. on level.
20½ m.p.g. at constant 80 m.p.h. on level.
19 m.p.g. at constant 90 m.p.h. on level.
16 m.p.g. at constant 100 m.p.h. on level.
(Direct top gear)
31 m.p.g. at constant 30 m.p.h. on level.
29½ m.p.g. at constant 40 m.p.h. on level.
26½ m.p.g. at constant 50 m.p.h. on level.
23½ m.p.g. at constant 60 m.p.h. on level.
20½ m.p.g. at constant 70 m.p.h. on level.
18 m.p.g. at constant 80 m.p.h. on level.
16½ m.p.g. at constant 90 m.p.h. on level.

Overall Fuel Consumption for 1,632 miles, 86.8 gallons, equals 18.8 m.p.g. (15.0 litres/100 km.)
Touring Fuel Consumption (m.p.g. at steady speed midway between 30 m.p.h. and maximum, less 5% allowance for acceleration). 21.6 m.p.g.
Fuel tank capacity (maker's figure) 12 gallons.

STEERING
Turning circle between kerbs :
Left .. .. 33¾ ft.
Right .. .. 33¼ ft.
Turns of steering wheel from lock to lock 3

BRAKES from 30 m.p.h.
0.93 g retardation (equivalent to 32 ft. stopping distance) with 75 lb. pedal pressure.
0.67 g retardation (equivalent to 45 ft. stopping distance) with 50 lb. pedal pressure.
0.27 g retardation (equivalent to 111 ft. stopping distance) with 25 lb. pedal pressure.

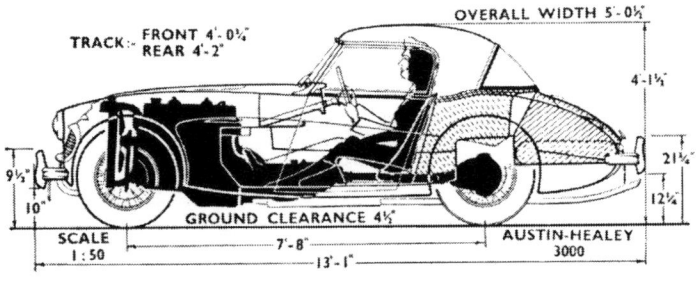

TRACK :- FRONT 4'-0¾" REAR 4'-2"
OVERALL WIDTH 5'-0½"
4'-1½"
9½" 10"
21¼" 12¼"
GROUND CLEARANCE 4½"
SCALE 1:50   7'-8"   13'-1"   AUSTIN-HEALEY 3000

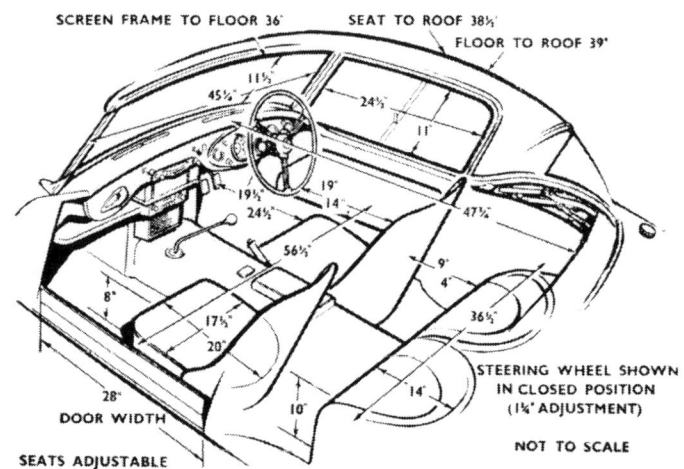

SCREEN FRAME TO FLOOR 36"   SEAT TO ROOF 38½"
FLOOR TO ROOF 39"
11½" 45½" 24½" 11"
19½" 19" 14" 47½"
24½" 14" 56½" 9" 4"
8" 36½"
17½" 20" 14"
28" 10"
DOOR WIDTH
SEATS ADJUSTABLE
STEERING WHEEL SHOWN IN CLOSED POSITION (1¾" ADJUSTMENT)
NOT TO SCALE

ACCELERATION TIMES from standstill
0-30 m.p.h.	3.4 sec.
0-40 m.p.h.	5.7 sec.
0-50 m.p.h.	8.5 sec.
0-60 m.p.h.	11.7 sec.
0-70 m.p.h.	15.5 sec.
0-80 m.p.h.	19.9 sec.
0-90 m.p.h.	27.2 sec.
0-100 m.p.h.	39.3 sec.
Standing quarter mile	17.7 sec.

ACCELERATION TIMES on Upper Ratios
	Overdrive top gear	Direct top gear	3rd gear
10-30 m.p.h.	—	6.8 sec.	5.0 sec.
20-40 m.p.h.	8.6 sec.	6.6 sec.	5.1 sec.
30-50 m.p.h.	9.0 sec.	6.8 sec.	5.0 sec.
40-60 m.p.h.	8.9 sec.	6.6 sec.	5.5 sec.
50-70 m.p.h.	10.1 sec.	7.6 sec.	7.0 sec.
60-80 m.p.h.	11.7 sec.	8.7 sec.	—
70-90 m.p.h.	16.5 sec.	12.4 sec.	—
80-100 m.p.h.	20.0 sec.	—	—

HILL CLIMBING at sustained steady speeds
Max. gradient on overdrive top gear	1 in 8 (Tapley 280 lb./ton)
Max. gradient on direct top gear	1 in 6.2 (Tapley 355 lb./ton)
Max. gradient on overdrive 3rd gear	1 in 5.9 (Tapley 375 lb./ton)
Max. gradient on direct 3rd gear	1 in 4.8 (Tapley 460 lb./ton)
Max. gradient on 2nd gear	1 in 3.2 (Tapley 665 lb./ton)

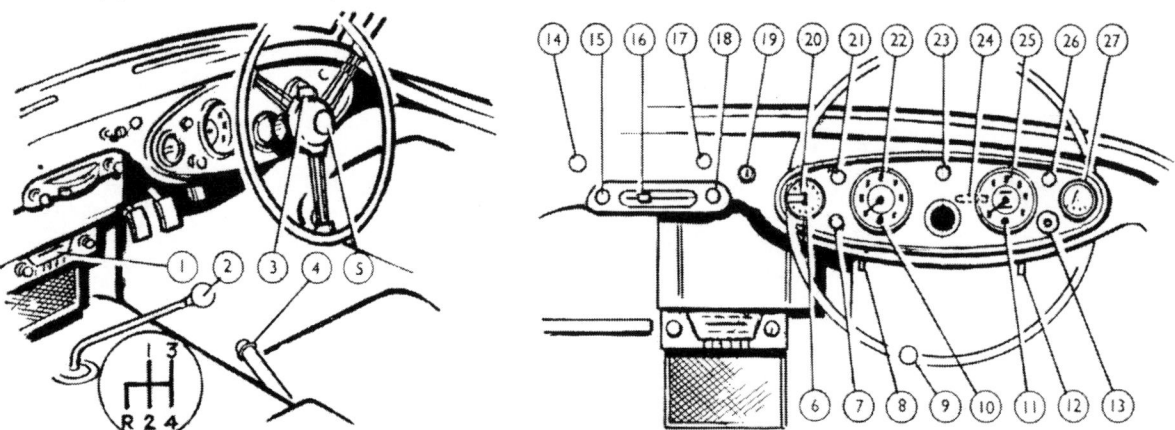

1. Radio controls. 2. Gear lever. 3. Direction indicator switch. 4. Handbrake. 5. Horn button. 6. Water thermometer. 7. Windscreen wipers control. 8. Panel light switch. 9. Dip-switch. 10. Dynamo charge warning light. 11. Headlamp high beam warning light. 12. Trip resetting knob. 13. Overdrive switch. 14. Screenwasher button. 15. Cold air control. 16. Heater control and fan switch. 17. Choke control. 18. Hot air control. 19. Ignition switch. 20. Oil pressure gauge. 21. Starter. 22. Tachometer. 23. Direction indicator warning light. 24. Bonnet catch release. 25. Speedometer. 26. Lights switch. 27. Fuel contents gauge.

The Austin-Healey 3000 Hardtop

An Occasional Four-seater Tested in Overdrive Form

SINCE the Austin-Healey "Six" was last tested, numerous small changes have been made in both the mechanical and body specifications. In conjunction with a 10% increase in engine size, bringing the capacity to just over 2.9 litres, the final drive gearing has been raised by 5%, a closer ratio overdrive fitted, and disc brakes have been adopted on the front wheels only. The particular car tested had the occasional four-seater body that now supplements the two-seat version and the well designed hardtop that effectively converts it to a closed car when the weather makes this expedient. All performance figures were taken with this fitted.

An unexpected by-product of these changes, which may be indicative of carburetter modifications, was the 5 to 15% improvement found in the overdrive top gear fuel consumption at speeds below 70 m.p.h. Less surprising, in view of the very smooth shape of the new hardtop, is the increase of 7 m.p.h. in maximum speed to the creditable figure of 115 m.p.h. It is probable that even better figures for acceleration and speed might have been obtained from a well-used model as the car tested

had done only 2,500 miles at the time and both engine and gearbox were relatively stiff.

In order to depress fully a long-travel clutch, it is necessary for the driver to sit quite close to the steering wheel, and for a person of average height the extended-arm steering position is out of the question, in spite of an adjustable steering column which allows the wheel to be moved quite near to the facia. The close conjunction of windscreen and driver is reminiscent of older sports cars and, despite a low seating position and a long broad bonnet, provides excellent visibility and a view of the road surface surprisingly close ahead. In addition, dirt or rain on the glass reduce visibility much less than with a distant screen and better protection is obtained

from the wind when the car is open; in this form the Austin-Healey is a very pleasant machine, and with the sidescreens erect it is possible to cruise at speeds in the region of 80 m.p.h. without undue buffeting or turbulence, although with considerable wind noise as must be expected in an open car.

The small bucket seats give unusually good lateral support but have very upright backs and almost horizontal seat cushions. Many people would prefer to have the seats tilted bodily backwards with some extra padding to support the small of the back which tends to ache on long journeys.

With standard tyre pressures, the car is perhaps a little heavy to drive on slow, twisty roads, and although the wheels adhere firmly to the ground, hard driving

TOP REMOVED.—The aluminium-framed detachable sidescreens have sliding Perspex windows, and the self-parking wipers do not obstruct the view from the low driving position. The knock-off wire wheels are an optional extra.

In Brief

Price (including overdrive and hardtop as tested) £935 17s. 6d., plus purchase tax £391 1s. 6d., equals £1,326 19s.
Price without overdrive and hardtop (including purchase tax), £1,175 10s. 10d.
Capacity ... ... 2912 c.c.
Unladen kerb weight ... 22 cwt.
Acceleration:
  20-40 m.p.h. in top gear ... 6.6 sec.
  0-50 m.p.h. through gears 8.5 sec.
Maximum direct top gear gradient 1 in 6.2
Maximum speed ... 115.0 m.p.h.
"Maximile" speed ... 107.1 m.p.h.
Touring fuel consumption 21.6 m.p.g.
Gearing: 19.0 m.p.h. in top gear at 1,000 r.p.m. (overdrive, 23.1 m.p.h.); 32.5 m.p.h. at 1,000 ft./min. piston speed (overdrive, 39.6 m.p.h.).

POWER.—The 3-litre engine fills most of the available space but leaves the major components accessible for servicing. Two large semi-downdraught S.U. carburetters feed a cylinder head with six separate inlet ports.

is mild pinking at full throttle using ordinary premium grade fuel. This disappears with the use of 100 octane fuel or if the lowest part of the r.p.m. range is avoided by means of the gearbox. At the other extreme, the engine runs quickly and smoothly up to the limit of 5,200 r.p.m. which is marked with a red line on the tachometer.

Mechanically, this is a very quiet unit, but this advantage is rather negatived by a hard and purposeful exhaust note from the twin pipes which, although intrinsically pleasing, attracts a lot of attention and raises the internal noise level to a point where it can become tiring on a long, fast journey, particularly with the hardtop in use. The small "pancake" air filters do little to eliminate carburetter intake roar, and sudden throttle opening is accompanied by a pronounced gasping noise.

The quiet gearbox has very satisfactory close ratios, but at first it was not found light to operate. To some extent this was caused by the stiffness that is common with new boxes, and later in the test it became freer to the extent that leisurely changes slipped through very easily, but to force through a really quick change against the effective synchromesh still called for some effort.

The amount of gear changing required, of course, is greatly reduced by the wide torque range of the engine and by the optional Laycock overdrive fitted to the car submitted for test and which provides an immediate 18% reduction in engine speed. Operated by a facia switch, which is most convenient for finger-tip operation without moving the right hand from the wheel, this overdrive is very smooth in action. Available on top and third gears only, an interconnection prevents engagement on the overrun with a completely closed throttle, whilst full power changes were perceptible by little more than the change of exhaust note.

produces some scream from the Dunlop Road Speed tyres. With the extra 6 lb./sq. in. all round which is recommended for prolonged driving at speeds over 85/90 m.p.h., tyre noise is very hard to provoke, the steering is light, roll negligible and wheel adhesion and behaviour of the Panhard-rod-located back axle on bumpy roads remains extremely good. Quite heavy use of the throttle induces very mild oversteer and enables a series of bends to be negotiated very fast with relatively small movements of the steering, so that the close driving position necessitates little passing of the wheel from hand to hand. On wet and slippery roads, however, the accelerator must be treated with some discretion to avoid sudden breakaway at the back.

Although the steering displays very little feed-back from bumps and camber changes, the driver is aware of continual movement of the wheel in his hands due to a slight lateral shake from which the scuttle suffers on bad roads, and which also causes some bonnet movement and chattering from the sidescreens in open form, particularly with the high tyre pressures. Comfortable riding qualities, however, have not been sacrificed to gain good roadholding and the notable freedom from roll; although fairly hard

ACCOMMODATION.
—The hood folds away neatly and remains permanently on the car whether the hardtop is fitted or not, and a tonneau cover, with central zip fastener, is supplied. The pockets in the doors will accept quite large flat parcels.

when travelling slowly, the ride flattens out at high speed to give an excellent compromise, free of pitch, too well damped for float, and transmitting sharp vertical movements only on substantial irregularities when the suspension approaches the end of its fairly limited travel.

Very easy to start from cold, the engine is rather slow to warm up and tends to spit back through the carburetters for the first mile or two unless the choke, which has a fast idling interconnection with the throttle, is pulled out slightly; thereafter it is notable for the effortless ease with which it produces a very impressive performance. Tuned for high torque in the low and medium speed ranges, it will pull strongly and smoothly from very low speeds although, driven in this unusual way, there

VISIBILITY.—A very large plastic window in the smooth and elegant hardtop affords an excellent rear view. The sidescreens close on to very effective rubber seals.

First impressions of the Girling brakes (disc front) suggested that a servo might be desirable to reduce the pedal pressures. It soon appeared, however, that a little warming up of the linings improved the efficiency very considerably and normal fairly hard driving keeps them at a temperature where they are pleasantly light to operate. As with many disc systems, gentle use sometimes caused a high-pitched squeal, but much more important was the fact that the heaviest operation in road use never produced any loss in braking power or balance.

Pedal Points

On a car of this sort, heel and toe operation of the accelerator and brake is a most useful facility which the Austin-Healey layout did not permit; the operation of the accelerator could have been improved by elimination of initial free play together with more progressive opening thereafter. Other minor points which the driver may criticize include a mirror mounted too near the windscreen so that it chatters against the glass when correctly adjusted, and a fuel gauge which is extremely sensitive to acceleration or gradient.

A spell of warm weather which coincided with our test revealed that ventilation, even with the sliding windows open, is not adequate for these conditions. How-ever, in the circumstances most owners would remove the hardtop, which is a very rapid and simple process involving two quick-action toggles and two wing nuts. Refitting is almost equally easy, and it is probably quicker to fit or remove the hardtop than it is to raise or lower the hood which, although quite straightforward, necessitates some care in stowing the fabric to ensure that it folds neatly into the space allotted. The doors rise as they open to avoid high kerbs and have been fitted with rather stiffly set friction hinges to hold them at any position. When closed, the side windows seat on soft rubber seals which are effective in excluding rain and draughts.

Although the occasional back seats look small, they are in fact adequate for two adults sitting rather high in the airstream when the car is open, but with the hardtop fitted, headroom is enough only for small children. In many cases this space will be used for carrying extra luggage as the boot itself is fairly small. A most useful feature is the fitting of a battery master switch inside the boot, which is the only part of the car which can be locked, so that valuable articles can be left in the boot and the whole car immobilized when it is parked.

A little attention to seating comfort and a few modifications to some of the minor controls would still further improve a car which now offers quite extraordinary performance in relation to its cost, taking performance in its broadest sense to include acceleration, maximum speed, roadholding and braking. The winning of the team award, amongst other striking successes, in the recent Alpine Rally, shows that durability is another attribute that must be added to this list.

The World Copyright of this article and illustrations is strictly reserved © *Temple Press Limited, 1960*

Specification

Engine

Cylinders	6
Bore	83.36 mm.
Stroke	88.9 mm.
Cubic capacity	2,912 c.c.
Piston area	47.1 sq. in.
Valves	Pushrod o.h.v.
Compression ratio	9/1
Carburetter	Two S.U. H.D.6
Fuel pump	S.U. electric
Ignition timing control	Centrifugal and vacuum
Oil filter	Tecalemit full-flow
Max. power (net)	124 b.h.p.
at	4,600 r.p.m.
Piston speed at max. b.h.p.	2,680 ft./min.

Transmission

Clutch	Borg and Beck s.d.p. 9 in.
Top gear (s/m)	3.91 (overdrive, 3.20)
3rd gear (s/m)	5.12 (overdrive 4.19)
2nd gear (s/m)	8.02
1st gear	11.45
Reverse	14.78
Overdrive	Laycock-de Normanville
Propeller shaft	Hardy Spicer open
Final drive	Hypoid 11/43
Top gear m.p.h. at 1,000 r.p.m.	19.0 (Overdrive, 23.1)
Top gear m.p.h. at 1,000 ft./min. piston speed	32.5 (overdrive, 23.1)

Chassis

Brakes	Girling disc front, Girling drum rear
Brake diameters	Discs 11¼ in. dia. Drums 11 in. dia.

Friction areas: 112 sq. in. of friction surface working on 383 sq. in. of rubbed area.

Suspension:
  Front: Independent by coil springs and wishbones.
  Rear: Rigid axle with semi-elliptic leaf springs and panhard rod.

Shock Absorbers:
  Front: Armstrong hydraulic lever-type.
  Rear: Armstrong hydraulic lever-type.

Steering gear	Cam and peg
Tyres	5.90-15 Dunlop Roadspeed

Coachwork and Equipment

Starting handle	Yes
Battery mounting	Off-side of boot
Jack	Screw type
Jacking points	Under front and rear suspension

Standard tool kit: Jack and handle, starting handle, plug spanner and bar, ignition combination tool, ignition key, valve key, copper hammer.

Exterior lights: Two head, two side/indicator, two tail/stop/indicator, rear number plate.

Number of electrical fuses	2
Direction indicators	Flashing, self-cancelling
Windscreen wipers	Lucas single speed self-parking
Windscreen washers	Tudor Manual
Sun visors	None

Instruments: Speedometer with decimal trip distance recorder, revolution counter, fuel gauge, oil pressure and water temperature gauge.

Warning lights: Dynamo and headlamp main beam.

Locks:		
With ignition key		Boot
With other keys		None
Glove lockers		None
Map pockets	One in each door	
Parcel shelves	One below facia	
Ashtrays	One on transmission tunnel	
Cigar lighters		None
Interior lights		None

Interior heater: Optional extra. Smiths fresh air type with demisters.

Car radio: Optional extra. H.M.V. Push button.

Extras available: Hard top, overdrive, wire spoked wheels, heater, radio.

Upholstery material	Hide
Floor covering	Rubber-backed carpet
Exterior colours standardized:	6 single, 5 two tone.
Alternative body styles	Open 2-seater

Maintenance

Sump	11¾ pints, S.A.E. 30 (including filter)
Gearbox:	5 pints, S.A.E. 30 plus 1½ pints for overdrive.
Rear axle	3 pints, S.A.E. 90
Steering gear lubricant	S.A.E. 90
Cooling system capacity	19 pints (2 drain taps)

Chassis lubrication: By grease gun every 1,000 miles to 14 points.

Ignition timing (static)	5° b.t.d.c.
Contact-breaker gap	.014-.016 in.
Sparking plug type	Champion N.3
Sparking plug gap	.025 in.

Valve timing: Inlet opens 5° b.t.d.c.; Inlet closes 45° a.b.d.c. Exhaust opens 40° b.b.d.c.; Exhaust closes 10° a.t.d.c.

Tappet clearances (Hot):

Inlet	.012 in.
Exhaust	.012 in.
Front wheel toe-in	1⁄16-⅛ in.
Camber angle	1°
Castor angle	2°
Steering swivel pin inclination	6½°

Tyre pressures: Front 20 lb. Rear 23 lb. (or 26 lb. with full load).

Brake fluid	Girling

Battery type and capacity: 12 volt, 57 amp. hr.

Policeman's Delight

Our test car was by no means new. In this photograph it is climbing the Gavia pass in the 1959 Liège-Rome-Liège Rally wearing extra lights but no bumpers.

WATCHING the works Austin-Healeys motoring spectacularly fast on the soaking Brands Hatch circuit at the end of the R.A.C. Rally aroused our curiosity about the development that has made these three-litre machines into such formidable G.T. cars during the past two rally seasons. Mentioning only a few highlights, the Pat Moss/Ann Wisdom team followed up their 2nd place in the 1960 Alpine with an outright win in the Liège-Rome-Liège; in both events the Healeys took the team prize as they did in the recent R.A.C. Rally in which the Morley brothers finished 3rd and the Riley/Ambrose crew 11th.

On the whole, successful competition people are a disillusioned lot, given more to sorrow over the failings of their motorcars than to recognition of any virtues, and it was rather impressive, therefore, to find amongst the team members a genuine respect and admiration for the cars, a feeling that their performance was

The navigator has his own switches, one of which is for the flexible map reading light clipped out of the way behind the screen. He also has a selection of grab handles and a personal horn button, operated by the left toe, which is not shown in the photographs.

a match for any G.T. car competing in rallies and their durability much greater than most.

The season having finished, most of the cars had been sold, but we were fortunate to be able to borrow the one with which John Gott (now Chief Constable of Northamptonshire) and Rupert Jones finished 10th in the Liège-Rome-Liège. This car, with a long history of events in 1959 as well as in 1960, was being rebuilt for sale to John Gott, and some of the special rally fittings had been removed, including the usual row of auxiliary lamps. An ordinary boot lid was fitted instead of the special one which allows two spare wheels to be carried for certain events, and a plain bonnet replaced the one with large louvres in the top. The latter proved rather a disappointment anyway, as the openings turned out to be in a high-pressure region and, instead of the hot under-bonnet air emerging through them, the flow was in the opposite direction. As on the ordinary production car, bonnet, boot lid and wings are all made of steel, and the fairly small remaining area of the "top deck" of the body is aluminium. The weighbridge showed that SMO 746 was half a hundred-weight heavier than the standard car we road tested last year (The Motor, July 13, 1960) so that the competition cars do not gain their performance by extensive and expensive lightening.

The outside of the Healey reveals little that is non-standard. The twin exhaust system ends in front of the nearside wheel to avoid the loss of ground clearance inevitable when pipes have to pass below the rear axle, the wire wheels have 60 spokes instead of 48 and reveal Girling disc brakes all round, and there is an air intake on the scuttle, together with an opening ventilator in the roof.

The Competition Department makes a point of using the maximum possible number of standard parts (not necessarily from the same B.M.C. model) to reduce costs and to simplify the spares position, and the modified engines have standard but carefully balanced crankshafts, connecting rods and pistons. A special (B.M.C.) camshaft operates ordinary valve gear with stronger springs and the 6-port cylinder head is gas-flowed, re-shaped and polished, leaving the compression ratio unchanged at 9 to 1. Three 2 in. S.U. carburetters on long inlet pipes replace the ordinary 1¾ in. pair. The engine drives through a 10-in. single-dry-plate Borg and Beck clutch with strong springs to a special B.M.C. gearbox with very close ratio straight-cut gears, and the standard Laycock overdrive is wired to work on 2nd, 3rd and top. At the flywheel the engine is claimed to give 180 b.h.p. at 5,200 r.p.m., but we were also shown some figures taken at the back wheels on a chassis dynamometer. For reasons connected with cooling problems and the power consumption

A lap-strap for the driver and harness for the navigator supplements the built-in shaping of the luxurious seats. A headlamp flasher switch projects near the left-hand rim of the wheel, the overdrive switch can be flicked by the fingers of the right hand, and the rev-counter has special red-light illumination.

Getting the Measure of a Works Austin-Healey Rally Car

The quick filler cap, roof ventilator, reversing light and short exhaust system are special features visible in a picture which conveys some sense of the car's urgent function.

of tyres on rollers, these dynamometers usually seem to give rather pessimistic results, but even so, figures of 142 b.h.p. at 4,900 r.p.m. and 145 at 5,500 are indicated. In passing it is amusing to note that our technique for quick but unobtrusive passage through towns was to use the gearbox freely but keep the revs right down in the 1,500 to 2,500 r.p.m. band. The dynamometer figures show that even then 40 to 70 b.h.p. were available at the back wheels.

Suspension modifications include heavier coil springs at the front, with standard dampers re-valved to increase the damping by about 20%, and a stronger anti-roll bar. The rear dampers are replaced by the "click adjusting" Armstrong type DAS 10, and the normal 7-leaf semi-elliptics give way to special springs with 14 (thinner) leaves which are better able to resist the rude assault of Yugoslav roads passing very quickly underneath, whilst supporting two spare wheels and a petrol tank up to 20 gallons in capacity. Both ends of the car are raised about an inch to increase ground clearance, and the special rear springs are not advised for light loads as there is then little rebound clearance between the back axle and the underslung chassis.

(Below) Thick heat-insulating washers separate the big S.U. carburetters from the bifurcated inlet stubs. The neat arrangement of the very progressive throttle linkage is interesting. Note the wired-on oil and water filler caps and the spare coil.

All the cars have the same very comfortable special seats, but alterations to their mountings and to the pedal positions are necessary to accommodate say, Pat Moss on the one hand or the enormous John Gott on the other. The Healey does not lend itself to the long reach driving position now favoured in racing, but it is doubtful whether this would be appropriate to very long rallies. An exaggerated arms'-length steering position becomes rather tiring long before the sun has set for the third time, and the 99% concentrated effort of the race circuit is only necessary for parts of a long road event. One of the team thought that the Alpine Rally probably demanded the greatest percentage of really hard driving, and estimated the proportion of such motoring as about one-third of the total. In most events, darkness, rain, snow, fog or dust in various combinations will create conditions in which it is a great advantage to sit fairly close to the screen; not only does visibility through the glass improve but the greater angular spread of vision subtended by the width of the screen wiper arcs helps in negotiating hairpin corners.

As soon as one drives this car away it becomes apparent that the feel is entirely different from that of the ordinary Healey 3000. The touring character of the latter has entirely vanished in favour of the hard, taut feeling of the sports-racing car. Although one knows at once that this is an impressive car, it is not one with which the conductor establishes an immediate *rapport*. The reasons for this are by no means clear, and certainly after a few hundred miles it leaves the driver very thoroughly and completely at home and with a firmly established liking and respect for the car; it is tremendous fun to drive in a way which has almost vanished with the passing of the bigger sports-racing cars of the post-war decade. The exhaust, which has a deep bathplug gurgle at tickover, develops the most purposeful hard and hollow ring as soon as the revs start to rise, almost drowning the crescendo howl of straight-cut gears. A clutch which is immensely positive, not unduly heavy and yet needs only the token movements of a pre-war Austin 7, a gearbox with very close ratios, powerful synchromesh and short, light movements and a carefully arranged progressive throttle linkage all combine to provide the most enjoyable gear-change we have encountered on a large-engined car and one which we used far more than necessary just for the fun of it.

In fact, the engine is very flexible and the car can be driven happily through London traffic using mostly overdrive top or direct top gear in which it will accelerate smoothly and rapidly from under 10 m.p.h., but excellent torque at low r.p.m. is succeeded by even better torque which comes in half way up the speed range. The rev. limit is 5,500 r.p.m., with permission to use a momentary 6,000 on occasions, but during our performance tests we

25

exceeded by only a small margin the lower figure, above which the engine sounds less happy. Conditions were far from ideal for the acceleration runs, with a wet track on which take-off from rest was both difficult and slow. In these circumstances a standing ¼ mile (with full test load) in 16.7 sec. with 100 m.p.h. appearing after 23.9 sec. is a remarkable performance but one which the car could better considerably on a dry surface using one of the lower axle ratios fitted for some rallies. These figures were registered without using overdrive at all, overdrive top being selected at just over 100 m.p.h.; a full throttle change at peak revs into overdrive second gear would have improved the ¼ mile time, but gives the unit a very limited life.

At this time of the year it is most difficult to get reliable maximum speed figures for such a fast car in this country, and one attempt was abandoned when it was found that a sliding Perspex side window departed on a quickly diverging course at a speed in excess of 115 m.p.h. This speed was reached after accelerating for only about ⅞ mile from rest, and from the way in which it was still rising it seems likely that the terminal velocity must be in the region of 125 m.p.h. (about 5,700 r.p.m.), but suitable conditions to confirm this never arose again. From the competition point of view this is significant only in the Monza speed test of the Alpine Rally; generally the range up to 100 m.p.h. or less is the important one, although on the Acropolis very high averages are called for on the straight but undulating roads through the foothills of the mountains where 100-110 m.p.h. may be held for some time.

It is, however, in the handling and the ride that the general feel differs most markedly from that of the touring version. The steering is remarkably light for a 22½ cwt. car wearing Dunlop Duraband tyres, and there is no very obvious reason why this should be so. It has the benefit of skilled assembly, careful maintenance and frequent greasing, but the steering box is the standard one made by Cam Gears, the castor angle is not reduced and the general geometry is altered only as a by-product of the suspension raising. At first we ran the tyres at standard Duraband pressures (23 lb. front and 26 lb. rear) but later, on advice from B.M.C. Competition Department, we raised them to 30 and 35 respectively with improvement to directional stability, but for straight running at very high speeds on bumpy roads the Healey is not as good as some more softly sprung vehicles.

The ride is definitely hard and, thinking of the appalling surfaces of some of the more obscure mountain passes that have to be taken against the clock, we were rather surprised until we reflected that a hard spring which never bottoms is probably less destructive to the car than a better insulator which occasionally crashes to the limits of its travel; the crews are obviously very durable. On English main roads this ride is far from unpleasant. Except for a bonnet lid which floated in its recess, it failed to provoke any shakes or rattles from the structure. The whole car feels immensely solid and in one rigid piece and sits down at speed with a steadiness that inspires the greatest confidence.

Having encountered nearly all weather conditions during our test (but mostly bad) we would summarize the silent and almost completely roll-free cornering as being outstanding in the dry, good on wet surfaces and indifferent on ice, a gradation very common with sports cars which seldom feel as controllable when the coefficient of friction is really low as some family saloons do. Driving near the limit of adhesion in wet weather calls for some experience of the car, as the braced-tread tyres characteristically fail to indicate the proximity of the approaching stall and the car continues to feel "on rails" until the moment the back wheels break away; rather confusing is the occasional loss of steering resistance which feels like front-end breakaway but is, in fact, caused by the drop in self-aligning torque which is experienced prematurely with this type of tyre. The Girling brakes which are boosted by a Dewandre Mot-A-Vac servo unit, seem to be very good indeed on all kinds of surface, and simultaneous operation of brake and throttle is possible but not easy.

It was a considerable surprise to find that heaters are never fitted to the team Healeys, but engine and exhaust heat kept the interior tolerably warm in December and January. Even with all the vents closed the car keeps reasonably free of mist when travelling quickly, and the driver has the assistance of an electrical de-mister on his side of the screen. In summer events, for which the Healeys are mostly used, the problem is to keep the occupants below melting point; various bits of asbestos insulation are to be seen on the engine side of the bulkhead, a raised intake just ahead of the windscreen discharges air in controllable quantities through ducts on to the feet and legs and there is a small opening vent in the roof.

After more than 1,500 miles of very varied motoring, at an overall fuel consumption of 19 m.p.g., we handed the car back to competitions manager Marcus Chambers with real regret. Most of the really fast cars that pass through our hands are relatively large and luxurious touring machines. The rare combination of tremendous performance with real sports-car compactness and agility is something to remember.

C.H.B.

THE AUSTIN-HEALEY 3000 RALLY TEAM CAR

TEST DATA

World copyright reserved; no unauthorized reproduction in whole or in part.

CONDITIONS: *Weather: Cold and wet with light wind. (Temperature 35°-36° F., Barometer 29.0-29.3 in. Hg.). Surface: Wet tarmacadam. Fuel: Premium pump petrol (96 Octane Rating by Research Method).*

INSTRUMENTS

Speedometer at 30 m.p.h.	1½% fast
Speedometer at 60 m.p.h.	1½% fast
Speedometer at 90 m.p.h.	3½% fast
Speedometer at 110 m.p.h.	5% fast
Distance recorder	1½% fast

WEIGHT

Kerb weight (unladen, but with oil, water and fuel for approx. 50 miles)	22½ cwt.
Front/rear distribution of kerb weight	50/50
Weight laden as tested	26¼ cwt.

MAXIMUM SPEEDS

Speed in gears (at 5,500 r.p.m.)

Max. speed in overdrive top	See text
Max. speed in direct top gear	99 m.p.h.
Max. speed in overdrive 3rd gear	101 m.p.h.
Max. speed in direct 3rd gear	83 m.p.h.
Max. speed in direct 2nd gear	57 m.p.h.
Max. speed in 1st gear	41 m.p.h.

FUEL CONSUMPTION

(Overdrive top gear).

30½ m.p.g. at constant 30 m.p.h. on level.
29 m.p.g. at constant 40 m.p.h. on level.
28 m.p.g. at constant 50 m.p.h. on level.
25½ m.p.g. at constant 60 m.p.h. on level.
23½ m.p.g. at constant 70 m.p.h. on level.
22 m.p.g. at constant 80 m.p.h. on level.
19½ m.p.g. at constant 90 m.p.h. on level.
17½ m.p.g. at constant 100 m.p.h. on level.

(Direct top gear).

26½ m.p.g. at constant 30 m.p.h. on level.
26 m.p.g. at constant 40 m.p.h. on level.
24½ m.p.g. at constant 50 m.p.h. on level.
22½ m.p.g. at constant 60 m.p.h. on level.
21 m.p.g. at constant 70 m.p.h. on level.
19 m.p.g. at constant 80 m.p.h. on level.

Overall Fuel Consumption for 1,519 miles, 79.9 gallons, equals 19.0 m.p.g. (14.9 litres/100 km.).

Touring Fuel Consumption (m.p.g. at steady speed midway between 30 m.p.h. and maximum, less 5% allowance for acceleration). 21.3 (approx.)

Fuel tank capacity (maker's figure) ... 15 gallons

ACCELERATION TIMES from standstill

0-30 m.p.h.	4.2 sec.
0-40 m.p.h.	5.7 sec.
0-50 m.p.h.	7.6 sec.
0-60 m.p.h.	10.2 sec.
0-70 m.p.h.	13.0 sec.
0-80 m.p.h.	16.0 sec.
0-90 m.p.h.	19.8 sec.
0-100 m.p.h.	23.9 sec.
0-110 m.p.h.	31.9 sec.
Standing quarter mile	16.7 sec.

ACCELERATION TIMES on Upper Ratios

	Overdrive top gear	Direct top gear	3rd gear
10-30 m.p.h.	—	6.0 sec.	5.2 sec.
20-40 m.p.h.	7.4 sec.	6.0 sec.	5.2 sec.
30-50 m.p.h.	7.8 sec.	5.8 sec.	5.0 sec.
40-60 m.p.h.	8.5 sec.	6.1 sec.	5.3 sec.
50-70 m.p.h.	8.6 sec.	6.2 sec.	5.5 sec.
60-80 m.p.h.	8.1 sec.	6.1 sec.	5.8 sec.
70-90 m.p.h.	8.5 sec.	7.0 sec.	—
80-100 m.p.h.	9.6 sec.	7.9 sec.	—
90-110 m.p.h.	13.7 sec.	—	—

HILL CLIMBING at sustained steady speeds

Max. gradient on o/d top gear
1 in 7.8 (Tapley 285 lb./ton)

Max. gradient on direct top gear
1 in 5.9 (Tapley 375 lb./ton)

Max. gradient on 3rd gear
1 in 4.8 (Tapley 460 lb./ton)

Max. gradient on 2nd gear
1 in 3.3 (Tapley 650 lb./ton)

SPECIFICATION

Engine

Cylinders	6
Bore	83.36 mm.
Stroke	88.9 mm.
Cubic capacity	2,912 c.c.
Piston area	47.1 sq. in.
Valves	Pushrod o.h.v.
Compression ratio	9/1
Carburetter	3 S.U. type H8
Fuel pump	S.U. electric
Ignition timing control	Centrifugal
Oil filter	Tecalemit full-flow
Max. power (gross)	180 b.h.p.
at	5,200 r.p.m.
Piston speed at max. b.h.p.	3,030 ft./min.

Transmission

Clutch	10 in. Borg & Beck s.d.p.
Top gear (s/m)	4.10 (Overdrive, 3.47)
3rd gear (s/m)	4.90 (Overdrive, 4.02)
2nd gear (s/m)	7.06 (Overdrive, 5.80)
1st gear	9.90
Overdrive	Laycock-de Normanville
Propeller shaft	Hardy-Spicer open
Final drive	Hypoid
Top gear m.p.h. at 1,000 r.p.m.	18.0 (Overdrive, 21.9)
Top gear m.p.h. at 1,000 ft./min. piston speed	30.8 (Overdrive, 37.5)

Chassis

Brakes	Girling disc with Dewandre Mot-A-Vac servo
Brake diameters	11¼ in.

Suspension:
Front: Independent by coil springs, wishbones and anti-roll bar.
Rear: Rigid axle with semi-elliptic leaf springs, panhard rod.

Shock Absorbers:

Front:	Armstrong lever type
Rear:	Armstrong lever type DAS 10 (adjustable)
Steering gear	Cam and peg
Tyres	Dunlop Duraband 6.5 × 16

The author and Bill Shepherd in their Austin-Healey 3000 on a typical loose Alpine col. Under these conditions crews have to average no less than 38 m.p.h.

Clean Sweep

by John Gott

With the outright BMC victory in the Liège–Rome–Liège Rally still very much in mind, the BMC Team Captain looks back to the 'Alpine' which preceded it, in which the Austin-Healey 3000s won every class and team award open to them

THE B.M.C. Competitions Department always supports the Coupe des Alpes (better known, perhaps, as the 'Alpine') in strength. Not only is it one of the top rallies, but it is a driver's event in which luck plays little part in the results and consequently much can be learnt about the mechanical weaknesses of the competing cars. This latter factor is, of course, one of the chief reasons why go-ahead manufacturers enter works cars in rallies; it is far better that a works driver should break down on some inaccessible mountain-top and point out the reason, which can then be put right, than that John Motorist should do so on his Continental tour.

As far as mechanical stress was concerned, the 1960 'Alpine' was one of the toughest of recent years. The course was the usual 2000-mile 'figure-of-eight' from Marseilles to Cannes via Monza, but it had only one night stop (at Chamonix) instead of the usual three, whilst the average speed was increased and the sections shortened. The Automobile Club de Marseille et Provence also reverted to a scheme they used some

years ago whereby the fastest car in the class set the 'bogey' time in the tests and any car was penalised if outside 5 per cent. of that time, and/or not within 10 and 7 per cent. of the times of the fastest cars in the Touring and G.T. Categories respectively. This meant, of course, that it was risky not to drive the tests 'flat', so that the cars got little respite.

It also called for much hard thinking by Marcus Chambers and myself as to the best cars to use, and the degree of tune for them. Eventually we concluded that, as an Austin-Healey '3000' had been 8th in the Tulip, 4th in the R.A.C. and 2nd in the Deutschland (with the class wins as a matter of course), it was about ripe for an outright win, although we appreciated that the 'Alpine' competition would be much tougher than in any of the other three events. Four '3000's were accordingly prepared with the emphasis on maximum performance, by the use of modified heads and manifolds with three S.U. carburetters. This naturally entailed a considerable 'calculated risk'. It is not too difficult

considerably to increase engine output, but only actual experience can show whether the other components will stand up to the increased strain. That we were going to find out!

The cars, incidentally, were two of last year's team and two new 1960 models; being a sentimentalist where cars are concerned, I was delighted to have the car which I had used in 1959 to finish 2nd in class and 7th in G.T. category.

To back up the Austin-Healey striking force there were three Mini-Minors and two Sprites. The Minis were driven by Gold/Hughes, Pitts/Ambrose and Jones/James, whilst the Sprites were handled by Tommy Wisdom/Jack Hay and John Sprinzel/Stuart Turner.

The '3000' crews were Pat Moss/Ann Wisdom, who are not only the fastest lady drivers in the game but are more than able to see off mere males, the Tulip-winning Morley twins, who have taken to the big Austin-Healey like ducks to water (they were 4th in the R.A.C. on their first outing in one), myself with Bill Shepherd (who

27

had won a Coupe on a Healey in 1958), and Ronnie Adams with John Williamson, who had been Bill's partner in 1958. Ronnie was new to Healeys, but he is very experienced and won the 'Monte' in 1956. The 'Alpine', however, has not been his luckiest event, and 1960 was to prove no exception.

TOUGH OPPOSITION

On arrival at Marseilles we found that we were going to be up against some very tough opposition. There were full works teams from Citroën, Ford, Sunbeam, Triumph and Volvo, with works-prepared teams from Jaguar, Porsche and Renault. Even more formidable was the Alfa Romeo team on special S.S. Giuliettas, prepared and looked after by Conrero himself. And in case the works teams didn't keep us busy enough, there was a 250GT Ferrari to deal with. Another big headache was the Ford team, manned by the redoubtable Harrison family, Gerry Burgess, Anne Hall and Vic Preston, a Safari winner. These cars turned out to have three-carburetter, light alloy heads, disc brakes, gearboxes with overdrives giving five forward speeds, and much lightened coachwork; their b.h.p. was reputed to be 152, and they performed as though that estimate were about right.

The quality of the crews was as high as that of the cars. In addition to Britain's top rally drivers, the Continental rally stars were there in force. Amongst other famous names, France was represented by Paul Coltelloni and Annie Soisbault, reigning European Rally Champions, backed up by Roger de Lageneste, Henri Oreiller, Robert Buchet and José Behra (Jean's brother); Sweden had Ewy Rosqvist, the 1959 European co-champion, Gunnar Andersson, the 1958 Champion, and Erik Carlsson, the 1959 runner-up. Schock and Moll had entered, but they had so great a lead in the Championship that Mercedes had scratched them; however, they left in Bohringer and Socher, who had been second in the 'Monte'. Drivers of this calibre are only interested in cars and crews which, they think, have a good chance. At scrutineering we were therefore gratified to note their keen interest in our cars, but rather amused by their shrewd questions, designed to elicit details of the cars' performance and of our tactics.

These were, in fact, largely left to individual crews. At our final team conference where the route, the passes, the tests, the weather, the schedule and the opposition was carefully evaluated—we reckoned the Alfas and the Porsches were liable to give us the most trouble—Marcus had succinctly summed up by saying, 'We're here to win everything we can. You are all experienced enough to know how to do that without blowing up or crashing your cars. Good luck to us all'.

This gave us all a pretty free hand, and, at our private crew conference the night before the start, Bill and I decided that the rally would be won and lost on the Quatre Chemins section in the last 100 miles. We planned our drive, therefore, to make each section and test 'clean' by the barest margin, so that car and crew would be in as good a trim as possible for this all-important stage.

THE FIRST TEST

That others hadn't got quite the same plan of campaign was proved next morning. Within 20 miles of the start came the first test, a twisting 5¼-mile climb on the Col Ste. Beaume. The record (by a single-seater racing car) is 8 min. 15.2 sec. Oreiller's Alfa (a rally car, be it remembered) did 8 min. 17 sec., followed by our Miss Moss in 8 min. 27 sec. This blistering pace penalised all the cars in our class except the Austin-Healeys and the Ferrari, and obviously was a severe shock to the Ford team; more particularly to Edward Harrison, who was hoping for that coveted trophy, a Gold Coupe, awarded for un-penalised runs in three consecutive years. It was a little galling to be penalised within 20 miles, for, although the penalisation would be finally calculated upon the total times in all tests, the first climb is always a pointer to the ways things are likely to go.

The Ste. Beaume results were confirmed by the next test, 13½ miles on Mont Ventoux, one of the European Hill-Climb Championship courses. Having made second F.T.D. last year, I was pleased to return a time well below last year's F.T.D.—but that wasn't fast enough for 1960. Oreiller made F.T.D., and this time his Alfa team-mate, Roger de Lageneste, and the Ferrari managed to beat Miss Moss, but no other mere male could manage it. Oreiller's *average* for the climb to 6000 feet was, incidentally, just under 60 m.p.h., and on the lower stretches the Austin-Healeys were doing around 110 m.p.h.

So far it seemed as though the A.C.M.P. had adopted the Tour de France scheme of a leisurely tour from test to test, with the emphasis upon speed rather than reliability. The run to the Italian frontier at Mont Genèvre was, however, a really tough stage in the old 'Alpine' tradition; i.e., some very tight sections over poor road surfaces. The climb at dusk up and over the Col de Menée was particularly difficult, as it was only 28 km. (16½ miles) long, of which five kilometres were appallingly rough. This penalised most of the small cars, and, not long after, Les Leston slid off the road. As Slotemaker had earlier retired with axle trouble, the formidable Triumph team was no longer a threat.

Trouble, however, wasn't to be confined to the Triumph team. Apart from a tyre burst when the Morleys hit a rock which had rolled into their path on Mont Ventoux, the Austin-Healeys had been running like clockwork. But at the Mont Genèvre control the Morleys came in to report that they had lost third gear. This was dealt with by converting their gearbox to over-drive on all gears, which gave them over-drive second to replace the lost third gear. The conversion throws a terrific strain on the gearbox and is only to be recommended

Pat Moss and Ann Wisdom exuberantly collected together all the trophies won by the Austin-Healey team in the 'Alpine' and posed with them displayed on the dusty bonnet of their car

as a temporary expedient—but they had 1500 tough miles to go. No sooner was this crisis dealt with than Ronnie came in to report that he had lost all gears except bottom and top. This meant his retirement, for although the car could be driven back to Cannes in this state, it could never have got over the passes ahead. Never before in either the 'Alpine' or Liège-Rome-Liège had we had gearbox trouble, but it was now obvious that the increased b.h.p. was proving too much for the old gearboxes. We had, of course, fulfilled one branch of our assignment (*i.e.*, trouble-shooting), but we hadn't expected trouble to strike quite as soon as this. Although we did our best to hide it from the other équipes, there was some gloom in the Healey team, and Bill and I spent the next few hours imagining noises in our own gearbox!

A HIGH-SPEED DEMONSTRATION

This gloom was somewhat dispelled by the test at Monza, where, in groups of ten, the cars had to cover four timed laps on the road circuit, of which the fastest alone counted. The Austin-Healeys being in the last group, we knew what we had to beat before going on the track. Oreiller had done just under 2 min. 17 sec. and the Ferrari 2 min. 20 sec. As the fastest Austin-Healey lap to date was 2 min. 19 sec. by Jack Sears, Marcus felt that 2 min. 20 sec. would be fair enough. We had other ideas, however. The three red Austin-Healeys streaked round in line ahead, opening out on the second lap to keep out of each others' way and closing in again on the last lap to finish in line astern. Pat did just under 2 min. 15 sec., Donald Morley did 2 min. 16 sec., and I did 2 min. 17 sec. Pat's average speed was just under 95 m.p.h., and all the Healeys were touching just on 122 m.p.h. by rev. counter on each straight. This high-speed demonstration put us in tearing spirits for the infamous Vivione and Gavia.

In fact, we managed these without undue difficulty. On the Vivione all three Healeys caught the Ferrari, which had started 2 minutes ahead of the Morleys. The Swiss Ferrari crew were real sportsmen, for they pulled right over to let us all past and, at the start of the Gavia, offered to leave a minute after the girls (and so lose 60 marks) to avoid holding them up. Needless to say, the girls did not accept this offer, but the Ferrari stopped to let them past as soon as the Austin-Healey hove in sight. We were all delighted to see these great sportsmen do so well later in the Six-Hour G.T. race at Clermont Ferrand.

The rest of the stage to Chamonix, apart from the passage of the Grand St. Bernard in cloud, was tiring rather than difficult motoring, so we managed to make up enough time to have a quick lunch and a refreshing swim in the lake at Lecco. The cars were not neglected either; they were carefully checked over and found to be in good fettle, whilst the tyres were changed as a precaution, for the run to Cannes was going to be very hard on them.

That night the rally hotel in Chamonix was a miniature Tower of Babel, with crews recounting their experiences in six languages. Good stories were rife, and I particularly liked the one about the small Italian boys who urged a rally car to go faster, only to turn as white as sheets and fall backwards over a wall when the car's tail slid viciously as the driver responded too enthusiastically to their urgings. Marcus capped this by recounting how he had come into an Italian village to be cheered by the villagers on sighting his Rally Service plate. but booed on exit because he didn't drift the bend and was only doing about 70 m.p.h. The Italians like drivers to go fast!

From what we could learn over a Dubonnet, the Austin-Healeys didn't seem to be doing too badly, and Bill and I retired fairly satisfied for eleven hours' solid sleep.

LEADING OUR CLASS

The official results issued on the following morning showed that the team was doing better than we had thought. Of the 66 crews which had started from Marseilles, 49 had reached Chamonix, of whom 23 were unpenalised; of these latter only 15 had managed to keep within the test percentage. Included amongst these were the Austin-Healeys, which were 1, 2 and 3 in their class, whilst the girls were second to Oreiller/Masoero in the G.T. category. As far as the team awards were concerned only the Healeys and the Citroëns were unpenalised, whilst Alfa, Jaguar, Porsche, Volvo and Triumph no longer had full teams.

It is perhaps superfluous to add that our girls were firmly in command of the Ladies' Section, in which Anne Hall (accident) and Annie Soisbault (wheel off) had retired.

I have done every 'Alpine' since 1947 but cannot remember a harder run-in than the 1960 one. We started in brilliant sunshine to tackle the twisty 4000-foot cols around the Lake of Annecy, and at dawn were up in the high Alps around Briançon. The 8000-foot Galibier was particularly tricky, as the upper hairpins glittered with ice, and we saw from marks on the rocks that more than one driver had 'lost' it. Throughout that gruelling night we had passed cars whose rally was run, either from accident or mechanical failure, but the Austin-Healeys rumbled tirelessly on. Then, on the 7300-foot Allos, trouble hit us. On the way up we passed Rupert Jones standing dejectedly by his Mini-Minor, which had obviously come off second-best in an argument with a rock. Worse still, at the control at the foot we saw what we had been subconsciously expecting for some time—the Morley's car having difficulty in getting away. Bill and I ran up to hear that they only had top gear left. Fortunately they were over the steepest passes, but they had 200 miles to go and the Quatre Chemins still to come. Giving them a shove off, we took up station astern to make sure that they finished. The torque of that Austin engine was staggering, for it pulled the car

uphill past tourists who must have thought they were standing still. Don Morley drove superbly, for despite the handicap he lost no time at all up to the start of the Quatre Chemins.

TWENTY SECONDS TO SPARE

Bill and I regard this as the tightest section we have done in more than sixty Continental rallies. It was only 21 miles long and ran over no pass higher than 4000 feet, but the longest straight was only about 100 yards and the road was only occasionally wide enough for two cars. The route ran through a gorge where the air shimmered with the heat, which had melted the tar on the bends, so that each was taken in a slide as a private calculated risk. I gave the Austin-Healey all it could take and it responded magnificently except towards the end when the terrific under-bonnet temperature caused a slight miss at peak revs. We passed the Ferrari, Gerry Burgess's Ford and Coltelloni's Citroën; each overtaking cost us valuable seconds, although the drivers did their best to give us free passage. However, at the top of the Col de Bleine, with four kilometres to go, we had 20 seconds in hand. The section seemed to be in the bag, but, as so often happens, it didn't turn out that way! Coming downhill very fast, I didn't realise until too late that there was loose gravel on the far side of one corner. The resultant slide wasn't caught quite quickly enough and we ended broadside across the road. Even with the knowledge that one may be collected at high velocity by another competitor, it takes a long time to straighten up on a 15-foot road with a 13-foot car, and flat-out driving for the rest of the section couldn't prevent us from being 23 seconds late.

Our Coupe des Alpes was gone, but what of the team? Pat came through with a thumbs-up; the girls had done it by 9 seconds! Then came the Morleys with a broad grin, which well they might have. On top gear only they had lost but 4 minutes—a staggering drive when the best Ford performance, with all five gears, was 3 minutes late!

And so, in team order, the Austin-Healeys drove quietly into the finish. Their successes are possibly the best ever obtained by a works team in the 'Alpine'. We finished 1, 2 and 3 in our class, won every team and class prize open to us, and Pat and Ann were only beaten in General Classification by a fine car, magnificently driven, which, however, probably cost more than all our team put together! To round it off, the Gold/Hughes Mini-Minor won its class—in which, indeed, it was the only survivor.

Finally, we provided the information which the 'boffins' wanted for their stress calculations. But, for me, the 1960 'Alpine' will always be the supreme example of a justified calculated risk which came off for the team but not for the individual—and the former is more important than the latter!

Externally the Healey 3000 can not be distinquished from its immediate forerunner, the 100-6

ROAD TEST

Austin-Healey 3000

IT is difficult when you look at the current Austin-Healey 3000 to believe that this basic vehicle has been on the roads of Britain and the world for something approaching ten years. The lines of the body are of a classic simplicity which has only been slightly refurbished over the years since it was introduced in 1952. Certainly the character of the car has changed, but not excessively so. In the beginning the original Healey 100 had that sturdy four-cylinder Austin engine which had so many admirers. Now it has an equally robust six-cylinder unit which has many of the characteristics of the four. Handling has been considerably improved since those early days and, more important still perhaps, the car now boasts Girling disc brakes on the front wheels, giving it a stopping power equal to its get-up-and-go.

We have not conducted a full-scale road test since the days of the 100-Six, which was a car of 2½-litre capacity as against the 3000's 2,912 c.c., and it was a most pleasant experience to make re-acquaintance with the car. It frequently seems to be the lot of the tester to get open cars in the middle of winter and ill-ventilated saloons in the height of the summer. The Healey arrived with hood snugly erected but with no glass fibre hardtop (optional extra). On the very first evening of the test the weather was fine and experience of the previous few months indicated that this happy state of affairs might not pertain for long. Accordingly the hood was lowered, not without some exasperation for the Healey has yielded no ground to the convertible philosophy, its hood remaining simply a fabric covering and "sticks". After disassembling the outfit it seemed impossible that this would all fit into the very small space provided behind the occasional rear seats. This was eventually achieved, the whole operation taking some 12 minutes. Not, we concluded, the most delightful undertaking to reverse the procedure in the event of a sudden heavy shower. Nevertheless, the hood was down and the thought of putting it up again was somewhat daunting. Accordingly almost the entire test was carried out with the car in an open state, and remarkably well-protected we found it to be. Our observations lead us to conclude that the majority of sports car drivers only lower their hoods or remove their hardtops for two or three weeks in the year: perhaps it is not, as we had previously concluded, fear of fresh air but dread of getting entangled in a contrivance such as the aforementioned.

First you put the sticks in,   quite upright

Then you put the fabric over   and you pull it tight

The pleasing appearance of the car with hood erected makes it all well worth while!

Despite its long currency and no change in basic design the Austin-Healey has managed to keep abreast of the times regarding interior comfort, instrumentation and performance as well as good looks. Only one or two small items, which we shall refer to from time to time, mar this overall impression. Perhaps the most important of these is the seating position. Those accustomed to sitting in modern cars, be they saloons or sports cars, will find the low seating position of the Healey disconcerting from two points of view, firstly getting in—you almost have to step down from the kerb—and secondly from ease of vision. Indeed, it would certainly be necessary for a really short person to have the seat built up to give adequate forward visibility. The screen also is rather low and set close to the driver by the standards of recent years. Phrased thus, these points are defects, but they have their good side also. The low seating position, whereby the shoulder comes scarcely above the level of the door or the back of the car, affords a protection from the wind better than any car of its type that we have tested. Similarly, the nearness of the flat screen makes raindrops, smears, squashed flies and other such fauna and phenomena less of a hazard. When the hood is up, and presumably also when the hardtop is in position, there is a reasonable amount of headroom for the average driver. With this low seating position the legs are perforce stretched forward well under the scuttle, and the pedals seem a very long way off. The shortest member of our staff could not reach the pedals without having the steering wheel too close to his chest for comfort. Even an average sized person of some 5 ft. 10 in. could not adopt an arms-length driving position and still be able to operate the pedals adequately. Only the tallest driver, in fact, could take up a seating position in the modern manner. The seats themselves are well made, close-fitting bucket ones giving such good grip and location that they are immediately forgotten—about the highest recommendation one can make for a seat! Instruments, consisting of speedometer and tachometer with supplementary dials for fuel gauge, combined water temperature and oil pressure, together with various warning lights, are grouped on a panel in front of the driver and beneath the protruding edge of the facia which effectively prevents reflection in the wind-screen. Also on this panel are various control switches, not all of which are as easy of access as they might be. On the passenger's side is a grab handle, and a large parcel tray which also accommodates the windscreen washer bottle: not in our opinion the best position for this container. A sprung steering wheel of 17 in. diameter has a horn button in the centre and indicator switches mounted above. A very worthwhile improvement would be a change to the steering-column arm-type of control with which could be incorporated a flasher for the headlamps, which is absent at present. The standard of the interior trim is on a high level with good quality carpets and well upholstered seats. There is a pocket in each door, and the backs of the seats fold forward for access to the diminutive seats in the back. These vestigial back seats are of the very occasional variety, and any adult sitting in them is about as exposed as the north face of Kanchenjunga. For children the situation is not quite so bad, although two volunteer guinea-pigs aged six and three turned a delicate shade of heather blue in approximately 11 minutes of fairly brisk motoring on a crisp winter's afternoon. On a hot summer's day of course the situation would be much improved, and the wind force should not be too disconcerting since the main blow comes from the back rather than the front. The main drawback of these small seats is that they are of necessity positioned rather too high to give the snug protection that the front seat occupiers enjoy. On the pure two-seater version the spare wheel rests in the space occupied by the seats on the occasional-four with consequent improvement in the size of the luggage boot. On the car tested the spare wheel, which was of the spoked type, sits in the luggage boot and severely restricts the available space. The battery also has perforce to be moved to the boot so that two adults and two children could not tour in the car without additional luggage facilities, although the space behind the front seats can be used when only two persons occupy the car.

So much for the general amenities of the car. On starting the engine you are delighted or dismayed, according to temperament, by the throaty burble which issues from the exhaust pipe. At low to medium revolutions indeed the exhaust is brutally healthy, probably due to resonance in the system, since as the revs mount higher the noise goes down. We must confess to finding some joy in all this, for if a car looks like a sports car and goes like one, why shouldn't it sound like one? Not only that, a snappy change-down in town traffic clears pedestrian crossings better than any device we have yet encountered. The clutch was adequately progressive, although the throttle pedal had quite a lot of lost motion at the beginning of its travel. The brakes, which are Girling disc at the front and drum at the back, have no servo assistance and consequently pedal pressures are reasonably high. Due to the very good angle of attack for exerting strong pressure, this was no inconvenience, and the very good stopping power could be used to the full. Indeed, the Healey not being an excessively light car, the effectiveness of this disc braking system makes us wonder whether the servo systems used on many disc-braked cars are an unnecessary complication. The hand brake at first seemed to be sadly out of adjustment since the lever, which is of the fly-off type, moved a full eight inches before the brake shoes bit on the drums. This left it at an awkward angle for release, particularly for the technical editor (who is the shorter party mentioned earlier).

The gearbox was reasonably quiet and the change swift and positive without being inspired. The gearing left, we felt, something to be desired when the optional overdrive was fitted as on the test car. This operates on third and top gears and gives a variety of ratios that can take care of any road conditions whatsoever. Our feeling was that the incorporation of the overdrive called for a rather higher back axle ratio, despite the fact that overdrive top is 0·822 to 1, with a back axle of 3·91 to 1. Our feeling that the ideal gear ratios, or more accurately combination of gear ratios, has not been found for the car is borne out by a comparison of the ratios for the non-overdrive gearbox and the overdrive one. On the overdrive car the lower back axle ratio gives lower overall ratios throughout the gearbox (where the ratios are the same) except for overdrive third and overdrive top. But overdrive third is only seven per cent of a ratio lower than direct top and is therefore, for all normal purposes, unnecessary. Indeed, our acceleration tests showed that through-the-gears acceleration was better if overdrive third was ignored altogether. We still have approximately 20 per cent of a ratio difference between third, top and overdrive top, close enough ratios in all conscience for most purposes. The overdrive top gear gives a theoretical maximum speed some 10 per cent better than the non-overdrive box, i.e. 110 m.p.h. as against 100 m.p.h. Doubtless therefore the engine would be unlikely to pull an overdrive gear which was very much higher, and our own solution to the problem would be the fitting of an overdrive on top gear

only in conjunction with the non-overdrive back-axle ratio.

So much for the theoretical considerations. In practice the joys of driving the Austin-Healey are such as to make these points rather academic, and it is always better to have a multiplicity of gear ratios at your command rather than a paucity. Whatever gear you happen to find yourself in, a stamp on the throttle pedal gives scalding acceleration over a very wide range of engine revolutions. 80 m.p.h. can be seen in 18″ from rest, and mild gradients have little effect on the Healey's road-eating propensities. 60 m.p.h. is a ten-second job and a clear run at 100 m.p.h. will see the magic ton on the clock in not much over 30 seconds. At 100 m.p.h. in overdrive top, incidentally, the engine is only turning at little over 4000 r.p.m. and a maximum speed of 110 m.p.h. can be reached in a reasonable length of road. Acceleration tests were undertaken with the hood erect to improve the aerodynamics of the car (although of course a hood is inferior in this respect to a hardtop) and there was considerable wind noise and hood slap at high speeds. In its open form, it should be emphasised, the wind noise does not impinge over the cheerful crackle of the exhaust.

The fitting of anti-roll bars at both front and rear has improved the high-speed cornering of the Healey 3000 noticeably over the earlier model. Although the springing could not be termed hard for a sports car, there is very little roll on corners and the steering characteristics do not alter noticeably during hard pressure. The steering is a very pleasant feature of the car's handling, being very positive, not over-castored and transmitting just sufficient road shock to give the "feel" that is so useful under bad conditions.

It is not difficult to understand why the Austin-Healey has remained such a popular car over a long period of time. It provides at a not immodest cost real fire-eating performance allied with fine finish, good road-holding and reasonable carrying capacity. In one respect we have the strongest possible criticism to make: why, oh why has the exhaust system come down to within about two inches of the road throughout the eight years' currency of the model? We can recall driving behind an Austin-Healey coming away from Snetterton in 1953 or '54 and watching sparks flying from the silencer every time the car went over the slightest bump. Although this test car was never driven on anything but main metalled roads, the exhaust system hit the ground on three occasions, once so hard that we were momentarily convinced that the whole assembly had become detached. A brief inspection of the underneath of the car reveals that there is indeed not a lot of space to accommodate silencer or pipes, but surely during this period of time some solution to the problem should have been found. The specification, incidentally, gives a ground clearance of 4½ in. which our test car did not achieve even in an unloaded condition, although admittedly the measurement was not taken until after the exhaust system had been banged two or three times and it might therefore have been deranged.

This point excepted, the car certainly shows the benefits and refinements of a long period in use throughout the world. When its successor is introduced we can hope that the design will incorporate this experience blended with a dynamic reappraisal of what the markets of the world are likely to require of a sports car in the future. High on this list, we would hazard a guess, will be more silence, better carrying capacity of passengers and luggage, and roadholding that is more than equal to tremendous performance which, in all probability necessitates an independent rear end.

SPECIFICATION:

ENGINE:

Six cylinders; bore 83.36 mm. (3.282 in.) stroke 89 mm. (3.5 in). Cubic capacity, 2,912 c.c. Overhead valves, push-rod operated. Compression ratio, 9 to 1. Maximum b.h.p., 130 (gross) at 4,750 r.p.m. Maximum torque, 175 lb. ft. at 3,000 r.p.m. Twin S.U. H.D.6 carburettors; S.U. electric fuel pump; tank capacity, 12 gallons. Cooling system by fan and centrifugal pump with thermostat control; capacity, approx. 20 pints. Pressurised lubrication system, Tecalemit full-flow oil filter; sump capacity, approx. 12 pints. 12 volt battery.

TRANSMISSION:

Single dry-plate 10in. dia. clutch. Four-speed gearbox with Laycock-de Normanville overdrive on third and top, giving six forward gears. Overall ratios: 1st, 11.45; 2nd, 8.02; 3rd, 5.12; o/d 3rd, 4.19; top, 3.91; o/d top, 3.20. Centrally mounted gear lever. Hypoid 11/43 final drive.

CHASSIS:

Suspension: front, independent by coil springs and wishbones, with anti-roll bar; rear, semi-elliptic leaf springs and anti-roll bar. Armstrong hydraulic lever-type shock absorbers front and rear. Girling hydraulic brakes, disc at front, drum at rear. Cam and peg steering gear; 17in. steering wheel with three spring spokes. Knock-off wire wheels; Dunlop RS5 tyres; size, 5.90-15.

Well-stocked engine compartment, showing the twin semi-downdraught S.U.s.

Driving compartment is business-like if slightly disordered

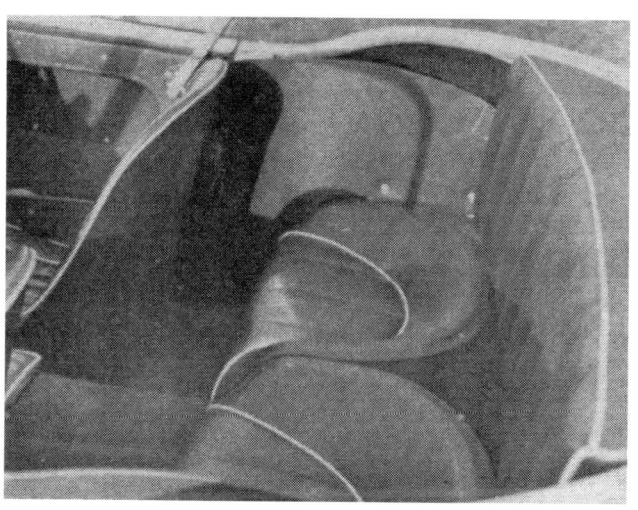

On the left is shown the back seat area for children or touring luggage

A good-sized boot is impinged upon by spare wheel and battery on the four-seater

DIMENSIONS:

				ft.	in.
Wheelbase	...	...	...	7	8
Track: front	...	...	4	0¾
Track: rear	...	...	...	4	2
Overall length	...	...	13	1½
Overall width	...	...	5	0½
Overall height: hood up	...	4	2
	hood down	3	10
Ground clearance	...	...		4½
Turning circle	...	...	35	0
Kerb weight	...	...	22 cwt.

PERFORMANCE:

Acceleration through gears:

m.p.h.	secs
0— 30	2.9
0— 40	5.2
0— 60	10.6
0— 80	17.2
0— 90	25.4
0—100	35.6

Maxima in gears (as used for test):

1st	30 m.p.h.
2nd	45 m.p.h.
3rd	70 m.p.h.
O/D 3rd	90 m.p.h.
top	95 m.p.h.
O/D top	110 m.p.h.

Overall fuel consumption during test: 18.5 m.p.g.

960 BOJ

Deutschland-Rallye

The story
by Tony Ambrose
of a team effort
in the International
German Rally.
Ecurie Safety Fast
took a class
one-two-three
and two
class seconds

THE 2nd International Deutschland Rally, held from 29 September to 1 October, gave the B.M.C. works team an opportunity to underline the list of successes recently scored in the Liège-Rome-Liège Rally. Our team entries (the only ones from Britain) consisted of Pat Moss/Ann Wisdom, David Seigle-Morris/Stuart Turner and Donald Morley/Barry Hercock, all in Austin-Healey '3000's, and Peter Riley and myself in an M.G.A. 1600. John Sprinzel was also competing, together with his sister Norma, in the Austin-Healey Sprite with which he and John Patten finished third overall in the Liège-Rome-Liège. The only other British-made car entered was the 2.6-litre Austin-Healey of Metzker and von Schulmann from Dusseldorf.

The start was at Freiburg in southwestern Germany at 6 a.m. on an uninviting morning with steady rain and low cloud, providing little encouragement for the crews to leave their warm beds in the excellent Colombi Hotel, but as the rain eased the crews' enthusiasm gained strength. While the cavalcade made its way in a well-ordered procession to the foot of the Freiburg-Schauinsland hill-climb, we were able to take stock of the opposition in the three classes with which we were concerned. The big Austin-Healeys were very impressive, their twin side exhausts heralding their arrival at the foot of the hill.

STIFF OPPOSITION

Number 1 in the rally and the only other car in their class was the Mahle/Ott works Mercedes 300SL; what the class lacked in quantity was more than compensated by the quality of the entries. As expected, Mahle achieved fastest time of the rally in the first climb with a time of 9 min. 01.8 sec., followed by David Seigle-Morris with

9 min. 13.9 sec. Donald Morley did well to climb in 9 min. 32 sec. with an engine which was firing on only five cylinders, and Pat Moss's climb in 9 min. 40.6 sec. showed that the Austin-Healeys might well be a force to be reckoned with on hills where the local knowledge of the Germans was not so great.

In the class for Grand Touring cars from 1301–2000 c.c., the M.G. had for opposition a formidable array; no less than nine Porsches in various states of tune. In the Freiburg climb the M.G. was not particularly impressive, achieving eighth fastest time in 10 min. 11.8 sec. compared with the fastest Porsche Carrera's 9 min. 35.6 sec. John Sprinzel, whose Sprite was competing against a diversity of cars such as two Conrero-tuned Alfa Romeos and a D.B., climbed in 10 min. 36.4 sec. to take third place in his class.

After the climb the rally route quickly left German soil, crossing the Rhine just south of Strasbourg and passing into a complexity of narrow lanes in the Jura. This type of route suited the British crews, whose experienced navigators demonstrated to their less able Continental counterparts that 'a map is a map in any language', and a rather self-satisfied B.M.C. team arrived at Pontarlier having made light of the tricky route, while members of the Mercedes and Citröen works teams were seen to take several wrong turnings.

CROSSING THE ALPS

The rally continued at a leisurely 50 k.p.h. average, the scheduled speed for the entire route, heading south for Annecy where a half-hour stop was allowed, during which the sun came out and revealed the beauties of early autumn in Haute Savoie in their full splendour. As dusk fell the cars approached the control at St. Etienne

en-Devulay which was the start of the first potentially difficult section. This was of 140 kilometres, embracing the Col du Glandon, Col de Croix de Fer, Col Telegraphe and Col du Galibier, with the final control at the Col de Lauteret. The first two cols, in typical Alpine Rally terrain, are known to British competitors as 'Hellfire Loop', but on dry roads a 50 k.p.h. average was well within the capabilities of our contingent. Rumours of snow and ice on the upper reaches of the Galibier (8,300 ft.) were not without foundation, we found, but most crews had sufficient time in hand to treat the icy roads with respect and still avoid penalties.

The rest of the night was spent in some fairly hectic motoring taking in such famed Cols as the Izoard, Cayolle, Allos and Noyer. It was on the Cayolle that electrical troubles beset two of our cars, the Seigle-Morris/Turner Austin-Healey and our M.G., and in each case as headlights began to fail the cars tagged on to the most convenient competitor in order to get a 'tow'.

HEALEY SANDWICH

David Seigle-Morris was able to choose Pat Moss's similar car, but Peter Riley and I had to make do with the Porsche Super 90 of Heyse/Schuler. At the control at Annot, just before the Col d'Allos, it was necessary for us to leave before the Porsche, and, in the light of the last glimmer from its battery, the M.G. was hurled up the slopes in pursuit of the Austin-Healeys. Owing to an error in the distance quoted on the route card for this section, it was obvious that a true average of about 54 k.p.h. was needed to avoid penalty. By half-distance, however, we had caught the Austin-Healeys, and the rest of the journey to the summit was achieved by sandwiching

*David Seigle-Morris
and Stuart Turner move
up for a close look, as
the Morley twins try to
overtake a low-flying
cow on a twisty section
of the route*

**Photos
by Stuart Turner**

the two blind mice between the two far-seeing Healeys.

The run down to the control on the far side of the pass was taken in leisurely fashion, as by this time the entire team was well ahead of schedule. Unfortunately for us, the results of this section, on which about half the entry was late, were not taken into consideration in calculating the final results due to the error in the distance.

Dawn once more brought heavy rain and low cloud. At one point, where the route had been diverted due to a landslide, we had to cross a raging torrent flowing over a recently bull-dozed dirt track. By the time John Sprinzel's Sprite reached this the flow of water had increased, and, as the Sprite was negotiating the river (passing a Citroën which had stalled its engine) it was lifted clear of the road by the current and only rescued by the manhandling of generous fellow-competitors. It was here, also, that the German-entered Austin-Healey was retired with a damaged sump.

By mid-morning on the second day the cars had reached Mont Ventoux for the second speed hill-climb. Unfortunately only the lower eight kilometres were free from cloud, and many performances were spoilt by minor excursions from the road. The first of these was made by Mahle/Ott (300SL Mercedes), whose excursion into the shale allowed the Morley/Hercock Austin-Healey to take first place with a climb of 16 min. 5 sec.—six seconds faster than the Mercedes. Seigle-Morris climbed in 16 min. 15.4 sec., and Pat Moss in 17 min. 0.4 sec. after going a short distance up a wrong fork in the cloud. Our M.G. achieved 18 min. 12.2 sec., which was fourth fastest in the class.

A short section on narrow roads taking in a difficult new pass, the Col. de Pennes,

which will surely be used again by other organisers, brought competitors to the foot of the Col de Rousset for the third timed climb. The three Austin-Healeys and the Mercedes were remarkably consistent in their performance here, less than 1 per cent. separating the fastest, Mahle/Ott, from the slowest.

FASTEST IN THE CLASS

As soon as the cars reached the northern slopes the light rain which had been falling steadily turned to a torrential downpour, causing the mountainsides to ooze brown liquid mud which flowed across the road in waves of slime. There was considerable speculation on whether the fourth speed test on the St. Jean 'circuit' would be held in such conditions, but fortunately the course for this special stage was sheltered from the full force of the storm. This stage was a very severe test of a driver's ability

to handle his car under appalling weather conditions and it is pleasing to note that the Austin-Healeys were all faster than the Mercedes by more than 10 per cent. And our trusty M.G., I'm glad to say, also put up a pretty remarkable performance, for we beat the fastest of the Porsches by 45 sec.

The competitors then made their way across country on minor roads to Charbonnières, just west of Lyon. Navigation was tricky and not helped by floods and fog. Again many of the Continentals showed their fear of navigational sections by choosing to use main roads, risking fear of elimination for missing a secret control; they were either very lucky or extremely well-informed, as no check was established. However, on this section the Nyffeler/Lambart Porsche made a navigational error, losing six minutes and allowing our M.G. to climb to second place in the class. After a three-hour rest at Charbonnières, competitors were routed across country via St. Claude and Pontarlier and then were made to follow, in the opposite direction, the route from the Rhine used on the outward journey.

Arrival at the attractive spa of Baden-Baden revealed success yet again for *Ecurie Safety Fast.* The Austin-Healey '3000's of Seigle-Morris/Turner, Morley/Hercock and Pat Moss/Ann Wisdom took the first three places in their class in that order. With the M.G., Peter Riley and I retained second place in the 2-litre class, to the embarrassment of a whole bevy of Porsche drivers, and the Sprinzels' Sprite was also second in its class (which included cars of up to 1300 c.c.), underlining very firmly its recent third place in the Liège-Rome-Liège.

*The three Austin-Healeys in procession
through a German village, with the
population out to watch — or at least the
junior element !*

The Cambodian crest.

A HEALEY WITH EXTRA STING

RIDE IN AUSTRALIA'S ONLY AUSTIN-HEALEY 3000, WITH HARDTOP COMFORT AS WELL

Badge on left of grille is in Cambodian colors.

Distinguishing word "3000" under the writing "Austin Healey".

CANBERRA is the ideal city for motoring enthusiasts with the flock of exclusive cars on display there — all owned by members of Diplomatic Corps and usually sporting left-hand drive. On a recent visit to the Albury International meeting we dropped off at the Cambodian Embassy, in Vancouver Street, Canberra, where the secretary (Mr Doeuskoma Poc) is the owner of Australia's first Austin Healey 3000, with a hardtop adding to trimness and comfort.

Being a Sydneysider I did not know the existence of a 3000 in our land, so I asked the Austin agents, Larke Hoskins, through their publicity man Ron Gill, when the first of the handful could be expected. I was told the 3000's were being brought out to order only, but the Cambodian Ambassador Mr Poc had one already. I dispatched a letter to Mr Poc requesting a test of his flyer and eagerly awaited results.

A week later I visited Sydney's luxury Chevron-Hilton Hotel to farewell BMC team manager Arthur Grogan and his team on the pre-release run to Perth and back in the Morris 850. Outside the hotel I sighted a newcomer to Sydney streets — a cream hardtop sports car, with the undoubted lines of a Healey. Then I saw the number plates, DC999, and realised my quarry was in Sydney, so that I might not have to make the trip to Canberra afterall.

Next morning I found the owner, Mr Doeuskoma Poc, nephew of the Cambodian Ambassador (Mr. Thieun Poc). Mr Doeuskoma Poc was in Sydney while his wife was in hospital. Between visiting hours and business appointments he found it hard to talk motoring, but he was most helpful. However, the car had only 3000 miles on the speedo and needed another 2000 before he considered it should be driven at top speed.

But we arranged to take some color shots for Sports Car World cover before Mr Poc departed for Canberra on the Sunday morning. The morning came up with the skies opened up and continual rain. Still I took a shot of the Healey during a shower. But it was too dark and not up to the standards of our SCW covers. I had to wait another month for the 3000 to be fully run in.

Mr Poc rang just prior to the Albury International meeting, so that I was able to drop in at Canberra en route to the NSW-Victoria border. Unfortunately, racing petrol was not available in Canberra and we were unable to get the best out of this potent machine.

While waiting for Mr Poc at the Embassy I learnt a little about the country of Cambodia. One of the smallest Asian countries still strictly neutral in the "cold" war. There are four Cambodian families in Australia—three at the Embassy and another in Adelaide. Yet this tiny independence is very happy to have its team of diplomats in Australia just for the sake of good relations. After 80 years under French rule, Cambodia now has been independent for eight years.

Soon after, the cream Healey, with hardtop giving it an exclusive look for Australia, swung through the Embassy gates and I was invited to take the controls. Body work is the same as in the previous 100-Six model.

The left-hand drive was a novelty to me and I took extreme care for the first few miles as we swung towards a deserted road just outside of Canberra where we could carry out our speed runs in safety.

I was particularly careful to give way to the left, a very strict rule in Canberra, despite the fact we carried the DC numberplates and their immunity from traffic conditions. As we wound through the picturesque streets Mr Poc told me his ambition was to own an Aston Martin. But he could not afford one, even with the free-of-tax price to members of the Diplomatic Corps. Next best, in his opinion, was the Healey. He had raced previously in France and was a friend of Maurice Trintignant. His ambition was to race the Healey at Warwick Farm. I arranged for Australian Automobile Racing Club secretary Mr Geoff Sykes to send him an entry form on my return to Sydney.

The roof, made of fibreglass, had padding underneath to guard against bumps on a bad road. It rattled slightly at high speeds, but so slight that I would not have noticed it if Mr Poc had not pointed it out.

The left-hand drive proved no problem, in fact I felt it had advantages as you could go right to the edge of the road with safety, and would be especially good on narrow roads. But it would have its problems. On one occasion Mr Poc turned the car round and placed it on the right-hand side of the road, probably remembering his days in Paris and Washington.

The rev counter was ideally placed and could be seen through one side of the steering wheel, with the speedo through the other. Revolutions were red lined at 5200, which we decided would be the limit for our tests, though it went up to 6000 rpm for anyone who wanted to thrash such a machine.

With a compression ratio of 9.03 to 1, the 3000 reaches its maximum power of 124 bhp net (or 130 gross) at 4600 rpm and maximum torque of 167 lb/ft at 2700 rpm.

With this compression ratio there was knocking at top speed, which would be eliminated by the use of a racing fuel such as Shell

A potent machine with twin exhausts ready to roar into action.

Upward view of the lights and grille.

100 with ICA. Fuel experts also calculated this fuel should raise top speed by about six miles per hour, that is at Canberra, where the height above sea level cuts down speed nearly two mph, despite the boost of the lesser air resistance. This probably accounts for the excellent rolling resistance figures recorded by the 3000.

Our best speed in one direction was a true 109 mph with an average both ways of 107. This was well ahead of the Healey 100-Six which averaged 98.9 in fourth and 104.2 in overdrive when tested by

37

SPORTS CAR WORLD in June, 1957. But even then we felt the 3000 could have done better with a longer run up as the speedo needle was still climbing when we had to ease down due to road conditions. Mr Poc has done 110 with his wife and son Eric (aged eight), while tests in England regularly reach 115 mph.

Acceleration of the 3000 was well ahead of the 100-Six times, while slightly slower than overseas tests using racing fuel. The speedo was really accurate, being two miles out at 30 mph, one at 40 and 50, then right on the dot for the higher speeds.

The gear lever, placed a little over towards the passenger's side perhaps as the Healeys are made in England generally with right-hand drive, took a little getting used to. As a result acceleration times (even by Mr Poc) were slow early until he had the real feel of the car. There was no synchromesh on first gear. Our changes were generally made when the 3000 reached the 4600 rpm mark, or its maximum power.

Braking with all anchors out was really good and shaded some of the fine sports cars we have tested in the past. Using our Bronder Brake Graph, it took only 15 ft 7 in to stop the 3000 from 20 mph, which rates excellent. However, Mr Poc felt the Healey would be made safer still by the fitting of disc brakes on all four wheels, not just on the front as in the standard version.

Opening the bonnet one is struck by the two SU carburettors which are fed by an SU pump. Though sporting a big motor for an engine compartment of its size the 3000 is still fairly accessible. Boot space is somewhat restricted, but what sports car isn't? As well as the spare wheel it has to carry side covers and has tucked away to one side the usual Healey safety switch to turn off your petrol when parked.

Inside the twin bucket seats are most spacious, but room behind is most occasional, only being big enough for the carriage of adults on extremely short trips, or for children. The 3000 boasts big pockets in each of the widely arced doors, as well as a parcel tray under the passenger's side of the well padded dashboard. Other controls are for choke, push starter and trafficators. Oil and water gauges also are set before the driver.

As extras Mr Poc had fitted a HMV imported radio and a cigarette lighter. Selling at £2300 (inc. tax) for a canvas top model the 3000 is £140 dearer than the 100-Six model, putting it even further into the luxury class.

A real man's car that goes as expected by the Healeys, the 3000 won last year's Liege-Rome-Liege Rally, when it was driven by two women — Pat Moss and Ann Wisdom. But who would deny that this pair can drive as well as any two men.

The Healey 3000 celebrates its second birthday this month, so that it is strange that more of this potent vehicle have not found their way to our shores. Bearing the type name BN7, it is hard to pick from its predecessors without being close enough to read the inscription on the radiator grille or on the boot.

Finally just a few comparisons between the old and the new Healeys. The 3000 marked the first appearance of the BMC C type engine of 2912 cc, which later was used in the full range of six-cylinder cars offered by this manufacturer. Capacity formerly was 2639 cc. The change over increased net power output from 117 bhp to 124, using a compression ratio of 9.03 to 1.

Rear axle ratio on the 3000 is 3.545 to 1, which gives a road speed of 20.9 mph for every 1000 rpm. Overdrive is available at extra cost, but it was not installed on Mr Poc's car. #

Heart of the Healey 3000, and the boot with safety petrol device and spare wheel.

AUSTIN HEALEY

PERFORMANCE

TOP SPEED:
Two-way average .... 107 mph
Fastest one way .... 109 mph

ACCELERATION:
(Test limit, 4600 rpm)
Through gears:
0-30 mph .... 3.5 sec
0-40 mph .... 5.3 sec
0-50 mph .... 8.0 sec
0-60 mph .... 10.9 sec
0-70 mph .... 14.2 sec
0-80 mph .... 19.2 sec
0-90 mph .... 27.5 sec
0-100 mph .... 31.1 sec

MAXIMUM SPEEDS IN GEARS (Calculated):
(at 5200 rpm)
I .... 37.6 mph
II .... 52.7 mph
III .... 81.1 mph
IV .... 108.6 mph

SPEEDOMETER ERROR:
30 mph actual — indicated 32 mph.
40 mph actual — indicated 41 mph.
50 mph actual — indicated 51 mph.
60 mph actual — indicated 60 mph.
70 mph actual — indicated 70 mph.
80 mph actual — indicated 80 mph.

TAPLEY DATA:
Maximum pull in gears:
I .... 550 lb ton at 25 mph
II .... 520 lb/ton at 40 mph
III .... 370 lb/ton at 60 mph
IV .... 290 lb/ton at 65 mph

ROLLING RESISTANCE:
90 mph .... 100 lb/ton
80 mph .... 58 lb/ton
70 mph .... 49 lb/ton
60 mph .... 30 lb/ton
50 mph .... 25 lb/ton

BRAKING:
Stop from 20 mph: 15 ft 7 in (excellent).
FADE:
Nil.

CALCULATED DATA:
Weight as tested (2 men) 23½ cwt.
Max bhp, 124 at 4600 rpm (130 gross)
Max torque, 167 lb/ft at 2700 rpm
Lb/hp (nett) 21.2
Mph/1000 rpm top gear, 20.9.
Mph at 2500 ft/min piston speed top gear, 89.2.
Cub cm/lb ft torque 17.4
BHP/litre 42.5
BHP/ton as tested 105.5
Piston speed at max bhp 2995

SPECIFICATIONS

PRICE:

£2300 (inc tax), with canvas hood.

ENGINE:

Type .... 6 Cylinders, water cooled
Valves .... pushrod overhead
Capacity .... 2912 cc
Bore and Stroke .... 83.34 x 88.9 mm
Piston area .... 50.7 sq in
Compression ratio .... 9.03 to 1
Carburettors: Two SU (type HD6).
Fuel Pump: SU (Type LCS)
Spark Plugs: Champion N5.
Oil Filter: Tecalemit or Purolator full flow.

CHASSIS:

Wheelbase .... 7ft 7¾ in
Track, front 4ft 0¾in
        rear .... 4 ft 2in
Suspension, front .... Coil and wishbone independent
        Rear .... Half-Elliptic
Shock absorbers .... Armstrong piston type
Brakes: Type .... Girling Hydraulic
        Operation: Disc front ..... (11¼ in diameter);
        Drum rear .... (11 in x 2¼ in)
Steering: Cam and peg.

TRANSMISSION:

Clutch .... 10 in Borg and Beck.

GEAR RATIOS:

I 10.209
II 7.302
III 4.743
IV 3.545
Synchromesh on 2, 3, 4.

GENERAL:

Length overall .... 13 ft 1½ in
Width .... 5 ft 0 in
Test weather: Fine, dry.

All test runs made on dry, bitumen-bound gravel road
with driver and one passenger aboard.

Austin-Healey **3000** *Mark II* ◀ · · ·

Vertical slats of the Healey Mk. II grille are reminiscent of earlier models, although the shape of the opening is not the same. This re-styling clearly distinguishes the three-carburettor from the two-carburettor cars

AT the same time as their announcement of the Austin-Healey Sprite II, British Motor Corporation also introduce modifications to the well-established Austin-Healey 3000 model, affecting both its performance and apearance. By the addition of an extra carburettor to the 2·9-litre engine, maximum output has been increased by 8 b.h.p. Styling changes to the radiator grille distinguish this model from the two carburettor version. At the same time servo-assisted braking is to be offered as an optional extra.

For some time, competition Healey 3000s have been using three carburettors, so their adoption for the production model is not unexpected. The three now fitted are 1½in. HS4 S.U.s, replacing the two 1¾in. HS6s of the earlier model. To suit the different characteristics of these three carburettors and the redesigned inlet manifold, a new camshaft giving higher lift to the inlet valves and a longer dwell to the exhaust valves has been adopted. Stronger outer valve springs and a timing chain damper steady pad look after the increased loads involved. The result of these modifications is an increase in maximum b.h.p. from 124 net at 4,600 r.p.m. to 132 b.h.p. net at 4,750 r.p.m. Maximum torque remains at 167 lb ft but the engine speed at which it is attained rises from 2,700 to 3,000 r.p.m. The compression ratio remains at 9 to 1.

When redesigning the induction manifold and throttle linkage, the opportunity was taken of improving the choke control. This is still cable operated, but the main control cable now runs to a central distri-bution unit mounted on top of the manifold. A simple lever arrangement there operates three separate cables to the carburettor choke levers. The effort required to use the choke is now reduced.

A 10in. diameter single plate Borg and Beck clutch was introduced at the same time as the 2·9-litre engine and no change to this unit has been necessary to cope with the extra power of the three-carburettor engine. Gear ratios and rear axle ratios remain unaltered.

For those who find the brake operation rather heavy, a Girling servo-assisted braking system will be offered as an optional extra at a later date. The vacuum cylinder fits neatly into the recess between the right hand frame member and the bonnet side, forward of the scuttle. As this system requires new brake pipes, dif-ferent brake pads and rear brake linings, it will normally be a factory fitting, installed before the car leaves the works.

Apart from the change from horizontal to vertical grille slats to distinguish this car from the two-carburettor version, there is a redesigned bonnet motif incor-porating the Mark II designation. As with the new Sprite, safety strap attach-ments are a standard fitting and modifica-tions to the frame, side floor panels, wheel arches and centre tunnel have been made to provide secure anchorages for these. The price is unchanged.

This view of the Mk. II engine compartment shows the new carburettor arrangement and the dis-tribution unit for the choke control, which is mounted on the carburettor balance pipe

BRIEF SPECIFICATION

Engine: No. of cylinders, 6 in line; Bore and stroke 83·3 x 88·9 mm (3·28 x 3·5in); Displacement 2,912 c.c. (177·7 cu in.); Valve position and operation, pushrods and rockers; Compression ratio 9·0 to 1; Max. b.h.p. (net) 132 at 4,750 r.p.m.; Max. b.m.e.p. 142 p.s.i. at 3,000 r.p.m.; Max. torque 167 lb ft at 3,000 r.p.m.; Carburettors, three S.U. type HS4; Fuel pump, S.U. electric type LCS; Tank capacity, 12 Imperial gallons (55 litres); Sump capacity 12·75 pints (7·25 litres); Cooling system, pump, fan and thermostat; Battery 12 volt, 57 amp hr.

The NEW AUSTIN-HEALEY

3000 Mark II !

Still more power for this rally-winning 3-litre sports car! Now with three carburetters, the engine output goes up from 124 to 132 b.h.p.

New frontal treatment (above) gives the Austin-Healey '3000' Mark II an even bolder look, while under the bonnet (below) three S.U. carburetters help it to pack a bigger punch than ever

ALREADY an outstandingly successful, high-performance sports car, the Austin-Healey '3000' now appears in still more powerful form, as the '3000' Mark II. The experience gained in rugged Continental rallies now goes into this luxury roadster to give still more effortless power for overtaking, hill-climbing and high-speed highway cruising.

Externally, the change is apparent in the new, bolder front grille and the distinctive bonnet motif. In the cockpit there are now built-in fittings for equipping your car with the added security and comfort of seat belts.

But under the bonnet there are now three S.U. carburetters instead of two. New manifolding, special valve springs and a redesigned camshaft combine to give a power output of no less than 132 b.h.p., compared to 124 b.h.p. of the earlier model—and this increase, believe it or not, is accompanied by an appreciable *reduction* in fuel consumption!

Three carburetters have for some time been part of the specification of the specially-prepared versions of the Austin-Healey '3000' which have been available to carefully selected private owners for competition use, and of course this configuration has also contributed to the remarkable run of successes by the works team cars in Continental rallying. In 18 months of competition, these cars won their class nine times in International events, including the impressive outright victory in the Liège-Rome-Liège Rally last year, driven by Pat Moss and Ann Wisdom.

The three-carburetter Austin-Healey '3000' Mark II is for the time being available only for export.

Make: Austin-Healey **Type:** 3000 Mark II 4-seater (with overdrive and hardtop)

Makers: The Austin Motor Co., Ltd., Longbridge, Birmingham

Test Data

World copyright reserved; no unauthorized reproduction in whole or in part.

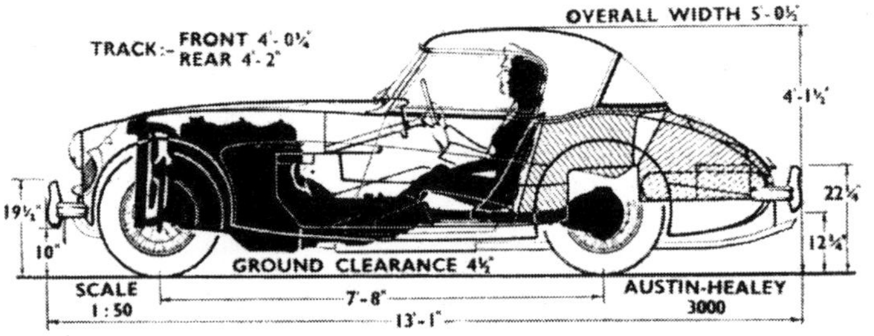

CONDITIONS. *Weather: Mild and damp, calm for maximum speed trials with wind rising to 10-15 m.p.h. later. (Temperature 54°-58°F. Barometer 28.8-29.0 in. Hg.) Surface: Damp concrete and tarred macadam (dry for braking tests). Fuel: Premium grade pump petrol (approx. 97 Research Method Octane Rating).*

INSTRUMENTS

Speedometer at 30 m.p.h.	accurate
Speedometer at 60 m.p.h.	4% fast
Speedometer at 90 m.p.h.	4% fast
Distance recorder	2% slow

WEIGHT

Kerb weight (unladen, but with oil, coolant and fuel for approx. 50 miles)	22¾ cwt.
Front/rear distribution of kerb weight	48½/51½
Weight laden as tested	26½ cwt.

MAXIMUM SPEEDS

Flying Mile

Mean of four opposite runs	112.9 m.p.h.
Best one-way time equals	113.6 m.p.h.

"Maximile" Speed. (Timed quarter mile after one mile accelerating from rest.)

Mean of four opposite runs	107.8 m.p.h.
Best one-way time equals	108.4 m.p.h.

Speed in gears (at 5,200 r.p.m.)

Max. speed in direct top gear	97 m.p.h.
Max. speed in overdrive 3rd gear	90 m.p.h.
Max. speed in direct 3rd gear	74 m.p.h.
Max. speed in 2nd gear	47 m.p.h.
Max. speed in 1st gear	33 m.p.h.

FUEL CONSUMPTION

(Overdrive top gear)

34 m.p.g. at constant 30 m.p.h. on level
33 m.p.g. at constant 40 m.p.h. on level
30 m.p.g. at constant 50 m.p.h. on level
28 m.p.g. at constant 60 m.p.h. on level
25 m.p.g. at constant 70 m.p.h. on level
22½ m.p.g. at constant 80 m.p.h. on level
20 m.p.g. at constant 90 m.p.h. on level
16 m.p.g. at constant 100 m.p.h. on level

(Direct top gear)

31½ m.p.g. at constant 30 m.p.h. on level
28 m.p.g. at constant 40 m.p.h. on level
25½ m.p.g. at constant 50 m.p.h. on level
23½ m.p.g. at constant 60 m.p.h. on level
22 m.p.g. at constant 70 m.p.h. on level
19½ m.p.g. at constant 80 m.p.h. on level
17 m.p.g. at constant 90 m.p.h. on level

STEERING

Turning circle between kerbs

Left	32½ feet
Right	32½ feet
Turns of steering wheel from lock to lock	3⅛

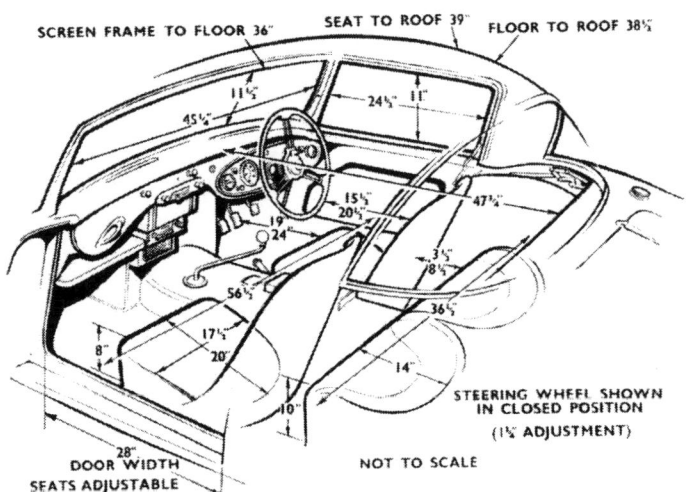

TRACK:- FRONT 4'-0¼" / REAR 4'-2" OVERALL WIDTH 5'-0½" 4'-1½" 22¼" 12¾" 19½" 10" GROUND CLEARANCE 4½" SCALE 1:50 7'-8" 13'-1" AUSTIN-HEALEY 3000

SCREEN FRAME TO FLOOR 36" SEAT TO ROOF 39" FLOOR TO ROOF 38½" 11½" 24½" 11" 45½" 47¼" 15½" 20½" 19" 24" 3½" 8½" 56½" 36½" 17½" 20" 14" 8" 10" 28" DOOR WIDTH SEATS ADJUSTABLE STEERING WHEEL SHOWN IN CLOSED POSITION (1½" ADJUSTMENT) NOT TO SCALE

Overall Fuel Consumption for 3,767 miles, 181.3 gallons, equals 20.8 m.p.g. (13.6 litres/100 km.)

Touring Fuel Consumption (m.p.g. at steady speed midway between 30 m.p.h. and maximum, less 5% allowance for acceleration) 23.5 m.p.g. Fuel tank capacity (makers' figure) 12 gallons

ACCELERATION TIMES from standstill

0-30 m.p.h.	3.8 sec.
0-40 m.p.h.	5.8 sec.
0-50 m.p.h.	8.3 sec.
0-60 m.p.h.	10.9 sec.
0-70 m.p.h.	14.3 sec.
0-80 m.p.h.	19.2 sec.
0-90 m.p.h.	25.9 sec.
0-100 m.p.h.	36.4 sec.
Standing quarter mile	18.3 sec.

ACCELERATION TIMES on Upper Ratios

	Overdrive top gear	Direct top gear	Direct 3rd gear
10-30 m.p.h.	8.8 sec.	6.8 sec.	4.9 sec.
20-40 m.p.h.	9.2 sec.	7.0 sec.	5.3 sec.
30-50 m.p.h.	9.8 sec.	7.2 sec.	5.5 sec.
40-60 m.p.h.	10.5 sec.	7.4 sec.	5.7 sec.
50-70 m.p.h.	11.2 sec.	7.9 sec.	6.3 sec.
60-80 m.p.h.	11.8 sec.	8.9 sec.	—
70-90 m.p.h.	13.4 sec.	10.9 sec.	—
80-100 m.p.h.	18.8 sec.	16.7 sec.	—

BRAKES from 30 m.p.h.

1.00 g retardation (equivalent to 30 ft. stopping distance) with 120 lb. pedal pressure.
0.95 g retardation (equivalent to 31¾ ft. stopping distance) with 100 lb. pedal pressure.
0.71 g retardation (equivalent to 42½ ft. stopping distance) with 75 lb. pedal pressure.
0.47 g retardation (equivalent to 64 ft. stopping distance) with 50 lb. pedal pressure.
0.22 g retardation (equivalent to 137 ft. stopping distance) with 25 lb. pedal pressure.

HILL CLIMBING at sustained steady speeds.

Max. gradient on overdrive top	1 in 8.7	(Tapley 255 lb./ton)
Max. gradient on direct top	1 in 6.9	(Tapley 320 lb./ton)
Max. gradient on overdrive 3rd	1 in 6.5	(Tapley 340 lb./ton)
Max. gradient on direct 3rd	1 in 5.1	(Tapley 430 lb./ton)
Max. gradient on 2nd gear	1 in 3.3	(Tapley 645 lb./ton)

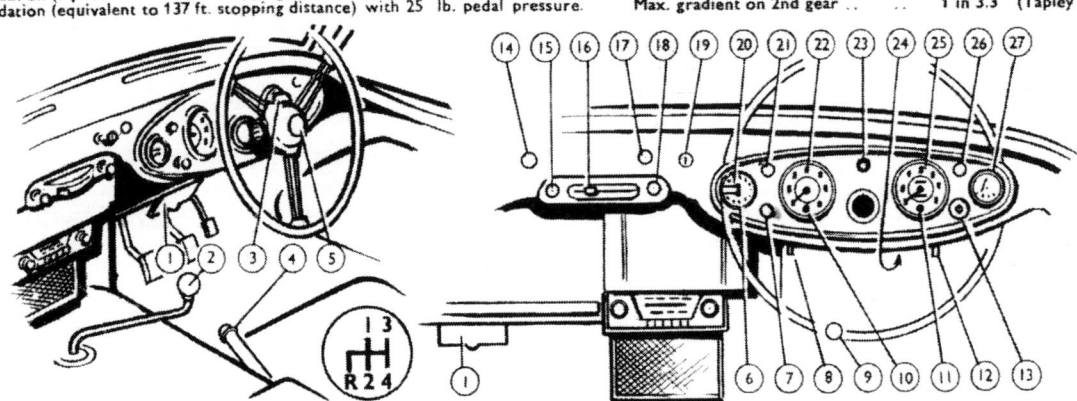

1, Heater air outlet shutters. 2, Gear lever. 3, Direction indicator control. 4, Handbrake. 5, Horn button. 6, Water temperature gauge. 7, Wipers switch. 8, Panel light switch. 9, Dip switch. 10, Dynamo charge warning light. 11, High beam warning light. 12, Trip reset. 13, Overdrive switch. 14, Screen washer. 15, Cold air control. 16, Heater temperature control and fan switch. 17, Choke. 18, Heater air-intake control. 19, Ignition key. 20, Oil pressure gauge. 21, Starter. 22, Rev. counter. 23, Direction indicator warning light. 24, Bonnet release. 25, Speedometer. 26, Light switch. 27, Fuel gauge.

The Austin-Healey 3000 Mark II

(with overdrive)

Velvet-gloved High Performance from the Latest Triple-carburetter 4-seater

POWER in ample quantities over a wide range of engine speeds makes the big Austin-Healey a quick and effortless mountaineering car, although ground clearance is limited for rough surfaces such as this one on the Great St. Bernard Pass.

EXTENDING our test of the Austin-Healey 3000 to something more than 4,000 miles, and sampling this triple-carburetter Mark II version of the British Motor Corporation's fastest model in France, Italy and Switzerland as well as in Britain, we found ourselves with quite extraordinarily mixed reactions. One might say that 85% of what we felt was keen enthusiasm for this car; it is capable of well over 110 m.p.h. on level road, has acceleration and braking to match its top speed, is quite pleasantly controllable, and delights both driver and passenger by providing a really comfortable ride in two excellent seats. The remaining 15% of our reaction was dismay that a company which has big resources and has been developing this series of Austin-Healeys for eight years is still delivering cars with two familiar and quite serious, but demonstrably curable, shortcomings in respect of ground clearance and heat in the cockpit.

From the fact that differences between a Mark II Austin-Healey and its immediate predecessors centre around a third carburetter and a high-lift camshaft, one might be forgiven for expecting this version to put all the emphasis on high performance. In actual fact, whilst an ability to reach 100 m.p.h. from rest in 36.4 sec. and less than ¾-mile of road testifies to the reality of its performance, smooth running and easy riding are the characteristics which really distinguish this model from other fast cars. Its primary appeal may be sporting, as appearances suggest, but the comfort and driving ease which accompany a delightful power to accelerate clear of obstructive traffic could make this a better "executive's car" than are many more cumbrous saloons.

Built as low to the ground as it is, the Austin-Healey 3000 has almost complete natural immunity from body roll on corners, and is able to ride on comfortably flexible springs. Although the suspension is slightly firmer than on most modern saloons, excellent matching of the front and rear springs gives a delightfully flat ride at all times; even with the extra-high tyre pressures advised for very fast driving, the car is very comfortable on British roads and not unduly lively over the fast but rough roads of northern France. Greater curvature of the backrest might save the driver from a tendency to rest one shoulder against the body side when cornering fast, but the seats are comfortable even when judged from the passenger's side during fast progress along secondary roads. The doors extend reasonably far forward and down to floor level, making this a tolerably easy car to enter or leave in spite of its low roof.

With all its emphasis on riding comfort, this is, nevertheless, an easy car to swing along winding roads, its Dunlop RS5 tyres having excellent adhesion on most sorts of

THREE carburetters with individual air filters make an impressive looking array, and with a new camshaft they put extra emphasis on power in the upper-middle range of r.p.m.

In Brief

Price (including overdrive, wire wheels and hardtop as tested), £960 17s. 6d. plus purchase tax £401 9s. 10d., equals £1,362 7s. 4d.

Price without extras (including purchase tax), £1,175 10s. 10d.

Capacity		2,912 c.c.
Unladen kerb weight ...		22¾ cwt.

Acceleration:

20-40 m.p.h. in top gear ...	7.0 sec.
0-50 m.p.h. through gears	8.3 sec.

Maximum direct top gear gradient		1 in 6.9
Maximum speed ...		112.9 m.p.h.
"Maximile" speed ...		107.8 m.p.h.
Touring fuel consumption ...		23.5 m.p.g.

Gearing: 18.6 m.p.h. in top gear at 1,000 r.p.m. (overdrive, 22.6 m.p.h.); 31.8 m.p.h. at 1,000 ft./min. piston speed (overdrive, 38.8 m.p.h.).

43

OCCASIONAL rear seats add to the usefulness of this Austin-Healey in its four-seater form, can accommodate children under cover or will carry adults when the car is open. Cockpit details include an effective pull-up handbrake and an oddly-shaped but sturdy central gear lever.

road surface, and the car slides only gradually when pushed towards the limit. Although the steering is not quite quick enough in its gearing or free enough from lost motion to satisfy the most fastidious sporting tastes, the light control with some feel but very little kick-back pleases a majority of drivers.

At times, the controls seem disappointingly clumsy to use, as all three pedals have a rather long travel and are arranged so that toe-and-heel operation of brake and accelerator is impossible; the gear lever curves oddly from the left side of a broad gearbox cover, and the overdrive switch is irritatingly farther to one side of the steering wheel rim than it could have been on a less stylized facia panel. Gear ratio spacings which are not ideal (1st and 2nd are surprisingly similar ratios) matter little with such a flexibly powerful engine, and occasional complaints of a poor gearchange are usually traceable to incomplete declutching, the long pedal travel being rather awkward from a straight-leg driving position. Most initial complaints concerning the controls are soon forgotten, this

being an untiring car in which to drive 500 miles when the weather is reasonably cool.

Should the weather be even moderately hot, some cockpit surfaces become fairly warm (despite a substantial amount of asbestos sheeting, visible only when the car is raised on a hoist), and a most unwelcome volume of hot (but not smelly) air from the engine blows into the body through concealed bonnet hinges, around the doors or past the corners of the facia panel. Using our test model to follow and report the French Alpine Rally, which was won by a factory-entered Austin-Healey 3000 fitted with neat-looking additional hot-air outlets alongside the engine and additional air inlets and outlets for the cockpit, we wondered very much why production cars could not be similarly equipped: our test car's engine did not overheat, but its passengers (who had retained the removable hard-top as an anti-theft protection for their photographic equipment) certainly did.

A contrast with the team cars was also very evident in respect of ground clearance, and whilst a great increase could not be

obtained without sacrificing some of the spring travel which lets production models ride so comfortably, it would not be difficult to eliminate vulnerable projections below the flat underside of this model's sturdy chassis. The low-set exhaust pipes have already been arranged and mounted so that frequent use of them as toboggan runners does no harm, as a moderately well laden car will ground them occasionally even on main road undulations, and very frequently on bad roads; but during our test mileage the electrical wiring to all the rear lights was severed and there were visible signs of abrasion on the clutch operating hydraulic pipe, the main petrol pipe and the steel sump of the engine.

Triple carburetters in place of the former two have brought a useful improvement in power over the upper-middle range of engine speeds, giving enhanced acceleration through-the-gears and from 70 m.p.h. in top. Lower in the engine r.p.m. range, a twin-carburetter car which we tested a year ago showed even better acceleration than this Mark II model although it was very much harsher in feel. As the triple carburetters reduce accessibility under the bonnet, give very poor throttle response during the first mile after a start from cold and have little overall effect on petrol consumption, one can reasonably suggest that other rally-developed features should have been applied to production cars in advance of this one.

Regardless of delicate comparisons with the preceding model however, this car really does accelerate quickly, anywhere in its speed range. The overdrive top gear in which it was timed at a two-way mean speed of 112.9 m.p.h. also gave acceleration from 10 to 30 m.p.h. in only 8.8 sec., demonstrating the torque which this

NEAT lines of the removable hardtop, secured by four clamps and leaving the folded hood frame in position, are shown here. Centre-lock wire wheels are an optional extra.

3-litre 6-cylinder engine develops right down to the bottom of the speed range. In traffic on de-restricted roads, second gear provides really ferocious acceleration up to nearly 50 m.p.h. before the red mark on the rev counter dial is reached, or third gear will swing the speed from 20 m.p.h. up to 70 m.p.h. in under 14½ sec. before the driver need consider changing up into either overdrive third or direct top. Such quick acceleration over a wide range of speeds allows a driver to get clear away from awkward groups of traffic at times when with less performance it might be unsafe to overtake.

Oddly, and not as a matter of any practical importance, this Mark II Austin-Healey was slower by 2 m.p.h. than the far-less-refined example which we drove in 1960. On a hot, dry day in Italy measured kilometres were timed at a mean speed of 112.7 m.p.h., and on a cool day in Britain with the road damp, measured miles were timed at a mean speed of 112.9 m.p.h., with the engine turning over at about 5,000 r.p.m. which is rather short of the suggested r.p.m. limit. On an autostrada or motorway, cruising at 80, 90 or 100 m.p.h. does not seem to be hard driving although above 75-80 m.p.h. there is rather a lot of wind noise. Equally, one potters quietly through speed limits in overdrive top gear; exhaust noise from the mechanically quiet engine is never conspicuous for long because when the exhaust does become fairly loud, the Austin-Healey is a rapidly disappearing object. The strange gobbling sounds which the three carburetters emit during acceleration at some speeds and throttle openings neither tire nor offend.

Comfortable as a two seater, this car can only be called a four-seater when neither

LOCKABLE accommodation for luggage will take two week-end bags, which in the four-seat model must fit alongside the battery and above the spare wheel: an alternative two-seat version has more room in its luggage locker.

the hardtop (secured by 2 clamps and 2 screw attachments) nor hood are in use, although two small children can ride in the back under cover, and it is not impossible for one adult to coil himself into the rear compartment. This model has less luggage space in the rear locker than the two-seater in which the spare wheel and battery are mounted farther forward, but two week-end bags can be stowed under lock and key. Despite a fabric cover to the battery, over-filling of this component can lead to luggage being damaged by acid.

Although our 4,000-mile test showed up certain assembly details which an owner would have had rectified under guarantee (tightening numerous nuts to eliminate rattles or thuds from sidescreens, bonnet, rear axle U-bolts and other points) no breakages whatever occurred, and once going well this model has a reputation for sturdiness. Oil consumption in brisk touring was around 3,000 m.p.g., although frequent use of maximum engine r.p.m. could treble this rate of consumption. The brakes, of self-adjusting disc pattern at the front, and with drums which do not quickly go out of adjustment at the rear, gave excellent power without ever fading, and on a good surface they could swing a brake meter to the end of its scale before any trace of rear wheel locking occurred. Brake pedal pressures, in the absence of any servo, were slightly higher than is nowadays normal, and when warm the front brakes sometimes squealed very loudly indeed.

We have felt it necessary to criticize some aspects of this Austin-Healey quite strongly, and we know many owners of slightly earlier models are equally critical about the same faults of cockpit overheating and underside vulnerability which could and should be cured. We also know that despite these complaints many an Austin-Healey is changed only for a later model of the same car, because owners would rather put up with the faults than forgo the unique combination of comfort and high performance which this car offers at a very reasonable price. Despite its shortcomings, many other people (whether graduating from a smaller car, or seeking a faster and more entertaining alternative to a luxury saloon) will find that this model ranks as their "best buy."

Specification

Engine

Cylinders 6
Bore ... ... 83.34 mm.
Stroke ... ... 88.9 mm.
Cubic capacity ... ... 2,912 c.c.
Piston area ... ... 50.7 sq. in.
Valves ... ... Overhead (pushrods)
Compression ratio 9/1
Carburetter ... 3 inclined S.U. type HS.4
Fuel pump S.U. electrical, rear mounted
Ignition timing control ... Centrifugal and vacuum
Oil filter Full-flow (Tecalemit or Purolator)
Max. power (net) ... ... 132 b.h.p.
at ... ... 4,750 r.p.m.
Piston speed at max. b.h.p. 2,770 ft./min.

Transmission

Clutch ... Borg & Beck 10 in. s.d.p.
Top gear (s/m) ... ... 3.909 (overdrive, 3.205)
3rd gear (s/m) ... ... 5.12 (overdrive, 4.20)
2nd gear (s/m) 8.02
1st gear 11.45
Reverse 14.78
Overdrive ... ... Laycock-de Normanville
Propeller shaft ... ... Hardy Spicer single-piece open
Final drive ... ... 11/43 spiral bevel (without overdrive, 11/39)
Top gear m.p.h. at 1,000 r.p.m. 18.6 (overdrive, 22.6)
Top gear m.p.h. at 1,000 ft./min. piston speed ... 31.8 (overdrive, 38.8)

Chassis

Brakes: Girling hydraulic, drum type at rear and self-adjusting disc type at front.
Brake diameters:
Front discs ... ... 11¼ in. dia.
Rear drums ... 11 in. dia. by 2¼ in. wide
Friction areas: 112 sq. in. of lining area working on 383 sq. in. of rubbed area.
Suspension:
Front: Independent by coil springs, transverse wishbones and anti-roll torsion bar.
Rear: Rigid axle, semi-elliptic leaf springs and Panhard rod.
Shock absorbers: Girling lever-arm hydraulic (front units form upper wishbone pivots).
Steering gear ... ... Cam and peg
Tyres 5.90—15 Dunlop Road Speed, tubed

Coachwork and Equipment

Starting handle ... ... None
Battery mounting ... ... In rear locker
Jack ... ... Rachet screw type
Jacking points Under front spring base plates and under rear spring leaves
Standard tool kit: Jack and handle, copper-head hammer, sparking plug spanner and tommy bar.
Exterior lights: 2 headlamps, 2 sidelamps, 2 stop/tail/flasher lamps, rear number plate lamp.
Number of electrical fuses ... 2
Direction indicators: Self-cancelling flashers combined with side and stop lamps.
Windscreen wipers ... Electrical twin-blade, self-parking
Windscreen washers Trico hand-pump type
Sun visors ... ... None
Instruments: Speedometer with total and decimal trip distance recorders, rev. counter, fuel contents gauge, oil pressure gauge, water thermometer.
Warning lights: Dynamo charge, headlamp main beam, turn indicators.
Locks:
With ignition key Ignition switch and luggage locker
With other keys ... ... None
Glove lockers ... ... None
Map pockets Two wide compartments in doors
Parcel shelves One below left half of facia
Ashtrays ... ... One on gearbox cover
Cigar lighters ... ... None
Interior lights ... ... None
Interior heater: Fresh-air heater and screen de-mister as optional extra.
Car radio Optional extra H.M.V. Radiomobile
Extras available: Wire wheels, overdrive, hardtop, heater, radio.
Upholstery material: Hide facings, leathercloth on non-wearing surfaces.
Floor covering ... ... Pile carpet
Exterior colours standardized: 5 single colours and 5 duotone combinations.
Alternative body styles 2-seater

Maintenance

Sump ... 11¼ pints, S.A.E. 30 above freezing
Gearbox 5 pints plus 1⅓ pints in overdrive, S.A.E. 30
Rear axle ... 3 pints, S.A.E. 90 hypoid oil
Steering gear lubricant ... S.A.E. 90 gear oil
Cooling system capacity 19 pints (2 drain taps)
Chassis lubrication ... ... By oil gun every 1,000 miles to 17 points
Ignition timing ... 12° before t.d.c. static
Contact-breaker gap ... 0.014-0.016 in.
Sparking plug type: Champion N3 (fast driving) or N5 (town use), 14 mm. long reach
Sparking plug gap ... ... 0.025 in.
Carburetter jet needles ... ... Type DJ
Valve timing: Inlet opens 5° before t.d.c. and closes 45° after b.d.c.; exhaust opens 51° before b.d.c. and closes 21° after t.d.c.
Tappet clearances (hot):
Inlet and exhaust ... ... 0.012 in.
Front wheel toe-in ... ... 1/16-⅛ in.
Camber angle ... ... 1°
Castor angle ... ... 2°
Steering swivel pin inclination ... 6½°
Tyre pressures:
Front ... ... 20 lb.
Rear 23-26 lb. according to load (increase front and rear pressures by 6-8 lb. for sustained high-speed driving).
Brake fluid Girling, or to S.A.E. spec. 70R1
Battery type and capacity 12-volt, 50 amp. hr.
Miscellaneous: Top up carburetter dashpots with S.A.E. 20 engine oil.

Austin-Healey

*Three carbs mean added power, and
suspension changes give this
'62 model even better handling*

by Bob Russo

INITIAL THE NAME Austin-Healey and you come up with something like "AH," which, except for a few misgivings, describes our reaction to BMC's new "3000" roadster. This is not simply a rash reaction, either, but a solid opinion gained during a cross-country, six-state driving test that even included a run over the fabulous world speed record course at Bonneville and a trip up Pikes Peak.

Since its birth in 1953, the Austin-Healey has scored heavily with sports car buffs in this country, due mostly to its perky performance on road racing courses and its deep-throated roar of performance on the street. Its basic design has always made it readily adaptable for racing and fun. With a few exceptions, it has captured the hearts of sportsmen and enthusiasts alike.

The new "3000" for 1962, which BMC bills as the successor to the 100-Six, is not too noticeably different from the '61 model. Except for slight grille modifications, in fact, it is difficult to distinguish the '62 from the '60. Under the hood, however, there is a marked difference — one of great improvement insofar as performance is concerned.

Officially designated the Austin-Healey 3000 Mark II, the '62 houses a stepped-up six-banger equipped with triple SU carburetors, a new camshaft and stronger valve springs. Horsepower has been increased from 124 hp (put out by the previous, twin-carburetor version) to 132 hp, which is especially noticeable at the top end.

Going along with the horsepower increase is improved handling — a marked improvement at that. Suspension remains nearly the same, with independent wishbones and coil springs in front and leaf springs, solid axle and panhard rod at the rear. But the sagging,

almost unstable feeling experienced with the previous model has been replaced by a solid, more secure feeling under hard cornering. The harder we pushed it, in fact, the better the car felt, especially in the winding Rockies that were part of our extensive test route. A stronger stabilizer bar and a slight change in shocking are the reason.

Domestic car exponents and even some sports car buffs will argue that an Austin-Healey is definitely not a cross-country car. Limited luggage space, the roar of the engine and exhaust, the lack of ventilation in the cockpit are all points of contention. We found some of this to be true. Traveling any great distance is a problem where luggage is concerned, and cockpit ventilation is poor. Still, we had no problem fitting in suitcases and even a picnic lunch, and for the most part the journey was a real ball.

Healey's cornering ability is improved this year through minor chassis changes. Its mild tendency to rock and roll has been completely eliminated.

3000 Road Test

RUSSO PUT THE CAR THROUGH ITS PACES IN MANY PLACES — INCLUDING PIKES PEAK AND HERE ON BONNEVILLE'S WELL-KNOWN SALT FLATS.

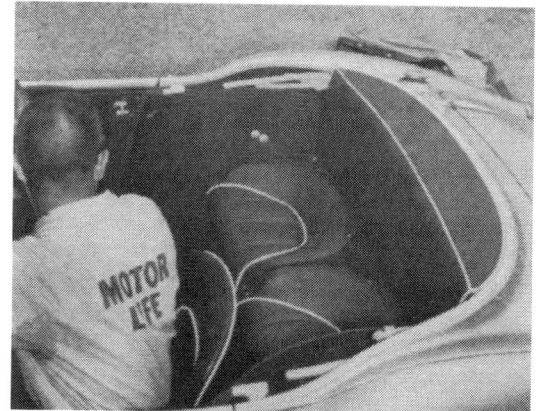

Jump seats are too small to reasonably carry adults, but they're fine for luggage and hauling small items.

Telescopic steering wheel may be adjusted while car is in motion, gives driver a variety of stances on long journeys.

Although limited in space, the Healey is surprisingly comfortable for two adults. True bucket seats with individual long-track adjustments accommodate long or short legs and provide needed support and comfort for long periods of travel. Adding to this, an adjustable steering column is easily set to nearly any desired driving position, which may be changed while traveling to help ease strain after many hours behind the wheel.

While our test car was what is designated as "an occasional four-seater tourer," with two jump seats in the rear, use of these extra seats by anyone but a pygmy is highly impractical. These seats do come in handy for stowing luggage or other cargo that has to be taken on an extensive trip. Or they can be used on a short trip to the grocery store, since trunk space is very limited. Spare tire and battery take up most of the room.

As mentioned, cockpit ventilation is inadequate and was a particular problem in desert country. The Mark II is equipped with a heater/ventilating system that draws air through ducts on either side of the engine, but there simply was not enough volume — and what there was, wasn't distributed to the right places. Even in cool weather, the driver is bothered with lack of heat dissipation on his throttle foot. Ventilating doors in each fender would be a great improvement.

Fully convertible with a soft top that folds behind the rear jump seats, the '62 Healey may be purchased with a fiberglass hardtop although it is our opinion that this detracts slightly from the out-and-out sports car look and feel. Portions of our cross-country hop were made with the top folded, but long periods under a broiling sun didn't always make this a practical way to travel. For short trips and in-city driving, though, the open air comfort is hard to beat on hot days.

Removable, plexiglass side curtains (which stow in the trunk when not in use) are necessary under extremely cold conditions, but are hardly worth the effort of installing on brisk days. Turning up the heater and wearing a good windbreaker works almost as well.

Two features, in addition to fine handling, are particularly impressive with the Mark II. One is braking, with Girling hydraulic discs in front and drums in the rear; and the other is an electrically controlled overdrive unit. Both of these items add greatly to the safety, comfort and economy of one's trip.

Braking with the Girlings was devoid of any sudden swerves and, most of all, without fade of any kind. We paid particular note to this, avoiding the downshift in many cases in order to give the brakes full emphasis. In panic-stop tests at 60 mph, the car came to a halt in less than 130 feet.

The overdrive unit, which helped bring our mileage figure to 26 mpg on the open highway, is electrically operated through a toggle switch on the instrument panel. Flip it up and the transmission shifts into a higher gear. Flip it down and the gearbox shifts back to top. In heavy traffic or for passing, this simple device saves time and effort. Rear axle ratio is 3.91 with overdrive and 3.54 for conventional. Transmission is a standard four-speed with synchromesh in all but first gear. Control is by a floor-mounted, short stick.

One other outstanding feature of the '62 Austin-Healey is an "immobilization" device situated in the trunk. This consists of a knob which, when turned, cuts off the power supply from the battery. Once the power is turned off and the trunk is locked, the car may be left without fear of theft, a major consideration since the doors themselves cannot be locked.

It's been eight years now since the Austin-Healey went on the market, and the tastes of motorists have changed a great deal. But there can be little doubt that, when it comes to a pure sports car, aimed directly at the sportsman/enthusiast, the Healey has nestled into a permanent niche of popularity that shows no sign of abating. BMC has taken great pains to preserve this popularity without drastic changes from its original design — and, if the Mark II is any yardstick, their efforts have been successful. •

Major engine change is the new three-carburetor set-up which contributes to engine's 132 hp. Formerly the ohv Six had 124 horses. Other changes include different cam and valve springs.

Top is a one-man operation, stores out of sight behind the jump seats. Hard top is extra.

AUSTIN-HEALEY 3000
2-4-passenger roadster

Options on car tested: Overdrive, wire wheels

Odometer reading at start of test: 1578 miles

Recommended engine red line: 5000 rpm

PERFORMANCE

ACCELERATION (2 aboard)

0-30 mph	....	4.1 secs.
0-45 mph	....	7.7
0-60 mph	....	12.2

Standing start ¼-mile 19.7 secs. and 74 mph

Speeds in gears @ 4800 rpm

1st	.... 27 mph	3rd	...............63 mph
2nd	..............41 mph		

Speedometer Error on Test Car

Car's speedometer reading	30	45	50	60	70	80
Weston electric speedometer ..	30	45	50	60	70	80

Miles per hour per 1000 rpm in top gear (actual meter reading) ....23 mph
(Overdrive 20.9 mph)

Stopping Distances — from 30 mph, 39 ft.; from 60 mph, 127 ft.

SPECIFICATIONS FROM MANUFACTURER

Engine
Ohv, in-line Six
Bore: 3.282 ins. Stroke: 3.5 ins.
Displacement: 177.7 cubic inches
Compression ratio: 9:1
Horsepower: 132 @ 4750 rpm
Ignition: 12-volt battery/coil

Gearbox
Manual 4-speed, floor stick

Driveshaft
Open

Differential
Ring gear and pinion
Standard ratio 3.54:1
Overdrive ratio 3.91:1

Suspension
Front: Independent with wishbones, coil springs,
hydraulic shocks,
anti-roll bar

Rear: Semi-elliptic leaf springs,
hydraulic shocks,
panhard rod

Wheels and Tires
Standard 15-in. steel discs —
optional wire knock-offs
5.90 x 15 Dunlop tires

Brakes
Girling hydraulics
Front: 11¼-in. discs
Rear: 11-in. drums

Body and Frame
Box-section frame; aluminum and
steel body
Wheelbase 92 ins.
Track, front 48.75 ins.,
rear 50.0 ins.
Overall length 157 ins.
Dry weight 2390 lbs.

Side curtains are plexiglass with aluminum frames. They have wing nuts which hold them fast. Door compartment is for maps.

(Above) Trunk is cramped, will carry little more than a small suitcase. Switch shuts off battery and makes car theft-proof.

(Below) The Healey has always attracted sporting types, and as such may be seen on the racecourse, on the road, or in town.

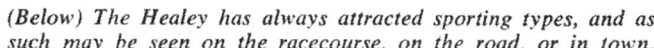

AUSTIN-HEALEY MK II
ROAD TEST/22-61

The new Mk. II has much more to offer than simply a face-lift

ALONG WITH THE OTHER BMC CAR LINES, the Mark II tag has been placed on the latest 3-liter Healey and — as their press release states — "It can be readily distinguished by its slightly modified radiator grille which now has vertical slats." But it hasn't been all play and no work for their styling department; there are other, more subtle changes.

The real difference lies beneath the hood, however, where output has been upped from 124 bhp to 132 by the addition of (among other things) a third SU carburetor. This is a successful improvement since it increases performance and mileage without decreasing any other factors. Example: the throttle can be dumped wide open at any speed without the usual gasping associated with full-potential carburetion. Starting is almost instantaneous and idling exceptionally smooth. Our acceleration times didn't quite equal those claimed by the factory, but were still fast enough to be impressive *and* convincing that the Mk II is a powerful machine.

Ride and comfort in the new Healey are optimum, without sacrifice in roadability. The slightly-rubbery-but-still-firm feel that we identified with previous models remains, but it's even softer, yet just as controllable. The increased production of the four-seater with its two molded-in back seats behind the regular seats will be a blessing to Healey fanciers with families, providing their offspring are small in stature. The additional cut-away makes the entire cockpit feel a lot roomier, as well. Positioning of controls remain about the same, however, and we have our share of gripes with these. Even with column adjustment tight against the dash, a fairly short driver still finds the big steering wheel tangling with his nose if he has the seat adjusted far enough forward to reach the pedals. This positioning had, in the past, been somewhat of a British trademark, but many other cars, including some made by BMC have a more realistic distance between face and steering wheel. Magnifying the discomfort for short folk is the fact that the wheel is mounted high to lift it away from the driver's legs. The gearshift lever is no improvement either, with its long, flexing shaft making positive shifts a matter of chance. Instrumentation is good, as are hand controls. These remain unchanged from previous models. Seat belt attachment points are now standard equipment on all Healeys.

Stopping power of the Mk II is excellent. High-speed braking required some pedal pressure, but the stop was extremely rapid and stable. So was the second, and the third. On the fourth, however, one of the big, 11¼-inch disc brakes started to chatter and it was 15 minutes before an ear-splitting squeak disappeared. This was likely a peculiarity individual to the test car and possibly was caused by some external factor such as dirt or grease on the pads. When the squeak disappeared it stayed gone even under some later rough use. No trouble with the drum brakes on the rear, though.

While quite a bit of play was present in the engine and driveline mounting during hard initial acceleration, the clutch, etc., were able to cope with the torque and moved the big car off the line very positively. A new camshaft and stronger valve springs are other improvements incorporated in the Mk II engine along with the triple, 1¾-inch carburetors, and they undoubtedly contributed to the strong

PHOTOS: RANDY HOLT

acceleration we were able to get from the very new test unit. The Healey engine as it comes off the regular production line is not a high twister, being red-lined still at 5200 rpm. In fact most Healeys, except those prepared with competition with the optional cam, will definitely sign off before 5500 revs are reached. The performance comes from sheer brute torque. This is the most noticeable aspect of the big six-holer; it comes on low on the rpm scale, so low in fact that second gear can be used for starts with some regularity if the clutch and throttle are properly coordinated.

Handling remains as good as ever, with typical initial understeer. It is an easy car to drift, with excellent adhesion on most surfaces. The Dunlop RS5 tires do a very creditable job of sticking, with minimal noise. Gone forever is the old tendency of fast, chattering rear end breakaway. The Healey is definitely a car that must be powered through a corner — or rather out of it and the remarkable torque output makes this a relatively simple operation. The best technique in hard driving as in competition with the Healey is to use the very excellent brakes going into the turns, motoring through and then climbing back on the throttle as soon as the car is lined up for the exit — but please, not too early. Too much, too soon especially in too low a gear, can result in some pretty spectacular spinning, generally toward the inside, in which case it's best to concentrate on where the car is going to end up rather to make any wild attempts to pull off a complete save. So low is the Healey's center of gravity that it usually takes something in the nature of a derrick or a wheel-tripping curb or ditch to turn one over. These things don't happen on the road unless the driver is indulging in some pretty goofy foolishness but they can happen on the race track.

There are certain small detail changes in the new Mk II that are worthy of comment. One is the top. Healey tops, especially four-seater tops, in the past have been something to make strong men weep in angry frustration. On earlier four-seaters the top frame was hinged to the car and the front bow had no connection with the rest of the frame. It still doesn't but the frame is not attached to the top fabric either. The frame is removable now and separate from the top itself a-la Sprite. The top is an envelope that fits over the frame, snapping at the rear and fastening, still with that tricky bow, at the windshield. Putting it up and down is still time consuming but no longer an exercise in finger-breaking.

Another detail is in the overdrive. Normally the Laycock unit is instantaneous when the switch is flipped — it's either in or out just like that. Injudicious use of this switch has in the past resulted in damaged overdrives. Not so with the new Healey. Now the switch acts almost as a pre-selector. To go into overdrive from direct the switch is flipped up and the throttle backed off slightly. It'll go in without backing off but there's short time lag that makes it silly not to adjust engine speed to the upward change. In going out of overdrive the switch is flipped down and the throttle kicked. In this case it won't go out until the throttle is depressed to pick up the slack and take the shock out of the driveline. Very likely this little change will save a few OD repair bills due to damage from sloppy downshifts out of overdrive into direct.

All in all the new Mark II is fit continuation of a line that has been successively and successfully improved since it was introduced. With all its muscle and good handling qualities the latest Austin Healey is probably the most car for a given amount of money, taken in terms of amount of car received per dollar spent, that can be bought today.

TEST DATA

VEHICLE	Austin-Healey	MODEL	MK II
PRICE (as tested)	$3639.00	OPTIONS	Adj. steering $15
	POE L.A., inbound		

ENGINE:

Type	6 cylinder, in-line, 4 cycle, water-cooled
Head	Removable, cast-iron
Valves	Ohv, pushrod/rocker actuated
Max. bhp	132 @ 4750 rpms
Max. torque	n.a.
Bore	3.281 in. 83.34 mm.
Stroke	3.5 in. 88.9 mm.
Displacement	177.7 cu. in. 2912 cc.
Compression Ratio	9.1 to 1
Induction System	3 SU 1¾" HD6
Exhaust System	Cast manifold into double muffler
Electrical System	12V Lucas, single distrib.

CLUTCH:	Borg-Beck single	**DIFFERENTIAL:**	Salsbury
Diameter:	10½ in.	Ratio:	3.9 to 1
Actuation:	hydraulic disc	Drive Axles (type)	Live, enclosed, semi-floating

TRANSMISSION:	4 speed, synchro top 3 — Laycock de Normanville OD
Ratios: 1st	2.94 to 1
2nd	2.058 to 1
3rd	1.32 to 1
4th	1.0 to 1
3rd O.D.	1.075 to 1
4th O.D.	.822 to 1

STEERING: Turns Lock to Lock	3¼
Turn Circle:	35.7 ft.
BRAKES:	Drum rear, 2¼" width
Disc front	2" pad width
Drum or Disc Diameter	11.25 & 11.0 in.
Swept Area	302.16 sq. in.

CHASSIS:

Frame:	Box section, conventional
Body:	Steel, semi-unit
Front Suspension:	Unequal control arms, coil springs
Rear Suspension:	Live, leaf springs, arm shock
Tire Size & Type:	5.90 x 15 Dunlop RS5

WEIGHTS AND MEASURES

Wheelbase:	91.7 in.	Ground Clearance	4.6 in.
Front Track:	48¾ in.	Curb Weight	2465 lbs.
Rear Track:	50 in.	Test Weight	2765 lbs.
Overall Height	46 in.	Crankcase	7½ qts.
Overall Width	60 in.	Cooling System	12½ qts.
Overall Length	157½ in.	Gas Tank	14.4 gals.

PERFORMANCE:

0-30	3.5 sec.	0-70	15.0 sec.
0-40	5.9 sec.	0-80	20.3 sec.
0-50	8.6 sec.	0-90	26.6 sec.
0-60	11.9 sec.	0-100	— sec.

Standing ¼ mile 16.3 sec. @ 72 mph

Speed Error	30	40	50
Actual	31	41	50

Top Speed (av. two-way run) 112 mph

	60	70	80	90
	60	70	79	89

Fuel Consumption Test:	19 mpg
Average	25 mpg
Recommended Shift Points:	
Max. 1st	32 mph
Max. 2nd	47 mph
Max. 3rd	79 mph

RPM Red-line	5200 rpm
Speed Ranges in gears:	
1st	0 to 32 mph
2nd	15 to 47 mph
3rd	35 to 79 mph 3rd. O.D. 88
4th	43 to top mph 4th. O.D. 50-top

Brake Test: 78 Average % G, over 8 stops.
Squeal encountered on 6th stop.

REFERENCE FACTORS:

Bhp per cubic inch	0.745
Lbs. per bhp	18.7
Piston Speed @ Peak rpm	2771 ft./min.
Swept brake area per lb.	0.1225 Sq. In.

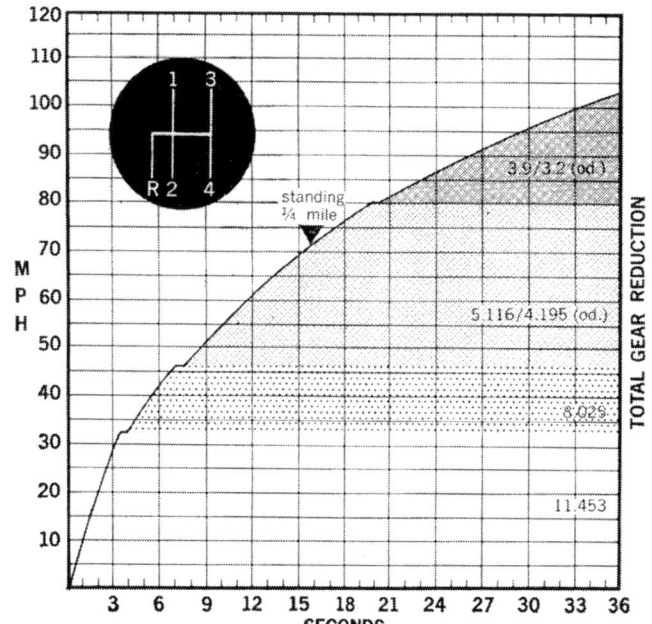

Detail modifications—including radiator grille and the air intake on the bonnet top—have been made, but the basic outline of the "big" Healey remains much the same as when it was introduced in 1952. In certain ways, the Healey preserves earlier British sports car traditions

AUSTIN-HEALEY 3000

No. 1852

WHEN the Healey 100 made its début at the Earls Court Show of 1952, fitted with the four-cylinder 2·6-litre engine used in the Austin A.90 Atlantic coupé, it was clear that the car was destined for a successful competition career. However, one doubts whether anyone foresaw its becoming, eight years later, one of the most successful rally cars in the world, winning outright the tough Liège-Rome-Liège and Alpine rallies. Except for detail changes, the clean, attractive lines of the car have remained very much the same. Mechanically, the changes have centred largely around the power unit, the Austin-Healey 100 becoming the Austin-Healey 100-Six in 1957, when the four-cylinder engine was replaced by a six of similar capacity.

Three years later it became the Austin-Healey 3000, when the capacity was increased to 2,912 c.c., and this year the Mark 2 was introduced. Apart from a restyled radiator grille, the latest car is fitted with three 1½-in. HS4 S.U. carburettors in place of the two 1¾-in. HS6s of the previous model, together with a redesigned inlet manifold and a new camshaft giving higher lift to the inlet valves and a longer dwell to the exhausts. All this has brought the production car allegedly into line with the specification of the successful competition cars used by the B.M.C. Competitions Department. Thus, through the years, the engine output has increased from the 90 b.h.p. of the Healey 100 to the 132 b.h.p. of the Mark 2 Austin-Healey 3000, with the weight increasing from 1,960lb to 2,526. The b.h.p. per ton figure, therefore, has been increased only from 102 to 117.

First impressions of the car are that it is comfortable, has plenty of leg room, is moderately well appointed, and

Central pull-up handbrake, all-black finish, near-vertical steering wheel, and full instrumentation—this is very much a "competition" cockpit

52

The engine compartment is packed, yet everything that matters—carburettors, hydraulic reservoirs, distributor and radiator cap—are readily accessible. The screenwash bottle is mounted inside the cockpit

Austin-Healey 3000 . . .

is immensely strong and rigid. Also, it has a pleasant, long-legged feeling of being able to lollop along all day at a cruising speed of 90 m.p.h. or more with very little effort.

The cockpit is very well arranged and is finished throughout in black leather, or leather-cloth where wear is light. The driving seat on the car tested was hard and seemed to have inadequate upholstery; this, together with one or two other points, suggested that the 10,000 miles indicated in the speedometer window had been fairly strenuous ones. For a tall person the forward visibility is excellent; but, with the seat so compressed, a shorter driver had his view interrupted by the top of the large steering wheel. The instruments are comprehensive and well set out, while all the "driving" controls are within comfortable reach. Instrument lighting is good, without being so bright as to worry one, though there is no rheostat control. The screen pillars are slim and the extremities of both front wings are seen easily, so that placing the car in heavy traffic is no problem.

The hard-top was draught- and water-proof, making the interior of the car snug and warm. This is an optional extra, costing £60, the conventional soft hood being standard equipment; with either in position, the occasional rear seat(s) can be used only for short runs, headroom being decidedly cramped. Rigid, aluminium-framed transparent plastic sidescreens are fitted, the rearmost panels of which slide forwards. There is no method of locking the driving compartment, and no lockable glove locker, so that valuables should not be left in the car. By turning off the battery master-switch in the boot, and locking the boot lid, the car can be made secure against a thief in a hurry.

Large pockets are provided in the doors, and there is a parcels shelf above the foot-well on the passenger's side. This would be much more useful if it did not house the screenwash bottle, for which there is no room in the very full engine compartment. The heating-demisting system is most efficient, as is the fresh-air cooling system, and one

is no longer worried by the high cockpit temperatures found in earlier models of this car. The range of seat adjustment for both passenger and driver is considerable, and desirable if the rear seats are to be used. However, if one sets the driving seat to achieve a "straight-armed" position, the pedals become out of reach, despite the provision of an adjustment in steering column length of around 3in. The situation is not improved by the unusually long travel in the clutch pedal and gear lever. Adding to the impression that the particular car tested had seen a very active life was the fact that the synchromesh was practically non-existent, particularly on top gear.

The hand-brake is of the pull-up type, conveniently placed between the front seats. When the car is travelling forward it is extremely efficient, and will apply the rear drum brakes with sufficient force to lock the rear wheels; it will also hold the car from running forwards on a 1-in-3 test hill. Surprisingly, however, it will not prevent the car from running backwards on the 1-in-4 test gradient.

Cold Starting

With use of the choke, the engine starts quickly and easily from cold, though it reaches its working temperature somewhat slowly. It does not appreciate a diet of premium-grade fuel, on which it pinks and tends to run-on after being switched off. With the compression ratio of 9.0 to 1 this is scarcely surprising, and both faults were eliminated by using super-premium fuel. It is extremely smooth and flexible, and has plenty of torque at low speeds. It will pull the car away in top gear without hesitation or snatch from the surprisingly low speed of 8 m.p.h., so that it is able to trickle through traffic happily in third gear. It is reasonably quiet and unobtrusive up to 3,000 r.p.m., but above this speed there are some intake roar and roughness.

The clutch is light in operation, and very smooth in take-up; there was no prolonged slip when the standing-start figures were taken, nor when full-throttle changes were made, and it had no trouble in moving the car off quickly and cleanly on a 1-in-3 test gradient. The Laycock-de Normanville overdrive, which is available as an optional extra and was fitted on the test car, works on top and third gears. It is invaluable in keeping the engine speed down, and thus saving petrol; and it helps one to avoid the critical engine speed of 3,000 r.p.m. at which there is a noticeable resonance in the exhaust system. The transmission as a whole is very quiet, and there are no vibration periods throughout the speed range.

In general "feel" the car inspires great confidence, being undoubtedly very safe indeed and entirely without whims or idiosyncrasies. It has excellent directional stability, and will hurry along at 100 m.p.h. or more "hands off," without any desire to wander off-line. It has a slight—and de-

Very much an "occasional four-seater," the Healey offers limited space for rear passengers; headroom beneath the hard-top is cramped

The rear bumper wraps round to give good protection. Ground clearance is limited below the exhaust pipe where it runs beneath the rear cross member. The hard-top is optional

sirable—understeering characteristic; and, except when speeds are so high that the engine has run out of power, it is always possible to help the tail round by means of the throttle. If the rear wheels do begin to slide—which they will do fairly easily at the manufacturers' recommended high-speed tyre pressures of 26 p.s.i. front and 29 rear—the response to opposite lock is immediate, the car quickly straightening up. So "right" does the handling feel that one gets the impression that it would be difficult even for an inexperienced driver to get into any serious trouble. The steering is light though one would prefer slightly higher

Luggage space, if the rear seats are to be used for passengers, is strictly of the "toothbrush-and-pyjamas" variety, though when the car is used as a two-seater—as it normally would be on long runs—there is plenty of space behind the front seats

gearing than its present 3¼ turns from lock to lock. Self-centring action is pleasantly strong.

Second gear is too low, maximum speeds in the gears being 34, 48, 77, and 106 m.p.h.—and 98 in overdrive third. The gear-change is precise, and smooth in operation. In taking the standing-start acceleration figures it was difficult to avoid wheelspin on the initial take-off, even on a dry road, and in the wet one had to be decidedly gentle with the throttle.

Although surprisingly soft, the suspension is sufficiently damped to avoid much roll when the car is cornering fast, and ride comfort is excellent. Not only does it iron out the normal, main road long-frequency irregularities completely, but it rides well over the shorter bumps, such as

potholes. Very little road noise is transmitted to the interior of the car. On a rough, pavé-type surface, however, the occupants are bounced about to some extent at slow speeds, though the ride levels off as the speed is increased; on such surfaces there is reasonably little outward patter of the wheels on cornering. On the washboard test surface, the whole body structure of the car was amazingly stable, confirming the impression that it is very rigidly built. Coupled with the safe handling characteristics of the Healey, the first-class ride makes it a very restful car for long-distance travel.

Reliable Brakes

From start to finish the brakes inspired great trust, giving plenty of "feel," always pulling the car up in a straight line, and never showing signs of fade, even after repeated stops from high speeds. The car has always been sound in this particular aspect; of the drum brakes fitted to the car tested in 1953 it was said that they were "entirely suitable," and the same was said of the rear drums and front discs of the car tested last year—equipment which the Mark 2 also uses. A brake servo was not fitted to the car tested, though this is available as an optional extra, and pedal pressures were therefore somewhat high, as shown by the meter readings. Due to the angle of the pedal, however, or the relative positions of the seat and brake pedal, one never appeared to be pressing particularly hard; it seems that the use of a servo is scarcely justified, even if the car is to be driven exclusively by a woman.

There are several points about the car which, though in keeping with its honest-to-goodness, no-frills character, seem somewhat out of place in a £1,200 car in 1961. There are, for example, no automatic supports for the bonnet or boot lid when they are open; instead one has to reach for their props and fit them into the slots provided. The doors are stiff to open, due to the use of friction-damper-type devices to stop them from swinging shut; and wheel-changing involves the use of an old-fashioned screw-up jack and the business of groping underneath the car for a suitable jacking point. The forepart of the hardtop is sensibly padded, to protect the occupants' heads—yet, proud of the padding, protrude potentially dangerous sharp clips which secure the roof to the windscreen. If the Austin-Healey were an out-and-out competition car one would readily forgive a lack of concessions to creature comforts, but it is essentially a fast sports-tourer, at least in its production form.

Luggage accommodation is rather meagre, the spare wheel and battery occupying most of the boot. For long-distance touring, however, when carrying space is at a premium, the car must in any case be regarded as no more than a two-seater, and the compartment behind the front seats will take a substantial amount of baggage. The fuel tank capacity is 12 gallons, giving the car a range between fill-up stops of about 200 miles. The lighting equipment is in keeping with the performance, the headlamps giving a powerful enough beam almost for the daytime cruising speeds to be maintained. They are foot-dipped by a switch alongside the clutch, where the left foot normally rests. This space, in fact. is larger than it needs to be—and the pedals could with advantage have greater separation; it would be difficult to drive the car wearing wide shoes.

Though there are a few points of criticism, the Mark 2 Austin-Healey is a good quality, strongly built sporting car with great charm and an amazing aptitude for hard work. It has a lively performance in standard trim, a performance to which the figures achieved by this far from new car scarcely do justice; almost all of them are appreciably down on those recorded by its predecessor, road-tested last year. The general quality of finish, and attention to detail is first class, except for those points mentioned. That it is capable of giving a much enhanced performance—for those who seek it—is shown by its remarkable run of successes in International rallies.

AUSTIN-HEALEY 3000

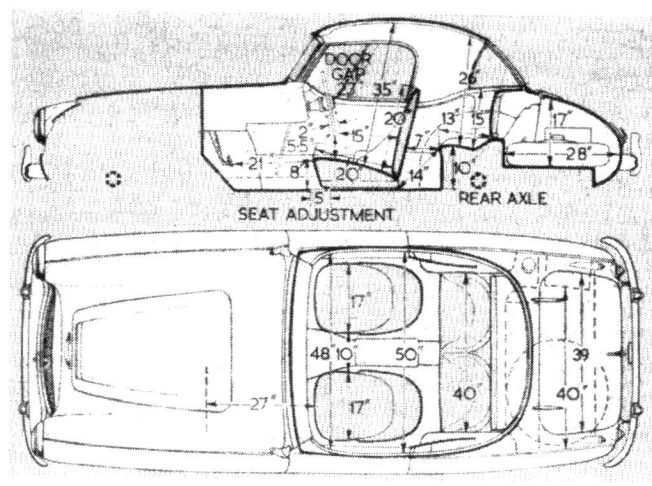

Scale ¼in. to 1ft. Driving seat in central position. Cushions uncompressed.

━━ PERFORMANCE ━━

ACCELERATION TIMES (mean):
Speed range, Gear Ratios, and Time in Sec.

m.p.h.	3·21* to 1	3·91 to 1	4·2* to 1	5·12 to 1	8·05 to 1	11·26 to 1
10– 30	—	—	—	7·0	4·1	3·5
20– 40	11·0	8·6	7·9	6·2	4·0	—
30– 50	11·3	8·3	8·1	6·2	—	—
40– 60	11·2	7·8	7·9	6·3	—	—
50– 70	13·1	8·9	8·8	7·6	—	—
60– 80	13·6	10·0	9·7	—	—	—
70– 90	15·0	13·2	13·9	—	—	—
80–100	18·5	17·5	—	—	—	—

* Overdrive

From rest through gears to:

30 m.p.h.	..	3·7 sec.
40 ,,	..	6·2 ,,
50 ,,	..	9·3 ,,
60 ,,	..	11·5 ,,
70 ,,	..	15·6 ,,
80 ,,	..	22·0 ,,
90 ,,	..	30·0 ,,
100 ,,	..	36·9 ,,

Standing quarter mile 18·8 sec.

MAXIMUM SPEEDS ON GEARS:

Gear			m.p.h.	k.p.h.
O.D. Top	(mean)		112·5	181·1
	(best)		115·0	185·1
Top	..	..	106	170
O.D. 3rd	..		98	158
3rd	..	..	81	130
2nd	..	..	50	80
1st	..	..	37	60

TRACTIVE EFFORT (by Tapley meter):

		Pull (lb per ton)	Equivalent gradient
O.D.	..	260	1 in 8·6
Top	..	340	1 in 6·5
O.D. Third	..	355	1 in 6·4
Third	..	445	1 in 5·0
Second	..	670	1 in 3·2

SPEEDOMETER CORRECTION: m.p.h.

Car speedometer:	..		10	20	30	40	50	60	70	80	90	100	110	120
True speed:	..	..	9	19	28	37	47	57	66	75	84	94	106	115

BRAKES (at 30 m.p.h. in neutral):

Pedal load in lb	Retardation	Equiv. stopping distance in ft
50	0·31g	97
75	0·47g	64
100	0·72g	42
125	0·84g	36
130	0·94g	32·1

FUEL CONSUMPTION (at constant speeds):

		Direct Top	O.D. Top
30 m.p.h.		30·5 m.p.g.	31·3 m.p.g.
40	,,	27·2 ,,	30·0 ,,
50	,,	25·1 ,,	28·0 ,,
60	,,	23·3 ,,	26·0 ,,
70	,,	21·2 ,,	24·2 ,,
80	,,	19·1 ,,	23·3 ,,
90	,,	15·0 ,,	18·0 ,,
100	,,	11·0 ,,	15·1 ,,

Overall fuel consumption for 1,223 miles, 17·7 m.p.g. (16·0 litres per 100 km.).

Approximate normal range 13–20 m.p.g. (21·7–14·1 litres per 100 km.).

Fuel: Super premium grades.

TEST CONDITIONS: Weather: Damp surface.
0–5 m.p.h. wind.
Air temperature, 55 deg. F.
Model described in *The Autocar* of 2 June. 1961.

STEERING: Turning circle:
Between kerbs: L, 34ft 4in.; R, 35ft 4in.
Between walls: L, 35ft 4in.; R, 36ft 4in.
Turns of steering wheel from lock to lock, 3·25.

━━ DATA ━━

PRICE (basic), with four-seater body, £829. British purchase tax, £381 3s 11d. Total (in Great Britain), £1,210 3s 11d. Extras (inc. p.t.): Radio, £35. Heater, £22 12s 1d. Overdrive, £69 7s 3d. Hard-top, £87 10s. Wire wheels, £36 9s 2d.

ENGINE: Capacity, 2,912 c.c. (177·7 cu. in.) Number of cylinders, 6.
Bore and stroke, 83·36 × 89·0mm (3·28 × 3·5in.).
Valve gear, overhead, pushrods and rockers.
Compression ratio, 9·0 to 1.
B.h.p. (net), 130 at 4,750 r.p.m. (b.h.p. per ton laden 100·7).
Torque (net), 167 lb. ft at 3,000 r.p.m.
M.p.h. per 1,000 r.p.m. in top gear, 20·9; in overdrive, 23·1.

WEIGHT (with 5 gal fuel): 22·8 cwt (2,555 lb).
Weight distribution (per cent): F, 48·8; R, 51·2.
Laden as tested, 25·8 cwt (2,891 lb).
Lb per c.c. (laden), 0·9.

BRAKES: Type, Girling, disc front, drum rear, hydraulic.
Disc diameter: 11·25in.
Drum dimensions: 11in. diameter; 2·25in. wide.
Swept area: F, 228 sq. in.; R, 155·5 sq. in. (297 sq. in. per ton laden).

TYRES: 5·90—15in. Dunlop RS5.
Pressures (p.s.i.): F, 20; R, 23 (normal); F, 26; R, 29 (fast driving).

TANK CAPACITY: 12 Imperial gallons.
Oil sump, 12 pints.
Cooling system, 20 pints (plus 1 pint if heater fitted).

DIMENSIONS: Wheelbase, 7ft 8in.
Track: F, 4ft 0·75in.; R, 4ft 2in.
Length (overall), 13ft 1·5in.
Width, 5ft 0·5in.
Height, 4ft 6in.
Ground clearance, 4·5in.

ELECTRICAL SYSTEM: 12-volt; 50 ampère-hour battery.
Headlamps, 50–40 watt bulbs.

SUSPENSION: Front, wishbones and coil springs, anti-roll bar.
Rear, live axle, half-elliptic springs and Panhard rod.

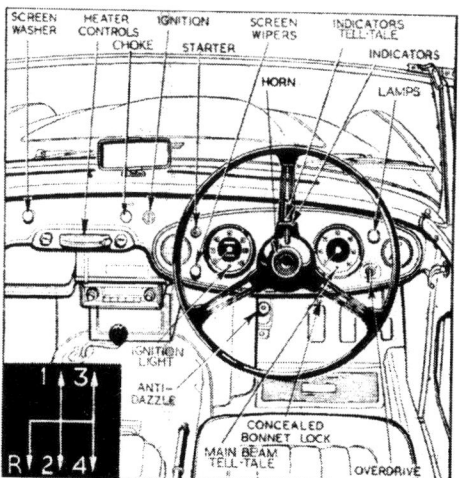

1963 CARS

Austin-Healey 3000 sports convertible

With the accent on comfort

STEADILY developed over the past 10 years—and with an extremely successful team of rally cars always pointing the way ahead—the big Austin-Healey has been further improved for the coming season. This time, the accent is mainly on added comfort and weather protection, although changes have also been made to the engine and chassis.

The new model, which is known as the Austin-Healey 3000 Sports Convertible, is an occasional four-seater and replaces both the two-seater and occasional four-seater Mark II models.

Both the body shape and the seating accommodation are virtually identical to the Mark II occasional four-seater, but its rounded screen and all-weather equipment are entirely new. Frameless winding door windows, with hinged ventilating panels on their leading edges replace the former sliding side screens. The winders are conveniently placed below the interior door handles and, despite the need to accommodate drop windows within the doors, map pockets have been retained.

The sloping rear edges of the windows give a wide field of side vision from the front seats. Rearward vision is also good, through a large, flexible backlight attached to the hood by fasteners so

Top: The curved and sloping screen, hood and frameless winding side windows distinguish the new model. *Below:* The hood is simple to stow or erect, and this can be done from inside the car.

that it can be dropped into the hood-well for increased ventilation in hot weather.

The head design makes one-man operation very simple. The drill for lowering it consists of pulling the rear squab forward slightly, undoing a pair of toggle fasteners securing the backlight and folding the latter into the hood-well, releasing the two toggle fasteners attaching the hood to the screen and then swinging the hood back into its well by a handle on the top rail. No tricky folding is needed and the whole job can be done from inside the car in a minute or so. The driver need alight only if he decides to button the hood envelope in place. The appearance with the hood down is not quite so "concours" as some, but the design is far more practical than most for those who like to take advantage of fine weather.

With the hood closed there is generous headroom and neat appearance. The driver's head does not come immediately below a hood iron and soft, circular-section rubber seals suggest freedom from draughts and water leaks. But despite the comparative security of the interior there are no door locks, the only lockable space being the boot.

Two adjustable bucket seats are provided as before, but better foot room has been achieved by re-designing the gearbox tunnel to give comfortable pedal spacing with plenty of room for the driver's left foot to the side of the clutch pedal. The tunnel is of glass fibre which gives better insulation from both heat and noise. It is not, strictly, a 1963 innovation, having been introduced during production earlier this year to go with a new central, remote-control gear change, more conventional and positive than that previously used because the gearbox has been turned through 90° to bring the selectors to the top instead of at one side. As before, Laycock-de Normanville overdrive

At a glance . . .

ENGINE.—6 cyl., 83.36 mm. x 89 mm., 2,912 c.c.; o.h.v. (push rods); two S.U. HS6 carburetters; max. power, approx. 130 b.h.p. net at 4,750 r.p.m.; max. torque, 167 lb. ft. at 3,000 r.p.m.

TRANSMISSION.—10-in. s.d.p. clutch; 4-speed gearbox with synchromesh on 2-3-4. Ratios (normal): 3.545, 4.640, 7.278, 10.39; rev., 13.41. Ratios (with opt. Laycock-de Normanville overdrive): 3.91 (O/D 3.215), 5.118 (O/D 4.207), 8.027, 11.46; rev., 14.78. Road speed in top gear at 1,000 r.p.m., 20.9 m.p.h. (with O/D: direct, 18.94 m.p.h.; O/D, 23.1 m.p.h.).

RUNNING GEAR.—Girling hydraulic brakes, disc front/drum rear (vacuum servo optional extra); coil and wishbone i.f.s.; semi-elliptic rear springs; anti-roll bar front and rear; cam-and-peg steering; 5.90-15 Dunlop Road Speed tyres.

DIMENSIONS.—Length, 13 ft. 1½ in.; width, 5 ft. 0½ in.; turning circle, 35 ft.; weight, 21½ cwt.

PRICES.—Basic, £865 (total with P.T., £1,190 7s. 9d.). Extras (including P.T.): overdrive, £64 9s. 1d.; wire wheels, £34 7s. 6d.; tonneau cover, £13 15s.

Back to twin carburetters, mainly for the benefit of U.S. dealers who had difficulty in synchronizing three of them. Power and torque are unaffected by the change.

controlled by a switch on the facia board is an optional extra.

The reversion to two carburetters, instead of the three adopted for the Mark II model, is an interesting engine change. This has been done largely because U.S. dealers have complained of the complexity of three and the difficulty of synchronization. Imperfectly tuned, three instruments gave less satisfactory results than two larger, more easily synchronized carburetters. The $1\frac{3}{4}$-in. S.U. carburetters are of the latest HS6 type; and the new camshaft which was largely responsible for an increase in power on the Mark II is retained in the latest engine. In addition, the increased under-bonnet space given by the two carburetters permits better heat insulation (by means of both washers and an asbestos-lined metal shield). As a result, b.h.p. and torque figures are said to be unaltered despite a simplified specification.

The only other significant chassis change concerns the front suspension, the coil springs having been stiffened considerably in the light of competition experience. The spring rate at the wheel is now 115 lb./in. compared with the former 96 lb./in. and damper settings have been modified to suit. The effect is to transfer some roll load from the rear to the front, with a general improvement in cornering and a reduced tendency to rear-end breakaway. A short run on one of the new models suggested that the improvement has not been achieved at the expense of the ride.

One further innovation is the availability, as an optional extra, of a Girling vacuum servo which greatly reduces the pedal effort for the disc-front/drum-rear brakes.

A short straight gear lever, padded transmission tunnel, and the hood envelope are points to note in this picture. The rear seats are strictly occasional but useful for luggage.

Now the brilliant Austin Healey 3000 is a slicker, more practical 2/4 seater, with a quick-folding convertible top that stows away neatly round the top of the new back seat. We call it the Sports Convertible—and a dream of a sports car it is:—130 b.h.p.; disc front brakes (optionally servo assisted); twin carburettors. All give you—performance plus safety, plus luxurious styling. ☐ The Austin Healey 3000 was outright winner of the Alpine Rally in both 1961 and 1962. The Sports Convertible costs £1045.15.4 (£865 plus £180.15.4 purchase tax). At a price like that, it's a match for any sports car in the world. See it and drive it—at your Austin Dealer's showroom.

THE AUSTIN HEALEY 3000 SPORTS CONVERTIBLE

AUSTIN HEALEY 3000 MARK II
faster off the mark for three good reasons

Three reasons: Get into an Austin Healey 3000 Mark II. Accelerate. You feel a new response. A joyous surge-forward you never experienced before—not even in an Austin Healey 3000. The previous one didn't waste any time, but this one has an unfair advantage. It's got three carburettors where the other had two. That means in simple terms you've got 130 b.h.p. to play with as compared with the previous 124. That means an even finer rally car. An even finer pleasure car. And the extra price of the extra carburettor is frankly nil: the car costs £824 plus £378.18.1 Purchase Tax and Surcharge. **More points:** The Mark II is not only an even faster car, it's also an even safer car. It's still got disc brakes on the front of course, but as an optional extra the braking can now be servo-assisted. And inside the car are all the necessary fittings for seat belts. **Still more points:** New camshaft. New air cleaner. New heat shield for silencer. New grille and air-intake slats.

GET INTO AN AUSTIN AND OUT OF THE ORDINARY!

THE AUSTIN MOTOR COMPANY LIMITED · LONGBRIDGE · BIRMINGHAM · Personal Exports Division: 41/46 Piccadilly · London · W1

AUSTIN-HEALEY 3000
Sports Convertible

IN keeping with the current trend in sports car body design, the British Motor Corporation announce the Austin-Healey 3000 Sports Convertible as a replacement for the well-established 3000 Mark II model. Retaining the same body lines as that model it offers greatly enhanced weather protection. As a result of minor engine changes, the low speed behaviour of the car has been brought into line with its new role without, however, detracting appreciably from its top end performance. An internal re-arrangement of the gearbox has reduced the effective dimensions of that unit, resulting in slightly more toeboard space.

A new windscreen with a stout, chromium-plated frame is the main apparent change to the appearance of the car. The line of the screen bottom rail is continued along the top of the doors by the use of a stainless steel moulding—a trick which raises the waist line. Plated quarter-vent frames are functional as well as adding to the area of bright metal work; they have channels in their rear edge for the new curved side window glasses, which are frameless and wind down flush with the tops of the doors. Conventional window lifts are employed, with the handles set well forward on the doors, clear of the occupants' knees.

Internally, little is altered except that trim pads with map pockets replace the door compartments of the earlier model. There is also slight loss of width across the rear compartment because of the wider boxes required to house the more complex hood frame. The main trim change is in the upholstery material itself, which is a new porous, leather-grained plastic. This covering retains its flexibility in a wide range of temperature conditions. The upholstery is in a choice of colours to contrast with the main body paint.

Folded, the hood does not drop below the main body level but makes a neat line along the rear deck and should help to reduce back swirl of wind at speed. Although it is necessary to get out of the car to stow the hood neatly, it can be lowered from the driving seat by unfastening two over-centre clasps which hold it to the screen rail, and pushing it back with one hand. The hood frame is sturdy without being complicated and the covering, in stout black plastic, is sufficiently flexible to pull tight without wrinkles.

While enthusiasts may not approve of the reversion to two 1·75in. HS6 S.U. carburettors on basically the old inlet manifold, maximum power is reduced by only 1 b.h.p. With this change goes an improved torque curve which is now substantially flat between 2,800 r.p.m. and 3,700 r.p.m., a figure of 158lb./ft. (equal to a net b.m.e.p. of 135 p.s.i.) being

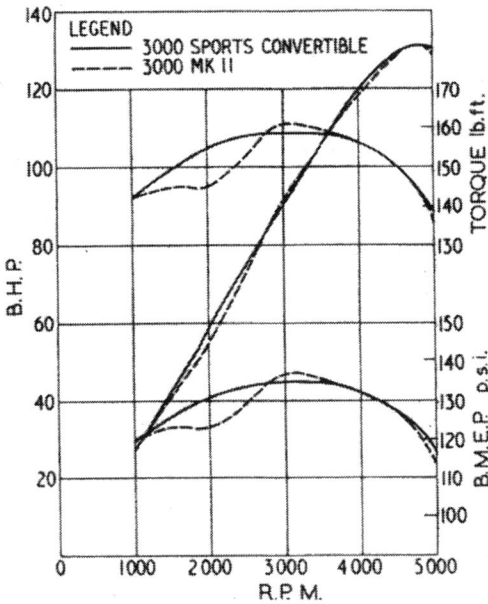

Left: Induction layout, using two 1·5in. HS6 S.U. carburettors in place of three 1·5in. instruments. It gives better accessibility for tuning, and two units are more easily synchronized

Comparative performance curves of the new and old engines, torque has been improved without significant top-end power loss

Left: Furled, the hood stands proud above the rear deck and forms a windbreak. The hood cover is standard equipment. Right: Introduction of wind-down windows has meant that the large door lockers of previous 3000 models have been lost in accommodating the window winding mechanism. However, map pockets are retained on both doors

Above: A useful feature in hot climates is the ability to roll down the rear window and obtain a flow of cool air through the car. The flexible clear plastic light is attached internally with press studs. Right: Suitable for one-man operation, the new hood is sturdy and neat. The heavy sponge rubber window seals can be seen along the edge of the frame

maintained within this range. Moreover, greater flexibility at very low speeds is claimed, and it was certainly possible to drive an early production model at less than 10 m.p.h. in top gear. Among the detail changes is a camshaft with slightly reduced dwell.

An engineering change, which considerably reduces the complication of the remote gear-change mechanism, has been a redesign of the gearbox casting to bring the selector mechanism to the top of the box. Previously this was at the side, a relic from the time when the gearbox was common to a B.M.C. model with steering column change. Apart from bringing the gear lever to the centreline of the car, the gear casing is narrower, permitting an increase of 0·75in. in toeboard width. A further improvement in this vicinity is that the transmission cover material has been changed to glass-fibre reinforced plastic, resulting in reduced heat transfer into the driving compartment.

To improve handling, the front roll stiffness has been increased by the incorporation of stiffer front springs and harder damper settings.

The incorporation of so many minor changes has had a marked influence on the character of the car. A brief run in an early production model confirmed that the level of refinement is noticeably higher because of greatly improved flexibility and increased quietness, and very little bite has been lost. The impression of refinement is owed partly to extra attention to soundproofing generally and in particular to the sound damping of the new door trim pads and side window glasses. At the moment production is concentrated on cars for the export market; however home buyers should not have too long to wait. As a result of these improvements, the basic price has increased by £36, or £49 10s with tax.

PRICES	Basic £	U.K. List £	s	d
Austin-Healey 3000 Sports Convertible..	865	1,190	7	9
Extras :				
Wire-spoke wheels			34	7	6
Radio			33	0	0
Heater			21	6	3
Servo brakes			13	15	0
Tonneau cover			13	15	0
Overdrive ..			64	9	1

AUSTIN HEALEY '3000'

goes convertible

A quick action disappearing hood, wind-up windows and wrap-around windscreen add saloon car comfort to an outstanding sports car

THE world's most successful sports car in international rallying, the Austin-Healey '3000', now makes its appearance in a new form as an occasional four-seater sports convertible with wrap-round windscreen, wind-up glass side windows, and quick-action folding hood.

This popular sports car thus develops what is truly a dual personality. The big six-cylinder 2912 c.c. engine, with its power output of 136 b.h.p. (gross) at 4,750 r.p.m., gives the outstanding performance which Austin-Healey owners have come to expect, and this can be enjoyed at its best in open form with the hood and side windows lowered. In a matter of seconds the hood can be raised to transform the Sports Convertible into a snug, all-weather car for high-speed motoring in comfort. Open or closed, the Austin-Healey '3000' will outperform most other sports cars on the road, yet the flexibility of the six-cylinder engine makes the car just as suitable for low-speed pottering if desired.

All the best features of the well-proved chassis specification have been retained in the new model. The power unit is largely

---

SPECIFICATION...

Engine: Six-cylinder 2912 c.c. (83.36 × 89 mm.) with four-bearing crankshaft and overhead valves operated by pushrods. Full-flow oil filter with renewable element. Centrifugal water pump with four-blade fan (six-blade fan available overseas). Ignition by coil and 12-volt battery; distributor with combined centrifugal and vacuum advance control. KE965 steel exhaust valves. Twin exhaust system. Twin semi-downdraught S.U. HS6 carburetters and S.U. electric fuel pump. Power output, 130 b.h.p. net (136 gross) at 4,750 r.p.m. Max. torque, 167 lb. ft. at 3,000 r.p.m. Compression ratio, 9.03 to 1.

Transmission: Single dry-plate clutch to four-speed synchromesh gearbox with short central gear-lever mounted on transmission tunnel. Open propeller shaft with needle-roller universal joints. Hypoid final drive, ratio 3.545 to 1 (3.91 to 1 with overdrive). Gearbox ratios: reverse, 3.72; first 2.88; second, 2.06; third, 1.31; overdrive third, 1.077; top, 1.0; overdrive top, 0.822 to 1.

Suspension: Independent front by coil spring and wishbone, with anti-roll bar. Non-independent rear by semi-elliptic leaf springs, with anti-sway bar. Hydraulic lever-type shock absorbers, front and rear.

Steering: Cam and peg, ratio 14 to 1. Spring-spoke steering wheel, 17 in. dia.

Wheels and brakes: Ventilated steel disc wheels with 590 × 15 in. Dunlop Road Speed tyres (wire-spoke wheels obtainable if preferred). Girling brakes: 11¼ in. disc type on front; 11 × 2¼ in. drum type on rear.

Bodywork: Occasional four-seater, two-door convertible with wind-down glass side windows and hinged ventilators. Forward-hinged doors with locking handles. Fixed wrap-round windscreen with stainless steel frame. Vinyl-treated fabric hood anchored to top of windscreen by two quick-release catches; folds completely behind rear seats when lowered. Lockable luggage compartment. Paint finish in single or dual colours.

Instruments: Grouped on driver's side of facia. Trip speedometer, tachometer, fuel gauge, combined water temperature and oil pressure gauge.

Leading dimensions: Wheelbase, 7 ft. 8 in. Track, 4 ft. 0¾ in. (front); 4 ft. 2 in. (rear). Length, 13 ft. 1½ in. Height (hood up), 4 ft. 2 in. Width, 5 ft. 0½ in. Turning circle, 35 ft. Ground clearance, 4½ in. Unladen weight, approx. 2393 lb.

Price: £865 basic (£1190 7s. 9d. with Purchase Tax in U.K.).

unchanged, but the enthusiast will welcome the new close-ratio gearbox with higher first, second and reverse gears—and especially the new short gear-lever mounted

**The Austin-Healey '3000'
Sports Convertible, Model BJ7**

With hood furled neatly, the new convertible version of the Austin-Healey '3000' is as exhilarating an open-air car as its predecessor, while the new windscreen gives even better visibility; the new side windows can be instantly raised or lowered and in conjunction with the swivelling quarter vents can provide complete control of cockpit ventilation

centrally on the transmission tunnel, giving a crisper and more positive gear-change than the previous type. High gearing (3.545 to 1 in top) gives the 'long-legged' gait which is so untiring for long journeys, and as before the Austin-Healey '3000' is obtainable with Laycock de Normanville overdrive on third and top gears, engaged at will by flicking a switch on the facia. Normal top gear gives 20.9 m.p.h. per 1,000 r.p.m. On overdrive models, a 3.91 to 1 final drive ratio provides 19 m.p.h. per 1,000 r.p.m. in normal top, rising to 23 m.p.h. per 1,000 r.p.m. when the overdrive is engaged.

The acceleration is outstanding, 30 m.p.h. being reached from a standing start in 3.7 seconds, 60 m.p.h. in 10.9 seconds, and 90 m.p.h. in 26 seconds. Mean maximum speed is 116 m.p.h., yet the Austin-Healey '3000' has returned 34 m.p.g. at a constant 40 m.p.h. in overdrive top. Normal fuel consumption under fast driving conditions averages 20 to 25 m.p.g. To this performance is added the safety of disc front brakes and Dunlop Road Speed tyres, while sturdy seat belt anchorages are built into the car during manufacture.

Although basically similar to its predecessor, the new bodywork gives improved aerodynamics and the lines are subtly sleeker. The wrap-around windscreen gives better visibility, and the wind-down side windows are combined with hinged ventilators to provide complete control over cockpit ventilation. The hood design is particularly ingenious, the frame being counterbalanced by concealed springs so that it can be raised or lowered in a moment, whether the side windows are up or down. In the lowered position, the hood folds behind the occasional rear seats, where it is concealed by a neatly-fitting cover. When raised, it is quickly attached to the windscreen frame by two quick-release catches.

A special feature of this hood is the new rear light, which is made of flexible plastic material and attached to the hood by fasteners. It can be quickly unfastened and lowered out of sight behind the seats, leaving the hood raised. In hot countries this provides the best possible form of ventilation for an open car.

With its new side windows, the Austin-Healey '3000' has now been provided with locks on both doors, that on the driver's side being operated by the ignition key from outside the car. As there is also a battery master switch located inside the lockable luggage boot, the Sports Convertible can safely be left unattended.

The price of the Austin-Healey '3000' Sports Convertible is £865, plus £325 7s. 9d. purchase tax in the U.K. Optional extras include radio, heater, overdrive, wire-spoked wheels, tonneau cover and servo-assisted brakes.

The wind-up side windows retract into the doors, but there is still a useful pocket for maps. Also in the cockpit view above is shown the remote control gear lever and the curved windscreen. On the right is seen the quickly detachable rear window incorporated in the new hood, giving the ideal hot weather combination of shade and through-ventilation

Austin-Healey 3000 MK. II SPORTS CONVERTIBLE 2,912 c.c.

BETWEEN the range of small four-cylinder-engined sports cars in the up-to-100 m.p.h. class and the true tiger cars, capable of travelling nearly half as fast again, is a select group of individualistic sports cars of which the cheapest is the Austin-Healey 3000. Over the years it has developed in power considerably from the form in which it was originally introduced as the 100 in 1952, but the recent modifications are the first real move to increase the refinement and convenience of the car as a whole, widening its appeal.

For simplification and ease of maintenance there has also been a reduction in the number of carburettors, from three to two, and this has been made without any apparent loss of peak engine performance. Instead, the Healey in its latest form proved considerably quicker throughout the performance range than the three-carburettor version which we tested at the end of last year. The twin-carburettor car saved 6sec in acceleration from rest to 100 m.p.h., which took just over half a minute, while its excellent time of 17·8sec for a standing start quarter-mile is a second less than the figure obtained with the previous model.

In terms of maximum speed, the latest car again proved faster by returning a best figure of 120 m.p.h., with a mean for a two-way run at 117 m.p.h., in overdrive top gear. At this top end of the performance range, the driver is certainly well aware of the rate of progress, and, while the car is still perfectly stable, the front begins to feel "light" at the steering, and there is a tremendous roar of noise from wind, engine and exhaust. Wind noise is sufficiently loud from about 80 m.p.h. onwards to discourage conversation.

Overdrive is an optional extra, operating on third and top gears, and is priced at some £64 including purchase tax. When this component is specified, the car is supplied with a 3·91 to 1 axle in place of the 3·55 unit. This is a pity in some respects, as it converts overdrive from a geared-up cruising ratio to an essential top gear. When the car had

to be used for some miles during the test with overdrive out of action as a result of an internal fault, it felt decidedly under-geared, and maximum speed was limited by engine revs. In overdrive top, the Austin-Healey runs at 25·4 m.p.h. per 1,000 r.p.m., compared with 23·1 m.p.h. in top with the all-direct drive version. If the standard 3·55 axle were retained, overdrive would give 28·1 m.p.h. per 1,000 r.p.m. and easy 100 m.p.h. cruising at only 3,570 r.p.m., which would seem more appropriate.

These comments need to be amplified by emphasizing the commendable smoothness and evenness of torque of the six-cylinder three-litre engine, which beg for high gearing; but there is advantage for the driver who does not like to bother with gear changing. The car may be taken away from rest in second gear, and will pull smoothly from 10 m.p.h. in third, which is pleasant and convenient even if out of character for a sports car. Above 30 m.p.h. one may make perfectly good progress using simply top gear and the overdrive switch, which may suit the habits and temperament of some less sporting owners. There is little difference in overall ratio between overdrive third and direct top gears, and when accelerating hard through the gears it is quickest to engage overdrive while remaining in third gear, at about 75 m.p.h., and then change straight to

PRICES				
2-door convertible	..	..	..	£865
Purchase tax	..	..	..	£325 7s 9d
	Total (in G.B.)			**£1,190 7s 9d**
Extras (including tax)				
Overdrive	.. ..	..	..	£64 9s 1d
Heater	.. ..	..	..	£21 6s 3d
Wire wheels	.. ..	..	..	£34 7s 6d
Brake servo	.. ..	..	..	£13 15s 0d
Radio	.. ..	..	..	£33 0s 0d
Tonneau cover	.. ..	..	..	£13 15s 0d

Leather is used for the wearing surfaces of the seats. The remainder, and the door and facia trim, are in p.v.c. A tiny ashtray is built into the transmission tunnel, part of which is padded

overdrive top gear after 90 m.p.h. An inhibitor switch prevents operation of the overdrive solenoid with the throttle closed.

Engine smoothness continues through the range up to the limit of just over 5,000 r.p.m. The unit is also quite quiet up to about 3,000 r.p.m., but begins to sound busy at the higher crankshaft speeds. A distinct induction hiss is audible from the carburettor air intakes in normal driving, even at a steady throttle opening, and there is a resonant boom from the exhaust around 2,500-3,000 r.p.m. The engine is an instant starter from cold, but considerable use of the choke is necessary for the first few minutes of running, and the power unit is slow to warm up, misfiring and hesitating if the choke is returned too early. A low-temperature thermostat was fitted in the cooling system of the test car, with the result that the engine was generally running below the ideal temperature. In traffic, however, with much ticking over, the coolant became decidedly hot but never actually boiled.

A new gear change with straight lever and remote control linkage replaces the cranked, direct-acting lever of earlier models. It is an accurate, sturdy gear change, which proves quite satisfying to use, and fast changes may be made. Yet the synchromesh on top gear is largely in-

B.M.C.'s big three-litre engine, now with twin carburettors, fills the under-bonnet space, but essential service points are accessible

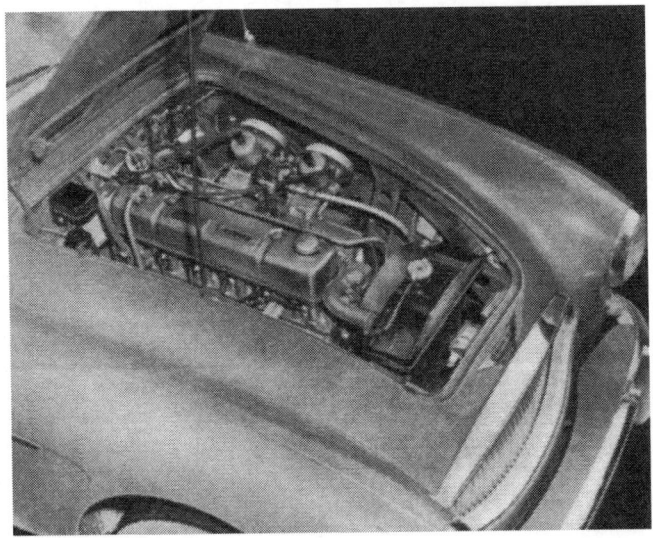

effective—a fault which was observed with the previous model—and the change from third to top has to be made slowly or with double-declutching if the gears are not to crash. There is no synchromesh on bottom gear.

Light pedal pressure operates the clutch, for which there is considerable pedal travel. The clutch is fully adequate for the engine torque available, and coupled to the fairly low bottom gear it enabled a very easy restart to be made on the 1-in-3 test hill. Some clutch judder with the test car occurred occasionally but may, perhaps, be blamed on the severe use which this demonstrator has endured. There was also a tendency to axle hop when the standing-start performance figures were being measured.

This model is the only sports car manufactured by B.M.C. which does not have rack-and-pinion steering, and although the control is fairly heavy and high-geared it does not have quite the degree of accuracy desirable for the very considerable performance potential. Slight movement of the wheel may be made when travelling straight without influencing the car's course; but the directional stability is really excellent, and little steering correction is necessary to hold the car to a straight line even in severe side winds.

Appreciable understeer is balanced by a ready tendency for the rear wheels to lose adhesion on a rough or slippery surface; at high cornering speeds the Healey still remains properly controllable and is delightfully quick to respond to steering correction.

Tauter than before, the suspension gives a decidedly harsh and bumpy passage even on fairly smooth town surfaces. There is some flattening out of the ride above 60 m.p.h., and the tautness and resistance to roll undoubtedly pay dividends in the predictable and responsive handling characteristics at high speed, though on rough roads it is evident that the wheels make a poor job of following the surface contours. The car is certainly designed for rapid travel on good roads, but increased tyre pressures recommended for maximum performance naturally amplify the hardness of the ride.

Girling disc front and drum rear brakes are retained, and the test car was fitted with a vacuum servo, priced at £13 15s extra including tax. This relieved much of the effort of applying the brakes, which set a standard of excellence leaving little room for improvement; and it is highly commendable that a load of 100lb on the brake pedal at 30 m.p.h. resulted in the theoretical maximum efficiency of 1 g, which could be repeated for demonstration again and again without any need to cool the brakes. Firmer pressure on the pedal simply resulted in rear wheel locking,

Chromed door fillets with winding windows and a true convertible hood make the car more practical for changeable climates, while the familiar Austin-Healey outline is retained. Winking indicator lights are still shared with the side and tail lamps; the rear reflectors are separate

but without any loss of control or serious reduction in braking effort.

A chromium-plated lever between the driving seat and the propeller shaft tunnel operates the handbrake. It has to be pulled through a considerable arc of travel, but provides tremendous leverage. The figure of 0·4g recorded is the maximum achieved before the handbrake locked the rear wheels, which occurred readily on a dry road, while a perfectly normal application was sufficient to hold the car securely on 1 in 3.

Great strides have been made, compared with the previous model, to improve the weather protection, and it may be said straight away that the operation of the p.v.c. hood of the new Cabriolet is delightfully simple. The flexible rear window is attached by two over-centre catches at the top which, when released, allow it to lie flat in the well formed behind the backrests of the occasional seats. This is normally done before lowering the hood, but it is quite pleasant to drive the car with the rear window open.

With the rear window lowered one simply releases the two over-centre windscreen catches—each of which has a simple threaded adjustment for tensioning—and then pushes the screen rail back. This normally involves getting out, though a passenger can do the job from inside with the car travelling very slowly. A neat hood cover is provided, and stowed in the luggage locker when not in use, to attach to press studs over the lowered hood. It can be

The spare wheel and battery occupy the lion's share of the luggage locker. A prop holds the boot lid open. Below, right : The rear window may be lowered, as here

fastened without a struggle or the need to pull it tremendously tight. When open the Healey is particularly enjoyable to drive, and the fixed quarter-lights and winding windows allow the occupants to enjoy the maximum of fresh air in really hot weather, or to have little more than a cheering back draught at restricted speeds with the side windows wound up.

There remain some points which call for further attention. For example, there is too much rattling of the hood mechanism and supports over any but the smoothest surfaces. On the test car the side windows were extremely stiff to wind up or down, and although the frameless glass butts against a thick rubber surround attached to the hood a strong draught entered from the trailing edge on each side above about 40 m.p.h. The doors are held in any position by adjustable friction stops which accordingly make them rather stiff to open; with the side windows down care is needed when entering the car to avoid the sharp edge of the quarter-light frame.

Apart from replacement of the roomy door pockets of the previous model by map pockets (on account of the space taken by the window mechanism) there are few changes to the interior, and some old criticisms still apply. The pedals are sited too close together for most drivers, and the steering-wheel is too big and too high, so that its upper rim interferes with forward vision of short-in-the-body drivers.

About two inches of telescopic steering-wheel adjustment are available when the locking hand-wheel is slackened. The bucket seats are somewhat thinly padded, but give good lateral support for cornering. The backrests tilt forward to give access to the rear compartment, which will accommodate two small children or one adult (sitting

Austin-Healey 3000 Mk. II...

slightly sideways) without too much complaint on short trips during a rail strike.

A parcels tray with shallow lip is fitted beneath the facia on the left, but a locking cubby-hole would be more welcome, especially as there are still no locks on the doors, even though the car is now essentially a convertible. For one of our test staff this inexcusable omission was highlighted when some of his property was, in fact, stolen from the car. The only locked compartment is the luggage boot, which is so filled by the spare wheel and battery that there is space for little more than a small portmanteau. An anti-theft precaution is to turn off the battery master switch, provided the parking lights are not required, and then to lock the boot lid.

Instruments, in addition to the speedometer—which has a trip mileometer—and the rev counter, include gauges for oil pressure, water temperature and fuel level. The tank is fairly flat in shape, and the fuel gauge is greatly influenced by the attitude of the car, and by acceleration and braking, so at best its indications are only a vague guide to the state of the tank.

Hard driving, such as the Healey invites and obviously enjoys, formed the majority of the test mileage, with the result that fuel consumption was decidedly heavy—only just over 17 m.p.g. for more than 2,000 miles. This distance included a fast drive from London to Scotland and back,

and a number of high-speed runs on M1. Owners may expect consumption in the region of 18 m.p.g., the most favourable figure of 24 m.p.g. being obtained only in very subdued driving, never exceeding 60 m.p.h. As the fuel tank holds only 12 gallons, stops for petrol have to be made inconveniently often on a long journey, and usually will be less than 200 miles apart.

Different material is now used for the insulation of the bulkhead, but considerable engine heat still comes back to the passenger compartment in warm weather. A fresh air heater is available, and was fitted to the test car. It is difficult to adjust so as to admit small quantities of warmed air, but has tremendous capacity for keeping the car snug in winter, perhaps even with the hood down on fine days.

Normal Lucas 700 headlamps are fitted, which restrict the amount of performance which may be used at night owing to their limited penetration and unduly short throw when dipped. No fewer than 17 grease points require attention every 1,000 miles. Only five pints of oil were consumed in 2,264 hard miles.

While there are many relatively minor points open to criticism on this car, there are other much more significant and less tangible factors which are decidedly creditable. They resulted in the Austin-Healey 3000 always being in demand while in our care, especially for long journeys. The more one drives it, the easier it becomes to understand the long and successful competition career of the type, especially in those gruelling continental rallies fought for days on end.

Specification

Scale: 0·3in. to 1ft.

Cushions uncompressed.

ENGINE

Cylinders	...	6
Bore	...	83·34mm (3·28in.)
Stroke	...	88·90mm (3·50in.)
Displacement	...	2,912 c.c. (177·7 cu. in.)
Valve gear	...	Overhead, pushrods and rockers
Compression ratio		9·0-to-1
Carburettor	...	Twin S.U. H56 semi-downdraught
Fuel pump	...	S.U. electric
Oil filter	...	Tecalemit full flow, replaceable element
Max. power	...	130 b.h.p. (net) at 4,750 r.p.m.
Max. torque	...	167 lb. ft. at 3,000 r.p.m.

TRANSMISSION

Clutch	...	Single dry plate, Borg and Beck, 10in. dia.
Gearbox	...	Four speed, synchromesh on 2nd, 3rd and top, central floor change
Overall ratios	...	OD Top 3·21, Top 3·91, OD 3rd, 4·20, 3rd 5·12, 2nd 8·02, 1st 11·45, Reverse 14·78
Final drive	...	Hypoid bevel, 3·91 to 1

CHASSIS

Construction	...	Steel and aluminium body welded to boxed, cruciform frame

SUSPENSION

Front	...	Independent, wishbones and coil springs, Armstrong lever arm dampers and anti-roll bar arm
Rear	...	Semi-elliptic leaf springs, Armstrong lever arm dampers and anti-roll bar arm
Steering	...	Cam Gears, cam and peg. Wheel dia., 17in.

BRAKES

Type	...	Girling, hydraulic, disc front, drum rear; vacuum servo.
Dimensions	...	F. 11·25in. dia. discs; R. 11in. dia., drums, 2·25in. wide shoes
Swept area	...	F. 228 sq. in.; R. 155·5 sq. in. Total: 383·5 sq. in. (296 sq. in. per ton laden)

WHEELS

Type	...	Pressed steel disc, 5 studs
Tyres	...	5·90-15in. Dunlop RS5

EQUIPMENT

Battery	...	12-volt 50-amp .hr.
Headlamps	...	Lucas 36-48 watt
Reversing lamp	...	None
Electric fuses	...	2
Screen wipers	...	Single speed, self parking
Screen washer	...	Standard, manual plunger
Interior heater	...	Extra, Smith's fresh air, with electric booster
Safety belts	...	Extra, anchorages provided
Interior trim	...	Hide on wearing surfaces
Floor covering	...	Carpet
Starting handle	...	No provision
Jack	...	Screw type
Jacking points	...	4, on suspension
Other bodies	...	None

MAINTENANCE

Fuel tank	...	12 Imp. gallons (no reserve)
Cooling system	...	20 pints (including heater)
Engine sump	...	12 pints. Change oil every 3,000 miles; Change filter element every 6,000 miles
Gearbox and over-drive	...	5·3 pints SAE30 Change oil every 6,000 miles
Final drive	...	3 pints SAE90. Change oil every 6,000 miles
Grease	...	17 points every 1,000 miles
Tyre pressures	...	F. 20; R. 23 p.s.i. (normal driving) F. 25; R. 28 p.s.i. (fast driving); F. 20; R. 26 p.s.i. (full load)

Make · AUSTIN-HEALEY Type · 3000 Mk. II Sports Convertible

Test Conditions

Weather ... Heavily overcast with 5-10 m.p.h. wind
Temperature .... 60 deg. F. (16 deg. C.).
                 Barometer 29.2 in. Hg.
Dry surfaces for standing start acceleration and
                    braking tests.

Weight

Kerb weight (with oil, water and half-full fuel tank)
            22.9cwt (2,562lb-1,162kg)
Front-rear distribution, per cent F, 49; R, 51.
Laden as tested ...... 25.9cwt (2,898lb-1,309kg).

Turning Circles

Between kerbs .... L, 36ft 5in.; R, 34ft 3in.
Between walls .... L, 37ft 7in.; R, 35ft 5in.
Turns of steering wheel lock to lock 3

Performance Data

Overdrive top gear m.p.h. per 1,000 r.p.m.... 25.4
Top gear m.p.h. per 1,000 r.p.m. 20.9
Mean piston speed at max. power ... 2,775ft/min.
Engine revs. at mean max. speed ...... 4,500 r.p.m.
B.h.p. per ton laden 102.6

FUEL AND OIL CONSUMPTION

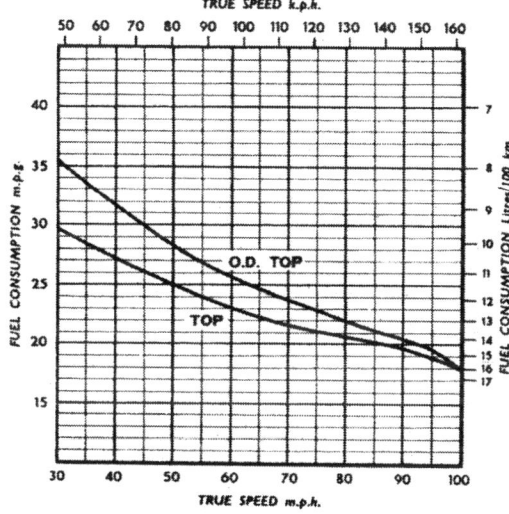

FUEL.........................Premium Grade
                       (97 octane RM)
Test Distance........................ 2,264 miles
Overall Consumption .... 17.1 m.p.g.
                   (16.6 litres/100 km.)
Normal Range.................. 16-24 m.p.g.
                 (17.7—11.8 litres/100 km.)
OIL: S.A.E. 30 ... Consumption: 3,600 m.p.g.

HILL CLIMBING AT STEADY SPEEDS

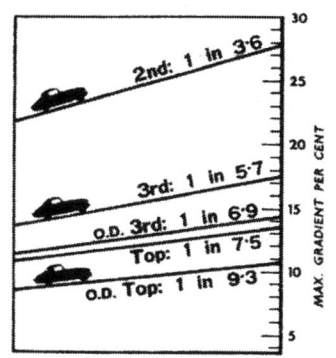

GEAR	O.D. Top	Top	O.D. 3rd	3rd	2nd
Tapley Reading (lb per ton)	240	295	320	385	600
	1 in 9.3	1 in 7.5	1 in 6.9	1 in 5.7	1 in 3.6
Speed range (m.p.h.)	59-64	53-58	52-57	50-55	38-43

MAXIMUM SPEEDS AND ACCELERATION (mean) TIMES

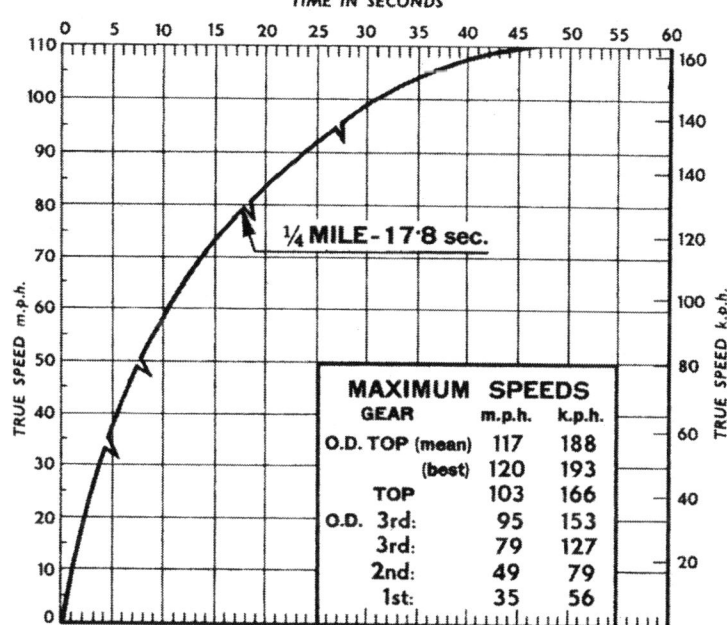

¼ MILE - 17.8 sec.

MAXIMUM SPEEDS		
GEAR	m.p.h.	k.p.h.
O.D. TOP (mean)	117	188
(best)	120	193
TOP	103	166
O.D. 3rd:	95	153
3rd:	79	127
2nd:	49	79
1st:	35	56

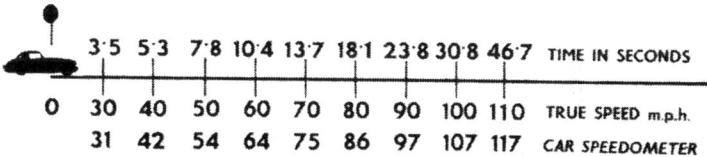

	3.5	5.3	7.8	10.4	13.7	18.1	23.8	30.8	46.7	TIME IN SECONDS
0	30	40	50	60	70	80	90	100	110	TRUE SPEED m.p.h.
	31	42	54	64	75	86	97	107	117	CAR SPEEDOMETER

Speed range and time in seconds

m.p.h.	O.D. Top	Top	O.D. 3rd	3rd	2nd	1st
10— 30	—	—	—	5.9	3.9	2.9
20— 40	—	7.3	7.4	5.6	3.7	—
30— 50	9.2	8.1	7.5	5.2	—	—
40— 60	10.3	7.3	6.6	5.3	—	—
50— 70	9.1	7.1	7.2	5.7	—	—
60— 80	10.2	8.0	7.8	—	—	—
70— 90	11.8	9.5	10.2	—	—	—
80—100	17.1	12.7	—	—	—	—
90—110	25.1	—	—	—	—	—

BRAKES

	Pedal Load	Retardation	Equiv, distance
(from 30 m.p.h. in neutral)	25lb	0.20g	150ft
	50lb	0.55g	55ft
	75lb	0.85g	36ft
	100lb	1.0g	30.2ft
Handbrake		0.40g	75ft

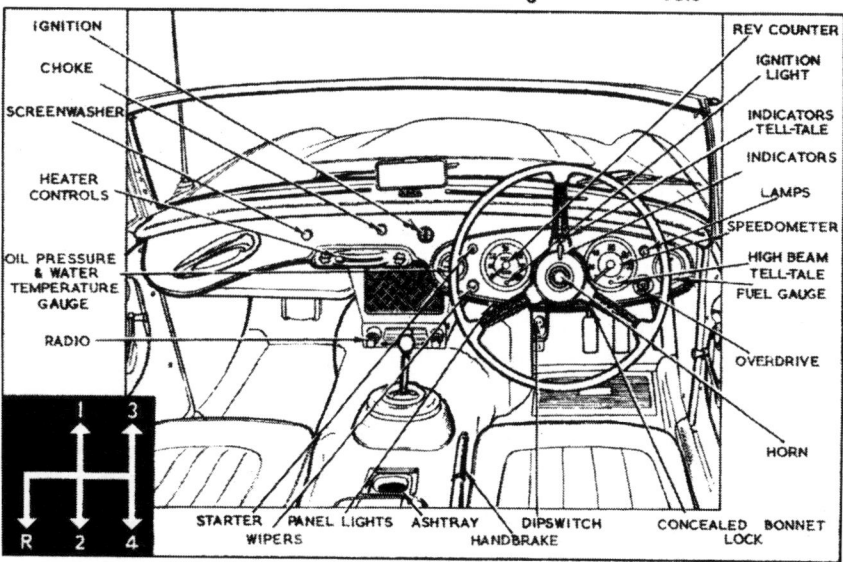

IGNITION
CHOKE
SCREENWASHER
HEATER CONTROLS
OIL PRESSURE & WATER TEMPERATURE GAUGE
RADIO
REV COUNTER
IGNITION LIGHT
INDICATORS TELL-TALE
INDICATORS
LAMPS
SPEEDOMETER
HIGH BEAM TELL-TALE
FUEL GAUGE
OVERDRIVE
HORN
STARTER WIPERS
PANEL LIGHTS
ASHTRAY
DIPSWITCH HANDBRAKE
CONCEALED BONNET LOCK

AUSTIN-HEALEY 3000

For a decade, and more, the Austin-Healey sports roadster has been in production, and it has always been a favorite. It was introduced at a time when little choice existed between the extremes represented by the XK-120 Jaguar and the MG-TD, and the Austin-Healey was sold by the boatload here in America. The fact that the car was powered by a truly Stone-Age 4-cyl. engine and had a rather fragile 3-speed transmission did little to inhibit sales; the Austin-Healey was the nicest looking machine available and occupied a spot high on the enthusiast's list of preferred automobiles.

To keep pace with overall advances in automobiles, the lumbering old 4-banger was replaced with a 2.6-liter, in-line 6 (and the car's wheelbase was simultaneously stretched a couple of inches to accommodate the six's length). With the change in engines, and to extend the appeal of the Austin-Healey, the spare tire was relocated and the passenger compartment enlarged to include "occasional" seating behind the driver and passenger seats. And the old 3-speed transmission was exchanged for a more sturdy and versatile 4-speed unit.

Subsequent upgradings have seen the engine further enlarged (to just under 3-liters) and a host of detail improvements; none of which really changed the character of the car very much. Both 2- and 3-carburetor versions (from two 1¾-in. to three 1½-in. SU carburetors in 1961) of the "3000" have been produced and the car's performance has been steadily improved, along with the creature comforts.

This year, the greatest improvement of all has been made: a change to roll-up windows, the *sine qua non* of the modern sports car. Getting the sliding glass and the cranking mechanism into those thin roadster doors must have been a pretty good trick, but it has been done. The cranking system is fairly direct acting, and the new windows zing up and down in a flash, which is certainly an improvement over the old side-curtains—and there are small, pivoting wind-wings that can be opened for draft-free ventilation. To those of us who remember the infamous "side-flap" model of the early days, these concessions to easy-arm-signals and fresh air are enough to bring tears of relief.

We did, however, discover that (probably due to the scarcity of space within the doors) the side windows were rather poorly braced. When cranked up, they would flutter and rattle, and the frame around the wind-wing—which had a channel to guide and steady the window—was not strong enough to stop the shaking. Only when the top was up and the windows cranked all the way up into the top frames, did the tremors cease.

The top itself is new, too. Unlike the earlier efforts, the top that goes with the roll-up windows is a true convertible, as opposed to roadster, top. It attaches securely to the bodywork around the back, and has linkages that really do guide it into place. No guessing games or step-by-step instructions or anything; just grab the convenient handle on the windshield bar and haul it up into place. A pair of simple, over-center latches are provided to dog it down. When up, it is air-tight, water-tight and (here is a novelty) it does not drum much. Added to these virtues is a big back window, which on warm days may be dropped down (by releasing a couple of catches) to give yet more fresh air.

Unfortunately, here again someone suffered a lapse, or something. When the time comes to drop the top back down into its well (where it can be stowed neatly and well out of sight) there is a serious snag. If the top is just tossed back—as it very easily can be—the folding links will scissor ragged little holes in the top material and the owner will say something heartfelt and forceful. Naturally, this top-tearing does not occur every time the top goes down, but it will happen about every third or fourth time, and that is certainly often enough to make an owner pretty grouchy. So, do be careful, and make certain that the fabric is held clear of the framing as you lower the top.

Of lesser importance than the top and side windows is the new windshield. Previous Austin-Healey windshields were nearly flat; the new one (still a simple curve) wraps around and fairs into the window posts a lot more smoothly. Better vision and less wind turbulence are claimed. We are not certain about these factors, although the vision was excellent, as was the case in the older model, and it does *look* more streamlined. Certainly, the new windshield is more modern and attractive.

Mechanically, the latest version of the Austin-Healey is very little changed over last year's car. The engine is essentially the same, and produces the same power, but the 3-carburetor setup (1½-in. SUs) has been abandoned and the engineers have reverted to 2 (1¾-in. SU) carburetors. This would seem, on the face of it, to be a regression, but the

car's performance does not seem to have been reduced by the change. Indeed, in comparing reports on the 3-carburetor car with the figures we obtained with this new machine, we found evidence that the engine may be slightly more powerful with one less carburetor.

The transmission has been slightly re-designed—given a new shift mechanism that is more positive and smoother than before. Externally, this change manifests itself in the shift lever, which was rather long and snaky, but is now straight and grows right up out of the transmission tunnel next to the driver's knee. Unfortunately, the re-design was not carried far enough to eliminate the pronounced gear-whine, and there is still no synchromesh on first gear: a curious deficiency considering the car's price.

The rear suspension, an ordinary live axle carried on leaf springs, has not been changed, but the A-arm type front suspension has been given slightly stiffer coil springs to improve the car's roadability. That is, at least, the purpose of the change in spring rate, but we are not convinced that it has actually improved things. The Austin-Healey has never been the fastest-cornering car in this world, but it always had great stability. Now, (and we checked this on two different examples of the new car) the car is just a trifle twitchy when pushed hard, and it is persuaded to travel in a straight line only with some difficulty. Even on a smooth road, and in relatively still air, the Austin-Healey would wander from side to side, and the driver is forced to make endless small corrections to hold his course.

Interior layout and appointments in the Austin-Healey are good—but with a couple of minor points of irritation. The seats follow the classic bucket pattern closely, with a contoured cushion on which one sits and a seat back that wraps well around at the sides to give lateral support. These seats were comfortable, but would have been better if they had been raked back more. As they were (and there was no adjustment for rake) one is forced to sit very upright, which may be good for the posture but is not entirely comfortable. The back seats, such as they are, cannot be seriously intended for occupancy by anyone but children, and as we were unable to get any children to render an opinion, we cannot report on that part of the seating package.

Trunk space in this car is all but non-existent—unless you happen to be filling it with sand, or some other substance that will flow into all kinds of irregular corners. The spare tire, which was crowded down to the trunk floor when the Austin-Healey was converted into a 2/4-seater, effectively prevents

The unexciting but exceedingly reliable Austin "six."

The Austin-Healey was, and is, a nice-looking car.

AUSTIN-HEALEY 3000

the stowage of hard luggage; a soft duffle bag could be accommodated, but that is about all.

Serviceability is a mixture of good and bad: all of the points requiring attention are easily reached, but if the driver's handbook instructions are followed, the points are going to be often reached, too. For example, the manual calls for attention to no less than 25 lubrication points every 1000 miles. With the passing of 3000 miles, the ritual becomes even more involved, and at 12,000 miles there is a check list to be followed that would keep a corps of mechanics busy for a fortnight. They will be even busier at 24,000 miles, when the manual politely requests that, in addition to everything else, the sump be removed and cleaned. This kind of hypochondria contrasts rather oddly with the modern trend toward sealed, self-lubricating bearings and minimal service. On the other hand, the Austin-Healey has demonstrated a rather impressive reliability over the years; whether this is because the owners follow the service procedures, or in spite of the fact that they ignore them, we are not prepared to say.

As a touring car, the Austin-Healey has a great many virtues. Its big 6-cylinder engine does not have to work very hard to propel the car down the road, and the overall drive ratio provided by running in overdrive gives a relatively low engine

The new top offers good weather protection, visibility.

speed even at 100 mph (4200 rpm, to be exact).

We would have strongly preferred that there not be quite so much mechanical noise at high speeds, and other cars have proved that a harsh ride like that of the Austin-Healey is not really essential to good road manners, but apart from those objections it was all right. The only thing that bothers us is that the Austin-Healey is going to have to sit on the same showroom floor with BMC's MG-B, and it is in all respects save performance substantially inferior to that new model. Perhaps it is time for an Austin-Healey "B." ⬢

Instruments are clustered and can be easily read.

An old-fashioned prop holds open the trunk lid.

AUSTIN-HEALEY 3000

SCALE: 10" DIVISIONS

DIMENSIONS

Wheelbase, in.	92.0
Tread, f and r	48.7/50.0
Over-all length, in.	157.5
width	60.5
height	50.0
equivalent vol, cu ft	274
Frontal area, sq ft	16.8
Ground clearance, in.	4.5
Steering ratio, o/a	n.a.
turns, lock to lock	2.5
turning circle, ft	35
Hip room, front	2 x 18.0
Hip room, rear	36.0
Pedal to seat back	43.0
Floor to ground	9.0

CALCULATED DATA

Lb/hp (test wt)	20.3
Cu ft/ton mile	94.5
Mph/1000 rpm (o/d)	23.7
Engine revs/mile	2535
Piston travel, ft/mile	1480
Rpm @ 2500 ft/min	4290
equivalent mph	101
R&T wear index	37.5

SPECIFICATIONS

List price	n.a.
Curb weight, lb	2430
Test weight	2760
distribution, %	48/52
Tire size	5.90-15
Brake swept area	n.a.
Engine type	6-cyl, ohv
Bore & stroke	3.28 x 3.50
Displacement, cc	2912
cu in	177.7
Compression ratio	9.03
Bhp @ rpm	136 @ 4750
equivalent mph	112
Torque, lb-ft	167 @ 3000
equivalent mph	71

GEAR RATIOS

o/d (0.82)	3.20
4th (1.00)	3.91
3rd (1.31)	5.12
2nd (2.05)	8.02
1st (2.93)	11.5

SPEEDOMETER ERROR

30 mph	actual, 29.2
60 mph	59.4

PERFORMANCE

Top speed (4850), mph	115
best timed run	n.a.
3rd (5200)	77
2nd (5200)	49
1st (5200)	34

FUEL CONSUMPTION

Normal range, mpg	15/21

ACCELERATION

0-30 mph, sec	3.5
0-40	5.5
0-50	8.2
0-60	11.2
0-70	14.7
0-80	19.8
0-100	37.0
Standing ¼ mile	17.6
speed at end	77

TAPLEY DATA

4th, lb/ton @ mph	265 @ 54
3rd	365 @ 48
2nd	540 @ 41
Total drag at 60 mph, lb	120

ENGINE SPEED IN GEARS

O.D.
4th
3rd
2nd
1st

R 3 1
2 4

2000 3000 4000 5000
ENGINE SPEED IN RPM

MPH
90
80
70
60
50
40
30
20
10

ACCELERATION & COASTING

SS¼
4th
3rd
2nd
1st

5 10 15 20 25 30 35 40 45
ELAPSED TIME IN SECONDS

The interior, above left, is basically unchanged. The new door design does not interfere with available space. Top is covered by this snap-on boot in its folded-down position.

Above is the biggest change in the '63 Healey; the roll-up windows. Glass is nicely tapered. Note the long pocket in the door bottom, redesigned hardware, new latch mechanism.

At left, the wide rear window fastens in place with two clips and has a metal frame at top. The transparent material is of a heavy gauge, yet very flexible and more scratch-resistant.

As solid and strong as its predecessors and a lot more weathertight, the BJ7 smoothly negotiates a corner on broken road surface. The ride is firm but comfortable. Stiffened by new bows and framing, the top is tight and rattle-free at all times.

THE PAST TWO OR THREE YEARS have seen little change in the stalwart Austin-Healey. Though not hurting from a sales-volume standpoint, dealers have made the almost singular request for roll-up windows. The factory was apparently in accord with these suggestions, as the biggest change over the previous models incorporated in the '63 is — you guessed it — roll up windows! It is a welcome change, too, as we feel the day of the side-curtain is long since past and only excusable on economy-type roadsters at the bottom of the price scale. The Healey has been, since its inception, a quality sports car and should have incorporated the windows with the first 3-liter model.

Our test car was a 2-plus-2 similar to the '62 model we analyzed in the October 1961 issue of SCG; a *family* sports car, if there is such a thing. But the small, neatly-molded seats built over the rear-axle hump do an admirable job of holding the youngsters, and it was the first time in quite a while that this writer could pile wife and two pre-teen boys in comfortably for an extended cruise in sporty-type equipment. What also made it interesting was the comparison of acceleration figures. The new model has one less carburetor and this has made such a tremendous improvement in low-end response that its times are noticeably better throughout the entire range, with practically no sacrifice in top speed, and an improvement in gas mileage to boot. This is a classic example disproving the common theory that, if two carburetors work well, three will work even better! The '63 Healey idles smoothly, starts eagerly, is hard to stall, and the usual "spit-back" tendency has been almost entirely eliminated in cold-starts.

Installing windows naturally dictated some door modifications and this has been accomplished neatly, without noticeable loss of interior room. The upholstery is nicely styled and durably fastened, includes a long-but-shallow pocket in

ROAD TEST/35-62

AUSTIN HEALEY BJ7 3-liter

If you're looking for a "family sports car," the 1963 Austin Healey is hard to beat indeed!

PHOTOS: RANDY HOLT

AUSTIN-HEALEY BJ7

the bottom. All the hardware, including the latch mechanism, is new and modern. The inside door handle is easy to operate but the window crank, by necessity, is a bit too near the seat cushion and best operated with the door open. There is nothing noteworthy about the narrow vent window except that it appears durable. On our test unit, rushed through inspection, there were slight rattles with the window rolled all the way down. It is probable that this could be eliminated by tightening or realigning the felt channels. The convertible top is *much* improved, with a latched-in, semi-framed rear window and the molding incorporated for the sidewindows. Relatively simple to fold down, the top does not sink into the rear boot, but lays above it and only looks neat when the snap-on cover is in place. This is probably not the case with the regular two-seater, but we've been unable to see one as yet.

No changes in suspension or steering were mentioned by the factory, so we concluded that the front end of our test car had less than standard caster settings. Steering was very light in comparsion with the normal Healey "feel" and we found this very pleasing. There was a sacrifice in high-speed stability, however, as the car had a tendency to wander around a bit above 70 mph, unlike the usual Healey steadiness at speeds well in excess of this.

With the up-dating of the Sprite in 1962, the remodeled MG in 1963, it's highly probable that this is the last year for the now-classic Healey body style. There's also a V-6 engine kicking around BMC, though we don't know what size it is or will be. Meanwhile, they have a solid, well-developed product in the 1963 Healey, with the weatherproofing and low-end performance bringing it a lot nearer perfection.

— *Jerry Titus*

How 'bout that; less for more money! Engine is equipped with one less carburetor than previous but is a lot more responsive in all aspects; starting, idling, and acceleration.

TEST DATA

VEHICLE	AH 3000 BJ7	MODEL	Convertible
PRICE (as tested)	$3730	OPTIONS	Radio $50

ENGINE:

Type: ....6-cylinder, in-line, 4-cycle, water-cooled
Head: ....Cast-iron, removable
Valves: ....OHV, pushrod/rocker actuated
Max. bhp ....136 @ 4750 rpm
Max. Torque ....167 lbs. ft. @ 3000 rpm
Bore ....3.281 in. 83.34 mm.
Stroke ....3.5 in. 88.9 mm.
Displacement ....177.7 cu. in 2912 cc.
Compression Ratio ....9.0 to 1
Induction System: ....2 SU type HS6 carburetors
Exhaust System: ......Cast manifold into dual pipes and mufflers (tandem)
Electrical System: ....12V Lucas distributor ign.

CLUTCH: Borg & Beck, single disc, dry
Diameter: ....10.5 in.
Actuation: ....Hydraulic
TRANSMISSION: ......4-speed, top 3 synchronized

Ratios: 1st ....2.879 to 1
      2nd ....2.06 to 1
      3rd ....1.304 to 1
      4th ....1.0 to 1
      O.D. 0.822

DIFFERENTIAL:
Ratio: ....3.9 to 1
Drive Axles (type): ....enclosed, semi-floating
STEERING:
Turns Lock to Lock: 3.25
Turn Circle: ....35.7 ft.
BRAKES:
Drum/rear Disc/front
Diameter ....11.25 in.
Swept Area ....302.16 sq. in.

CHASSIS:

Frame: ....Box section conventional
Body: ....Steel semi-unit
Front Suspension: ....Unequal A's, arm shocks, coil springs, anti-sway bar
Rear Suspension: ....Live, leaf springs, arm shocks
Tire Size and Type: ....5.90 x 15 Dunlop

WEIGHTS AND MEASURES:

Wheelbase:	91.7 in.	Ground Clearance	4.6 in.
Front Track:	48.75 in.	Curb Weight	2490 lbs.
Rear Track:	50.0 in.	Test Weight	2783 lbs.
Overall Height	46 in.	Crankcase	7.5 qts.
Overall Width	60 in.	Cooling System	12.5 qts.
Overall Length	157.5 in.	Gas Tank	14.4 gals.

PERFORMANCE:

0-30	3.1 sec.	0-80	17.5 sec.
0-40	5.5 sec.	0-90	22.5 sec.
0-50	7.7 sec.	0-100	28.4 sec.
0-60	10.0 sec.	Standing ¼ mile 15.9 sec. @ 77 mph	
0-70	13.8 sec.	Top Speed (av. two-way run) 110 mph	

Speed Error	30	40		50	60	70	80	90
Actual	30	40		50	59	69	79	89

Fuel Consumption:
Test: ....21 mpg   Average: ....26 mpg

Speed Ranges in gears:
1st .... 0 to 32 mph   3rd ....35 to 79 mph
2nd ....15 to 47 mph   4th ....43 to top mph

Brake Test: 74 Average % G, over 10 stops. Fade encountered on 9th stop.

REFERENCE FACTORS:

Bhp per Cubic Inch 0.77
Lbs. per bhp. 18.3
Piston Speed @ Peak rpm ....2771 ft./min.
Swept Brake area per Lb. ....0.121 Sq. In.

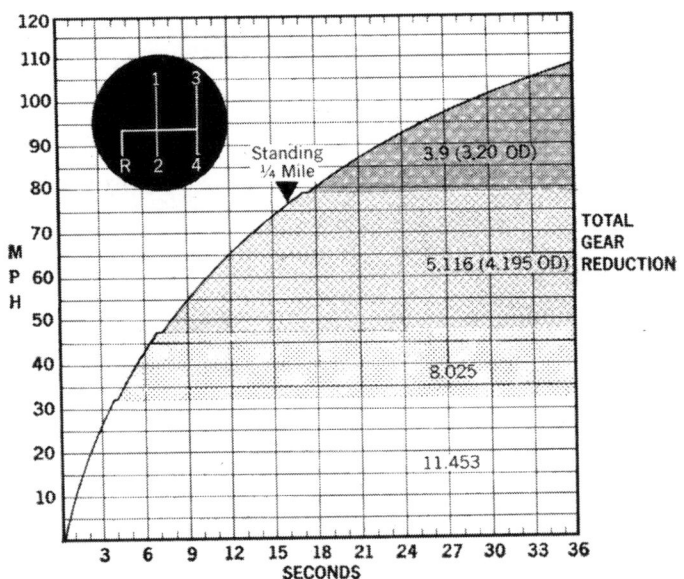

CAR and DRIVER
ROAD TEST
Austin Healey 3000

A long hood covers the powerful six-cylinder engine, which is set well back in the chassis. The forward slope provides a good view from behind steering wheel.

Aerodynamic Edwardian with roll-up windows

Capping a three-year period which has seen BMC score a series of truly dramatic engineering and marketing breakthroughs with cars like the Mini-Minor, the MG/Morris 1100, and the MGB, the new Austin-Healey is a bit of an anachronism. It really doesn't seem to be in keeping with the newly won BMC reputation for brilliantly executed dream-cars-come-true. It's marvelous fun to drive, it makes a great whomping six-cylinder noise, and it has all the qualities one traditionally associates with wind-in-the-face sports cars. But somehow these qualities, of themselves, aren't enough to keep us from being a trifle disappointed with the over-all result.

When first introduced at the London Motor Show of 1952, the Austin-Healey was an overnight sensation. This creation, inspired by Donald Healey and designed by B. Bildy and G. Coker, has withstood the test of time, and the body lines remain basically the same, although the car has undergone numerous mechanical changes through the years. British Motor Corporation ceased to enter it in sports-car races when the six-cylinder engine replaced the old Austin 16-based four, but it is now a contender for international rally honors.

With a hard-to-beat combination of great structural strength and booming performance, the Austin-Healey has been a consistent top finisher in the hands of drivers like Pat Moss and David Seigle-Morris. The sight and sound of Pat Moss howling over an Alpine pass in hairy-looking Healey, sans bumpers and loaded with lights, is a never-to-be-forgotten thrill. In more than one rally the straight-line performance of the Healey has given it the edge over many more sophisticated, more expensive automobiles.

Repeated efforts to up-date the car have been successful in that its appeal has been broadened and sales have continued at a high level. But looking at the 1963

version one sees much evidence of a 10-year-old design. This is particularly true of the suspension, which provides a harder ride than many lighter and later sports cars. The main attraction of the Austin-Healey 3000 lies in its powerful and untemperamental engine—a sports version of the BMC C-type unit that powers the Austin A-110, the Wolseley 6/110 and the Vanden Plas Three-Liter. The latest Austin-Healey version has two carburetors instead of the three that have been standard equipment for three years—BMC has managed to cut manufacturing costs and simplify maintenance without

Wind-up windows and a central gear lever set the interior of the new model apart from earlier Austin-Healey versions.

accepting any reduction in performance. The big and heavy engine develops maximum torque at 3,000 rpm and begs for high gearing. A good compromise has been found by using a 3.91-to-one rear axle ratio and fitting a Laycock-de Normanville overdrive unit on the transmission. In this manner, normal top gear gives brisk acceleration while overdrive top provides economical and relatively silent high-speed cruising. The engine is quiet up to about 3,000 rpm; after that noise seems to increase in direct proportion to rpm.

A new centrally located gear lever has replaced the cranked direct-working side lever of previous models, but the remote-control linkage is no quicker than the offset mechanism, and during warm-up requires much more muscle than the old linkage. As on so many BMC models, the main complaint in the transmission department remains the absence of synchromesh on bottom gear. The gate itself is the same as before, and reverse engagement is excellent. You positively cannot get reverse by mistake, yet when you want it a sharp sideways tap on the lever brings it over the catch so easily as to make parking almost a pleasure.

In many ways the fun of driving a Healey is directly traceable to this transmission and its Laycock de Normanville overdrive. Running fast in third and fourth, using the overdrive switch like another shift lever, can be pure joy. The shift lever's action is stiff but accurate, and declutching to switch the overdrive in and out, though quite unnecessary, results in crisp, fast shifts that are a delight to the ear and the seat of the pants. The ponderous nature of all the controls is a factor which lends a kind of appealing massive masculinity to the car. Again, this is traditional, harking back to those days when sports cars were meat for men only and the ladies rode reluctantly if at all or, better yet, stood timidly and admiringly by the side of the road.

On older Austin-Healeys, competition-minded customers often installed special higher-rate springs to improve high-speed cornering. New standard springs on the 1963 model are an approximation to those, and steering characteristics are improved throughout the speed range. As before the Healey understeers mildly up to the point where the rear lets go, but directional stability is better. Stiffer springs have done nothing to eliminate road shocks reaching the steering wheel, and bumps on a corner can affect the car's stability to an uncomfortable degree.

Body roll is as absent as ever on the 3000. There are no complications about seeing your line through a turn, since you sit in exactly the same vertical position regardless of how many times you may have to alter your direction. This is an inherent quality of the Austin-Healey which probably has served to endear it to more

An engine produced in large volume in its single-carburetor form provides a highly reliable power plant for a sports car.

AUSTIN-HEALEY 3000

Price as tested: $3,535 POE N.Y.
Importer: Hambro Automotive Corporation
27 West 57th Street,
New York 19, N.Y.

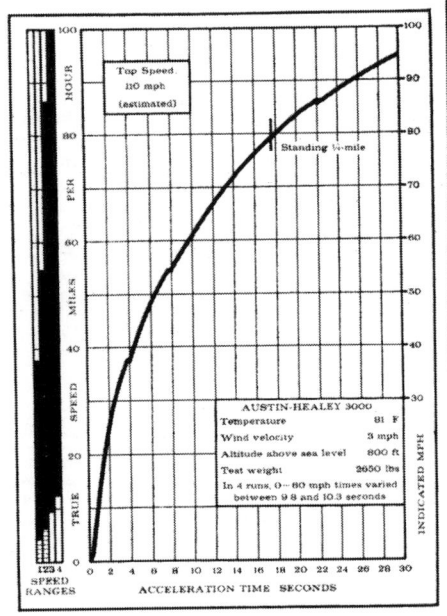

ENGINE:

Displacement.............177.7 cu in, 2,912 cc
Dimensions...6 cyl, 3.28-in bore, 3.50-in stroke
Valve gear: Pushrod-operated overhead valves
Compression ratio..................9.03 to one
Power (SAE)..............136 bhp @ 4,750 rpm
Torque.............167 lb-ft @ 3,000 rpm
Usable range of engine speeds....650-6,000 rpm
Carburetion: Twin semi-downdraft SU HS-6 carburetors
Fuel recommended.................Premium
Mileage..................14-22 mpg
Range on 14.2-gallon tank.......200-315 miles

CHASSIS:

Wheelbase.............................92 in
Track.......................F 49 in, R 50 in
Length..........................157.5 in
Ground clearance.....................4.5 in
Suspension: F: Ind., wishbones and coil springs, anti-roll bar. R: Rigid axle, semi-elliptic leaf springs, anti-roll bar.
Steering....................Cam and peg
Turns, lock to lock.......................3
Turning circle diameter between curbs....35 ft
Tire size....................5.90 x 15
Pressures recommended........F 26, R 28 psi
Brakes, Girling 11¾-in disc front, 11-in drums rear, 192 sq in swept area
Curb weight (full tank)..............2,465 lbs
Percentage on the driving wheels...........52

DRIVE TRAIN:

Clutch..................10-in single dry plate

Gear	Synchro	Ratio	Step	Over-all	Mph per 1000 rpm
Rev	No	3.78		14.80	−5.01
1st	No	2.93	43%	11.46	6.47
2nd	Yes	2.05	49%	8.03	9.24
3rd	Yes	1.31	21%	5.12	14.47
3rd OD	Yes	1.08	8%	4.23	17.65
4th	Yes	1.00	22%	3.91	18.94
4th OD	Yes	0.82		3.21	23.10
Final drive ratio					3.91 to one

AUSTIN-HEALEY 3000
Temperature   81 F
Wind velocity   3 mph
Altitude above sea level   800 ft
Test weight   2650 lbs
In 4 runs, 0—80 mph times varied between 9.8 and 10.3 seconds

Top Speed
110 mph
(estimated)

Standing ¼-mile

Luggage space is not the Healey's strong suit. However, the occasional rear seats can be easily pressed into service.

One of the car's happiest features is its good-looking, tight-fitting top. It goes up or down with truly minimal effort.

drivers than has any other one of its good qualities.

As for habitability, there are new improvements. We all remember the great step forward initiated in 1957, when the top could be put up or down by one man alone. Now he can complete this operation without getting out of the driver's seat. And instead of side curtains the car now has roll-up windows. These refinements, coupled with the Healey's two occasional rear seats, make genuine sports-car driving acceptable to a new class of customer. The extra seats are, of course, just as occasional as those in a Porsche 356-B or a Volvo P-1800, and on a long trip should be considered just storage space.

We have always had difficulty in trying to drive straight-armed in an Austin-Healey. The short seat travel makes it almost impossible even in the 1963

model, and the muscular force required to turn the wheel makes it inadvisable anyway. The large-diameter steering wheel provides good leverage for taking sharp turns, however, and the steering ratio is high enough to enable women to drive it enthusiastically.

Whether the car, as a two-seater, provides any enjoyment that, for instance, the MGB does not give, is questionable. With a top speed perhaps 10 mph higher, and taking about one second less over the standing quarter-mile, the Austin-Healey is so closely matched to the MGB in performance as to make you wonder about the monetary value of two occasional seats.

Servo brakes are optional at extra cost, but we found that the Girling system, with discs front and drums rear, required pedal pressures so normal that power assistance seemed quite superfluous. Stopping distances were minimal, and no fade could be provoked.

As for maintenance, the car has not stayed with the times. There are 17 grease points that require attention every 1,000 miles. The fuel tank holds only 14.2 gallons, which gives a range below average for any type of car.

We drove a couple of cars in the course of this test. They were identical, differing only in color. Our impressions of the Healey are drawn from several hundred miles of all kinds of driving on all kinds of surfaces. We found the car to be a nearly perfect expression of the pre-war two-seater brought up to date. It has the same kind of go-to-hell rakishness we all loved in the TCs and Healey Silverstones, but it tempers these characteristics with wind-up windows and creature comfort that those semi-classics never knew. As we've pointed out, it's strong and reliable. We just wish that it had a more modern chassis and suspension system to match its up-to-date mates in the BMC model line-up.

Though its basic design is a decade old, the Healey will still find an eager audience with the more traditionally minded enthusiast. It is a true sporting machine in the sense that it looks fine, sounds fierce, and goes fast. If it rides hard and crosses cracks in the road with a loud thump, so what? We can remember when unyielding suspension and continual tightening of all the nuts and bolts on the automobile were status symbols to be treasured by any true aficionado. **C/D**

Roll-up windows and vent panes! Creature comfort and convenience come to the traditional sports car, English style.

THE Motor

TEST DATA:

MAKE: Austin-Healey *TYPE:* 3000

MAKERS: Austin Motor Company Ltd., Longbridge, Birmingham

ROAD TEST • No. 14/63

World copyright reserved: no unauthorized reproduction in whole or in part.

CONDITIONS: *Weather: Mild, dry, 10 m.p.h. wind. (Temperature 42°-46°F., Barometer 29.1-29.2 in. Hg.) Surface: Damp tarmacadam and concrete. Fuel: Premium grade pump petrol (98 Octane by Research Method.)*

MAXIMUM SPEEDS

Flying Mile

Mean of four opposite runs .. .. 116·0 m.p.h.
Best one-way time equals .. .. 119·1 m.p.h.

"Maximile" Speed: (Timed quarter mile after one mile accelerating from rest)

Mean of opposite runs .. .. 112·3 m.p.h.
Best one-way time equals .. .. 114·1 m.p.h.

Speed in gears (at 5,200 r.p.m.)

Max. speed in direct top .. .. 97 m.p.h.
Max. speed in overdrive third .. 90 m.p.h.
Max. speed in direct third .. .. 74 m.p.h.
Max. speed in second .. .. 47 m.p.h.
Max. speed in first .. .. .. 33 m.p.h.

ACCELERATION TIMES From standstill

0-30 m.p.h.	3·2 sec.
0-40 m.p.h.	5·1 sec.
0-50 m.p.h.	7·2 sec.
0-60 m.p.h.	10·3 sec.
0-70 m.p.h.	12·9 sec.
0-80 m.p.h.	16·7 sec.
0-90 m.p.h.	21·3 sec.
0-100 m.p.h.	29·4 sec.
0-110 m.p.h.	45·3 sec.
Standing quarter mile	17·3 sec.

ACCELERATION TIMES on upper ratios

	Overdrive Top gear	Direct Top gear	Overdrive 3rd gear	Direct 3rd gear
10-30 m.p.h.	9·6 sec.	7·5 sec.	6·9 sec.	5·5 sec.
20-40 m.p.h.	9·6 sec.	7·2 sec.	6,9 sec.	5·2 sec.
30-50 m.p.h.	9·9 sec.	7·2 sec.	6·8 sec.	5·1 sec.
40-60 m.p.h.	10·0 sec.	7·4 sec.	6·6 sec.	5·1 sec.
50-70 m.p.h.	11·1 sec.	7·8 sec.	7·2 sec.	5·9 sec.
60-80 m.p.h.	11·2 sec.	8·2 sec.	8·0 sec.	—
70-90 m.p.h.	12·1 sec.	9·1 sec.	8·8 sec.	—
80-100 m.p.h.	14·9 sec.	—	—	—
90-110 m.p.h.	24·8 sec.	—	—	—

FUEL CONSUMPTION

Overall Fuel Consumption for 1,184 miles, 66·8 gallons, equals 17·8 m.p.g. (15·82 litres/100 km.)

Touring Fuel Consumption (m.p.g. at steady speed midway between 30 m.p.h. and maximum, less 5% allowance for acceleration) 22·66 m.p.g.

Fuel tank capacity (maker's figure) 12 gallons

Direct top gear

29¼ m.p.g.	at constant 30 m.p.h. on level
28 m.p.g.	at constant 40 m.p.h. on level
25½ m.p.g.	at constant 50 m.p.h. on level
23 m.p.g.	at constant 60 m.p.h. on level
22 m.p.g.	at constant 70 m.p.h. on level
20½ m.p.g.	at constant 80 m.p.h. on level
18¾ m.p.g.	at constant 90 m.p.h. on level

Overdrive top gear

37 m.p.g.	at constant 30 m.p.h. on level
31½ m.p.g.	at constant 40 m.p.h. on level
28¼ m.p.g.	at constant 50 m.p.h. on level
26 m.p.g.	at constant 60 m.p.h. on level
24¾ m.p.g.	at constant 70 m.p.h. on level
21¾ m.p.g.	at constant 80 m.p.h. on level
20¾ m.p.g.	at constant 90 m.p.h. on level
18½ m.p.g.	at constant 100 m.p.h. on level

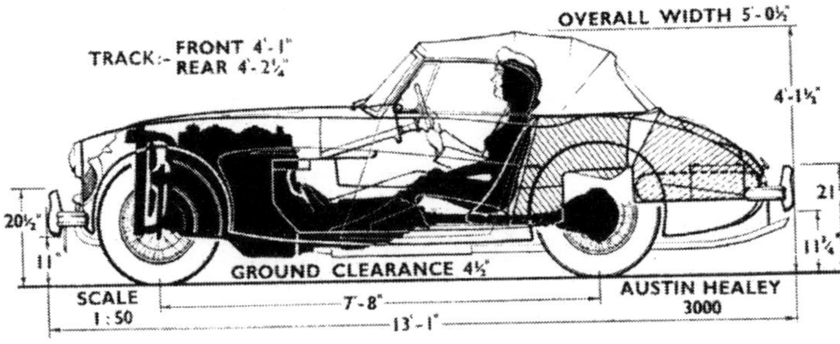
OVERALL WIDTH 5'-0½"
TRACK:- FRONT 4'-1"
REAR 4'-2¼"
4'-1½"
21¼"
20½"
11"
11¼"
GROUND CLEARANCE 4½"
SCALE
1:50
7'-8"
13'-1"
AUSTIN HEALEY
3000

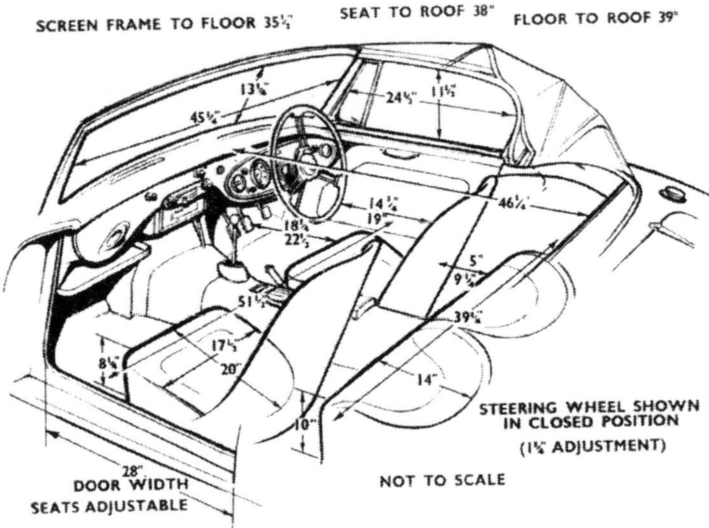
SCREEN FRAME TO FLOOR 35½"
SEAT TO ROOF 38"
FLOOR TO ROOF 39"
13¼"
45½"
24½"
11½"
14¼"
19"
46½"
18¾"
22½"
5"
9¼"
51½"
39¼"
17½"
20"
8¼"
14"
10"
28"
DOOR WIDTH
SEATS ADJUSTABLE
STEERING WHEEL SHOWN
IN CLOSED POSITION
(1½" ADJUSTMENT)
NOT TO SCALE

HILL CLIMBING

Max. gradient climbable at steady speed.

Overdrive top gear	1 in 9·2 (Tapley 240 lb./ton)
Direct top gear	1 in 6·5 (Tapley 340 lb./ton)
Overdrive third gear	1 in 6·1 (Tapley 365 lb./ton)
Direct third gear	1 in 4·8 (Tapley 455 lb./ton)
Second gear	1 in 2·9 (Tapley 680 lb./ton)

BRAKES

Deceleration and equivalent stopping distance from 30 m.p.h.

1·0 g with 85 lb. pedal pressure	(30 ft.)
0·99 g with 80 lb. pedal pressure	(30¼ ft.)
0·87 g with 75 lb. pedal pressure	(34½ ft.)
0·51 g with 50 lb. pedal pressure	(59 ft.)
0·27 g with 25 lb. pedal pressure	(110½ ft.)

STEERING

Turning circle between kerbs:

Left .. .. 32½ft.
Right .. .. 32¼ ft.
Turns of steering wheel from lock to lock 3⅓

INSTRUMENTS

Speedometer at 30 m.p.h.	1½% fast
Speedometer at 60 m.p.h.	2½% fast
Speedometer at 90 m.p.h.	3½% fast
Distance recorder	3% fast

WEIGHT

Kerb weight (unladen but with oil coolant and fuel for approximately 50 miles) .. 21¾ cwt.
Front/rear distribution of kerb weight 52/48
Weight laden as tested .. .. .. 25½ cwt.

Specification

Engine

Cylinders	6
Bore	83·36 mm.
Stroke	89 mm.
Cubic capacity	2,912 c.c.
Piston Area	50·7 sq. in.
Valves	Overhead (pushrod)
Compression ratio	9/1
Carburetter	2, S.U. type H.S.6
Fuel pump	S.U. electric
Ignition timing control	Centrifugal and vacuum
Oil filter	Tecalemit full flow
Maximum power (net)	130 b.h.p.
at	4,750 r.p.m.
Maximum torque (net)	167 lb. ft. at 3,000 r.p.m.
Piston speed at maximum b.h.p.	2,770 ft./min.

Transmission

Clutch, Borg and Beck, 10 in. s.d.p.

Top gear (s/m)	3·909 (Overdrive, 3·205)
3rd gear (s/m)	5·116 (Overdrive, 4·195)
2nd gear (s/m)	8·025
1st gear	11·453
Reverse	14·776
Overdrive	Laycock-de Normanville
Propeller shaft	Hardy Spicer, one-piece, open
Final drive	Hypoid bevel
Top gear m.p.h. at 1,000 r.p.m.	18·6 (Overdrive, 22·6)
Top gear m.p.h. at 1,000 ft./min, piston speed	31·8 (Overdrive, 38·8)

Chassis

Brakes: Girling hydraulic, disc front, drum rear

Brake dimensions: Front discs: 11¼ in. dia. Rear drums: 11 in. dia.

Friction areas: 112 sq. in. of lining working on 383 sq. in. rubbed area of discs and drums

Suspension:
Front: Independent by coil springs, transverse wishbones and anti-roll torsion bar
Rear: Rigid axle, semi-elliptic leaf springs, and Panhard rod

Shock absorbers:
Front } Rear } Armstrong lever hydraulic

Steering gear: Cam gears, cam and peg

Tyres: 5·90—15 tubed Dunlop Road Speed

AUSTIN-HEALEY 3000

SOME enthusiasts feel that the modern, refined, open two-seater is insufficiently masculine to qualify as a sports car. There are, however, some manufacturers who have not yet started making velvety, all-independent sporting machines with a sort of unobtrusive high performance. B.M.C. turn out the Austin-Healey 3000 which, despite a number of up-to-date attractions is a strong-willed survivor of a more hairy-chested era. It has a big, six-cylinder engine which revs lazily in a sturdy chassis and gives lots of smooth power and an exciting performance. Cornering is good without much body roll, the steering is light, and the brakes with the optional servo are first-class. The new hood is easy to fold away, although it does not stow completely out of sight, and the winding windows and more deeply curved screen are useful concessions to comfort. It is a pity the concessions do not extend to an improvement in driving comfort, but

the old problem of cockpit overheating seems to have been alleviated, although the persistent Austin-Healey shortcoming of restricted ground clearance remains. This is surprising as seasons pass with further rally successes by the works Austin-Healeys whose spectacular wins have demanded better clearance than the standard machine. One wonders why the rather obvious modifications necessary to give something more than a niggardly 4½ inches have not been made. Of the masculinity of the Austin-Healey 3000 there is no doubt; whether taming 130-odd horsepower is actually *liked* or not depends on the driver possessing the necessary skill and a certain amount of stout-heartedness. Certainly, on a performance/price basis, the car has few equals.

How it goes

THE "big Healey" makes a splendid noise. It *can* be driven quietly and in fact it is better to allow only moderate throttle openings and low engine speeds in towns or late at night. But the noise is by no means purely for effect because

The Austin-Healey's big straight six-cylinder engine takes up much of the available underbonnet space. There are two safety catches on the front-opening lid which is held open by a rod on the left.

In Brief

Price (including overdrive and servo brakes as tested) £925 plus purchase tax £193 5s. 4d. equals £1,118 5s. 4d.

Capacity	2,912 c.c.
Unladen kerb weight	21¾ cwt.

Acceleration:

20-40 m.p.h. in top gear	7.2 sec.
0-50 m.p.h. through gears	7.2 sec.
Maximum top gear gradient	1 in 6.5
Maximum speed	116.0 m.p.h.
Overall fuel consumption ..	17.8 m.p.g.
Touring fuel consumption ..	20.8 m.p.g.

Gearing: 18.6 m.p.h. in top gear at 1,000 r.p.m. (overdrive 22.6 m.p.h.)

the performance, right up to the maximum speed not very far short of 120 m.p.h. is rousing. Tuning and service problems have caused a reversion from three to two carburetters, but since a high-lift camshaft produced most of the last power increase, the loss of one of the 1¾ in. S.U.'s has only meant a decrease of 2 b.h.p. The performance seems a little flat under about 2,300 r.p.m. but thereafter the torque can really be felt right up to a red mark on the tachometer at 5,200. With such a deep note from the dual exhaust the engine doesn't sound as if it is working hard, and in fact it can easily be over-revved quite substantially. Cold starting is somewhat problematical with a reluctance to fire evenly on part choke and a determination to stall on no choke at all. This lasts for only a short time, however, a little over half a mile in traffic usually being sufficient to reach running temperature. Prolonged halts in traffic one mild, wet afternoon caused the engine temperature to rise to around 200°F., indicating that overheating might become something of a problem in a hot climate.

The clutch pedal has an unusually long travel, making it necessary to sit close to the steering wheel in order to operate the clutch properly. The full 6½ inches of movement have to be used up for every gear change, otherwise movement of the lever is difficult. The 10-inch diameter clutch takes up the drive smoothly and standing start acceleration tests showed that the most brutal methods were usually the best. There was very little slip when letting it in abruptly at 3,800 r.p.m., although the back axle dithered momentarily and there was a little wheelspin in first. Over-enthusiasm left black lines several feet long on dry concrete.

The gear change is distinctly heavy, and even when the clutch was being used properly, it was notchy and rather sticky. The lever no longer projects from the passenger's side of the tunnel, the gearbox having been turned through 90 degrees to bring the selectors to the top and provide a short, more sporting lever. The synchromesh, which is on the upper three gears, is very powerful, however, and fast changes require a firm push. Overdrive works on third and top and engages smoothly enough on an open throttle but downward changes on the overrun are made with a jerk; when making them it is preferable to blip the throttle. First and second gear ratios are very close; so are third and top. For the best results it is necessary to use second right up to peak r.p.m. or the gap between it and third becomes noticeable. Overdrive third is of little practical value because it is so close to direct top; it is only useful as a more easily selected gear. There is a little whine from first gear, but otherwise the transmission seems quite quiet.

A little body roll

THE Austin-Healey can be cornered very quickly on its RS5's and on fairly smooth surfaces the ride is outstandingly good for a firmly sprung sports car. On rough roads with closely spaced bumps, however, the rigid back axle becomes rather unruly and there is a good deal of scuttle shake. The effect is worsened by side windows which rattle in their guides, making this an uncomfortable car to drive over indifferent roads. Again one is surprised in view of the

AUSTIN-HEALEY 3000

Right: The cover for the furled hood is neat and easily fitted. In this picture the driver's seat is not at its rearmost adjustment, leaving some space between it and the rear "seat." The ashtray on the transmission hump has a neat cover to prevent the contents being blown out when the car is open.

Above: The spare wheel takes up a good deal of the boot which is the car's only lockable compartment. The master switch is on the right, aft of the battery.

Right: The floor of the Healey is fully carpeted and the facia has a padded roll along the top with a matt finish the same colour as the upholstery. There are slim map pockets in the doors. Switch on bottom right of the facia controls the overdrive and the ignition and starter are separate. The handbrake is not of the fly-off type.

Left: Open or closed, the Healey's broad-shouldered good looks are still elegant and only slightly "dated". Back-draught in the cockpit with the side windows up was quite moderate.

Upright driving position

A HIGH scuttle and steering wheel, the long travel of the clutch pedal, and the small, straight-backed seat heighten the Austin-Healey's "vintage" feel. Even quite tall drivers have to sit close to the wheel in order to press the clutch out far enough. The seat has a flat cushion and a curved backrest which is too short and upright, and it would be better if the whole seat were tilted backwards slightly to give a better reach to the pedals and a more long-arm driving position. The optional adjustable steering column would appear to give a driving position either for people with unusually long legs and short arms or a taste for sitting very close to the wheel indeed. The transmission tunnel (which is now made of glass fibre for better sound and heat insulation) takes up a good deal of space but there is plenty of room left for long legs. Clutch and brake pedals are rather close together with plenty of space for the left foot to rest, and "heel-and-toeing" is possible, if not very easy.

The two rear seats are meant for small children. Their shape makes them poor luggage carriers, as suitcases and boxes slide off them; some customers would probably be happier if they were optional, as this is now the only model of Healey 3000.

In the middle of a useful parcels shelf under the facia is the screen washer reservoir. It is not very accessible and has its control on the passenger's side. Not calibrated with the thoroughness sports car owners like (the speedometer reads in 10 m.p.h. divisions and the fuel gauge wriggles violently with the movement of petrol in the tank) the instruments are easy to see and comprehensive. An indicator switch in the middle of the steering wheel strikes one as rather old-fashioned, and a headlamps flasher would be welcomed.

Luggage space is restricted by the spare wheel in the boot and also the battery, which leave only enough capacity for a couple of small suitcases or some soft bags. There is a master switch which isolates the whole electrical system and the car can thus be left immobile with a locked boot lid, although there are no door locks. Engine accessibility is not very good, the space being quite narrow and crowded; replenishing with oil and water is comparatively simple and the dipstick is quite easy to get at. During the 1,184 miles of our test, almost all of which encompassed hard driving, the car used 5 pints of oil.

The hard driving also accounts for the quite heavy fuel consumption of 17.8 m.p.g.; on one run, however, at an average speed of 50 m.p.h., cruising mostly on fairly winding secondary roads in overdrive top at around 65 m.p.h. and avoiding wide throttle openings, 33 m.p.g. was recorded.

The big Healey is a good sports car. It is excellent value for money, fun, even exciting to drive, and provided one learns to accept the scuttle shake, low ground clearance and some of the other rather dated features that go with the car, it would be easy to live with. It is fast, safe, and has an appealing, "long-legged" character which suits the good riding qualities and makes it pleasant as a long-distance car.

rally record of the works Austin-Healeys. There is some body roll on corners and an initial understeer but the driver can confidently pile on power to hold a chosen line. The steering is very light and although perhaps a little insensitive to small movements of the steering wheel, it is accurate and pleasant to use. The brakes also inspire a great deal of confidence, although on a long descent without the engine supplying the vacuum servo mechanism, it became obvious how necessary the servo is. The pedal pressure needed to produce locking of the wheels from 40 m.p.h. without it was very high.

Stability at speed is excellent and there is every encouragement for cruising on motorways at near maximum except for the very high noise level. The exhaust note has already been mentioned, and above 90 m.p.h. wind noise makes conversation difficult; above 110 it becomes impossible except by shouting. The new hood is very rigid, however, and does not flap at any speed of which the car is capable, although near maximum gaps let in a draught at the tops of the side windows. It is particularly easy to dismantle and erect the hood; there are only two over-centre catches on the top windscreen rail and it folds away quite smoothly and easily, and can be managed comfortably by one person. A cover is provided for it in the closed position, and this fits neatly but the hood does not disappear flush with the body. During prolonged, very heavy rain taken at up to 110 m.p.h. there were no leaks or draughts except round the opening rear window in the hood. This seems rather casually fitted; although it may be nice to have an openable back window, one hardly expects gaps between the Vybak sheet and the hood cloth. Visibility forward is good, although the screen pillars and quarter lights are approaching saloon car standards of thickness and there are large blind areas in the rear quarters. The side windows fit neatly against rigid hood frames but they were stiff to wind.

Coachwork and Equipment

Starting handle .. .. None	Windscreen washers Manual, standard equipment	Ashtrays .. .. 1 on transmission tunnel
Battery mounting .. .. .. In rear boot	Sun visors .. .. None	Cigar lighters .. .. None
Jack .. .. Screw type	Instruments: Speedometer with total and decimal	Interior lights .. .. None
Jacking points .. Front spring base plates,	trip distance recorders, rev. counter, fuel gauge,	Interior heater .. Fresh air type; optional extra
rear spring leaves	combined water temperature and oil pressure	Car radio: Optional extra through B.M.C. Service
Standard tool kit: Jack, plug spanner, tommy bar,	gauge.	Extras available: Fresh air heater; servo-assisted
wheel nut hammer.	Warning lights: Main beam, dynamo charge,	brakes; wire wheels; overdrive; adjustable
Exterior lights: 2 headlamps, 2 sidelamps/flashers,	flashers.	steering column; tonneau cover.
2 stop/tail flashers, 1 number plate light.	Locks: With ignition key, ignition and boot	Upholstery material .. .. .. Hide
Number of electrical fuses 2	No other keys.	Floor covering .. .. .. Carpet
Direction indicators Self-cancelling flashers	Glove lockers .. .. None	Exterior colours standardized .. 6 single-tone,
Windscreen wipers .. Single-speed,	Map pockets .. .. .. 1 in each door	5 duo-tone
electric, self-parking	Parcel shelves .. .. .. 1 under facia	Alternative body styles .. .. .. None

Maintenance

Sump .. .. .. 12 pints, S.A.E. 30	Sparking plug type .. .. Champion N5	Camber angle .. .. 1°
Gearbox (including overdrive) 5¼ pints, S.A.E. 30	Champion N3 (high speeds)	Castor angle .. .. 2°
Rear axle .. .. .. 3 pints, S.A.E. 90	Sparking plug gap .. .. .024 in.	Steering swivel pin inclination .. .. 6¼°
Steering gear lubricant .. .. S.A.E. 90	Valve timing: Inlet opens 5° b.t.d.c. and closes 45°	Tyre pressures:
Cooling system capacity .. 20 pints (2 drain taps)	a.b.d.c. Exhaust opens 40° b.b.d.c. and closes	Front 20 lb.} Increase by 5 lb.
Chassis lubrication: By grease gun every 3,000	10° a.t.d.c.	Rear 25 lb.} for fast driving
miles to 15 points.	Tappet clearances (hot) .. .. Inlet .012 in.	Brake fluid .. .. Girling
Ignition timing .. .. 6° b.t.d.c. static	Exhaust .012 in.	Battery type and capacity .. .. Lucas 12-volt,
Contact breaker gap .. .. .014-.016 in.	Front wheel toe-in .. 1/16 in. to 1/8 in.	50 amp.-hr.

BEFORE I took delivery of the Austin-Healey 3000 various comments had led me to believe that this model was unpredictable in its handling, not particularly attractive and extremely thirsty. Perhaps this increased my pleasure when after only brief acquaintance I had already become quite fond of the big Healey, and found it to be a most pleasing and comfortable car.

The re-styled radiator grille and the wrap-round screen gives the Mark 2 a much more expensive look. In every way the car has been improved upon and is now very much the modern G.T. car. The wind-up windows with opening quarter lights exclude all draughts as they actually home into a channel in the hood supports. The wrap-round screen gives excellent forward and angled vision, the pillar blind spots being much reduced. The seats are more or less the same as on earlier models, giving good support to the back, but lacking lateral assistance in favour of ease of entrance. The steering wheel, which is adjustable, allows for a relaxed style of driving but does not quite permit the now popular straight arm position unless, of course, you have exceptionally long legs and short arms!

There is ample room for moderately sized luggage behind the seats in the "plus two" compartment—a space designed for children and legless dwarfs. The boot, which houses the battery and spare wheel, is rather inadequate for all but the smallest luggage.

The facia is well laid out with the rev. counter and speedometer directly in front of the driver. The oil pressure, water temperature and fuel gauges flank these major instruments. All these instruments are easily visible, the steering wheel causing little or no restricted vision.

The controls are much improved—especially the gear lever which now is placed conveniently to hand. The Abingdon people have done away with the old, long, cranked lever in favour of a remote control, which brings the lever into the optimum position. The accelerator pedal is not as close to the brake as

the AUSTIN-HEALEY 3000 Mark 2

it might be and, in order to heel-toe, it is important to have an extremely flexible ankle. A simple modification, however, would overcome this irritating but small point.

The engine is still the well-tried 3-litre which has seen a good deal of development since its introduction in 1959 and now produces 130 b.h.p. The gearbox has improved synchromesh, but the ratios remain as before with overdrive fitted to third and top. The overdrive is controlled by a conveniently placed panel switch.

Braking is provided by Girling 11¼ in. discs on the front with 11 in. drums on the rear. These are actuated through a single master cylinder and are servo assisted. The hand-brake, which is positioned alongside the propshaft tunnel, is on the driver's side.

One of the most pleasant features of this car is that long journeys can be accomplished with remarkably little driver fatigue. This is mainly due to the excellent torque characteristics of the big 3-litre engine, which enables the car to be driven with a minimum amount of gear changing. The car will happily toddle along at 30 m.p.h. in top and still accelerate away without complaint from either engine or transmission. The clutch takes up smoothly at all times and no slip was detected even under adverse conditions. The only criticism that can be made is the heavy clutch pedal pressure. The gearbox is extremely robust and, although greatly improved, the synchromesh is unable to cope with some unsynchronized gear changes by the driver. This feature makes heel-toe vital if advantage is to be taken of engine braking. Changing down does not necessitate double de-clutch as such but, unless one is prepared to wait, these down changes must be accompanied by enough revs. to synchronize the change. The brakes appear fade-free in normal road use and never gave the writer any disconcerting moments. After several really hard applications, if anything their efficiency was improved. At no time was there any tendency for the brakes to pull or grab.

With overdrive engaged, open road can be covered at well over the 100 mark without any apparent effort. It must be stated here, however, that the controlability of the car, which is excellent up to 110 m.p.h., when approaching its maximum is not so good, and between 110 and 120 road surfaces and side winds have adverse effects on the handling.

The performance of the car is such as to make it the fastest production car available at its price today. Maximum speed is 118.5 m.p.h. with the best one-way time of 120 exactly (7.5 secs. over the flying quarter mile). The 0 to 60 time is now 9.8 secs., whilst 30 m.p.h. is reached in 3.2 secs. and 50 m.p.h.

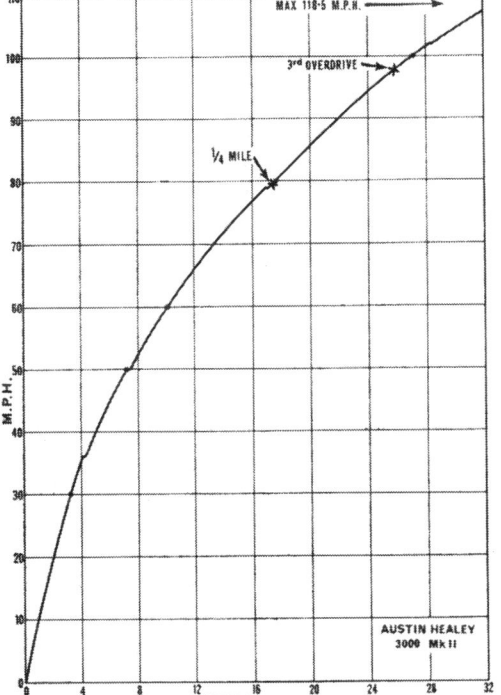

ACCELERATION GRAPH

SPECIFICATION AND PERFORMANCE DATA

Car Tested: Austin-Healey 3000 Mark 2 occasional four-seater. Price £1,064 including P.T. Extras on test car: overdrive, heater, wire wheels, radio.

Engine: Six cylinders, 83.36 mm. x 88.9 mm. (2,912 c.c.). Pushrod operated overhead valves. 9.03 to 1 compression ratio. 130 b.h.p. at 4,750 r.p.m. Twin HS6 semi-downdraught SU carburetters. Lucas coil and distributor.

Transmission: Single dry plate Borg and Beck 10 ins. clutch. Four-speed gearbox with synchromesh on upper three ratios with remote gear lever. Laycock-de Normanville overdrive. Open Hardy Spicer propeller shaft. Hypoid rear axle.

Chassis: Box section pressed steel frame. Independent front suspension by wishbones and coil springs with anti-roll torsion bar. Cam and peg steering gear, 14 to 1 ratio. Rigid rear axle on semi-elliptic springs with anti-sway bar. Hydraulic lever type shock absorbers. Girling hydraulic brakes, 11¼ ins. discs front, 11 ins. drums rear. Knock-on 4J wire wheels fitted 5.90 x 15 ins. tyres.

Equipment: 12 volt lighting and starting. Speedometer, rev. counter, oil pressure, water temperature and fuel gauges. Windscreen washer. Flashing indicators. Extra: heater and radio.

Dimensions: Wheelbase, 7 ft. 8 ins. Track (front), 4 ft. 0¾ in.; (rear), 4 ft. 2 ins. Overall length, 13 ft. 1½ ins. Width, 5 ft. 0¼ in. Turning circle, 35 ft. Weight, 1 ton, 1 cwt.

Performance: Maximum speed, 118.5 m.p.h. Best one way speed, 120 m.p.h. Speeds in gears: direct top, 102 m.p.h.; overdrive 3rd, 98 m.p.h.; 3rd, 79 m.p.h.; 2nd, 50 m.p.h.; 1st, 36 m.p.h. Standing quarter-mile, 17.5 secs. Acceleration: 0-30 m.p.h., 3.2 secs.; 0-50 m.p.h., 7.3 secs.; 0-60 m.p.h., 9.5 secs.; 0.80 m.p.h., 17.8 secs.; 0-100 m.p.h., 27.2 secs.

Fuel Consumption: 15-18 m.p.g.

scuttle shake had no apparent effect on the handling of the car—it was just annoying. This appears to be a characteristic of this model.

Fuel consumption was not bad at all and figures of 15 m.p.g. and 20 m.p.g. were recorded under different conditions, the overall consumption working out at a fraction over 17 m.p.g. Despite the large capacity sump, oil consumption was negligible.

The general impression gained of this car is that it is a first-class all-rounder. It is comfortable, relatively quiet and can be driven slowly with as much enjoyment as it can be driven quickly. For the man who wants a big car with plenty of power, the Austin-Healey 3000 Mark 2 fills the bill admirably.

takes 7.3 secs. The most impressive figure, however, is the 0-80, which is 17.8 secs.—this gives a very useful turn of acceleration. The 100, which tends to be an everyday feature of this car, takes just over 27 secs. These figures show a big improvement over the earlier 3000.

Whilst taking these figures, the following speeds in gears were used: first, 36 m.p.h.; second, 50 m.p.h. (into the red); third, 80 m.p.h. (into the red); third overdrive, 95 m.p.h.; fourth, 102 m.p.h. If speed proved the essence, for road use speeds of 30 m.p.h., 45 m.p.h., 70 m.p.h., 90 m.p.h. and 100 m.p.h. were more than adequate, for there was no advantage in going into the red.

The type of gear change employed made an appreciable difference to the performance figures and when one waited for the synchromesh the acceleration figures generally suffered by a second or so.

The much maligned handling of the 3000 proved, in fact, to be quite tolerable. Corners could be taken in grand style and the rear end had to be pushed out with a twitch of the wheel, but only needed the smallest fraction of opposite lock to bring it to order. The suspension gave a pleasant ride without the harsh characteristics normally found in a sports car. In the wet, a certain amount of discretion was needed but no more than any other car with three litres to propel it. The steering was perhaps a little heavy and the slightest bit remote, but it afforded excellent straight-line running manners. The castor return action was heavy but not aggressively so.

A criticism which must be made is the scuttle shake which sets in under certain conditions—namely, under power and fast cornering. Initially, I had attributed this shake to kick-back and judder on the steering but, on investigation, it proved to be caused by the lack of rigidity in the scuttle. It must be stated that this

AUSTIN-HEALEY 3000 MARK 2

THE AUSTIN HEALEY 3000—the "big Healey"—has held a high place in the affection of keen drivers for a long time: since the introduction of the original model it has enjoyed a reputation as a rugged, enduring sort of high performance sports car.

The latest in the long line of Austin-Healeys retains that impression of rugged strength, but, with it, has acquired rather more comfort than is possessed by some other cars of similar performance. With a maximum speed in overdrive top gear of comfortably over 120 m.p.h., it is an extremely fast car by any standards: the suspension gives a firm ride, and driver and passenger alike are conscious of sitting very close to the ground. Thick carpets, wind-up windows and "convertible top", as opposed to a hood, give the occupants a feeling of well-being which seems foreign to such a car.

The engine in this machine is the six-cylinder B.M.C. 3-litre unit of 2,912 c.c. with, in the Mark 2 Healey, a compression ratio of 9 to 1 and a power output of 136 b.h.p. at 4,750 r.p.m. This is mated to a four-speed and reverse gearbox with overdrive on 3rd and top

gears, and synchromesh on the upper three ratios. Suspension is entirely conventional, being independent, with coil springs at the front, and using semi-elliptic leaf springs at the rear.

The engine is extremely smooth, and the car can be driven in a really gentlemanly manner. Idling is smooth and reliable, and the considerable punch of 136 b.h.p. is delivered smoothly, with a steady "flow" of power throughout the engine speed range. It is an extremely flexible unit, and the car will potter along at 20 m.p.h. in top gear: only depression of the loud pedal and the flick of the overdrive switch is then necessary for brisk acceleration right up to 120 m.p.h. to be provided.

The gearbox now has its ratios selected by means of a centrally-mounted lever of traditional type and usual mounting, rather than the floor-mounted fitting used in earlier models. The lever is now comfortably placed, and falls easily into the hand, but the gearbox itself is spoiled by rather weak synchromesh: additionally, second gear is rather too low, and leaves a wide gap between 2nd and 3rd speeds. Overdrive was, on the test car, rather reluctant to

engage on 3rd gear, but was entirely satisfactory on top. The clutch is light, and the pedals are suitably arranged for "heel-and-toe" gear changing.

As we have said above, the suspension provided a ride which is firm to the point of harshness, and over rough surfaces the car hops about considerably. The ground clearance is rather too slight for fast motoring on any but first-class roads: the exhaust pipes scraped the ground on several occasions during the test, even at modest speeds, in country lanes which other cars have found far from rough. On the credit side, however, the driver retains a delightful feeling of being at one with the car, and from the performance standpoint the ride smooths out at high speed.

On this model, designated the "Sports Convertible", considerable trouble has been taken to provide occasional seats in the rear which are of real value as passenger accommodation. This endeavour has met with success, but it has meant that the driving position is a little cramped, even for a driver of average height and build. Although sufficient seat adjustment is available to make the legs comfortable, one remains rather too close to the wheel. All the controls are handily placed, however, and can be reached without contortions. The lateral support afforded by the seats could be much improved.

The instruments are placed in a nacelle immediately in front of the driver.

A rev.-counter reading to 6,000 r.p.m., and "red-lined" at 5,200 r.p.m., is matched by a speedometer reading to 120 m.p.h. It is distinctly unusual to find a car which is endowed with a maximum speed in excess of that to which the speedometer will read! Flanking these two large dials are a combined oil pressure/water temperature gauge, and a fuel contents gauge; warning lights are provided for head-lamp main beams and ignition charge, as well as for the flashing direction indicators which are controlled, in delightfully "vintage" style, by a switch mounted on the steering wheel boss. There is, unfortunately, no provision made for flashing the head-lights, which must be physically turned on by a "pull and twist" switch. The handbrake, which is not of "fly-off" type, is fitted between the driver's seat and the transmission tunnel, where it is occasionally inaccessible.

The whole of the interior is thickly carpeted, and the occasional rear seats are properly upholstered, with ample leg-room for two children. Visibility with the top erected is not as good as it might be: one sits very low down in the car, and forward vision is impeded noticeably by the rather high bonnet line, the parked screenwipers, and by the upper part of the steering wheel rim. An absence of transparent quarter panels in the hood seriously impedes rearward vision.

The test car was a hard-worked example, and had covered some 19,000 miles when it came into our hands. Thus it was not surprising to find several rattles and squeaks. The doors, however, closed well, and the car was waterproof in wet weather.

The brakes are the popular disc and drum combination, with $11\frac{1}{4}$ in. discs on the front wheels and 11 in. drums at the back. No servo is fitted as standard, although one is available as an option: without it, however, firm, powerful and progressive braking is provided for only light pedal pressure. The car's roadholding, despite an unfortunate reputation which it seems to have acquired for no very apparent reason, is in fact excellent. Directional stability at very high speed needs careful attention, but in other respects this big, powerful car can be driven hard with relative ease. It is, in fact, at its best on long, fast sweeping curves, when all four wheels will slide gently and controllably. Full use of the acceleration from rest promotes a good deal of axle tramp and wheel spin, while emerging quickly from tight corners also tends to get things moving at the back. Wheelspin in the wet is, understandably, readily provoked.

The acceleration itself is outstanding: its mean time of 16.75 seconds for the standing quarter-mile, together with a time from rest to 60 m.p.h. of well under ten seconds presents a picture of a very powerful car indeed: these figures could be improved considerably if the axle tramp at take-off could be eliminated. Acceleration from a standstill to 100 m.p.h. takes only 23.5 seconds—a time lapse at the end of which several medium-sized family cars are sometimes hard put to it to be travelling at 60 m.p.h.! Three figure speeds can be encompassed in each of the three upper ratios—overdrive third, direct and overdrive top gears. Once under way, easy 100 m.p.h. cruising speeds can be adopted at only 4,000 r.p.m. in overdrive top, leaving well over 1,000 revs. in hand and leaving the car completely easy: a machine with a very long stride, this. Travelling at 118 m.p.h.—4,500 r.p.m. in overdrive top—covers the ground with great celerity, but prolonged use of this sort of speed caused the oil pressure to start dropping, suggesting that for the man who likes to travel really fast an oil-cooler would be a worthwhile investment.

At high speed there is some scuttle shake on rough surfaces: patches of the M1 which have yet to recover fully from last winter's frosts induced this condition quite readily. Further, it is extremely warm in the driving compartment with the hood raised, and the opening quarter lights do little to alleviate this. The demister system is efficient, the lights powerful: a great improvement would be effected by the use of two-speed windscreen wipers.

SPECIFICATION AND PERFORMANCE DATA

Austin-Healey 3000 Mark 2 Sports Convertible. Price: £865, plus £180 15s. 4d. P.T.=£1,045 15s. 4d.

Engine: Six-cylinder, 83.36×89 mm. (2,912 c.c.). Compression ratio 9 : 1, 136 b.h.p. at 4,750 r.p.m. Twin SU HS6 carburettors; push rod operated overhead valves.

Transmission: Four-speed and reverse gearbox with synchromesh on upper three forward ratios and overdrive on 3rd and 4th. Central floor-mounted control. Single dry-plate clutch.

Suspension: Front, independent with wishbones, coil springs and stabilising bar. Rear, semi-elliptic leaf springs and anti-sway bar. Tyres: 5.90×15.

Brakes: Front, $11\frac{1}{4}$ in. discs; rear, 11 in. drums.

Equipment: 12-volt lighting and starting. Self-parking windscreen wipers. Windscreen washers. Speedometer, rev.-counter, oil pressure, fuel contents and water temperature gauges. Flashing direction indicators. Heating, demisting and ventilating equipment. Overdrive. Radio. Knock-on wire wheels.

Dimensions: Overall length 13 ft. $1\frac{1}{2}$ in.; overall width 5 ft. $0\frac{1}{2}$ in.; overall height 4 ft. 2 in. Ground clearance $4\frac{1}{2}$ in. Turning circle 35 ft. Weight 2,375 lb.

Performance: Maximum speed 122.1 m.p.h. (mean), 124.2 m.p.h. (best). Speeds in gears: 1st, 38 m.p.h.; 2nd, 55 m.p.h.; 3rd, 82.5 m.p.h.; overdrive 3rd, 101 m.p.h.; 4th, 110 m.p.h. Acceleration; 0–30 m.p.h., 3.4 sec.; 0–40, 4.0 sec.; 0–50, 6.0 sec.; 0–60, 9.1 sec.; 0–70, 12.9 sec.; 0–80, 15.4 sec.; 0–90, 20.2 sec.; 0–100, 23.5 sec. Standing quarter-mile: 16.75 sec. Fuel consumption: 17–19 m.p.g.

AUSTIN HEALEY'S REDOUBTABLE BULLDOG

ROAD IMPRESSIONS

English as "tea and crumpets", the revamped Austin Healey 3000 Mk2A has picked up a few Americanisms.

By CHRIS BECK

SIDEWAYS, ever sideways. This was the result of too much clog, too much lock into too much corner in the famous 100 series Austin Healeys that were familiar on Australian roads in the middle and late 1950s.

But the latest piece of big sports car machinery to come from this famed Longbridge lineage, the Austin Healey 3000 Mk 2A, a direct descendant of the 100 series, has had its suspension reworked, and so tamed this inherent lateral slippage to a point which now makes it almost conventional.

The older type Healeys were interesting, challenging cars to drive, and really needed to be driven; in every sense of the word. They were popular cars in this country until the early sixties, when suddenly, for some unknown reason, the demand for these highly desirable cars dwindled to a trickle. Now if you want one you virtually have to import it.

Recently a Sydney firm of sports car dealers, P. and R. Williams Pty Ltd, anticipated an upswing in the sales of big sports cars and made a speculative gamble by importing two of the latest Healeys, to feel out the market.

One car was a completely standard unit fitted with wire wheels, while the other had an overdrive as an optional extra. Not having driven a "big" Healey for some time and because SCW had not had a story on the latest model, I hot-footed it down to the dealers. A few well-placed words to the company's sales manager and everything was set for a road impressions run in the more expensive, overdrive, model of the two cars.

Next day I called to pick up the car and the last thing I heard as I drove away from the showroom was a hoarse salesman's voice pleading: "Don't take it above 3500 rpm in the gears." It was not necessary to exceed this limit, and I did not, but acceleration was still neck-snappingly good. Above 1700 rpm acceleration in all gears seemed so constant that one felt that the torque curve must be plateau-like. Delivering a lusty 130 bhp net at 4750 rpm the six cylinder 2.9 litre BMC C-series engine has a maximum torque output of 167 ft/lb at 3000 rpm. Compression ratio is high by Australian standards at 9.03 to 1 and the engine "pinked" low in the rev range and tended to run-on a little.

One of the main changes in this model from the Mk 2 is that the latter's three 1.5 in SU carburettors are replaced by two 1.75 in units, which will make the engine tuner's job easier. This really was the only major engine modification undertaken on the latest models.

When working, the noises of the four bearing motor — the thresh of the rocker and valve gear, the hiss of the carburettors and the throaty throb of the exhaust — mingle to produce a blood-stirring automotive symphony.

Ideally spaced ratios make the remote shift gearbox a delight to use and fairly fast shifts can be executed with precision. Only the stiffness of the new car seemed to hinder what would have otherwise been extremely rapid changes. Downward shifts, from fourth to third gear only, present a few problems as the gate seems to stop it falling into position — even double declutching does not help.

Sitting atop the seven inch chromium plated gear-lever is a patterned plastic ball - knob. Operating on third and top gears only, the Laycock de Normanville overdrive is excellent for the driver with a conscience and a heavy foot, and with its use the car would be easy to cruise around the 100 mph mark all day long — if the roads permitted — without harming the engine.

Clutch operation is by a single 10 inch dry plate unit which left little to be desired. The pedal needed to be depressed to different depths as take up varied right throughout the rev range.

Eleven inch disc brakes on the front and unfinned cast 11 inch drums on the rear take care of the car's stopping needs and effectively hauled it down from 80 mph (or 3500 rpm in top/overdrive), the highest speed attained during our run. A brake pedal sponginess, sometimes associated with discs, could be felt and the travel seemed a little more than in similar cars fitted with this form of braking; then again, of course, the system may have only needed adjusting.

Handling, as we said earlier, is a great improvement on earlier model Healeys and al-

Not a good-looking car by any means, the latest Healey retains the basic body lines of its predecessors.

though it is a little tricky when cornering near the limit, it does not spring any surprises. It becomes easily predictable with familiarity. But I couldn't help feeling that if you overstepped the mark through a corner and lost the car, there would be very little you could do to rectify the matter.

Like most English sports cars limit handling is the familiar initial understeer/final oversteer combination which can be quite tricky because the car is well on the way before you realise it. Judiciously used, the car's excess power can push it through a corner in many different ways and in varying attitudes — tail out or more lock. Once you have learned knack, power becomes a dominating factor in hard cornering and the sideways technique produces a rather queer sensation in such a large and heavy sports car.

Styling, to put it bluntly, would never win a designer's award and probably is not intended to. It is incongruous, bulbous and out of date by about seven years. Still the American and English sports car buying public must love the rugged, typically "John Bull" lines. Perhaps one of the primary reasons for the cars enduring success is that it has not undergone a major body change since the introduction of the original 100 series. Minor changes have been made over the years — different grills, a new bonnet with a small air intake has been fitted and many other unobtrusive details — but the basic form remains.

Maybe Americans do not like wrestling with hood ribs and soft tops in sudden rainstorms. This is the impression I gained after trying BMCs latest innovation for the 3000 — an American-type pull-up and clip convertible hood. When not in use it folds neatly and is stowed behind the two small rear passenger seats. Really suitable only for children, these seats could only be used to carry an average sized adult short distances.

For better weather-proofing, wind-up windows with quarter-lights replace those terrible unslidable, sliding side curtains on earlier models. Window winders, door handles and pulls are all chromed cast metal.

The dash panel is straightforward. There is a Smiths 120 mph speedometer on the right of the adjustable steering column, with on the left a 6000 rpm tachometer, redlined at 5250. Both were markedly free of flutter. To the right of the speedometer is a quarter-scale electric fuel gauge which tells one the contents of the 12 gallon petrol tank. On the left of the tachometer is a combined oil pressure and water temperature gauge. A spring spoked, 12 in diameter, plastic rimmed steering wheel is situated just short of the straight-arms position and the blinker light mechanism and the horn button are housed in the boss. Even by altering both the seat and the steering column I could not find a comfortable straight arms driving position. In the Healey tradition pedals are offset and pressures are fairly firm. The well-designed bucket seats provide excellent lateral support and are adjustable so that even a six-footer would have ample leg room.

In circuit racing the car would be completely outclassed, but that it is fast and tough is evident from its magnificent performances in high speed European rallies. On special stages and timed hill climbs it consistently whips all opposition, but this year the cars have been troubled by Ford Falcon Sprints fitted with a 4.2-litre V8 motor. As a fast, able-to-take-it car, it is hard to see why the popularity of the Austin Healey 3000 Mk 2A has diminished to such an extent in Australia.

Since we drove the Austin Healey 3000 Mk 2A — to once again enunciate its full and correct title — it has been purchased by well-known Sydney architect Andrew Findlay. At last reports he was learning to master that lateral slip and is as pleased as punch with the silver-blue and white car which is as British as tea and muffins or cricket on the village common on Saturday afternoons. It is the type of car I would like to own if I had a Georgian manor house, a stable of polo ponies and a dozen tweed jackets with leather elbow inserts.　　　　#

An unfamiliar insignia to Australians. This rear badge is often the only thing seen of the car by competitors in European rallies.

Austin-Healey 3000 Mk. III

PRICES

	Basic	Total (inc. P.T.)		
	£	£	s	d
Austin-Healey 300. Mk. III Sports Convertible	915	1,106	3	9

Extras (including P.T.)

Overdrive	£60 8 4
Wire wheels	£30 4 2
Fresh-air heater	£18 14 7
Adjustable steering column	£2 8 4
Tonneau cover	£12 1 4
Leather upholstery	Price not available

A YEAR and a half ago the Austin-Healey 3000 became a sports convertible with added comfort and refinement as its main features. Today B.M.C. go further along these lines by announcing the Mark III version with a more luxurious interior, better exhaust silencing and a 12 per cent increase in power. To cope with the extra performance, servo brakes are standard equipment. Externally the car is unchanged, but the price in Britain has been increased from £1,046 to £1,106.

The most obvious difference in the interior of the car is the facia design, now changed from the functional layout of earlier models to a symmetrical arrangement of wooden panels with a central console merging with the transmission tunnel. In front of the driver, on the walnut-veneered panel, are the speedometer and an electronic rev coun-

ter, visible through the spring-spoked steering wheel, and also the petrol gauge, water thermometer and choke control. On the passenger side is a glove box with a lockable lid.

Ignition and other switches are on a small strip on the console with the heater controls above them. Below the switch panel is a standard radio aperture and the speaker grille, blanked off when a radio is not fitted. Lower edges of the facia are finished with a plated bead, and the console is covered in black leathercloth.

The same arrangement of separate bucket seats at the front and miniature bucket seats for children in the back is retained. But the appearance of the trim is improved by fluting the centre panels of the seats with a new embossed Ambla two-way stretch leathercloth, giving the appearance of hand-tooled leather. Real leather upholstery is available at extra cost.

Suitcases and large objects carried on the back seats of earlier 3000s balanced precariously on the uneven platform

provided by the half-seats. Now those owners who normally travel two up will appreciate the new design of the rear seat backrest, which is made to double out forwards to form a large, flat, carpet-covered platform over the rear seats. Two sturdy bolts underneath its forward edge hold it firmly in place. A further addition is a small companion-box built into the armrest between the front seats.

Two engine modifications have increased power output from 136 b.h.p. (gross) at 4,750 r.p.m. to 154 b.h.p gross (148 b.h.p. net) at 5,250 r.p.m. One is a camshaft with longer dwell, which besides providing better cylinder filling has the advantage of giving the tappets an easier time. Secondly, the two 1·75in. HS6 S.U. carburettors fitted to the Mark II Healey have been replaced by a pair of larger HD8 2in. instruments. While the main gain in power has been at the top end of the speed range, it will be seen from the power curve that torque, which determines the accelerative ability, is much

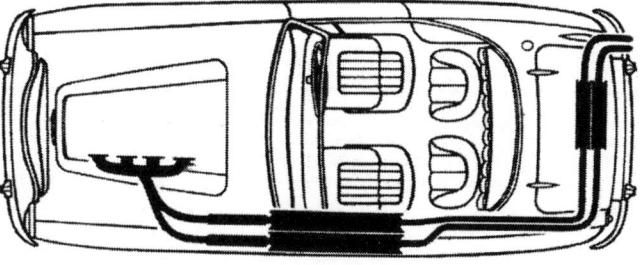

Layout of the new dual exhaust system

Below: New facia with walnut panels and centre console.

Right: Only external engine change is the substitution of larger S.U. carburettors

improved above 1,700 r.p.m. or 35 m.p.h. in top gear.

A short drive in a Mark III showed that the reduced exhaust noise increased the impression of power. In fact, the new dual exhaust system, made necessary by impending restrictions in the U.S.A. which could well be extended to this country, absorbs no more power than the old system. The gross power output figure was achieved with the new exhaust system fitted on the test bed but without fan and dynamo. Dual cast-iron manifolds are used and flexible down pipes lead the gases to a pair of straight-through silencers mounted amidships outside the left chassis side member. The dual tail pipes then follow the line of the side member and turn across beneath the tail of the car, where

the gases pass through dual expansion boxes.

A further improvement, which gives lighter clutch operation, is the adoption of a 9·5in. Borg and Beck diaphragm spring clutch. This modification was actually introduced some time ago to bring the Austin-Healey 3000 into line with other B.M.C. cars fitted with the C-series engine.

These changes confirm the Austin-Healey 3000 Mark III as a comfortable, high-speed touring car which will hold its own with most things on the road. The ruggedness of this model is a by-word—it is the only British model ever to have won the destructive Liège-Rome-Liège Rally—and its lines have a quality which should appeal to a buyer who likes to keep a car for several years.

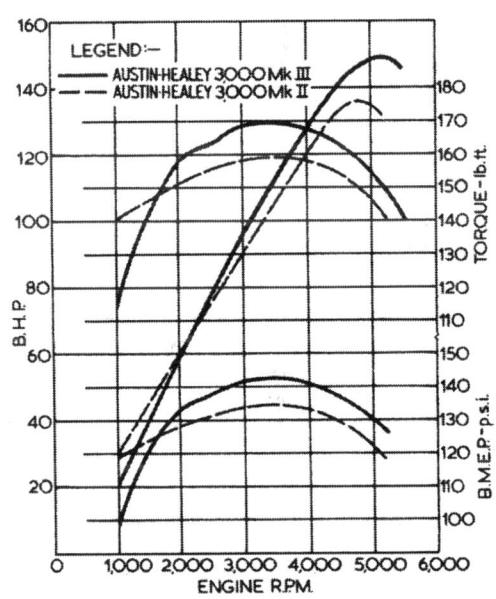

Gross performance curves for the new engine compared with the old

Specification

ENGINE (front-mounted, water-cooled)

No. of cylinders ...	Six in-line
Bore ...	83·4mm (3·28in.)
Stroke ...	89mm (3·5in.)
Displacement ...	2,912 c.c. (178 cu. in.)
Valve operation ...	Overhead, pushrods and rockers
Compression ratio	9·0 to 1
Max. b.h.p. (net) ...	148 at 5,250 r.p.m.
Max. b.m.e.p. (net)	140·2 p.s.i. at 3,500 r.p.m.
Max torque (net)	165·2 at 3,500 r.p.m.
Carburettors ...	Twin S.U. HD8
Fuel pump ...	S.U. electric
Tank capacity ...	12 Imp. gallons (54·5 litres)
Sump capacity ...	12·75 pints (10 litres)
Oil filter ...	Tecalemit or Purolator full-flow
Cooling system ...	Centrifugal pump, fan and thermostat, pressurized to 7 p.s.i.
Battery ...	12 volt, 57 amp. hr.

TRANSMISSION

Clutch ...	Borg and Beck diaphragm spring single dry plate, 9·5in. dia.
Gearbox ...	Four-speed, synchromesh on 2nd, 3rd and top; central floor change. Optional Laycock de Normanville overdrive

		Standard	Overdrive
Overall gear ratios	OD Top	—	3·14
	Top	3·55	3·91
	OD 3rd	—	5·12
	3rd	4·11	4·74
	2nd	7·73	8·05
	1st	10·21	11·26
	Rev	13·13	14·54
Final drive ...	Hypoid bevel 3·55 (3·91 with OD)		

CHASSIS

Brakes ...	Girling hydraulic, vacuum servo-assisted. Front discs, 11·25in. dia.; rear drums, 11in. dia.; 2·25in. wide shoes
Suspension: front	Independent, coil springs and wishbones, anti-roll bar
Suspension: rear	Live axle, half-elliptic leaf springs, Panhard rod
Dampers ...	Armstrong lever arm type
Wheels ...	Ventilated steel disc, 4in. wide rims
Tyre size ...	5·90—15in.
Steering ...	Cam and peg
Steering wheel ...	Three-spoke, 17in. diameter
Turns, lock to lock	3

DIMENSIONS

Wheelbase ...	7ft 8in. (234cm)
Track: front ...	4ft 0·75in. (124cm)
Track: rear ...	4ft 2in. (127 cm)
Overall length ...	13ft 1·5in. (400cm)
Overall width ...	5ft 0in. (152cm)
Overall height (unladen)	4ft 2in. (127cm)
Ground clearance (laden)	4·6in. (12cm)
Turning circle ...	35ft 7in. (10·8m)
Kerb weight ...	23cwt (2,548lb—1,145kg)

PERFORMANCE DATA

Top gear m.p.h. per 1,000 r.p.m. 20·72 (23·01 OD)
Torque lb. ft. per cu. in. engine capacity ....0·93
Brake surface swept by linings......... 383·5 sq. in.
Weight distribution: F, 49·3 per cent, R, 50·7 per cent.

Austin Healey 3000 mark III

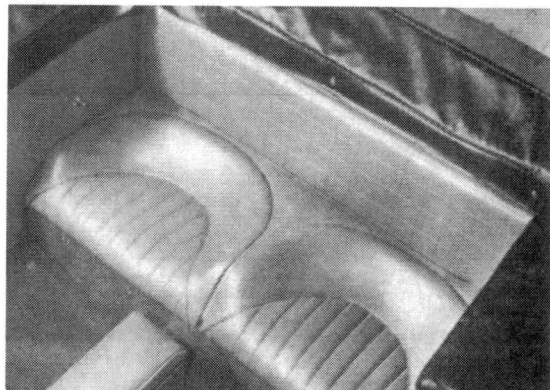

The cockpit is lavishly furnished now.
The central console incorporates minor controls,
radio installation, gearchange, ashtray and padded
glove-box, while the backrest of the 'jump-seat'
double-folds down to provide a carpeted luggage platform

...she looks the same, but under the skin there's still more power, still more luxury

YET another new and improved version of the rally-proved Austin-Healey 3000 was announced on 28 February. This is to be known as the Austin-Healey 3000 Sports Convertible Mark III and apart from a substantial increase in power output, the cockpit layout and trim has been completely redesigned to make this mile-eater even more luxurious than before.

The six-cylinder, 2,912 cc, C-Series engine now develops a full 150 b.h.p. (gross) at 5,250 r.p.m. compared with 136 b.h.p. at 4,750 r.p.m. previously, raising the maximum speed to around 125 m.p.h. with a corresponding boost in acceleration. Early production models have been timed to go from 0-80 m.p.h. in 15.5 seconds, yet smoothness and flexibility have not been impaired and fuel consumption figures are, if anything, slightly better than before. The power increase stems from the use of a new camshaft and the fitting of

twin HD8 S.U. carburetters, with 2 in. chokes, in place of the 1¾ in. S.Us. fitted to the Mark II. To provide comparable stopping power, the brakes (disc front, drum rear) are now equipped with vacuum servo assistance as standard, instead of as an optional extra.

In addition, a completely new silencing system has been developed, which actually contributes to the increase in power, but cuts the level of exhaust noise considerably, making the car much less tiring to travel in on a long journey. Several countries have (or are about to have) legislation governing vehicle noise and the new exhaust system meets all anticipated requirements.

The main feature of the interior trim is an entirely new fascia panel in polished wood veneers, with a central console, leathercloth covered, carrying switches and the optional radio installation. The console sweeps down between the seats and incorporates the

remote-control gear lever, a lidded ashtray and a glove-box, the padded lid of which forms an arm rest. On the passenger's side there is a large lockable glove compartment while in front of the driver is a 140 m.p.h. speedometer and an electric tachometer, with clear white figures on black dials, in addition to fuel, water temperature and oil pressure gauges. The ignition key now also operates the starter instead of a separate button being needed.

The bucket seats are luxuriously upholstered in 'Ambla' vinyl material with a smart new punched pattern on the centre panels, while the backrest of the occasional rear seat double-folds forwards to provide a flat and sturdy luggage platform. Leather upholstery is available as an optional extra.

The price in Great Britain is £915, plus purchase tax of £191 3s. 9d. total, £1,106 3s. 9d.

Power output has been raised to 150 bhp by means that include the fitting of larger carburetters.
The handsome new facia panel is finished in wood veneers, with black-faced instruments in front of the driver and a glove locker on the other side

more power, more comfort, less noise

Polished wood and four silencers for the Austin-Healey 3000

LEATHER coats and gauntlet gloves went out long ago for sports-car drivers. To be with it, the modern fun-motor has to feather-bed its driver and fan his passenger with gentle breezes from the heater; and all at a ton plus.

The new with-version of the Austin-Healey 3000 is known as the Mk. III and looks just like the Mk. II from the outside. They've even used the same picture for the cover of the latest catalogue; but the inside of the catalogue, like the inside of the car, reveals some notable changes; and the same goes for the technical bit at the end.

Power has gone up from 132 b.h.p. net to 149 b.h.p. net (with a little more torque as well), the noise level has come down with the aid of four cunningly contrived silencers, and light-footed braking no longer costs more because a vacuum servo is now standard. Inside the car, the former severely practical cockpit has been transformed into an equally practical driving compartment, with a central console to carry the switches, plus some polished woodwork on each side to house the instruments and a useful glove locker as well, adding a traditional touch of English luxury for the benefit of the 91.5 per cent of buyers who live overseas.

And the cost at home? £50 more on the price without tax, giving a basic figure of £915 and a total with British purchase tax of £1,106 3s. 9d.

Engine size and compression ratio are unchanged; the 13 per cent improvement in output comes from better breathing. Two HD8 S.U. carburetters with a choke diameter of 2 inches take the place of the former HS6 type with 1¾-in. chokes, and a new camshaft gives a total opening period of 252° for both inlets and exhausts compared with the previous 240°. The actual timing (with the previous figures in brackets) is: inlet opens 16° (10°) b.t.d.c.; inlet closes 56° (50°) a.b.d.c.; exhaust opens 51° (45°) b.b.d.c.; exhaust closes 21° (15°) a.t.d.c. Valve lift has been increased from 0.332 in. to 0.354 in.

Unlike many changes of this kind which boost the top-end performance at the expense of torque lower down, the new camshaft gives a useful improvement throughout the normal usable speed range; as the accompanying power curves of the Mk. II and Mk. III engines show, it is only below approximately 1,700 r.p.m. that there is any loss of torque.

Coinciding with these changes, much work has been put into reducing exhaust noise without loss of power. The latest system has been evolved in the light of West German and other European restrictions on exhaust noise which are likely to be followed by similar regulations in this country.

The new system has two pipes and four silencers—no easy matter to accommodate on a low-built sports car. The twin down-pipes

from the manifold go to a pair of silencers tucked away side by side below the driving compartment and then to a second pair of separate silencers housed across the car beneath the tail. Ground clearance remains at 4½ inches as before.

The only other mechanical change concerns the brakes, in which the vacuum servo, previously an extra, is standard.

There are lots of changes inside the convertible body. The 3000 is in fashion with a console connecting the transmission tunnel with its new facia board, to house the principal switches, heater controls and optional radio. The main instruments—speedometer, rev counter (now electrically operated), fuel gauge and combined thermometer and oil gauge—are still in front of the driver, now in a polished wood facia panel; a matching panel on the passenger's side holds a lockable glove box.

The console goes back between the seats and includes an ashtray and a neat combined arm rest and companion box with a magnetic catch. Other interior refinements include an improved type of vinyl upholstery material known as Ambla (leather is an optional extra) and a rearrangement of the rear squab so that it can be folded forward to form a luggage platform measuring 19¼ in. by 36½ in. when the occasional seats are not required.

A road test of the new model will be published shortly. The Mk. II clocked a mean speed of 116 m.p.h. and reached 100 m.p.h. from rest in 29.4 sec. The Mk. III should do even better—and with more "hush".

Bigger S.U. carburetters and better breathing help to increase power from 132 to 149 b.h.p. The 3-litre C-series engine remains fundamentally unchanged. Comparative figures are shown in the graph (far right).

A Pressing Getaway . . .

● *Snap impressions showed several big improvements. The getaway seemed to press the squab more firmly in one's back than ever, and although there was no opportunity for proper tests in a mere 20-mile run, 120 m.p.h. came up on the clock remarkably quickly. The new silencers have subdued the exhaust system to a point at which the occupants are no longer conscious of an exhaust note when the car is closed, but this, in turn has emphasized the fact that this is far from a silent car mechanically; a few extra pounds (sterling and avoirdupois) of sound-deadening materials might have been a good thing to add to the new specification for full measure.*

Bodywise, the modifications seemed all to the good. Altogether the best "Big Healey" yet.

Room for the kids. Rear seats fold forward to give flat luggage platform.

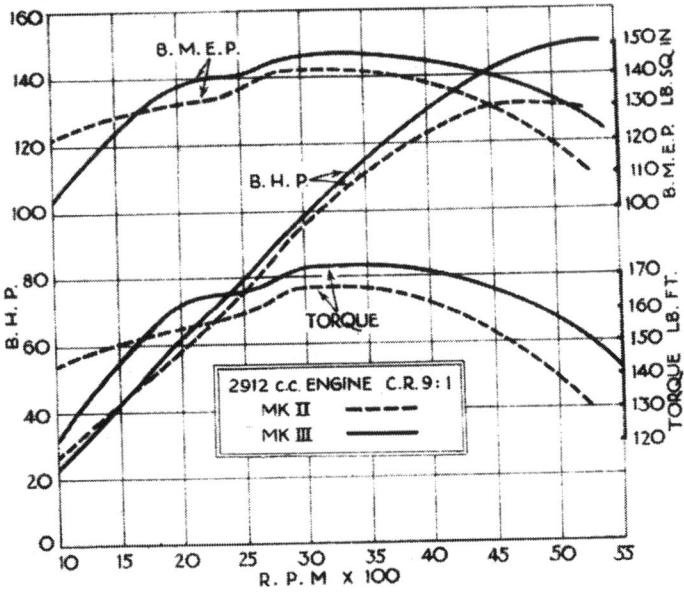

Bowing to the overseas buyers who want traditional British styling, the new Healey has a polished wood facia, central console and neat circular dials set in front of the driver.

IN BRIEF

ENGINE.—6 cyl., 83.36 mm. × 89 mm., 2,912 c.c.; o.h.v. (push rods); two S.U. HD8 carburetters; max. power, 149 b.h.p. net at 5,250 r.p.m.; max. torque, 173 lb. ft. at 3,000 r.p.m.

TRANSMISSION.—10-in. diaphragm-type, s.d.p. clutch; 4-speed gearbox with synchromesh on 2-3-4. Ratios (normal): 3.545, 4.644, 7.730 and 10.209; rev. 13.187. Ratios (with opt. Laycock-de Normanville overdrive): 3.909 (O/D 3.213), 5.120 (O/D 4.210), 8.052 and 11.257; rev. 14.541. Road speed in top gear at 1,000 r.p.m. 20.9 m.p.h. (with O/D: direct, 18.94 m.p.h.; O/D, 23.1 m.p.h.).

RUNNING GEAR.—Girling hydraulic brakes, disc-front/drum-rear with vacuum servo; coil and wishbone i.f.s. with anti-roll bar; semi-elliptic rear springs and Panhard rod; cam-and-peg steering; 5.90-15 Dunlop Road Speed tyres.

DIMENSIONS.—Length, 13 ft. 1½ in.; width, 5 ft. 0½ in.; turning circle, 35 ft.; weight 21¼ cwt. approx.

Number 13
MOTOR
TESTED
1301 MILES

" . . . a unique blend of vintage sports and modern GT . . . great fun to drive ".

PRICES
(including overdrive, wire wheels, heater as tested) £1,005 10s. plus purchase tax equals £1,223 10s. 1d. Price without extras (including p.t.) £1,106 3s. 6d.

AUSTIN - HEALEY
3000 Mk III

How they run . . .

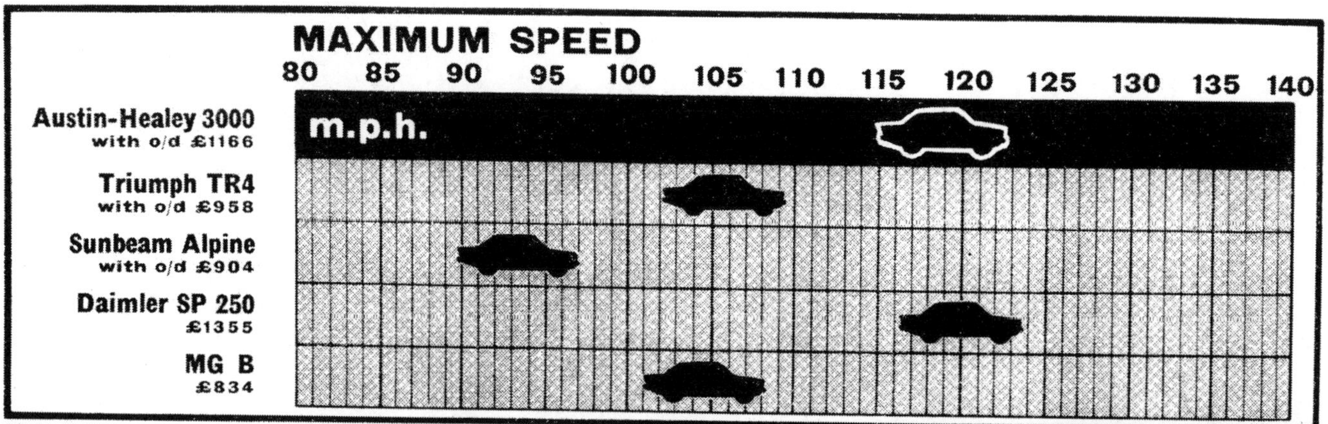

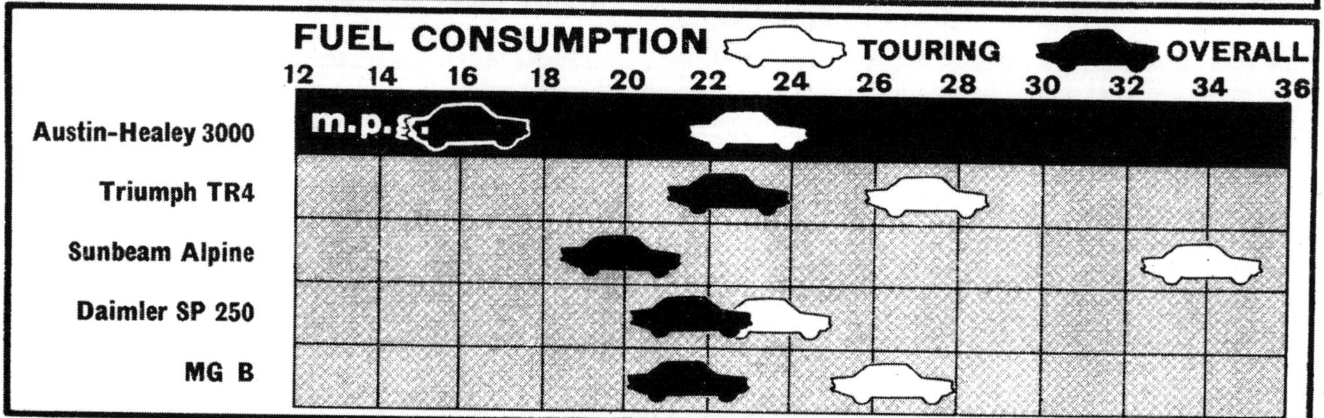

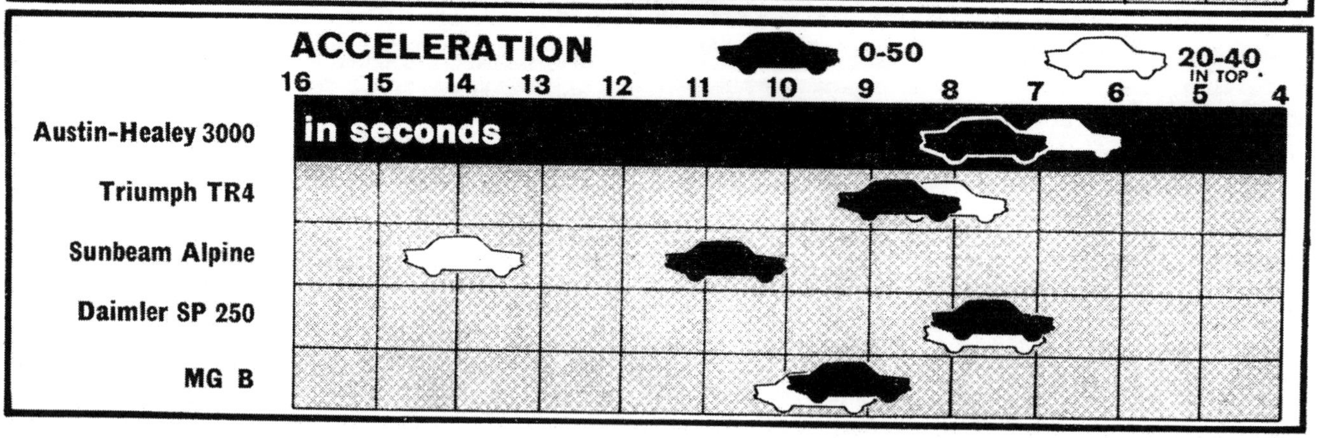

MAXIMUM SPEED

	80	85	90	95	100	105	110	115	120	125	130	135	140

m.p.h.

Austin-Healey 3000 with o/d £1166 — ~117

Triumph TR4 with o/d £958 — ~104

Sunbeam Alpine with o/d £904 — ~92

Daimler SP 250 £1355 — ~122

MG B £834 — ~103

FUEL CONSUMPTION — ☐ TOURING — ◼ OVERALL

	12	14	16	18	20	22	24	26	28	30	32	34	36

m.p.g.

Austin-Healey 3000 — overall ~16, touring ~23

Triumph TR4 — overall ~21, touring ~26

Sunbeam Alpine — overall ~19, touring ~34

Daimler SP 250 — overall ~20, touring ~24

MG B — overall ~21, touring ~27

ACCELERATION — ◼ 0-50 — ☐ 20-40 IN TOP

	16	15	14	13	12	11	10	9	8	7	6	5	4

in seconds

Austin-Healey 3000 — 0-50 ~8, 20-40 ~7

Triumph TR4 — 0-50 ~9, 20-40 ~8

Sunbeam Alpine — 0-50 ~11, 20-40 ~14

Daimler SP 250 — 0-50 ~8, 20-40 ~8

MG B — 0-50 ~10, 20-40 ~11

gets in the way. Even the passenger's grab handle has been replaced by a glove box. Gone too is the lovable bark. Two exhaust pipes and four silencers have subdued the noise to a pleasant grumble that is drowned at high speeds by the whirl of fan, intakes and wind.

Yet this is no cissy sports car. A top speed of 122.5 m.p.h. is fast by any standards and quite exceptional for £1,200. Moreover, it will accelerate to 120 m.p.h. in little more than a mile in satisfying surges that whip it across country at high average speeds. Handling and steering are by no means outstanding by modern standards but better than first acquaintance (and many old hands) would suggest and the car satisfies the sporting tradition by being great fun to drive even if it takes time and know-how to make firm friends.

In a nutshell, you now go much faster in greater (but by no means sumptuous) comfort on no more petrol—a fair return for long-term development.

MAKES and models come and go while the Big Healey still gathers momentum. With a production run reaching back 12 years to 1952, the car must surely be approaching the end of an unusually long and successful line that has bred international competition winners, earned a lot of dollars and, above all, provided relatively inexpensive high performance for enthusiasts throughout the world. In its latest form the combination of speed, refinement and character is still outstanding value.

In several easy stages, the Healey has matured over the years: it gained two more cylinders from the rationalized B.M.C. C-series engine, another gear, an extra 352 c.c., much more power and torque, better handling and brakes, more refinement and room, and various face lifts, until it reached the unique blend of vintage sports and modern GT in the Mk. III 3000 announced a month ago.

A little of the original Healey 100 still remains: the classic looks; firm ride; only marginal ground clearance; the vintage driving position and a take-off that few cars can equal regardless of price. In other respects it has mellowed with age reflecting the changing tastes of its ardent supporters—or perhaps a new, more sophisticated generation of sports car drivers. Popular demand has turned the original stark cockpit into a snug and fashionable office with polished wood on the facia and a dividing console down the middle that looks good but

Performance and Economy

THIS is the fastest production Austin-Healey yet made. Larger carburetters, a new camshaft and a more efficient (and quieter) exhaust system have raised the power of the 6-cylinder, 3-litre engine from 131 to 150 b.h.p. with a useful increase in torque above 1,700 r.p.m. Compared with the Mk. II car tested in April, 1963, it has gained nearly 7 m.p.h. in top speed (122·5 m.p.h.), knocked 6 secs. off the time needed to reach 100 m.p.h. (23.7 sec.) and pulls even better at low and moderate engine speeds. Sports cars do not usually attract lazy drivers but anyone who tires of changing gear can set it in top or third and motor smoothly on from 10 m.p.h. through traffic.

Surprisingly, this impressive performance has been achieved on less fuel, nearly all the steady-speed consumption figures showing a slight improvement. Only at very low r.p.m. when the big lazy engine is working below maximum efficiency is there a slight drop. High-speed motorway cruising is utterly relaxed if rather noisy, 4,000 r.p.m. corresponding to about 100 m.p.h. in overdrive top, so it is possible to amble along in the hundreds without any fear of overstressing the engine. Only when the tachometer needle approaches the red sector starting at 5,500 r.p.m. (the recommended rev. limit) do you begin to wince at the howl from beneath the bonnet, but there is seldom any need to use such high revs.

Flowing vintage lines and as fast as it looks: the latest Mk III will accelerate from a standstill to 100 m.p.h. and stop again in 29 seconds.

Performance figures

Test Data: World copyright reserved: no unauthorized reproduction in whole or part.

Conditions: Weather: Cold, calm and dry. (Temperature 40°F, Barometer 29.85 in. Hg.) Surface: Tarmacadam and concrete. Fuel: Super Premium (101 octane)

MAXIMUM SPEEDS

Mean of 4 runs (o/d top)	..	122.5 m.p.h.
Best one way ¼-mile	..	123.5
Direct top gear at 5,500 r.p.m.	..	114.0
O/d 3rd gear	..	..	..	104.0
3rd gear	..	..	..	85.0
2nd gear	..	..	..	52.0
1st gear	..	..	..	42.0

"Maximile" Speed: (Timed quarter mile after 1 mile accelerating from rest)

Mean	..	..	..	117.8
Best	..	..	..	120.0

ACCELERATION TIMES

0-30 m.p.h.	..	..	..	3.6 sec.
0-40	..	..	..	..	4.8
0-50	..	..	..	..	6.9
0-60	..	..	..	..	9.8
0-70	..	..	..	..	12.1
0-80	..	..	..	..	14.8
0-90	..	..	..	..	18.2
0-100	..	..	..	..	23.7
0-110	..	..	..	..	34.1

Standing quarter mile .. 17.0

	O/d		O/d	
	Top	Top	3rd	3rd
m.p.h.	sec.	sec.	sec.	sec.
20-40	9.0	6.0	5.5	4.3
30-50	10.5	6.8	6.4	5.1

AUSTIN - HEALEY 3000 Mk III

Twin pipes and a massive exhaust system look impressive but subdue the noise to a low growl. There is very little ground clearance beneath the silencers.

The spare wheel, held down by a rod and strap, steals a lot of boot room but there is enough space left for small cases or flexible bags. The two left-hand boxes fit behind the seats.

Our test car was an easy starter, although it would occasionally spit back through the twin 2-in. S.U. carburetters with a jerk if the choke was pushed home too soon after a cold start. There was pinking on premium grade petrol and the engine often ran on even if the throttle was blipped before switching off. Plenty of revs and clutch slip are needed to start on a 1 in 3 hill with the rather high first gear, and as an indication of the massive torque, 2nd will cope with a 1 in 4.

By absolute standards, the Healey is quite an expensive car to run, its overall fuel consumption of 17.7 m.p.g. representing a cost of £13 10s. per thousand miles on petrol at 4s. 9d. a gallon. During the first part of our test, it recorded an all-time high in oil consumption—about 45 miles to the pint. This was later rectified by B.M.C. who fitted new piston rings after the original ones were found to be excessively scuffed—possibly the result of incomplete running in.

Servicing demands are quite heavy too by modern greaseless standards, 13 points needing attention every 3,000 miles.

Transmission

AN unusually smooth-acting Laycock overdrive working on third and top gears gives six forward speeds to play with. Choice of ratios is never so critical when there is ample torque throughout the rev range, and five of the six are quite acceptable. The exception is second, which is so close to first that it is hard to detect any change of note when accelerating hard. The first three gears' maxima are about 42, 52 and 85

m.p.h. at 5,250 r.p.m.—mid-way through the tachometer's yellow warning sector. Something nearer 62 m.p.h. for second would seem to be a better gap filler. Overdrive third, 10 m.p.h. slower than direct top, is used more as an instant high town gear than an extra ratio when shifting through the box although we used all six gears when taking performance figures. Powerful but obstructive synchromesh works on the top three ratios, leaving accurate double-declutching to find first: most people settled for second instead—a point in favour of its low gearing. Unlike some sports cars on which the clutch is either in or out, the Healey's has a long travel and the gentle bite and smoothness of a touring car. What little whine there is from the gearbox and axle is soon drowned by other more aggressive noises.

Steering and handling

GIVEN sufficient practice and not a little nerve, it is possible to corner the Healey very fast indeed, but it is not the sort of car that you drive on the limit first time out. The steering

The narrow bonnet opening is crammed full of engine—a tuned version of the 2,912 c.c. C-series developing 150 b.h.p. Key to numbers: 1 brake reservoir, 2 coil, 3 distributor, 4 dip stick, 5 oil filler cap, 6 carburetters, 7 windscreen washer reservoir.

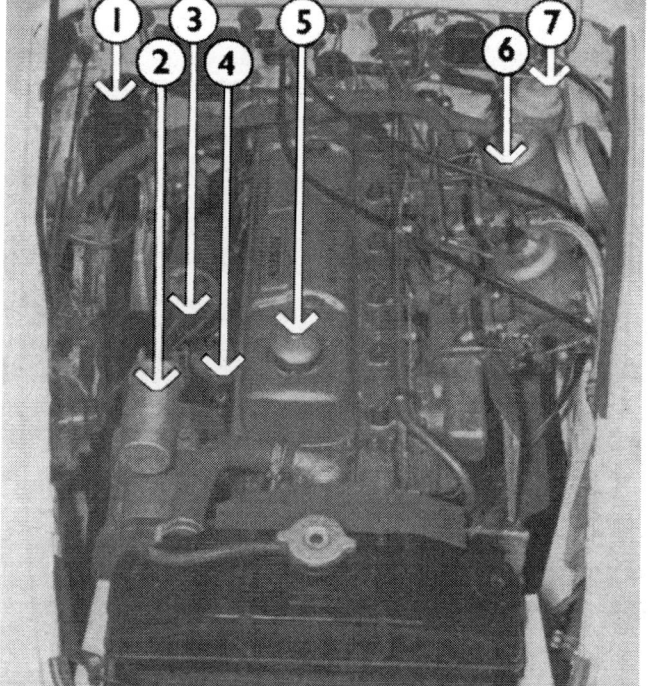

40-60	..	..	9.0	6.8	6.1	5.2
50-70	..	..	9.4	6.7	6.5	4.9
60-80	..	..	11.0	7.9	7.1	5.7
70-90	..	..	11.2	7.6	7.9	—
80-100	..	..	13.2	8.6	8.8	—
90-110	..		16.7	—	—	—
100-120	..		—	—	—	—

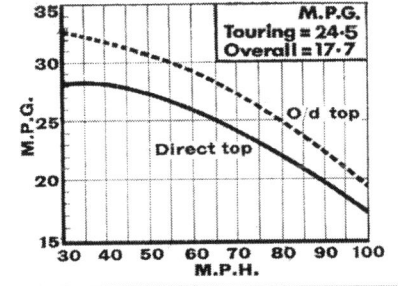

M.P.G.
Touring = 24·5
Overall = 17·7

O/d top
Direct top

HILL CLIMBING

At steady speed			lb/ton	
O/d top	..	1 in 12.1	(Tapley 235)
Top	..	1 in 7.0	(Tapley 317)
O/d 3rd ..		1 in 6.5	(Tapley 340)
3rd	..	1 in 5.4	(Tapley 412)
2nd	..	1 in 3.4	(Tapley 650)

FUEL CONSUMPTION

Total test distance	..	..	1,301 miles
17.7 m.p.g.		15.9 litres/100 km.

BRAKES

Pedal pressure, deceleration and equivalent stopping distance from 30 m.p.h.

lb.	g	ft.
25	35	86
50	65	46
75	90	33½
100	92	32½
Handbrake	35	86

STEERING

					ft.
Turning circle between kerbs:					
Left ..	..	..	..	..	32
Right	..	..	..	..	32
Turns of steering wheel from lock					
to lock ..	..	..	..	..	3¼

SPEEDOMETER

30 m.p.h.	..	..	..	1½% slow
60	..	..	..	1½% slow
90	..	..	..	2% fast
Distance recorder	..	..	3½% slow

WEIGHT

			cwt.
Kerb weight (unladen with fuel for approximately 50 miles)	..	..	23
Front/rear distribution	..	..	48/52
Weight laden as tested	..	..	26½

is averagely light and not particularly positive by sports car standards except when cornering quickly, when a delicate touch is needed on both the throttle and steering wheel, either of which can be used to direct the car. In this respect it is far removed from the typical understeering family saloon which remains stodgily stable with big sweeps of the wheel. This is not Healey technique and would soon land anyone who tried it in trouble. With a light throttle the steering is practically neutral but under power it reverts to oversteer and, in the extreme, a power slide although the vicious breakaway of earlier cars appears to have been cured: even in the wet, an impressive amount of torque can be turned on out of a sharp bend without sliding the tail. As a safety factor, lifting the throttle mid-way through a corner makes the front tuck in after a pause—like a front-wheel drive car in slow motion—by amounts depending on the speed and radius of the corner when indelicate opposite lock prevents the car from going sideways and tyre-scrub soon slows it down.

Firm suspension, which tends to twitch the car off course on roughish roads, emphasizes the need to concentrate quite hard to hold the right line when driving quickly. At lower speeds it just goes where it is aimed.

The old trouble of poor ground clearance is still there; you have to pick a careful path along rough tracks, and the right speed over hump-back bridges to avoid scraping the exhaust pipes. Even backing off a pavement ramp can make them touch the ground.

Big brakes (11¼ in. discs at the front, drums rear) need lots of push and a vacuum servo has now been standardized to take the he-man effort out of stopping. Most of the time the brakes felt powerful and reassuring but a front wheel locked before the best recorded stop of ·92g. The same locking brake probably accounted for the mild veering after being soaked by heavy rain, and twitching even in the dry when stopping from high speeds: we felt this was a peculiarity of our test car and not typical of the model. The handbrake would almost certainly have held on a 1 in 3 hill if another notch had been found by adjustment. It coped easily with 1 in 4.

Comfort and control

LIKE most good sports cars, the Healey has firm springing (independent coil and wishbone at the front and a leaf-sprung rear axle) that only feels unduly harsh over rough roads: sports car drivers will not complain. Two absurd failings mar the seats and driving position: the poor rearward adjustment which, despite a telescopic steering column, prevents drivers of any size from getting very far

The excellent hood can be erected without getting out, and it stows neatly in its own well.

New to the Mark III car are a wood veneer facia and central console with a small box.

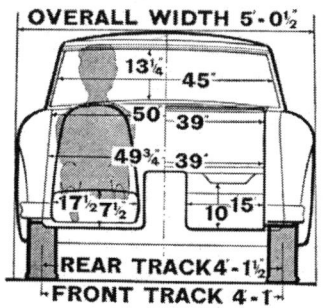

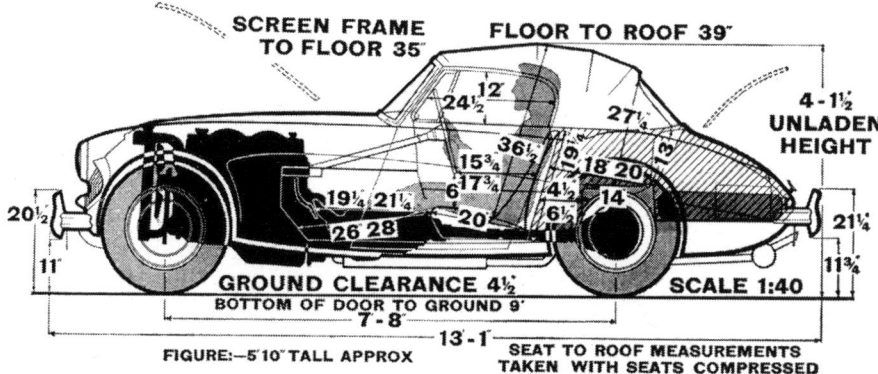

OVERALL WIDTH 5'-0½"

13¼ 45"

50 39"

49¾ 39"

17½ 7½ 10 15

REAR TRACK 4'-1½"

FRONT TRACK 4'-1"

SCREEN FRAME TO FLOOR 35"

FLOOR TO ROOF 39"

24½ 12

36½

15¾

17¾

19¼ 21¼

26 28

6¾

20

27½

18 20

4½ 14

6½

4-1½" UNLADEN HEIGHT

21¼

11¾

20½

11

GROUND CLEARANCE 4½"

BOTTOM OF DOOR TO GROUND 9"

7-8"

13-1"

SCALE 1:40

SEAT TO ROOF MEASUREMENTS TAKEN WITH SEATS COMPRESSED

FIGURE:—5'10" TALL APPROX

from the wheel if they want to; and the upright squab that compels a right-angled, elbows-out posture that most people did not like much although they soon got accustomed to it. A few extra shillings spent on longer runners and an adjustable squab angle would make far more people fit in greater comfort.

The combination of negligible body roll and good side support keeps you firmly in place when cornering hard: anyone in the back is so firmly wedged that no side-support is needed. On long journeys, the rear seats—little more than an upholstered ledge—are strictly for small children (a good excuse to retain a sports car *and* a growing family) and they are just tolerable for adults on short hops. Alternatively, the rear seat can be folded forward to form a useful luggage platform, supplementing a boot which is already half filled with spare wheel.

The low seating and large transmission hump/console have made the short gear lever rather high and it must be worked with the elbow raised and cranked. You soon get used to the position. The pedals are fairly comfortable but not very well placed for heel and toeing: many saloons are much better.

An easily erected and well fitting hood, wind-up windows and a heater make the Healey quickly adaptable to all weathers. Heavy rain revealed a small leak in the sealing which dripped cold water onto the gear lever. Otherwise, the inside is attractive and snug, air seepage rather than draughts giving the modest output of the heater plenty to fight on a cold day, but there is certainly never any need for the overcoats and gauntlets that were once essential sports-car wear. For such a low car, visibility is quite good, only the rear quarters of the hood making any objectionable blind spots. A large rear-view mirror on top of the scuttle gives a good view through a big plastic window and the lights are powerful if not outstanding.

There is no audible flapping of the taut hood but the noise rises with revs and speed until normal conversation ceases at about 75 m.p.h. and shouting is useless above 100 m.p.h. The optional radio would only be audible during fairly gentle driving, when a loud carburetter intake hiss can be heard above the woffle of the exhaust. Sound damping on the bulkhead would help to reduce this and other mechanical noises.

Fittings and Furniture

ALTHOUGH the new facia layout with its polished wood, neat dials and symmetrical switch gear looks neat and tidy, most drivers preferred the less stylish but more practical layout of the Mk. II car. The overdrive switch, for instance, which could formerly be flicked with a right-hand finger without lifting it from the wheel, is now grouped with four other toggle switches in the centre where it is easy to confuse with the wipers. On the other hand, it is now more logically placed near the gear lever.

Smallish dials for the almost accurate speedometer and rev counter are neatly calibrated but not angled towards the driver, making the top of the scales invisible. Well-fitted carpet covers the floor and vinyl cloth the seats, sides and the new central console which houses a radio and a small container for oddments. Its padded lid forms an armrest which got in the way of gearchanging so much that it was left permanently open. Any other luggage can be thrown behind the seats or, if small enough, locked in the passenger's cubby hole on the facia. Unlike the boot, the doors (stiff but self-supporting when open) cannot be locked, but the car can be immobilized by turning an electric master switch in the boot. There is no interior light; even worse, no headlamp flasher.

The B.M.C. safety belts are comfortable to wear and easy to adjust but only the anchorage points are standard fittings.

MAKE Austin-Healey • TYPE 3000 Mk III • MAKERS Austin Motor Co. Ltd., Longbridge, Birmingham.

ENGINE
Cylinders	6
Bore and stroke ..	83·36 mm. × 89 mm.
Cubic capacity ..	2,912 c.c.
Valves	O.h.v.
Compression ratio	9·03 : 1
Carburetter(s) ..	Twin S.U. HD8
Fuel pump ..	S.U. electric
Oil filter ..	Tecalemit or Purolator full flow
Max. power (gross)	150 b.h.p. at 5,250 r.p.m.
Max. torque (gross)	173 lb. ft. at 3,000 r.p.m.

TRANSMISSION
Clutch	Borg and Beck 9¼ in. single dry plate
Top gear (s/m) ..	3·545 (overdrive, 2·91)
3rd gear (s/m) ..	4·629 (overdrive, 3·81)
2nd gear (s/m) ..	7·341
1st gear	9·348
Reverse	12·021
Overdrive ..	Laycock-de Normanville electrically operated
Final drive ..	Hypoid bevel
M.p.h. at 1,000 r.p.m. in:—	
O/d. top gear ..	25·0
Top gear	20·5
O/d. 3rd gear ..	19·1

3rd gear	15·7
2nd gear	9·9
1st gear	6·05

MAINTENANCE
Sump	12¼ pints S.A.E. 30
Gearbox with overdrive ..	6¼ pints S.A.E. 30
Rear axle	3 pints S.A.E. 30
Steering gear ..	S.A.E. 90
Cooling system ..	18 pints (2 drain taps)
Chassis lubrication	Every 3,000 miles to 13 points
Ignition timing ..	10° B.T.D.C.
Contact breaker gap	0·014–0·016 in.
Sparking plug type	Champion UN12Y
Sparking plug gap	0·024–0·026 in.
Tappet clearances (cold) ..	Inlet 0·012 in.. exhaust 0·012 in.
Front wheel toe-in	1/16–1/8 in.
Castor angle ..	2°
Tyre pressures ..	20 lb. front, 25 lb. rear (fast driving, 25 lb. front, 30 lb. rear)

CHASSIS
Construction ..	Separate ladder frame

BRAKES
Type	Girling hydraulic, disc front, drum rear
Dimensions ..	11¼ in. front, 11 in. rear
Total friction area	112 sq. in. of lining working on 383 sq. in. rubbed area of discs and drums

SUSPENSION AND STEERING
Front	Independent coil and wishbone and an anti-roll bar.
Rear	Live rear axle located by Panhard rod and semi-elliptic leaf springs
Shock absorbers ..	Lever Armstrong
Steering gear ..	Cam and peg, ratio 15 to 1.
Tyres	Dunlop Road Speed 5·90-15

COACHWORK AND EQUIPMENT
Starting handle ..	Yes
Jack	Screw thread
Jacking points ..	4: beneath springs
Battery	Offside in boot
Number of electrical fuses ..	2
Indicators ..	Flashers, self cancelling
Screen wipers ..	Lucas electric DR3/A
Screen washers ..	Push button Tudor
Sun visors ..	None
Locks:	
With ignition key	Starter, boot and facia glove box
Interior heater ..	Smith fresh air (optional)
Extras	Heater, overdrive, wire spoke wheels, tonneau cover, leather seats, luggage carrier, whitewall tyres, etc.
Upholstery ..	Ambla vinyl
Floor covering ..	Fitted carpet
Alternative body types	None

The Healey's face-lifting over a decade has amounted to little, but weather protection at high speed is much improved

Austin-Healey 3000 Mark III

THE Austin-Healey 3000 is not a pretty sports car for pretty girls to drive, unless they stay within earshot of Knightsbridge or else possess the qualities that James Bond admires. In its Mark III form the car retains all the ruggedness that has made it a favourite among sportsmen during the past 11 years, but with the additional comfort of wind-up side windows. Servo assistance is now standard equipment for the braking system, and a pair of bigger HD8 SU carburettors combine with a new camshaft to raise the maximum power output to 150 bhp, resulting in spectacular performance up to 100 mph (in less than 23 seconds) and a maximum speed of 121 mph.

In all essentials the Healey is now a drop-head and not a roadster, but its sporting instincts are scarcely muted

This latest model is still a driver's car, feeling almost vintage so far as suspension and chassis design is concerned and demanding more concentration on control than is usual with the current run of high-performance models. Confidence thus comes with familiarity, and the potential of the Healey is clearly shown in the impressive list of competition successes in many different types of event.

Comfort and convenience

Seating is one of the very good features of the Healey, the two front seats being well padded and nicely shaped to support the body under hard cornering conditions. The upholstery, leather on our test car but normally 'Ambla' vinyl material, is punched on the centre panels to allow air to circulate, preventing too much body warmth on a hot day. The driving seat extends well back to allow straight-leg driving, but the steering wheel is still set near the body despite telescopic adjustment of the column.

There are two small, shaped seats in the back suitable for young children, and an adult could be inserted into this area for a short distance although with very little headroom if the hood is raised. When the seats are not being used the back folds flat to make a useful amount of room available for luggage; this is necessary for continental touring, for the big spoked spare wheel and the battery take up most of the usable space in the boot, leaving room for one small suitcase or a couple of hold-alls. There is no provision for locking the car, so valuables have to be locked in the fascia cubby hole or in the boot.

The fold-away hood merits high praise for ease of operation, erection taking but a few moments if there is a sudden downpour of rain. When stowed away the hood fits into a well and lies well down in the body-line, a cover being supplied to make a tidy job. The rear window zips into place and has to be three parts removed before the hood is stowed, so as to avoid damaging or distorting the clear plastic, and it is essential to re-secure the window before fastening the hood in its raised position, otherwise its tautness defeats the exercise. Two simple fasteners which batten the hood can be fixed by one person without assistance.

The rear window is usefully large and the mirror takes good advantage of the view, but when the hood is lowered the mirror is set too low and would be better suspended from the top rail or else on a vertical bar. The boot, which slopes rather sharply, is difficult to gauge for length when the car is reversed, but otherwise the all-round visibility is extremely good.

Under-bonnet accessibility is good, the bonnet aperture appearing narrow by modern standards but still offering good working space. Reversion to twin carburettors in the place of three has greatly simplified the process of tuning without sacrificing any power.

The Mark III version of the Healey is no more comfortable on the road than its predecessors, yet the many devotees who are loyal to the marque find sufficient compensation for this in the abundance of power which takes the car so far ahead of its price-rivals. The electric petrol pump in the boot clicks loudly enough to annoy new acquaintances; the carburettor intakes hiss louder than ever, and the scuttle shakes badly enough to make the instruments illegible on bad roads. At more than 70 mph wind noise concerts to drown all these aggravations, while at 100 mph conversation becomes quite impossible and thought nearly so. Ride comfort is poor except on roads of motorway standard. The short semi-elliptic rear springs transmit the feel of the road to the driver by the shortest route through his and the car's seat, preceded by advance warning through the steering wheel.

A revised dashboard is neat and sensibly laid out, while the old spring-spoke steering wheel holds its own against new-fangled rigid wood-rimmers

Few will remember it now, but the Austin Healey grille owes its abiding shape to the kite-like shape of early Riley-engined Healeys

Fittings and controls

Although exterior appearance of the Mark III is unchanged, the interior contains some improvements which suggest luxury to people who owned earlier models. Wood capping runs the width of the fascia panel, and a central console which is covered with leathercloth carries switches and the optional radio set. The console sweeps down astride the transmission tunnel, and the remote-control gear lever no longer needs to be raked, falling readily to hand. A box mounted rather far back between the seats is upholstered to serve as an armrest, the top flipping open to house maps and oddments. The handbrake is mounted on the right-hand side of the tunnel and is badly placed for easy operation.

Instruments are well grouped in front of the driver, and the combined water temperature and oil pressure gauge is appreciated for the ease with which the two functions can be checked during a split-second glance. Less happy is the petrol gauge which swings from full to empty and back during acceleration and braking, rendering the instrument practically useless.

Optional overdrive is operated by a switch on the fascia, and if a little less handy than is usual its operation soon became a natural movement. Foot controls are well placed, although the pedals are rather too close together for some drivers. Heel-and-toe gearchanges are soon mastered.

Surprisingly for such a fast car, there is no headlight flasher and the headlight switch is far away to the left,

causing the driver to rely on the powerful horn for early warning.

The jacking system is a suspect feature of this car. A puncture in the nearside rear tyre reduced ground clearance so drastically that we could find no way to place the jack under the axle spring (the recommended position) or any other reasonably solid piece of bodywork. Jacking the rear chassis cross member was possible, but did not lift the wheel from the ground. Garage assistance had to be sought eventually and we concluded a puncture was not a prospect we would relish for a wet night.

Performance

Docile as a lamb in traffic (the Healey *can* potter at 25 mph in overdrive top), full depression of the throttle transforms the car into a spirited beast on the open road. Clutch action is long and smooth, the throttle being equally progressive. Thus bad starts cannot be excused, and full performance is available only when the accelerator is pushed right to the floor.

The shapely rounded tail leaves little room for a boot, but who cares in a car meant for fun?

Tight-as-a-glove buckets are supplemented in the rear by two indentations more commode-like than commodious

A falsely spacious air is lent to the boot in our picture. The spare wheel was on the car, so we substituted a tyre to show positioning

It is a compliment to say that the Healey's bite is now worse than its bark, for the new exhaust system has reduced this source of noise to insignificant proportions. Instead, the driver is aware of the fan noise and a little gear whine—mainly in indirect ratios—vying with an acceptable level of mechanical chatter. Cockpit insulation is almost non-existent, and the driver gets full reward for his enthusiasm. Maximum power take-offs produce a little wheelspin, and a quick change into second gear suggests a nice, close-ratio gearbox. In fact second is really too low, taking the car from 42 mph in first gear to 52 mph before a change into third is necessary; the car badly needs a higher second gear, or else an overdrive ratio to bridge the gap up to third.

Care has to be taken not to stray from the tachometer's amber section—from 5,000 to 5,500 rpm—into the red in lower ratios, but in third overdrive the car runs easily up to 100 mph. Nifty manipulation of the gear lever and overdrive switch can, if need be, select direct top which rushes the car up to 117 mph, although for normal purposes overdrive top is the correct gear at more than 100 mph. At the ton the car is ambling along at 4,000 rpm and the natural cruising speed is in the region of 110 mph. When this speed is sustained on motorways the water temperature and oil pressure remain constant at satisfactory levels.

The gearlever moves easily through a fairly small gate, the powerful synchromesh completely overcoming any possible grating noises although introducing a certain amount of notchiness which slows the movement just a little.

Despite the introduction of a servo, the brakes require firm, but not really heavy pressure. Girling 11¼ in discs at the front are matched by 11 in drums at the rear, the system being entirely reassuring even on wet roads and virtually immune from fade in punishing conditions.

The six-cylinder engine is unlikely to work very hard unless the driver is normally in a considerable hurry, so petrol consumption figures should normally work out better than the 16 mpg obtained from our test car.

Handling

The scuttle vibration previously referred to is symptomatic of a degree of flexibility in the chassis which may well contribute to the Healey being an uncertain performer so far as handling is concerned. Greater familiarity is no doubt an asset, but even so the car is easily deflected from its course by bumps and undulations in the road, so that control requires a high degree of concentration at higher speeds.

Yet the car is undoubtedly rapid round corners, always

displaying a degree of oversteer which can be used to advantage. The majority of manufacturers instill understeer into their cars, at least at lower speeds, in the interests of accurate control and good straight-line running, but competent drivers soon find themselves at home with the Healey's characteristics. On wet roads a fair amount of discretion is called for, more restraint being needed in slow corners than in the fast ones, but in the dry the accelerator can be used to set the car up nicely for a corner and help it through on a good line. Cam and peg steering is employed, and this system gives accurate control with reasonable lightness, although some road shock reaches the steering wheel on particularly bumpy roads.

The Austin-Healey is not likely to be first choice for the majority of drivers, even the sporting ones, but anyone who strikes up a good friendship with it and is prepared to accept one or two basic faults is sure to be well satisfied with his choice.

SPECIFICATION

ENGINE:
Six cylinders; bore 83.36 mm (3.25 in), stroke 89 mm (3.52 in). Cubic capacity 2,912 cc. Compression ratio 9.03:1. Maximum bhp (gross) 150 at 5,250 rpm. Maximum torque 173 lb ft at 3,000 rpm; Twin SU HD8 carburettors. Overhead valves. SU electric fuel pump. Fuel tank capacity 10 gallons. Water capacity 18 pints. Sump capacity 12.75 pints. 12v battery of 57 amp/hr capacity.

TRANSMISSION:
Borg and Beck 9½ in dia. single dry plate clutch. Four-speed gearbox with synchromesh on 2nd, 3rd and top, and optional overdrive on 3rd and top. Overall gear ratios: 1st, 9.348. 2nd, 7.341. 3rd, 4.629. Top, 3.545. Gearing, 20.5 mph per 1000 rpm in direct top; 25.0 mph per 1000 rpm in overdrive top. Rear axle ratio 3.54 or 3.91 with overdrive.

CHASSIS:
Suspension: front, independent coil and wishbone and anti-roll bar. Lever Armstrong shock absorbers: rear, live rear axle located by Panhard rod and semi-elliptic leaf springs. Armstrong shock absorbers. Girling hydraulic brakes, disc front, drum rear. Cam and peg steering. 15 in disc wheels with wire spoke option. Dunlop Road Speed tyres, size 5.90-15.

DIMENSIONS:

	ft	in
Wheelbase	7	8
Track, front	4	1
Track, rear	4	1½
Overall length	13	1
Overall width	5	0½
Overall height	4	1½
Ground clearance		4½
Turning circle	32	
Kerb weight	23 cwt	

PERFORMANCE:

mph	sec
0-30	3.9
0-40	5.8
0-50	7.7
0-60	10.9
0-70	13.2
0-80	16.8
0-90	19.0
0-100	22.8

Maximum speed in gears:

1st	42 mph
2nd	52 mph
3rd	87 mph
Overdrive 3rd	103 mph
4th	117 mph
Overdrive 4th	121 mph

Fuel consumption: 16 mpg

PRICE:
£1,106 basic
£1,223 with extras as tested

FROM PERRANPORTH TO ABINGDON

IN June 1959 there came a new version of the B.M.C. six-cylinder C-type engine enlarged from 2.6 to 2.9-litres, and this was shortly followed by the announcement of a successor to the '100-Six', the Austin-Healey '3000'. By increasing the engine capacity to 2912 c.c. and raising the compression ratio to a little over 9 to 1, power output of the new model was rated at 124 b.h.p. compared with 117 b.h.p. of the '100-Six'. The '3000' thus offered greater pulling power and improved all-round performance. For the competition driver, the 2.9-litre engine obviously made better use of the International 3-litre class limit. The larger engine capacity, achieved by enlarging the cylinder bores, meant the use of an entirely new cylinder block and crankcase casting and, in line with the increased power output, there was a larger diameter clutch and stronger transmission gears. Improved braking was achieved with the use of Girling discs at the front. Apart from these mechanical improvements the '3000' was externally distinguished from its predecessor only by the flash on the radiator grille. As with the '100-Six' both two and occasional four-seater versions of the '3000' were available.

'3000' MARK II

Just the use of disc brakes on the works-entered competition '100-Sixes' had led to the fitting of front discs as standard equipment on the '3000', so the use of a triple-carburetter layout on certain competition cars during the 1960 season prompted the announcement of the triple-carburetter '3000' Mark II in May 1961. With three 1½″ S.U. carburetters installed on a new inlet manifold, and the use of modified valve springs and a redesigned camshaft, the power output of the '3000' was now quoted at 132 b.h.p. The additional power of the Mark II was most evident in the middle and upper ranges of engine speed. Most surprisingly, the fuel consumption of the triple-carburetter Mark II was slightly *better* than that of the twin-carburetter Mark I. The availability of servo-assisted brakes as an optional extra was a welcome feature. Later production models of the Mark II were fitted with a short, vertical, remote-control gear-lever and a glass-fibre gearbox cover, which helped to improve cockpit cooling and reduce transmission noise. Externally the Mark II wore a bolder radiator grille, vertical bars replacing the horizontal styling on the Mark I.

'3000' CONVERTIBLE

But the triple-carburetter Mark II proved, perhaps, just too much of a delicate essay in tuning for many owners, so in March 1962 came a return to twin carburetters with the announcement of the restyled '3000' Convertible. This, the most refined and

Pat Moss and Ann Wisdom climb Mount Ventoux in the 1962 Alpine Rally, to finish 3rd overall behind the Morleys' winning '3000'

Austin-Healey 3000

luxurious production Austin-Healey to date, presented the first major styling changes to the model since the introduction of the Healey '100' almost exactly 10 years previously. The '3000' was now brought into line with the present-day demand for a grand touring car offering saloon car comforts and appointments. A wrap-around windscreen was fitted and the doors had wind-down windows and quarter-lights. There was a new-styled quick-action one-piece hood complete with removable rear window panel. The Convertible was available only in occasional four-seater form. The return to twin carburetters represented a loss of 2 b.h.p., but the styling changes had improved the aerodynamics to compensate for this and the Convertible remains the fastest production Austin-Healey to date, excluding the '100 S' as a strictly competition machine. Handling of the latest '3000' was improved by fitting a stiffer anti-roll bar at the front and by using modified damper settings.

All the '3000' models have proved worthy successors to the '100-Six', both through sales in world markets and in the field of international rallying. Although the styling has remained basically unchanged for 11 years, in looks alone the current '3000' compares favourably with today's G.T. models from rival marques and no other production model offers better value for money in high-performance sports car motoring.

THE COMPETITION '3000'

Before reviewing the four years of outstanding competition successes achieved by the '3000' a brief technical description of a works rally car will not be out of place for, without exception, the premier achievements for the marque have been recorded by the familiar red cars prepared in the B.M.C. Competitions Department at Abingdon.

Naturally the specification of the works cars changes from event to event in the course of steady development, modifications being continually applied. Many of these ideas were later to appear on production models. The works rally cars are not one-off hand-built specials, but production models taken from the assembly lines and brought up to competition trim in the Competitions Department. Engine modifications begin with the balancing of crankshaft, flywheel, clutch assembly, and connecting rods. The cylinder head is gas flowed and polished and, on the current cars, the compression ratio is slightly raised to 9.5 to 1. The standard Mark II camshaft is used, together with the standard distributor. The standard inner valve springs are retained although stronger outer springs are fitted. A six-branch exhaust manifold is used and, to improve the ground clearance, the silencer is suitably modified with side pipes terminating in front of the near-side rear wheel. On the early competition cars, triple 2″ S.U. carburetters

were used, but more recently triple Weber carburetters have been found to give the optimum performance. Power output of the S.U. carburetted cars was 180 b.h.p., the Webers producing nearer 200 b.h.p. The clutch has stronger springs and the gearbox has close-ratio straight-cut gears.

To withstand the exceptional punishment inflicted on the underside of the car upon the rough rally roads, the sump is protected by welding an additional sheet of steel around the front and bottom. Similarly, all vulnerable wiring or hydraulic pipework is repositioned along the sides of the chassis members. Girling disc brakes are fitted at both the front and rear, and 60-spoke Dunlop wire wheels are used.

Suspension modifications are mainly designed to improve the ground clearance. At the front there is a heavy duty anti-roll bar with Mark II coil springs used in conjunction with packing pieces. At the rear the standard 7-leaf springs are replaced with thinner 14-leaf springs which are better suited to carrying the additional load of twin spare wheels and the 20-gallon fuel tank over rough going. Competition-type shock absorbers are fitted, adjustable type at the rear. Very little weight reducing is done on the works '3000'; in fact with full rally equipment they actually turn the scales at more than the production model. Body modifications include a hump in the boot lid to accommodate a second spare wheel, a less restricting wire radiator grille, and louvres in the front wings to assist engine cooling. There is a fresh air vent upon the scuttle and an extractor vent in the hardtop to assist cockpit ventilation. Instrumentation, seating and lighting are built up to the crews' personal preferences.

It says much for the sturdy design of the '3000' and the meticulous preparation of the Abingdon mechanics that (except for early gearbox troubles) it has been almost unknown for a works '3000' to retire because of mechanical failure, other than extensive crash damage which has crippled the car beyond immediate repair.

A fully detailed account of every international sortie for the '3000' would fill almost as many pages as our complete Healey history to date. Unlike those of past models featured in this series, the highlights of the '3000' competition successes have already been featured in SAFETY FAST through first-hand reports by the crews themselves. The following account, therefore, presents only a general year-by-year summary of the competition history of the '3000' to date. Those in search of more background information should read *Seven Year Twitch*, an absorbing and authoritative work by ex-B.M.C. Competitions Manager Marcus Chambers, who gives a mile by mile account of practically every international rally run by the works Austin-Healeys up to 1961.

1959—SETTING THE PACE

International competition debut for the new '3000' was in the 1959 Alpine Rally, a classic event later to become closely associated with Austin-Healey successes, rather as the Mille Miglia had been the happy hunting ground of the Warwick-built Healeys. The three works-entered cars for the Alpine ran in standard twin-carburetter form, the only modifications being the side exhaust system to improve ground clearance. Although the somewhat optimistically set average speeds meant that the larger G.T. cars were out of the running for the coveted Coupe des Alpes, the new 3-litre cars certainly proved that they now had the power to conquer such class opposition as the works Mercedes. John Gott/Chris Tooley only failed to win the class from a Triumph T.R.3 because of delays in repairing a punctured radiator. The rough going eliminated the other two works cars, a high-speed encounter with a deep gulley pushing the fan blades through the radiator of the Jack Sears/Sam Moore '3000' and similar road conditions crushing the sump on the Bill Shepherd/John Williamson car.

As the Alpine prompted the need for better underbody protection against the pounding of rough rally roads, so the next outing for the '3000', the Liège, emphasised the importance of a thorough pre-rally recce. Of the four works '3000' entered, navigational errors caused the retirement of two crews whilst the third entry was eliminated after a minor accident. Fortunately, Peter Riley/Rupert Jones saved the day for the Austin-Healey team by bringing the '3000' its first international class victory.

After a class win by Jack Sears in the Gold Cup meeting at Oulton Park (sadly the first and, to date, the lone international class victory for the '3000' upon the race track) came the German Rally, when the Pat Moss/Ann Wisdom partnership tried the new '3000' for the first time. Since they put up the fastest times on all but one of the speed tests, the girls obviously approved of the new Austin-Healey! The lone '3000' won its class, finishing second overall, and, of course, Pat and Ann collected the Ladies' Award. This was the highest overall placing ever gained by an all-ladies crew in a Rally Championship event—at that time.

Results of the 1959 R.A.C. Rally were somewhat overshadowed by delays in hearing protests, and the event was almost forgotten when it was confirmed that the works '3000's had taken first and second places in their class, the twins Don and Erle Morley winning the

Right: With wraparound windscreen and wind-down windows the '3000' Convertible offers saloon car comforts and appointments

Below: The triple-carburettor 132 b.h.p. power unit and gearbox used in the early '3000' Mark IIs

class honours in their first drive with the Austin-Healey team. The results might have been different had gearbox trouble not retired the John Williamson/John Milne car when it was leading the rally by a handsome margin. The 1959 season closed with the Portuguese Rally, when Pat Moss/Ann Wisdom entered a lone '3000' in search of points for the European Ladies' Championship. Although the girls gained their ladies' award, a somewhat unsporting gesture by a fellow competitor in withdrawing from the event meant that there were insufficient lady crews for the rally to count for the Championship. Pat and Ann were to have their revenge the following year!

AUSTIN-HEALEY ENTRIES IN INTERNATIONAL EVENTS

Phase Six: Austin-Healey '3000'

DATE	EVENT	DRIVERS	RESULTS
June 1959	Alpine Rally	J. Gott/C. Tooley W. Shepherd/J. Williamson J. Sears/S. Moore	5th in G.T. category, 2nd in class Retired Retired
September 1959	Liège-Rome-Liège Rally	P. Riley/ R. Jones J. Gott/K. James J. Sears/P. Garnier G. Burgess/S. Croft-Pearson	7th in G.T. category, 1st class Retired Retired Crashed
September 1959	Gold Cup Meeting Sports car race, Oulton Park	J. Sears	1st Class
October 1959	German Rally	P. Moss/A. Wisdom	2nd overall, 1st class, Coupe des Dames
November 1959	R.A.C. Rally	D. Morley/E. Morley J. Sears/W. Cave J. Williamson/J. Milne	4th overall, 1st class 17th overall, 2nd class Retired
December 1959	Portuguese Rally	P. Moss/A. Wisdom	53rd overall, 4th class, Coupe des Dames
March 1960	12-Hour Race, Sebring	G. Geitner/J. Louis-Spencer J. Sears/P. Riley F. Spross/ ——	15th overall, 2nd class 3rd class Crashed
March 1960	Circuit of Ireland	G. Parkes/G. Howarth P. Moss/A. Wisdom	1st class Retired
March 1960	Lyons-Charbonnières Rally	P. Moss/A. Wisdom	Crashed
April 1960	Geneva Rally	P. Moss/A. Wisdom	7th overall, 1st class, Coupe des Dames
May 1960	Tulip Rally	P. Moss/A. Wisdom D. Morley/E. Morley	8th overall, 1st class Coupe des Dames 21st overall, 3rd class
May 1960	Acropolis Rally	P. Moss/A. Wisdom P. Riley/A. Ambrose	Retired Crashed
June 1960	24-Hour Race, Le Mans	J. Sears/P. Riley	Retired
June 1960	Alpine Rally	P. Moss/A. Wisdom J. Gott/W. Shepherd D. Morley/E. Morley R. Adams/J. Williamson	2nd overall, 1st class, Coupe des Dames 8th overall, 2nd class 14th overall, 3rd class Retired (All Team Prizes)
August 1960	Tourist Trophy, Goodwood	P. Riley J. Bekaert	19th overall 25th overall
August 1960	Liège-Rome-Liège Rally	P. Moss/A. Wisdom D. Seigle-Morris/V. Elford J. Gott/R. Jones P. Riley/A. Ambrose	1st overall, 1st class Coupe des Dames 5th overall, 2nd class 10th overall, 3rd class Retired (All Team Prizes)
October 1960	German Rally	D. Seigle-Morris/S. Turner D. Morley/B. Hercock P. Moss/A. Wisdom	8th overall, 1st class 12th overall, 2nd class 16th overall, 3rd class
November 1960	R.A.C. Rally	D. Morley/E. Morley P. Riley/A. Ambrose R. Adams/J. Williamson P. Smith/G. Bryant D. Dixon/C. Bond-Smith L. Griffiths/G. Brown A. Griffiths/H. Liddon J. Casewell/H. Davenport	3rd overall, 1st class 10th overall, 2nd class 39th overall, 4th class 41st overall, 5th class 57th overall, 7th class 63rd overall, 8th class 94th overall, 10th class Retired (Team Prize)

Austin-Healey entries in International Events — *continued*

DATE	EVENT	DRIVERS	RESULTS
May 1961	Tulip Rally	P. Moss/A. Wisdom	11th overall, 1st class, Coupe des Dames
		D. Morley/E. Morley	14th overall, 2nd class
		D. Grimshaw/B. Melia	52nd overall, 5th class
		P. Smith/C. Bond-Smith	74th overall, 6th class
		M. Day/R. Douglas	76th overall, 7th class
		A. Vicat-Cole/H. Mainz	81st overall, 8th class
		D. Allen/J. Hill	95th overall, 10th class
		F. Powell/J. Tait	102nd overall, 11th class
May 1961	1000-kms. Race, Nürburgring	G. Gonzalo/G. van Opheim	35th overall
May 1961	Acropolis Rally	P. Riley/A. Ambrose	3rd overall, 1st class
		G. Parkes/J. Sprinzel	Crashed
June 1961	Midnight Sun Rally	P. Riley/A. Ambrose	12th overall, 2nd class
June 1961	24-Hour Race, Le Mans	J. Bekaert/D. Stoop	Retired
June 1961	Alpine Rally	D. Morley/E. Morley	1st overall, 1st class
		J. Gott/W. Shepherd	15th overall, 3rd class
		P. Moss/A. Wisdom	Crashed
		P. Riley/A. Ambrose	Crashed
		D. Seigle-Morris/V. Elford	Crashed
August 1961	Polish Rally	D. Astle/S. Turner	2nd Class
August 1961	Liège-Rome-Liège Rally	D. Seigle-Morris/A. Ambrose	6th overall, 1st class
		J. Gott/W. Shepherd	Retired
		P. Moss/A. Wisdom	Retired
		D. Grimshaw/R. Jones	Crashed
November 1961	R.A.C. Rally	P. Moss/A. Wisdom	2nd overall, 1st class, Coupe des Dames
		D. Seigle-Morris/A. Ambrose	12th overall, 2nd class
		D. Grimshaw/B. Melia	64th overall, 4th class
		D. Morley/E. Morley	Retired
November 1961	Tour of Corsica	P. Moss/A. Wisdom	17th overall, 1st class, Coupe des Dames
January 1962	Monte Carlo Rally	D. Seigle-Morris/A. Ambrose	18th overall, 1st class
		W. Marriott/R. Marriott	Retired
		D. Grimshaw/G. Humble	Retired
April 1962	Circuit of Ireland	G. Parkes/G. Howarth	3rd overall, 1st class
May 1962	Tulip Rally	D. Morley/E. Morley	14th overall, 1st class
		P. Riley/D. Astle	18th overall, 2nd class
		A. Verschoor/A. van Jaarsveld	6th class
May 1962	Acropolis Rally	P. Moss/P. Mayman	8th overall, 1st class, Coupe des Dames
May 1962	Police Rally	J. Gott/D. Nicholson	1st class
June 1962	Alpine Rally	C. Morley/E. Morley	1st overall, 1st class
		P. Moss/P. Mayman	3rd overall, 3rd class, Coupe des Dames
		D. Seigle-Morris/A. Ambrose	8th overall, 5th class
		P. Riley/D. Astle	Retired (Team Prize)
June 1962	24-Hours Race, Le Mans	R. Olthoff/J. Whitmore	Retired
August 1962	Polish Rally	P. Moss/P. Mayman	2nd overall, 1st class Coupe des Dames
August 1962	Liège-Rome-Liège Rally	L. Morrison/R. Jones	5th overall, 2nd class
		D. Seigle-Morris/B. Hercock	8th overall, 3rd class
		P. Hopkirk/J. Scott	Retired
		R. Aaltonen/A. Ambrose	Retired
November 1962	R.A.C. Rally	P. Hopkirk/J. Scott	2nd overall, 1st class
		P. Moss/P. Mayman	3rd overall, 2nd class, Coupe des Dames
		D. Morley/E. Morley	Crashed
		P. Riley/H. Nash	Crashed
		D. Grimshaw/G. Allen	Retired
		M. Day/M. Mobsby	Retired

DATE	EVENT	DRIVERS	RESULTS
January 1963	Monte Carlo Rally	T. Makinen/C. Carlisle W. Marriott/R. Marriott — Amy/— Casey	13th overall, 1st class Retired Retired
March 1963	12-Hour Race, Sebring	R. Olthoff/R. Bucknum P. Hopkirk/D. Morley	12th overall, 4th class 26th overall, 6th class
April 1963	Tulip Rally	D. Morley/E. Morley L. Morrison/R. Finlay D. Astle/D. Grimshaw	2nd G.T. category, 1st class Retired Crashed
April 1963	Circuit of Ireland	L. Morrison/R. Finlay	Crashed
May 1963	Police Rally	J. Gott/D. Nicholson	6th class
May 1963	G.T. Race, B.R.D.C. Silverstone	R. Olthoff	6th overall
June 1963	Alpine Rally	D. Morley/E. Morley T. Makinen/M. Wood P. Hopkirk/J. Scott L. Morrison/R. Finlay	Retired Retired Crashed Crashed
June 1963	Scottish Rally	G. Parkes/B. Whitmarsh	3rd class
June 1963	Midnight Sun Rally	T. Makinen/A. Ambrose	Disqualified
July 1963	Grovewood Trophy Race, B.R.S.C.C. Mallory Park	C. Baker	7th overall
September 1963	Liège-Rome-Liège Rally	P. Hopkirk/H. Liddon T. Makinen/G. Mabbs L. Morrison/M. Wood P. Moon/A. Cowan R. Aaltonen/A. Ambrose B. Russell/P. Scott	6th overall, 1st class Crashed Retired Retired Crashed Retired
October 1963	Geneva Rally	P. Moon/J. Davenport	11th overall, 1st class
November 1963	R.A.C. Rally	T. Makinen/M. Wood D. Morley/E. Morley P. Moon/R. Mackie B. Petch/H. Miller R. Aaltonen/A. Ambrose	5th overall, 1st class 9th overall, 2nd class Retired Retired Crashed

Perranporth to Abingdon

1960—FIRST FULL SEASON

First international outing for the marque in 1960 was to Sebring for the 12-Hour Race. Here a pair of '3000's entered by B.M.C. North America finished second and third in their class behind a Ferrari. Shortly after this came the Circuit of Ireland Rally, which brought Bobby Parkes/G. Howarth in a privately-entered '3000' a class win after the works car of Pat Moss/Ann Wisdom had retired with gearbox troubles. The girls were again out of luck on the Lyons-Charbonnières when Pat had a spectacular 100 m.p.h. crash at the Solitude circuit, and they had an equally unpleasant ride on the Acropolis when a navigational error took them into a forbidden military zone; they were fired upon by guards and later retired with the Austin-Healey's chassis smashed by the terrible roads. The

Geneva Rally, however, brought better fortune with a class win and the ladies' award for Pat and Ann, a performance which they repeated on the Tulip.

Returning to the Alpine, the stage was now set for the works Austin-Healeys to enjoy an unprecedented run of dominating class victories in Championship rallies. The incredible Pat and Ann, on the peak of their form, finished the Alpine second *overall*, gaining a Coupe des Alps, winning the class and yet another Coupe des Dames. The Austin-Healeys made it a 1-2-3 class victory, runners-up John Gott/Bill Shepherd missing their Alpine Cup by mere seconds after a spin on one of the final climbs. Don and Erle Morley completed the Austin-Healey trio despite gearbox troubles which also caused the retirement of the fourth works car, driven by Ronnie Adams/John Williamson. In addition to these class victories, the Austin-Healeys, now running under the banner of "Ecurie Safety Fast", collected all five team prizes.

After their performance on the Alpine it was clear that outright victory in a Championship rally was within the grasp of the Moss/Wisdom/'3000' combination, but few would have prophesied that they would achieve this ambition in the gruelling Liège-Rome-Liège Rally, the next event for the Austin-Healeys. The four works cars, now running in three-carburetter form, came to the starting line with improved gearboxes and transmission, the standard design having been unable to cope with the immense torque of the engine in tuned form. The Austin-Healeys were destined to enjoy their most successful outing, though they had no easy rally.

First, punctures delayed John Gott/Rupert Jones and David Seigle-Morris/Vic Elford on critical stages, then Peter Riley/Tony Ambrose had the throttle stick open, which later caused a fan-blade to fly off and wreck the radiator. Pat Moss/Ann Wisdom had the gearbox drain plug knocked out and Marcus

Chambers and his men removed the gearbox to attend to the clutch in less than an hour; a perfect example of the vital part played by the support team in the field of current international rallying.

Amongst the 13 survivors which returned to Liège—out of 81 starters—were three of the four Austin-Healeys, the incredible Pat and Ann achieving their greatest drive to be placed outright winners. Rallying history had truly been made. Never before had a British crew in a British car won the Marathon; never before had an all-ladies crew won

a Championship rally. The Austin-Healeys won the team prize for Britain for the second year running, Seigle-Morris/Elford and Gott/Jones completing the honours list by giving the '3000' another 1-2-3 class victory. Truly the marque's finest hour, and the first outright victory in a major international event for either a Healey or an Austin-Healey.

The remaining events in 1960 underlined the Liège and Alpine successes, David Seigle-Morris and the present B.M.C. Competitions Manager, Stuart

Turner, leading the Austin-Healeys to yet another 1-2-3 class victory in the German Rally. Then came the R.A.C. Rally when it was the Morley brothers' turn to lead the '3000' class domination, the Abingdon cars again collecting the team prize. The year closed with the highest honours being showered on Pat Moss and Ann Wisdom as joint Ladies European Rally Champions, coupled with their election by the Guild of Motoring Writers as 'Drivers of the Year'. The Austin-Healeys which had carried them to victory also received due praise, the run of international rally class wins totalling 10 out of 14 events since the '3000' was introduced in July 1959. The year 1960 had been the most successful season for B.M.C. to date and it certainly had not been a disappointing one for Austin-Healeys!

1961—FIRST ALPINE WIN

By 1961 the works Austin-Healeys had established such a reputation in international rallying that it was almost unheard of for the team to return to Abingdon without at least a class victory. Pat and Ann opened the season with a brilliant drive on the Tulip, the performance of their '3000' on the timed climbs and circuit tests being a feature of the event. As the overall placings were assessed on the "class improvement" basis, the '3000's did not feature high in the results. Nevertheless, the Austin-Healeys gained first and second places in the class, the girls winning the Coupe des Dames. In company with the Morleys' '3000' and the Sprite of Gold/Hughes, Austin-Healey again won the Manufacturers' Team Prize.

A thorough recce of the difficult terrain on the Acropolis rewarded Peter Riley/Tony Ambrose with a class win, their '3000' also being the highest-placed British entry. Close runners-up to the works car until a crash put them out of the event were the privateers Bobby Parkes/John Sprinzel.

Highlight of the year was the Alpine. The five Austin-Healey team cars, now at the peak of their development, must have been the most powerful entry with which B.M.C. has ever attacked an international rally. As always seems the case with the most successful outings, the event began badly for the team with Pat and Ann capsizing their '3000' in the early stages, Seigle-Morris/Elford also crashing not far from the start. Then brake troubles eliminated the Riley/Ambrose car on the Stelvio. These misfortunes were, however, completely overshadowed by the Morley's performance in leading the rally throughout to finish as the sole unpenalised crew, outright winners

---

Specification: *Austin-Healey '3000'*

Production Period:

'3000' Mark I (BN.7, 2-seater; BT.7, 4-seater) July 1959 to April 1961

'3000' Mark II (BN.7, 2-seater; BT.7, 4-seater) May 1961 to March 1962

'3000' Convertible, (BJ.7, 4-seater) March 1962 to date.

Main Dimensions:

Wheelbase: 7 ft. 8 ins.
Track: 4 ft. 0¾ ins. (front)
    4 ft. 2 ins. (rear)
Overall length: 13 ft. 1½ ins.
Overall width: 5 ft. 0½ ins.
Overall height: 4 ft. 1 ins.
Ground clearance: 4½ ins.
Unladen weight: 22½ cwt.

Engine:

Six-cylinder o.h.v. pushrod, 83.34 mm. × 88.9 mm. (2,912 c.c.)
Compression ratio, 9.03 to 1. 12-volt coil and battery ignition.

Mark I: Twin HD.6 1¾ ins. S.U. carburetters. 124 b.h.p. at 4600 r.p.m.

Mark II: Triple HS.4 1½ ins. S.U. carburetters. 132 b.h.p. at 4750 r.p.m.

Convertible: Twin HS.6 1¾. ins. S.U. carburetters, 130 b.h.p at 4750 r.p.m.

Transmission:

Borg and Beck 10 ins. single dry-plate clutch. Four-speed gearbox synchromesh on 2nd, 3rd and top gears. Laycock de Normanville overdrive on 3rd and top gears (optional extra). Open propeller shaft. Hypoid final drive.

Brakes:

Girling hydraulic. 11¼ ins. discs (front), 11 ins. drums (rear).
Brake servo, optional extra.

Suspension:

Front: Coil spring and wishbone with anti-roll bar.

Rear: Semi-elliptic leaf springs and Panhard rod.

Steering:

Burman cam and peg.

Wheels and tyres:

Steel disc or wire wheels with 5.90 × 15 ins. Dunlop Road Speed tyres

Performance:

	Mark I (*Autocar*)	Mark II (*Motor*)	Convertible (*Motor*)	Convertible (*Autocar*)
0—30 m.p.h.	3.5 secs.	3.8 secs.	3.2 secs.	3.5 secs.
0—50 m.p.h.	8.0 secs.	8.3 secs.	7.2 secs.	7.8 secs.
0—60 m.p.h.	11.4 secs.	10.9 secs.	10.3 secs.	10.4 secs.
0—70 m.p.h.	14.3 secs.	14.3 secs.	12.9 secs.	13.7 secs.
0—80 m.p.h.	18.9 secs.	19.2 secs.	16.7 secs.	18.1 secs.
0—90 m.p.h.	24.8 secs.	25.9 secs.	21.3 secs.	23.8 secs.
0—100 m.p.h.	32.8 secs.	36.4 secs.	29.4 secs.	30.8 secs.
Standing ¼-mile	17.9 secs.	18.3 secs.	17.3 secs.	17.8 secs.
Maximum speed (with overdrive)	114 m.p.h.	113 m.p.h.	116 m.p.h.	117 m.p.h.

and the only competitors to gain a Coupe des Alps. An off-course excursion on the final stages prevented John Gott/Bill Shepherd from finishing closer to the conquering Morleys.

The Liège brought hopes that perhaps Pat and Ann could repeat their 1960 victory, but unhappily they were retired with a broken chassis and it was left to Seigle Morris/Ambrose to win the class for Austin-Healey. Final 1961 Rally Championship event was the R.A.C. Rally. Here Pat and Ann found their past form to finish overall runners-up to Carlsson's Saab, their '3000', of course, winning the class and the Coupe des Dames. To close the season the girls took a lone '3000' to compete in the Tour of Corsica, perhaps in search of a little sunshine. But the foul British winter weather followed them south and the event was run in appalling conditions. Nevertheless, this did not deter them from winning their class and finishing as the highest-placed G.T. car.

Don and Erle Morley pose with their '3000' after winning the 1961 Alpine Rally— a performance which they repeated in the following year

1962—8 CLASS WINS IN 10 EVENTS

To keep pace with the consistent run of '3000' class wins in international rallies was by now becoming a task for the mathematicians. From 22 sorties the '3000' had gained 16 class wins, had three times won the marque team prize, and on only three occasions finished lower than second in their class. David Seigle-Morris/Tony Ambrose began the 1962 season by winning their class on the Monte Carlo Rally, the '3000' being runner-up to Lyndon Sims' Aston Martin on the Monaco circuit races. In April the privateers Bobby Parkes/G. Howarth repeated their 1960 effort by gaining a class win on the Circuit of Ireland. Then came the Tulip, when the Morley brothers, with Peter Riley/Derrick Astle in close company, defeated strong Jaguar and Mercedes opposition to be placed first and second in the large G.T. category.

Ann Wisdom having now become Mrs. Peter Riley, the Moss/Wisdom partnership came to a close. A newcomer to the B.M.C. team, Pauline Mayman, joined forces with Pat, this new combination on their first outing collecting a class win on the Acropolis; their '3000' was also the highest-placed British entry. Soon after the Acropolis; John Gott came out of retirement with his ex-works '3000' to compete in the International Police Rally, the Austin-Healey recording the fastest time on all speed tests and winning the class just like old times!

The Alpine was again the highlight of the season when the Morleys brought their '3000' through to score outright victory for the second year running, a truly brilliant performance. Pat Moss/ Pauline Mayman were third overall, collecting their usual Coupe des Dames. Despite a puncture on the Vivione, Seigle-Morris/Ambrose also finished and thus helped to bring the Austin-Healeys the team prize. On the Polish Rally, Moss/Mayman brought the '3000' its seventh consecutive international rally class win, Pat finishing overall runner-up to Bohringer's Mercedes. Hopes for another outright victory in the Liège were dashed when the leading '3000' of Seigle-Morris/ Hercock suffered a cracked chassis, and the second team car of Logan Morrison/ Rupert Jones had to concede class victory to the flying Bohringer. Seigle-Morris brought the crippled '3000' to the finish, achieving a personal triumph and a gold Liège award for finishing in three consecutive years on an Austin-Healey.

Two newcomers to "Ecurie Safety Fast" Paddy Hopkirk/Jack Scott, had their first success with the '3000' on the R.A.C. Rally by winning the class and finishing runners-up to Carlsson's Saab. Moss/Mayman followed Hopkirk into third place, adding yet another Coupe des Dames to their collection. The year 1962 had truly brought further impressive successes to the marque, the works '3000's claiming eight international rally class wins in nine events. Pat Moss and Pauline Mayman also clinched the Ladies' European Rally Championship, this being Pat's third Championship victory.

1963—LUCKLESS YEAR

Although last year did not bring the consistent run of achievements enjoyed by the marque in the earlier 1960s, there have been some remarkable drives, sheer bad luck robbing the '3000' of outright victory on two major events within sight of the finish. The season began well with the partnership of Timo Makinen and Christabel Carlisle winning their class on the Monte Carlo Rally, the '3000' being runner-up again in the circuit races at Monaco. In the warmer climes of Sebring the 12-Hour Race brought one of the all-too-few notable '3000' achievements on the race track when Bob Olthoff/Ronnie Bucknum finished fourth in class behind a trio of prototype Ferraris. The second '3000', driven by Paddy Hopkirk/Don Morley, finished sixth in the class. Digressing for a moment to

The victorious Austin-Healey team which dominated the 1960 Liège-Rome-Liège Rally by gaining outright victory, a 1-2-3 class victory and all team prizes. Left to right: the winning crew, Pat Moss and Ann Wisdom, with David Seigle-Morris/ Vic Elford and John Gott/Rupert Jones

review the international racing activities of the '3000', the marque has understandably been able to make little impression on the Ferrari domination of the 3-litre class. In three consecutive years mechanical troubles have eliminated the '3000' entry at Le Mans, the Bob Olthoff/John Whitmore effort in 1962 being the most creditable attempt, for their '3000' had reached eighth place overall before retiring only six hours from the finish. In less ambitious races, however, the efforts of private owners should be recorded here. Bob Olthoff, Mike Bond, David Dixon, Elizabeth Jones, John Gott, John Harris and Clive Baker are amongst those who have made '3000's perform exceptionally well on the track outside the field of international events. Particularly notable performances were Bob Olthoff's win in the 1962 Leinster Trophy and second place in the Rand Six Hours in South Africa.

Returning to the 1963 rally scene, the Morley brothers brought the '3000' its fourth consecutive class win on the Tulip, and when the Alpine Rally came around again there were high hopes that the popular twins would win this summer classic for the third consecutive year to gain the highest Alpine honour of all, the Coupe d'Or. The Alpine, however, turned out to be a disastrous outing for the marque and one of the almost unprecedented occasions when not one of the Austin-Healey team completed the course. The Morleys seemed assured of their third consecutive victory when, on the final night, failure of an experimental rear axle caused their retirement. The other members of the Austin-Healey team enjoyed equally bad fortune, crashes eliminating Paddy Hopkirk/Jack Scott and Logan Morrison/Ross Finlay, and a smashed hub putting Timo Makinen/Mike Wood out of the event.

The team's luck certainly did not change for the Liège. Rauno Aaltonen/Tony Ambrose crashed on the Vivione when leading the rally with only two more passes to come, and a very sporting effort by their team-mates, Paddy Hopkirk/Henry Liddon, failed to get the '3000' back on the road. Despite this delay, Hopkirk/Liddon finished and won their class. Mention must be made of the efforts of the private owners Peter Moon/Andrew Cowan, who put up a valiant performance but were finally beaten by the atrocious conditions. With John Davenport as his partner, Peter Moon fared better in the Geneva Rally when his ex-works car won the class. The final sortie for the works cars in 1963 was in the R.A.C. Rally, when Timo Makinen/Mike Wood led the big G.T. category with the Morleys in second place. For the record, this brought the Austin-Healey its 29th class win in international rallies.

This brief review of Austin-Healey '3000' competition activities has embraced some 50 international sorties covering four and a half years, a period of consistently successful competition which few other models can equal. During this time the '3000' has established itself as the world's most successful big G.T. rally car, and in the sphere of world sales the production '3000' has proved to be a worthy successor to the original Healey '100' of 1952. The marque continues to be in the forefront of Britain's best-selling sports cars and, with the '3000' still in full production and the prospect of perhaps newer '3000' models to appear in the future, we may expect further competition activities and no doubt there will be a sequel to this chapter of Austin-Healey history.

We haven't yet built a sportscar capable of flight. Meanwhile the Austin Healey 3000 offers you quite a take-off. 60 mph in 9.8 seconds.*

When motoring correspondents write about the Austin Healey 3000, they tend to let loose the adjectives. Flatterers like: Rugged. Muscular. Hairy-chested.

If you've ever driven an Austin Healey 3000 yourself, you won't quarrel with these descriptions.

Ruggedness is something Austin have been working on for thirteen years, the length of time it took to arrive at the present Mark III. By now the 3000 *should* be rugged.

The muscularity is a function of the famous BMC C-series engine, tuned to give 150 bhp at 5,250 rpm. This is a big, three-litre powerhouse: hence the long, sweptback rake of bonnet needed to conceal it.

The chief improvements, latterly, are details of finish. Wind-up windows, a convertible top, a more elegant cockpit. A back seat that folds forward to form a platform for extra luggage.

On the road the 3000 is a quieter car: dual exhausts reduce the noise without diminishing the power. And the disc brakes are servo-assisted to keep 120 mph plus under close rein.

Competition: The 3000 spoils for it. It's the only British sportscar ever to have won the Leige-Rome-Liege Rally, which is probably the most destructive test of them all.

It's also the only British sportscar ever to have won it twice!

*Motor, November 28, 1964.

AUSTIN

Austin Healey changes up!

All the way up to a faster, more comfortable, new 3000 Mark III!

THE BRITISH MOTOR CORPORATION LTD.

Austin Healey 3000 Mk. III Sports Convertible (including £192.3.9 P.T.)—£1,107.3.9.

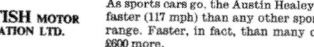

As sports cars go, the Austin Healey 3000 Mark II went faster (117 mph) than any other sports car in its price range. Faster, in fact, than many cars priced £500 or £600 more.

Now Austin Healey have taken the 3000 yet another step forward—to Mark III.

Brake horsepower is up from 136 to 150. And top speed now soars to a breathtaking 125 mph!

Other under-the-bonnet developments include twin carburettors, changed to deliver the extra power. Gear ratios modified to accommodate it. And an effortless new braking system, power assisted to cope with the improved performance.

Behind the wheel, too, you see a vastly different 3000. A sumptuous looking walnut fascia stretches all the way across the cockpit. The main controls are grouped together in a central console which descends to a transmission tunnel faced in leather.

There's a new look-up glove compartment. A new gadget box within easy reach of the driver. And the rear seat folds down to become a convenient platform for luggage.

The price, including £191.3.9 purchase tax, is £1,106.3.9. (Electrically operated Laycock overdrive is extra.) Which makes the new Austin Healey 3000 Mark III the fastest sports car you can own for less than £1,500!

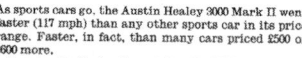

BACKED BY BMC SERVICE—EXPRESS, EXPERT, EVERYWHERE
THE AUSTIN MOTOR CO. LTD., LONGBRIDGE, BIRMINGHAM. BMC EXPORT SALES LTD., BIRMINGHAM AND 41-46 PICCADILLY, LONDON, W.1

 *you invest in an* **AUSTIN**

BACKED BY BMC 12-MONTH WARRANTY AND BMC SERVICE—THE MOST COMPREHENSIVE IN EUROPE
THE AUSTIN MOTOR COMPANY LIMITED · LONGBRIDGE · BIRMINGHAM Personal Exports Division · 41-46 PICCADILLY · LONDON W1 · REG 6000

AUSTIN-HEALEY 3000

MARK THREE

APART from various subtle body changes and a number of different power units, the big Austin-Healey has been with us for a very long time. Throughout its history, the car's competition record has been enviable and its popularity as a series-production sports car considerable. In spite of the undeniable fact that the car's greatest fan could scarcely describe it as refined with any degree of justification, the fact remains that it has always been a particularly satisfying car to drive.

The Mark III version was introduced earlier this year, and the principal changes from the Mark II model were new, larger carburettors, and a camshaft of improved design, together increasing the power output of the six-cylinder, 2,912 c.c. engine to 148 b.h.p. at 5,250 r.p.m.—nine more horse power, in fact, at an engine speed higher by five hundred revs. In addition, a diaphragm spring clutch is fitted (this feature was, in fact, included on some of the later models in the Mark II range), a vacuum servo is a standard fitting (having been an extra on earlier models) and the instrument panel, and in some cases the instruments themselves, have been redesigned. There is also a redesigned exhaust and silencing system.

As the years have passed, the big Healey has become more of a touring two-seater and has withdrawn from its early character as a sports car. The open model supplied for test is, in fact, officially designated the "convertible", and improved hood fastening arrangements tend to emphasise this aspect of its development. Despite all this, however, the car has lost none of its potency, and it remains an exhilarating machine

to drive: powerful, tractable and capable of an immense amount of hard work, it eats up the miles with astonishing rapidity.

The power unit is the basic B.M.C. 3 litre "C" series engine, of six cylinders with bore and stroke measurements of 83·4 mm. × 88·9 mm. (2,912 c.c.). With a compression ratio of 9 to 1, and the new S.U. HD 8 carburettors, power output is 148 b.h.p. at 5,250 r.p.m., with maximum torque of 165·2 lb./ft. at 3,500 r.p.m. Overhead valves are operated by pushrods, and there is a cast-iron cylinder head; the crankshaft runs in four main bearings. This large and, it must be admitted, fairly unrefined engine must now be nearing the limit of its potential development, although its smoothness at all speeds up to 5,000 r.p.m. is still its most outstanding feature, allied to quite remarkable flexibility. On the test car, the engine was noticeably rough once the rev-counter needle had passed the 5,000 mark, so much so that engine speeds in excess of this were employed only during the performance testing. Starting from cold was easy, although full use had to be made of the choke even in hot weather; the period required for the large mass of engine to warm through is long by current standards, and until proper running temperature was reached there was a tendency to spit-back through the carburettors: at the other end of the scale, there was frequent running-on after the ignition was turned off. The power unit is not excessively noisy in operation, although there is a pronounced hiss from the carburettor intakes, and while its exhaust note has never been more than a pleasant bark, the new exhaust system, with two silencers on the nearside of the car and a further pair mounted transversely under the boot, makes it even quieter from this aspect both inside and out. The new arrangement has not, however, improved the very poor ground clearance which has always been one of the car's faults, and at high speed on smooth roads there are still too many occasions when the silencers touch the ground. On poor surfaces, this factor must be taken into account and one's speed must be governed accordingly.

The clutch, with its diaphragm-type spring, is extremely light to operate and grips well, with no sign of slip even on full-power acceleration. The gearbox has four forward speeds and reverse and, on the test car, the optional Laycock de Normanville overdrive on third and top. No synchromesh is fitted to first gear, which is extremely difficult to select without crunching, while that on the upper three ratios is effective but rather heavy, making the gearchanges slow. This aspect is enhanced by the rather awkward arm movement needed by the position of the gear-lever. First gear is noisy, but the other ratios are quiet in operation: the ratios are not ideally chosen for a car of this type, and the wide gap between second and third is emphasised by the lower rear axle ratio employed where overdrive is fitted. In direct third 90 m.p.h. is possible: in second gear, however, only just over 50 m.p.h. can be achieved. This fault is offset to a large degree by the great flexibility of the engine, and in practice third and top gears are the only ratios employed, with their respective overdrives, once the car is on the move. The overdrive engages very smoothly, and is operated by a facia-mounted switch. The car will trundle along at around 20 m.p.h. in overdrive top without protest, while pressure with the right foot will increase this speed to the car's maximum of over 120 m.p.h. without delay.

The suspension remains conventional: at the front, coil

springs and wishbones, with lever-type shock absorbers and an anti-roll bar, provide independence, while at the rear, the live axle is sprung on semi-elliptic longitudinal leaf springs, with a panhard rod for lateral location. The ride is firm though not harsh, and uneven surfaces taken at speed set up noticeable scuttle shake, a fault from which the Mark II model was prone to suffer. The ground clearance, as we have said, is very limited, but the suspension settings are sufficiently firm not to allow this to worsen when the car is fully laden. On all surfaces the car is extremely sure-footed, and the model's road-holding, which has improved greatly over the years, now deserves to shake off once and for all its undeservedly poor reputation.

The big Healey is generously provided with brakes, and $11\frac{1}{4}$ in. discs on the front wheels are supplemented by 11 in. drums at the rear. Despite the vacuum servo now fitted as standard, heavy pedal pressure is still required, in exchange for which the big car can be stopped safely and swiftly from very high speeds. During the test there was no sign of fade however hard the brakes were made to work, and in general they gave confidence on wet and dry surfaces. Heavy braking

from high speed, however, was accompanied by slight weaving which, although not of dangerous proportions, was found to be unsettling, to say the least. The handbrake lever, mounted on the floor on the driver's side of the transmission tunnel, was found to be awkwardly-placed, though effective.

The redesigned cockpit layout and instruments add to the feeling of touring rather than sporting cars. The dashboard now has walnut veneer, and the centre of the facia extends downwards to form a console over the transmission tunnel, providing space for radio and speaker. The instrumentation is comprehensive, comprising speedometer, with total and trip mileage recorders, a new rev-counter, oil pressure, water temperature and fuel gauges. There is no ammeter, the speedometer is calibrated to 140 m.p.h. (on the Mark II model, the car was capable of a higher speed than that indicated on the speedometer dial) and the fuel gauge needle swings about so much as to render the instrument virtually useless. In all other cases, however, the instruments have steady needles, and are easy to read. Hand controls are mounted in the centre of the facia: all switches (for headlights, instrument lights, wipers and overdrive) are identical and rather too close together. Several times during the test the switch for the single-speed wipers was operated in mistake for the overdrive switch.

The driving position has a vintage feel: one sits close to the steering wheel (although an adjustment is provided it is still not possible to move the wheel close enough to the dashboard) and visibility, through a narrow windscreen, over a high bonnet line and high waist, is less "panoramic" than is nowadays common. Rearward visibility is restricted by the absence of transparent quarter-panels in the hood. The seats are small and rather hard, and provide only limited lateral support. A space behind them is upholstered to accommodate two small children, and the "squab" folds forward to provide a carpeted luggage platform when these occasional seats are not in use. This additional luggage space is particularly desirable since most of the available boot space is taken up by the spare wheel and battery. The boot also houses a battery master switch. Since no locks are fitted to the doors, it is possible to operate this switch and immobilise the car by cutting off the supply of electricity, the boot lid being then locked. Unfortunately, the switch also cuts off the supply for the side-lamps, so that one's field of parking after dark may thus be limited.

The hood fits well, and does not flap: the fastening arrangements comprise two over-centre clips on the screen top rail, so that it is almost a one-handed job to raise and lower the top. A hood cover is provided for the hood when it is folded: this adds greatly to the car's appearance, while if it is not fitted, the hood tends to rise through wind pressure at quite moderate speed, thus cutting off the rearward view through the rather small mirror. For summer motoring, the amount of engine heat which penetrates the passenger compartment is excessive, although no doubt a boon in colder weather.

The car's performance is impressive. A maximum speed of over 120 m.p.h. combines with a 0-60 m.p.h. acceleration time of exactly ten seconds to provide a car which will cruise effortlessly at high speed, while by no means wasting its time in getting to that speed. The acceleration times could be improved still further if a higher second gear were fitted. As it is, the car bowls along with a delightfully long stride: in overdrive top, 100 m.p.h. represents only about 4,000 r.p.m., and at this speed engine noise is not excessive and only the rushing wind noise indicates one's high rate of travel. The roadholding provides gentle understeer of the order which makes the keen driver itch to find fast open bends: there is, of course, plenty of power in hand to bring the tail round with a quick stab on the accelerator and at all times the car remains controllable. The steering is light and precise, although rather lifeless in feel: the scuttle shake already referred to also detracts from its better qualities. Fast getaways are, naturally, accompanied by spinning wheels, but the car is equally pleasant to drive in more "touring" fashion. During our test mileage our overall fuel consumption worked out at exactly 20 m.p.g., while the poorest figure we recorded was just over 17 m.p.g. Many owners, especially on long runs where much use is made of overdrive top gear, will undoubtedly be able to improve on this, while a twelve-gallon fuel tank provides a cruising range of well over 200 miles between refuelling stops.

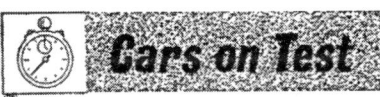 **Cars on Test**

THE AUSTIN-HEALEY 3000

Engine: Six cylinders, 83·34 mm. × 88·9 mm.; 2,912 c.c.; compression ratio 9 to 1; pushrod-operated overhead valves; two S.U. HD8 carburettors; 148 b.h.p. at 5,250 r.p.m.
Transmission: Diaphragm-spring clutch; four-speed and reverse gearbox with synchromesh on upper three ratios; overdrive on third and top on test car; floor-mounted gear-lever.
Suspension: Front, independent with coil springs, wishbones and lever-type shock absorbers. Rear, live axle with semi-elliptic leaf springs and panhard rod. Tyres: 5·90 × 15.
Brakes: Front, 11¼ in. discs; rear, 11 in. drums; vacuum servo assistance.
Dimensions: Overall length, 13 ft. 1½ ins; overall width, 5 ft. 0½ in.; overall height, 4 ft. 1 in.; turning circle, 35 ft. 7 ins.; ground clearance, 4 ins.; kerb weight, 22 cwt.

PERFORMANCE

	m.p.h.	ACCELERATION	secs.
MAXIMUM SPEED	—122·0	0— 30	2·8
Mean of two ways	—121·0	0— 40	5·1
SPEEDS IN GEARS		0— 50	7·4
First—	41	0— 60	10·0
Second—	52	0— 70	12·0
Third—	90	0— 80	15·0
overdrive third—	109	0— 90	17·8
Top—	112	0—100	25·0
		0—110	31·2
Fuel consumption	20 m.p.g.	Standing quarter-mile	—16·8

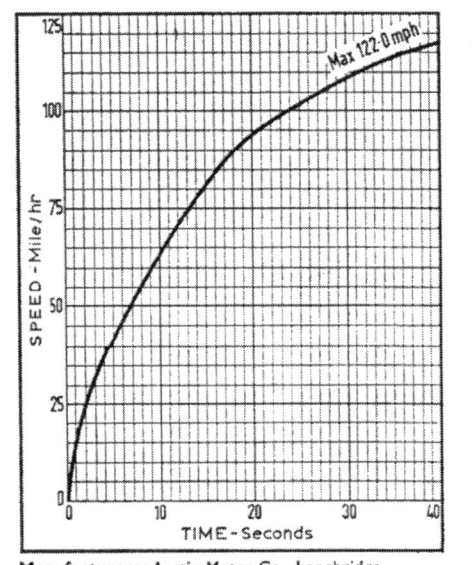

Manufacturers: Austin Motor Co., Longbridge, Birmingham.
Price: £1,045 including purchase tax.

113

AUSTIN-HEALEY
3000 MARK 3

Although based on a design that is some years old, the Austin-Healey 3000 has recently acquired extra engine power and is still a most potent force in rallies. It is a tough, rugged car, with the reputation of being nearly unbreakable. Now that it has winding windows and a really good hood, it can be regarded as a practical coupé rather than a "hairy" sports car, yet it is still primarily for the he-man.

The basis of the big Healey is a steel box-section frame which is carried close to the ground, passing beneath the back axle to which it is attached by semi-elliptic springs and a Panhard rod. In front there are wishbones and helical springs with a hefty anti-roll torsion bar. A cam and peg steering gear is fitted. Girling hydraulic brakes are used, servo assisted, with discs in front and drums behind. Knock-on wire wheels and overdrive, two worthwhile extras, were installed on the test car.

The six-cylinder engine, with cast-iron block and cylinder head, has push-rod-operated overhead valves and a four-bearing crankshaft. Steel-backed copper-lead bearings are used and the solid-skirt pistons have flat tops and a tin-plated finish. Twin S.U. downdraught carburetters, type HD8, permit sufficient breathing for 150 b.h.p. to be developed at 5,250 r.p.m.

The body is really a two-seater, though there are two extra seat pans without legroom. These may be covered to provide useful luggage space, the boot in the tail being largely occupied by the spare wheel. The hood is easy to raise and lower, the windscreen being curiously shallow by modern standards. However, the view all round is quite satisfactory. A raised section above the propeller shaft tunnel may be struck by the left elbow on occasion, but the gear lever is better placed than in the past. The adjustable steering column is an

114

excellent feature that should be found on many more cars.

When I first drove the Austin-Healey, the hood was raised and London traffic had to be negotiated. I was not impressed, for I thought that a six-cylinder engine might idle more smoothly and it seemed noisy when revved on the gears. In the open country with the hood down, however, it was a different story. The big machine had a wonderfully long stride and could put the miles behind it in a most effortless manner. In open form the tendency of the hood to magnify mechanical noises had gone, though the power unit still tended to be rather rough as maximum revolutions were approached. The large engine fills the bonnet and one is therefore conscious of its song.

The Mark 3 is much more stable than previous big Healeys, but at first one feels an occasional "wiggle" at speed which one later learns to ignore. The steering does not at first inspire confidence, but, again, it turns out to be much more accurate than appeared to be the case. The brakes are powerful, and though they smelt hot after a circuit test there was no fading.

The gears are easier to change with the new position of the lever. Third is a very useful ratio, which can be extended still further by the use of the overdrive. There is a large gap between third and second speeds, though first is quite high and curiously close to second. With the considerable torque of the big engine the gap is, in fact, not particularly noticeable.

A maximum speed of 118.4 m.p.h. was recorded on overdrive. It is possible that 120 m.p.h. could be exceeded on the direct drive, but as the timed runs would have entailed driving for several miles with the rev-counter needle on or near the red mark, I resisted the temptation. Obviously, 120 m.p.h. could be exceeded on overdrive with a favourable wind or gradient.

A cruising speed of 110 m.p.h. can be held with ease, though fuel economy may dictate a slightly lower speed. There is something most satisfying about the high-speed cruising, and a short burst on the direct drive can bring the car back into its stride when checked.

On Brands Hatch, the Austin-Healey cornered remarkably well. It "hung on," refusing to break away easily, and would take full throttle coming out of the corners without tending to run wide. I did not inflate the tyres especially for this exercise, as of course one would if one were doing it seriously, but it was obvious that the behaviour of the rear end was unusually good. Harder tyres would also increase the maximum speed. The car is too heavy to flick through a corner like a single-seater, but considered as the substantial sports convertible that it is the handling must be regarded as most satisfactory.

If the car is at its best with the hood folded away, it is also very cosy with the top up, and it is pleasant to be able to erect it quickly when the evening becomes chilly. Naturally, the sound of the engine is then more prominent, but this only becomes insistent during hard acceleration through the gears. The general impression is that the big machine is enjoying its work, which is very different from a poor little engine that seems to be in distress.

It took me several days before I could find reverse gear—a matter of using both hands! However, it was easy once I had got the knack, but I am informed that the test car was not up to standard in this respect.

Towards the end of my "ownership" the overdrive went out of action, but this may have been something trivial, such as a fuse.

The Austin-Healey 3000 is a car for long journeys. It will go anywhere, and fast, too, without wilting under the worst conditions. There are smoother and quieter town carriages, but for the man who likes to feel a big engine gobbling up the miles, this is an attractive buy.

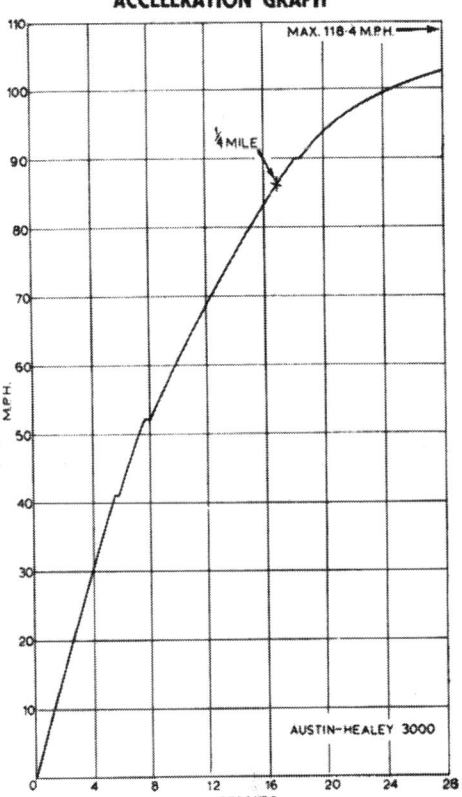

ACCELERATION GRAPH

MAX. 118·4 M.P.H.

¼ MILE

M.P.H.

SECONDS

AUSTIN-HEALEY 3000

SPECIFICATION AND PERFORMANCE DATA

Car Tested: Austin-Healey 3000 Mk. 3 Sports Convertible. Price, with fresh air heater, wire-spoked wheels, overdrive, and adjustable steering column, £1,217 19s. 2d. including P.T.

Engine: Six-cylinders 83.36 mm. x 89 mm. (2,912 c.c.). Compression ratio 9.03 to 1. 150 b.h.p. at 5,250 r.p.m. Twin S.U. carburetters. Lucas coil and distributor.

Transmission: Diaphragm type clutch. Four-speed gearbox, with central lever and synchromesh on upper three-speeds, plus Laycock-de Normanville overdrive. Ratios 3.205 (overdrive top), 3.909 4.195 (overdrive third), 5.116, 8.025, and 11.453 to 1. Open propeller shaft. Hypoid rear axle.

Chassis: Box-section frame, underslung at rear. Independent front suspension by wishbones, helical springs, and anti-roll torsion bar. Cam and peg steering gear with adjustable column. Rear axle on semi-elliptic springs with Panhard rod. Lever-type hydraulic dampers all round. Girling hydraulic brakes with servo assistance, 11¼ ins. discs in front, 11 ins. x 2¼ ins. drums at rear. 5.90 x 15 ins. Dunlop Road Speed tyres.

Equipment: 12-volt lighting and starting. Speedometer. Rev. counter. Fuel, water temperature, and oil pressure gauges. Heating and demisting. Flashing direction indicators.

Dimensions: Wheelbase, 7 ft. 8 ins.; Track (front), 4 ft. 0⅞in.; (rear), 4 ft. 2 in.; Overall length, 13 ft. 1½ ins.; Width, 5 ft. 0½ in.; Weight, 1 ton 1¼ cwt.

Performance: Maximum speed (overdrive), 118.4 m.p.h. Speeds in gears: Direct top, 118 m.p.h.; Overdrive third, 109 m.p.h.; third, 90 m.p.h.; second, 52 m.p.h. Standing quarter-mile, 16.8 secs. Acceleration: 0-30 m.p.h., 4 secs.; 0-50 m.p.h., 7.2 secs.; 0-60 m.p.h., 9.9 secs.; 0-80 m.p.h., 15 secs.; 0-100 m.p.h., 24.3 secs.

Fuel Consumption: 17 to 19 m.p.g.

Make · AUSTIN-HEALEY   Type · 3000 Mk. III (2,912 c.c.)

(Front engine, rear-wheel drive)

Manufacturers : Austin Motor Co. Ltd., Longbridge, Birmingham

Test Conditions

Weather ... Dry and sunny with 0-5 m.p.h. wind
Temperature .... 9 deg. C. (48 deg. F.)
Barometer .... 29·6in. Hg.
Dry concrete and tarmac surfaces.

Weight

Kerb weight (with oil, water and half-full fuel tank)
                    23·5 cwt (2,604lb-1,180kg)
Front-rear distribution, per cent F, 52; R, 48
Laden as tested ......26·5 cwt (2,940lb-1,333kg)

Turning Circles

Between kerbs ...... L, 35ft 0in.; R, 34ft 10in.
Between walls ...... L, 36ft 3in.; R, 35ft 10in.
Turns of steering wheel lock to lock 3

FUEL AND OIL CONSUMPTION

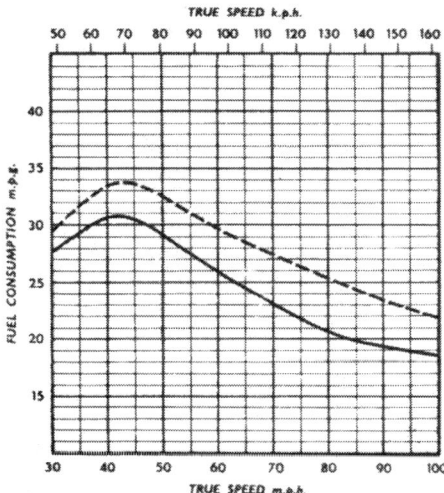

FUEL ....Super premium grade
                              (101 octane RM)

Test Distance .... 1,583 miles
Overall Consumption ...... 20·3 m.p.g.
                              (13·9 litres/100 km.)
Estimated Consumption (DIN) 24·9 m.p.g.
                              (11·4 litres/100 km.)
OIL: SAE 10W30 ... Consumption 1,600 m.p.g.

HILL CLIMBING AT STEADY SPEEDS

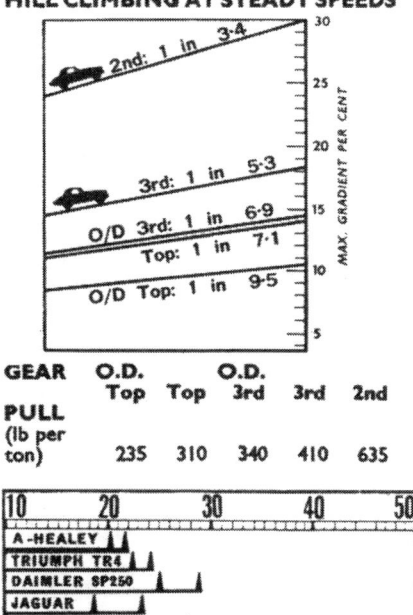

GEAR	O.D. Top	Top	O.D. 3rd	3rd	2nd
PULL (lb per ton)	235	310	340	410	635

M.P.G. Overall and Estimated (DIN)

A-HEALEY
TRIUMPH TR4
DAIMLER SP250
JAGUAR
RELIANT

MAXIMUM SPEEDS AND ACCELERATION TIMES

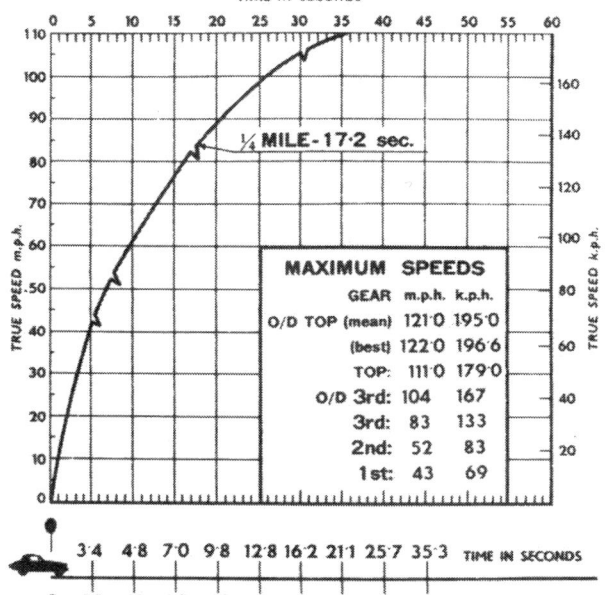

¼ MILE-17·2 sec.

MAXIMUM SPEEDS		
GEAR	m.p.h.	k.p.h.
O/D TOP (mean)	121·0	195·0
(best)	122·0	196·6
TOP:	111·0	179·0
O/D 3rd:	104	167
3rd:	83	133
2nd:	52	83
1st:	43	69

TIME IN SECONDS	3·4	4·8	7·0	9·8	12·8	16·2	21·1	25·7	35·3
TRUE SPEED m.p.h.	30	40	50	60	70	80	90	100	100
CAR SPEEDOMETER	28	40	48	58	70	80	93	104	114

Speed range, gear ratios and time in seconds

m.p.h.	O.D. Top (3·14)	Top (3·91)	O. Third (4·74)	Third (5·12)	Second (8·05)	First (11·26)
10—30	—	—	—	6·1	4·2	3·0
20—40	—	7·5	6·6	4·1	3·2	2·8
30—50	9·3	6·8	6·3	5·4	3·4	—
40—60	8·7	6·9	6·8	4·9	—	—
50—70	10·7	7·9	7·3	5·5	—	—
60—80	12·1	8·1	7·8	6·4	—	—
70—90	13·6	9·0	8·2	—	—	—
80—100	15·7	9·9	9·0	—	—	—
90—110	18·2	14·2	—	—	—	—

BRAKES (from 30 m.p.h. in neutral)	Pedal load	Retardation	Equiv. distance
	25lb	0·23g	131ft
	50lb	0·72g	42ft
	75lb	0·81g	37ft
	100lb	0·92g	32·8ft
Handbrake		0·37g	81ft

CLUTCH   Pedal load and travel—40lb and 6in.

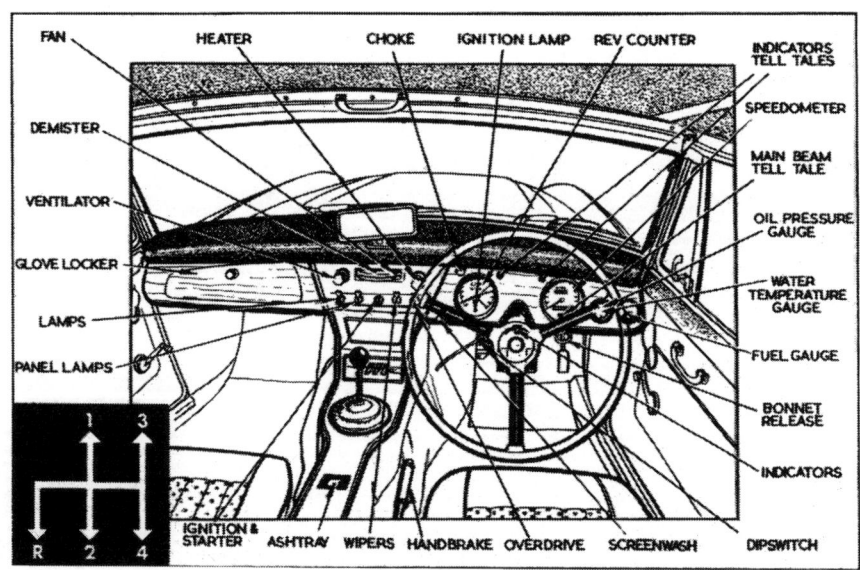

Austin-Healey 3000 Mk. III CONVERTIBLE 2,912 c.c.

SUN-CAPPED Dolomites and the distant roar and squeal of one of the works rally cars scrambling its way up the Gavia pass—this perhaps is the image that some people have of the big Austin-Healey at work. But there is a world of difference between those frequent winners, the former Spartan works rally cars, and the over-the-counter product of today—the 3000 Mk. III

For as long as many of us care to remember there has been a big Healey in the price lists. The car has been through several variations of engine size, but now, like an ageing but still beautiful dowager, repeated face lifts can no longer wholly hide the ravages of time and progress.

For many years a change in the model of the Healey has been marked with either the subtraction or addition of a carburettor; however, the Mk. III continues with two S.U. carburettors for the Series C 2,912 c.c. engine, with diameter increased by 0·25in. to 2in. With the new carburettors and a camshaft of improved design the power output of the engine has been raised from 137 b.h.p. at 4,750 r.p.m. to 148 b.h.p. at 5,250 r.p.m. Although this comparatively unsophisticated six-cylinder engine must now be very near the end of its development, it seems to have gained in flexibility and is virtually free from any temperament.

Provided full use is made of the choke, starting from cold is good. The engine takes a long time to warm through and

spits back through the carburettors if pushed at all hard before it is warm. The all-too-frequent trouble of running-on still persists and could only be prevented by opening the throttles wide as the ignition was switched off.

Although the big Healey has never been a noisy car in standard form, the latest design of exhaust system, with two silencers on the left side of the car and a further two set transversely under the boot floor, cuts the noise down to almost saloon car level at anything but near-peak engine

PRICES		£	s	d
Sports Convertible		915	0	0
Purchase tax		191	3	9
	Total (in G.B.)	1,106	3	9
Extras (including P.T.)				
Overdrive		60	8	4
Wire wheels		30	4	2
Fresh air heater		18	14	7
Telescopic steering column		2	8	4
Seat belts (each)		5	5	0

How the Austin-Healey 3000 Mk. III compares:

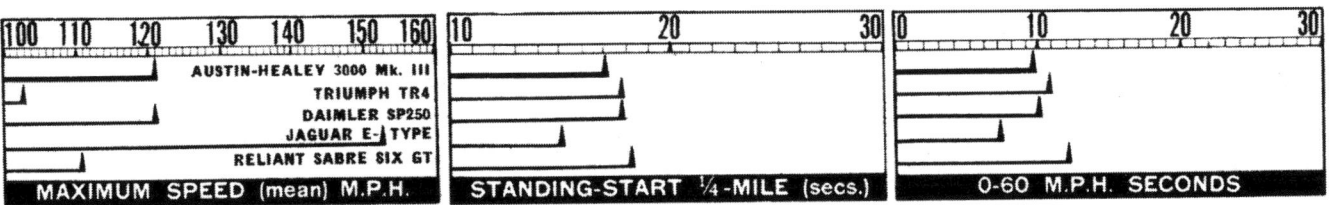

| AUSTIN-HEALEY 3000 Mk. III |
| TRIUMPH TR4 |
| DAIMLER SP250 |
| JAGUAR E-TYPE |
| RELIANT SABRE SIX GT |

MAXIMUM SPEED (mean) M.P.H. — STANDING-START ¼-MILE (secs.) — 0-60 M.P.H. SECONDS

*A central console,
wood-trimmed facia
and re-grouped
instruments are new
to the model; fixed
quarter-light frames
on the front doors
can be too close to
the occupants' head
when getting in*

revs. However, the car still suffers from very limited ground clearance and over rough roads one has to put up with bangs and thumps when the silencers touch bumps on the surface.

The test car was fitted with the optional extra Laycock de Normanville overdrive, working on third and top gears. With overdrive, a lower back axle ratio is used—3·91 in place of the normal 3·55 to 1 ratio. While this does make the car extremely flexible in the upper ratios at low engine revs, it tends to emphasize the large gap between second and third gears, with their respective maximum speeds of 52 and 83 m.p.h. Overdrive third gear produced a maximum of 104 m.p.h., direct top 111 m.p.h. and overdrive top gave a mean maximum speed of 121 m.p.h. Overdrive, operated by a switch on the facia, engages very smoothly indeed; to return to direct drive the engine has to be pulling before an inhibitor switch will release the overdrive. This prevents jolts in the transmission.

In practice, very high averages can be maintained on main roads by using just direct and overdrive top gears, the car wafting along at around the 90 mark with no more than 4,000 r.p.m. on the rev counter.

The big Healey's take-off from standstill is impressive. Without tyre squeal or wheel-spin, it reached 30 m.p.h. in 3·4 40 in 4·8, 60 in 9·8 and 100 in 25·7sec. At maximum revs—5,250 r.p.m. in this case—the combined noise of

engine, cooling fan, unsilenced carburettor air intakes and exhaust reaches almost Grand Prix levels and on the maximum speed runs the scream of wind round the windows and hood adds to the din. Prolonged motorway driving at very high speeds becomes tiring for this reason.

Clutch Improved

Later models of the Austin-Healey 3000 Mk. II were fitted with diaphragm spring clutches but this was the first model of the make we have been able to drive fitted with one. The pressure is light—only 40lb—and the length of travel and smoothness of engagement are more like those of a touring car than a 120 m.p.h. sports car. Effective, rather heavy synchromesh makes gear-changing a bit slow on the upper three ratios and it is almost impossible to get into first gear while on the move without crunching. The position of the gear lever is such that one has to use a cranked elbow action to make changes, but this soon becomes quite a natural movement.

The years of competition and development have certainly improved the car's handling. For normal motoring, the car has slight understeer, but when time is short, the right foot can turn this into an accurately controllable power oversteer. When cornering hard the driver has to beware of

*Left: The back of the rear seat folds forward to make a good luggage platform—which is needed
as the boot (right) is much taken up by spare wheel, battery and hood covers*

The unmistakable lines of the big Healey still suggest potency. The small upper rear "lamps" are reflectors

bumps in the road, which can throw the car off course with unexpected force. In the wet, an unwary jab on the accelerator can bring the tail of the car skating round and a good deal of caution has to be used on corners.

We were unable to test the car's handling on our special *pavé* track for fear of wiping off the exhaust system, but on a rough side road, the short suspension movements and firm damping make the car twitch about unless the driver concentrates on holding direction. The steering itself is heavy at low speeds, but once the car gets on to the open road it becomes a good deal lighter. At near-maximum speed, the car controls very well and holds a straight course.

Although a vacuum servo is standard equipment on the Mk. III models—it was an extra on the previous model—the brakes still feel heavy, but they are very powerful. Heavy braking from high speeds is accompanied by slight weaving; this never builds up to anything near dangerous proportions, but is nevertheless disconcerting. The pull-up handbrake, located between the driving seat and transmission tunnel held the car easily on a 1-in-3 hill, from where take-off was of the "rocket" variety, with spinning wheels.

Driving Position

In its appointments the Austin-Healey 3000 Mk. III is now more of a touring car than a sports car. The new panel design and the trim are attractive, almost luxurious. In these days of straight-arm steering, the driver of the big Healey has to get used to the old Vintage bent arm position again, with the huge 17in. diameter steering wheel only a matter of inches from his chest. On the test car the telescopic steering column (an extra) was fitted. If it had put the wheel 3in. *nearer* the facia it would have been more help. The pedals are small and set close together. If space and layout allowed the pedal group to be brought back three inches and the seat moved back a similar distance, the driving position would be far more comfortable. The seats are rather small and hard, with cushions that "set" after a few miles. At the end of a long drive you are glad to have a good stretch to restore the circulation.

The "traditional" British love of wood has extended to this Healey and the dashboard has walnut veneer on its two outer panels. The centre of the facia now extends downwards to form a central console with the deep transmission tunnel. There are spaces in this console for a radio and loudspeaker.

A comprehensive set of instruments is grouped behind the steering wheel and comprises a speedometer, with total and trip mileage recorders, rev counter, combined oil pressure and water temperature gauge and fuel gauge. While

driving, this last instrument swings freely between full and empty as soon as the tank contents have dropped to about three-quarters full. In the centre of the facia are four identical switches in pairs on each side of the ignition-starter switch; they control driving and panel lamps, and screenwipers and overdrive. A differently shaped toggle for the O.D. switch would make it more easily identifiable; at

Not a spare inch is wasted under the bonnet; the lid still has to be propped open with a stay

night it is easy to flick the wrong switch and start the single speed wipers working instead of selecting overdrive. A single quadrant control adjusts the temperature of the heater, distribution of flow between the car and windscreen being adjusted by two flaps set high under the back of the dashboard.

There is a large lockable cubby in the facia and a non-locking glove box on the transmission tunnel, with a padded top to form an armrest for driver or passenger. Two small seats for children are fitted in the back, and an adult, sitting sideways, could be packed in for short trips. The backrest of this seat folds forward and is held by two substantial bolts to form a large luggage platform, with a lip on the leading edge to prevent suitcases sliding forward. This platform is really valuable because the boot is mainly occupied by the spare wheel and battery and can hold only one small grip and some odds and ends. Now that winding windows are fitted and a hardtop is offered, B.M.C. ought to provide locks for the doors. They do provide a battery master switch in the boot which cuts off all current—including the side lamps for parking at night. A prop rod has to be slotted into a catch to hold the boot open.

In these days of international conformity over direction indicators, the big Healey still uses the side and tail lamps as indicators and at night they can be confusing to following traffic if one is braking and indicating at the same time. Twin horns with an impressive volume are fitted.

The well-fitting hood was rain-tight and did not flap at high speeds; it is held down on to the screen rail by two over-centre clips with ominously sharp projections. The convertible type hood can be folded back easily and in a matter of seconds, and a hood cover is provided. Fresh-air ventilation can be greatly increased in warm weather by un-zipping the whole of the back window and folding it down. In summer, the car still suffers from too much heat coming through from the engine and to help overcome this a cold air vent is fitted under the dash—on the left-hand side.

This car is much faster than the Mk. II version, and is more economical, averaging 20·3 m.p.g. overall. Commuting and a series of fast, short runs, where maximum revs were frequently being used, dropped the consumption to 18·7 m.p.g.; on everyday motoring, the fuel consumption is around the 22 m.p.g. mark. The 12-gallon fuel tank filled easily, without any blow back. During the 1,583 miles of testing eight pints of oil were used, but the car had been fitted with new piston rings shortly before it was handed over for test and probably they were still bedding-in.

Under the bonnet, the husky six-cylinder engine fills every inch of available space, with wires and cables running everywhere. The screenwasher bottle, which used to be inside the passenger cockpit, has now been moved under the bonnet. The lid is held shut by two safety catches and is held open with a stay.

Despite some dated features, the big Healey is still terrific fun to drive. Tractable, capable of an immense amount of hard work with reasonable economy, it will still have its devotees long after production has ceased.

Specification: Austin-Healey 3000 Mk. III Convertible

PERFORMANCE DATA
Overdrive top gear m.p.h. per 1,000 r.p.m. ... 23·0
Top gear m.p.h. per 1,000 r.p.m. ... 18·9
Mean piston speed at max. power ... 3,035 ft/min.
Engine revs. at mean max. speed ... 5,260 r.p.m.
B.h.p. per ton laden ... 111·2

▼ Scale: 0.3in. to 1ft. Cushions uncompressed.

ENGINE
Cylinders ... 6-in-line
Bore ... 83·4mm (3·28in.)
Stroke ... 88·9mm (3·50in.)
Displacement ... 2,912 c.c. (178 cu. in.)
Valve gear ... Overhead, pushrods and rockers
Compression ratio 9·0-to-1
Carburettors ... 2 S.U. HD8
Fuel pump ... S.U. electric
Oil filter ... Full flow, renewable element
Max. power ... 148 b.h.p. (net) at 5,250 r.p.m.
Max. torque ... 165·2 lb. ft. at 3,500 r.p.m.

TRANSMISSION
Clutch ... Borg and Beck diaphragm spring, 9·5in. dia.
Gearbox ... Four speed, synchromesh on 2nd, 3rd and Top; central control
Overall ratios ... O.D. Top 0·82, Top 1·00; O.D. Third 1·08, Third 1·31, Second 2·06; First 2·88; Reverse 3·72
Final drive ... Hypoid bevel, 3·91

CHASSIS
Construction ... Boxed cruciform chassis, with steel and aluminium body

SUSPENSION
Front ... Independent, coil springs and wishbones, lever arm dampers, anti-roll bar
Rear ... Live axle, half elliptic leaf springs, Panhard rod, lever arm dampers
Steering ... Cam and peg
Wheel dia. ... 17in.

BRAKES
Type ... Girling hydraulic, disc front drum rear, vacuum servo
Dimensions ... F, 11·25in. dia. R, 11·0in. dia., 2·25in. wide shoes
Swept area ... F, 228 sq. in.; R, 155·5 sq. in. Total: 383·5 sq. in. (286 sq. in. per ton laden)

WHEELS
Type ... Pressed steel disc standard, wire-spoked, centre-lock extra, 4·5in. wide rim
Tyres ... 5·90—15in. Dunlop RS5 with tubes

EQUIPMENT
Battery ... 12-volt 57-amp. hr.
Headlamps ... 36-48 watt
Reversing lamp ... None
Electric fuses ... 2
Screen wipers ... 2, single speed, self parking
Screen washer ... Standard, manual plunger
Interior heater ... Extra, fresh air, electric booster
Safety belts ... Extra, anchorages provided
Interior trim ... Ambla leathercloth
Floor covering ... Carpet
Starting handle ... No provision
Jack ... Screw type
Jacking points ... 4, on suspension
Other bodies ... None

MAINTENANCE
Fuel tank ... 12 Imp. gallons (no reserve)
Cooling system ... 20 pints (including heater)
Engine sump ... 12·75 pints SAE 10W30. Change oil every 3,000 miles; change filter element every 6,000 miles
Gearbox and overdrive ... 7 pints SAE 30. Change oil every 6,000 miles
Final drive ... 3 pints SAE 90EP. Change oil every 6,000 miles
Grease ... 11 points every 3,000 miles
Tyre pressures ... F, 20; R, 25 p.s.i. (normal driving). F, 25; R, 30 p.s.i. (fast driving)

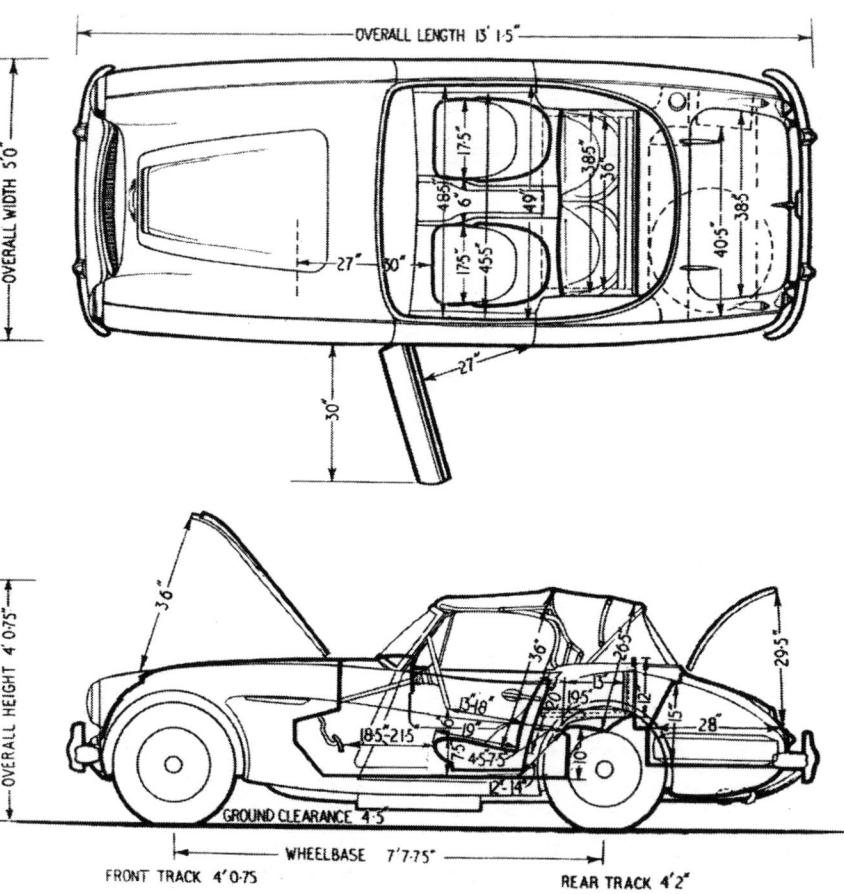

OVERALL LENGTH 13' 1·5"
OVERALL WIDTH 5'0"
OVERALL HEIGHT 4' 0·75"
GROUND CLEARANCE 4·5"
WHEELBASE 7'7·75"
FRONT TRACK 4'0·75"
REAR TRACK 4'2"

ROAD & TRACK
R&T
ROAD TEST

AUSTIN-HEALEY 3000 MK III

The latest model has an additional 11 bhp, a bit of tarting up and still retains that classic cowl shake

TEN YEARS AGO, the Austin-Healey 100 was first introduced to the American market. The man behind it was Donald Healey, who had previously built a limited quantity of very advanced and successful sports cars using Riley engines. The demise of the Riley and the many problems confronting the small manufacturer caused Healey to seek an easier way of making a living, so he sold the Austin company on the idea of using production Austin parts to build a sports car aimed specifically at the American market. The result was the Austin-Healey 100, which has been gradually updated during the ensuing years to become the Austin-Healey 3000 Mk III Sports Convertible.

In its original form, the Healey was a conventional low-priced sports car, which offered the fast and responsive rag-top-and-flapping-side-curtains type of driving demanded by the enthusiast of the day. Its 4-cyl engine was lusty and reliable, its 3-speed and overdrive transmission was a novelty and, even if the car did have some extremely annoying faults, at least it provided enjoyable and exciting driving at a time when the Detroit product was nothing short of ghastly.

In its 1964 form, the Healey is a much more refined car although it retains many of the characteristics of the original version, both desirable and undesirable. The major changes consist of a general tarting up of the interior, which now has walnut veneer on the instrument panel and much more luxurious finish and detailing throughout. The top is good by sports car standards because it can be erected from inside the car, and it is secured by two over-center clamps on the windshield pillars. The windows are of the wind-up variety so that the car

is well weatherproofed for the winter, at least in some climates.

BMC discarded the 4-cyl engine in 1956, substituting its rugged Six in the Healey, and this power unit has undergone a number of changes over the years so that it is now rated at 148 bhp. This is an increase of 11 bhp over the MK II version of the car, and the extra power is obtained from a different camshaft and the use of two 2-in. HD-8-SU carburetors. These carburetors require a lot of choke when starting from cold, and even then there is a tendency to spit back if too much throttle is used during the long warm-up period the engine seems to demand.

Another relatively insignificant but worthwhile improvement

AUSTIN-HEALEY 3000
AT A GLANCE...

Price as tested	$3828
Engine	6 cyl, ohv, 2912 cc, 148 bhp
Curb weight, lb	2650
Top speed, mph	116
Acceleration, 0–60 mph, sec	9.8
Passing test, 50–70 mph, sec	5.7
Average fuel consumption, mpg	19

ROAD TEST
AUSTIN-HEALEY 3000

SCALE: 10" DIVISIONS

PRICE

List price.................$3699
Price as tested..........$3828

ENGINE

No. cylinders & type....6 cyl, ohv
Bore x stroke, in......3.28 x 3.50
Displacement cc...........2912
  Equivalent cu in.........177.7
Compression ratio...........9:1
Bph @ rpm..........148 @ 5250
  Equivalent mph...........123
Torque @ rpm, lb-ft..165 @ 3500
  Equivalent mph............82
Carburetors, no. & make....2 SU
No. barrels & dia.......1–2 in
Type fuel required......premium

DRIVE TRAIN

Clutch type.single plate, diaphragm
  Diameter, in..............9.5
Gear ratios : o'drive (0.82)...3.21:1
  4th (1.00)................3.91:1
  3rd (1.31)................5.12:1
  2nd (2.06)................8.05:1
  1st (2.88)...............11.3:1
Synchromesh............on top 3
Differential type....hypoid bevel
  Ratio....................3.91:1
  Optional ratio..........3.55:1

CHASSIS & SUSPENSION

Frame type...separate ladder type
Brake type............disc/drum
  Swept area, sq in.........383
Tire size....Dunlop RS-5 5.90 x 15
Steering type........cam & lever
  Overall ratio.............15:1
  Turns, lock to lock........3.0
  Turning circle, ft........36.0
Front suspension: independent with
  A-arms, lever shocks, coil springs.
Rear suspension: live axle with
  semi-elliptic springs, lever
  shocks, Panhard rod.

ACCOMMODATION

Normal capacity, persons.......2
Occasional capacity............3
Seat width, front, in......2 x 17.5
  Rear....................2 x 16
Head room, front/rear...35.5/28.0
Seat back adjustment, deg...none
Entrance height, in...........44
Step-over height..........14.5
Door width, front..........26.5
Driver comfort rating :
  For driver 69-in. tall........85
  For driver 72-in.............65
  For driver 75-in. tall........45
  (85/100, good; 70/85, fair;
    under 70, poor)

GENERAL

Curb weight, lb...........2650
Test weight..............3020
Weight distribution (with
  driver), front/rear, %....47/53
Wheelbase, in.............92.0
Track, front/rear.......48.7/50.0
Overall length, in..........157.0
  Width...................60.0
  Height..................50.0
Frontal area, sq ft........16.7
Ground clearance, in.........4.5
Overhang, front/rear......25/41
Departure angle (no load), deg..14
Usable trunk space, cu ft......2.3
Fuel tank capacity, gal.......14.4

INSTRUMENTATION

Instruments: fuel, oil pressure,
  water temperature, 140 mph
  speedometer, 7000 rpm tachometer.
Warnings lights: high beam, ignition, turn signals.

MISCELLANEOUS

Body styles available: roadster as
  tested.

ACCESSORIES

Included in list price: overdrive,
  wire wheels, heater, windshield
  washers, full instrumentation,
  adjustable steering column, seat
  belt anchors.
Available at extra cost: seat belts,
  tonneau cover.

CALCULATED DATA

Lb/hp (test weight)..........20.4
Cu ft/ton mi................86.7
Mph/1000 rpm (overdrive)...23.3
Engine revs/mi.............2560
Piston travel, ft/mi........1490
Rpm @ 2500 ft/min........4280
  Equivalent mph..........100.3
R&T wear index............37.9

MAINTENANCE

Crankcase capacity, qt........7.5
  Change interval, mi.......3000
Oil filter type...........full flow
  Change interval, mi.......6000
Chassis lube interval, mi....3000
Tire pressure, front/rear, psi.20/25

ROAD TEST RESULTS

ACCELERATION

0–30 mph, sec................3.6
0–40 mph.....................5.1
0–50 mph.....................7.0
0–60 mph.....................9.8
0–70 mph....................13.0
0–80 mph....................17.1
0–100 mph...................27.4
Passing test, 50–70 mph.....5.7
Standing ¼ mi..............17.4
  Speed at end, mph.........82

TOP SPEEDS

Overdrive (5000), mph.......116
4th (5500)..................101
3rd (5500)...................81
2nd (5500)...................51
1st (5500)...................36

GRADE CLIMBING
(Tapley data)

Overdrive, max gradient, %.....9
4th.........................12
3rd.........................17
2nd.........................27
1st....................off scale
Total drag at 60 mph, lb......95

SPEEDOMETER ERROR

30 mph indicated.....actual 30.0
40 mph...................40.2
60 mph...................60.0
80 mph...................79.1
100 mph..................98.7

FUEL CONSUMPTION

Normal driving, mpg........16/21
Crusing range, mi.......230/302

ACCELERATION & COASTING

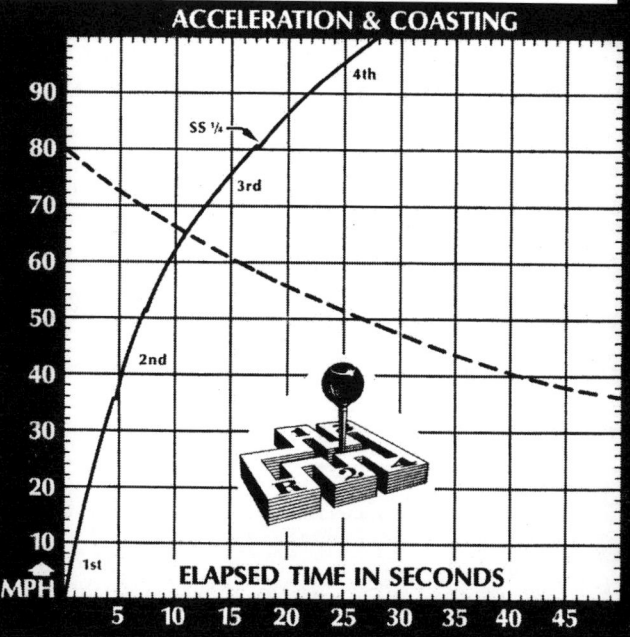

ELAPSED TIME IN SECONDS

AUSTIN-HEALEY 3000 MK III

concerns the rear suspension. Here the chassis frame has been curved to allow for additional axle movement, and springs of a lower rate are used. In order to control the movement of the axle more positively, it is now located by twin radius arms, and the results of these modifications are a better ride, improved handling and increased ground clearance.

Despite improvements to the rear suspension, the ride and handling of the Healey are still in the classic sports car tradition of the early '50s, before people like Chapman and Cooper had got in on the act. The ride is firm and there is some chassis flexing evident from the authentic cowl shake which occurs on any but the smoothest surfaces. In common with the rigidly sprung cars of the time, the road-holding of the Healey is quite good on smooth surfaces, but a fast turn on a poor surface may produce surprises, because the rear end has a tendency to jump and skip over bumps.

Under normal conditions, the Healey has slight understeer, but plenty of throttle opening in a corner will change this to oversteer, and the tail can be hung out a long way with delicate throttle control. However, one should select the road surface rather carefully before experimenting because any irregularity will throw the car off its line, and a wet surface tends to make the handling treacherous.

At low speeds the steering is comparatively heavy, but it lightens as the speed increases and the car holds its line accurately at normal cruising speeds, although there is a tendency for the rear end to twitch on rougher surfaces.

Due to the improved rear suspension and the slight rearward weight bias, one can apply a surprising amount of power when coming out of a slow turn without any tendency for the car to break away, lift its inside rear wheel, or lose traction. The Austin-Healey is no sluggard on the road, but one has to work hard and use some skill and experience to extract the maximum from it.

Although the car has an adjustable steering column, it is difficult for tall drivers to accommodate themselves comfortably, as a glance at the Driver Comfort Rating on the data panel will show. Apart from the driver and passenger seats, there is accommodation for two children behind, or, alternatively, one adult can be carried for short trips. This space can also be used to supplement the limited trunk space, which is almost entirely filled by the spare wheel and the battery. The controls are a mixture of ancient and modern. The transmission, in particular, needs updating because 1st is unsynchron-

ized, noisy and difficult to select, and the synchronization of the other three gears leaves a lot to be desired. On the other hand, the shifting of the overdrive is very fast and smooth, although the positioning of the control switch makes it hard to locate in a hurry.

The overdrive operates on 3rd and high so that in effect the car has 6 speeds. Although this would seem to provide a ratio for any occasion, there is actually an excessive gap between 2nd and 3rd, which is accentuated by the fact that if the overdrive switch is in the overdrive position, the overdrive ratio will be selected automatically as soon as one shifts up from 2nd to 3rd, thereby increasing the gap.

The clutch is a great improvement over previous Healey models and, in fact, over the majority of sports car clutches. It is of the diaphragm type, and its action is light and smooth in direct contrast to the early Healey units, which were very heavy and fierce, and had an annoying habit of breaking their linkages. The car is equipped with disc brakes at the front and drums at the rear and the brakes are generally very good, although the pedal pressure required is high despite the use of a booster in the system.

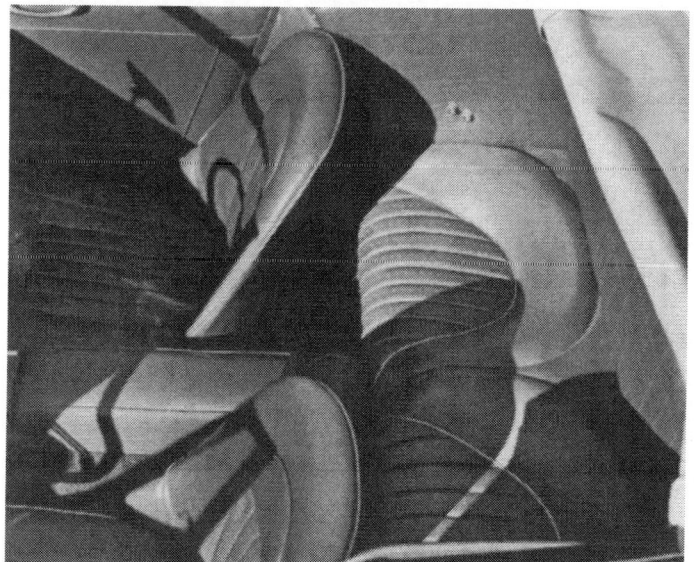

One of the most noticeable features of the Healey is the unduly high noise level, which commences at about 3000 rpm and makes normal conversation impossible by 4000 rpm. It takes the form of a loud roar which is a mixture of engine, fan, transmission, carburetor, and exhaust noises, and one can't help feeling that a lot of it could be eliminated by better attention to insulation. The noise coupled with the rather uncomfortable driving position and the stiff suspension makes the car tiring to drive on a long trip. The level of exhaust noise has been reduced by the addition of a pair of supplementary mufflers located transversely at the rear of the car. However, the eternal Healey problem of low ground clearance remains, and the primary mufflers are still located beside the left frame rail where they are far too low and consequently extremely vulnerable.

The Austin-Healey is now in its 12th year, which is a long span in an age of rapid automobile development. It has served its purpose well both on road and track, and as recently as 1962 a Healey got as high as 8th place at Le Mans before piston failure put it out. However, the existing model appears to have reached the point of honorable retirement, and perhaps BMC will soon come up with a worthy successor after starting from scratch with a clean sheet of paper.

AUSTIN HEALEY

3000 SPORTS CONVERTIBLE

Sprite MARK III

I T'S SURPRISING, really, just how short a time the Austin-Healeys have been with us. So far as the big car—nowadays called the 3000—is concerned, it seems like ages, though, because apart from various body changes—a good many of them hard to find—and the step up from four to six pots, it has been winning international rallies in much the same general form for most of its life. So far as the little one, the Sprite, is concerned, this has grown up in a big way since the first frog-eyed version was spawned five or six years back.

Recently we have been covering a bit of mileage in both of them, and we thought that this time we could do a lot worse than combine the two cars in one road test. Obviously, there is no comparison between the rough, lusty "big Healey" and the Sprite unless its in the way they've both become a good deal more touring than sporting.

Let's have a look at the big 'un first. This is something of a he-man's motor-car, Pat Moss-Carlsson aside: it is heavy, rough, slightly crude, noisy, and at high speed it takes a bit of driving. In fact, it's almost vintage, really, and you might think that there is no excuse for this sort of car nowadays apart from the trifling facts that it still sells as fast as they can make it, and it is still more than capable of winning any international rally you care to mention. On the credit side—and perhaps among the reasons why it is still so popular—it is fast, exhilarating and almost unbelievably tractable. The engine, as everybody must know, is the B.M.C. "A"-series unit, bore and stroke measurements of the six cylinders of 83.4 mm x 88.9 mm measuring up to 2,912 c.c. With a compression ratio of 9 to 1 and two S.U. HD8 carburettors, maximum power is 148 b.h.p. at 5,250 r.p.m. and there is 165.2 lb. ft. of torque at 3,500 r.p.m. This may not sound a lot when compared to the 3.8-litre Jaguar's 220 b.h.p. and 240 lb. ft. of torque, but it is, believe us, sufficient. In greater detail the power unit is a pretty unrefined slab of iron—four main bearings for the crankshaft, cast-iron head, push-rod overhead valves and so forth—and, once the needle goes past 5,000, is almost terrifyingly rough in standard unbalanced tune. But of course it never has to work terribly hard, produces an adequate amount of urge and, in general, keeps the Healey lolloping along at a brisk old trot in fine style. It isn't desperately thirsty, although you couldn't call 20 m.p.g. exactly economical. Few owners of this sort of car would mind that, though—if you

can afford the insurance premiums you ought to be able to pour the go-juice in alright.

The engine always starts easily, takes a long time to reach full working temperature unless its a very warm day, and spits back through the carbs until it's hot enough to get going. At the other end of the journey, it will very likely want to run-on after you switch it off, especially if you've been chasing it a bit. There isn't too much mechanical noise when its going, unless you count a very noisy hiss from the carburettors, while a complicated silencing arrangement—two silencers on the nearside of the car, with two more mounted tranversely under the boot—keep the bark from the twin tail pipes down to very sociable limits.

The gearbox is abominable, without any doubt, but in practice it doesn't matter so much—we'll explain that in a minute. First let's support that libel on the gearbox. For a start, bottom gear has no synchromesh, which is anachronistic these days. Then there is second gear—we are accustomed to second speeds which are too low by comparison with third, but on the Healey it reaches ridiculous proportions. In direct third you can do ninety, but in second the absolute top whack, before everything starts to fly to pieces, is only just over fifty—and that is a mere eleven miles an hour quicker than bottom gear itself. Both third and top have overdrive, and in overdrive third you can reach 109, which is a bit more like it, while in direct top it goes a little faster—112 m.p.h., to be exact. The overdrive engages very smoothly, and is operated by a fumbly dashboard-mounted switch which can take a bit of finding, even when you're used to distinguishing between that and, say, the screen wipers switch. So that's the gearbox—now why doesn't it matter? Well, the answer is in the extraordinary flexibility of the engine. Although maximum torque is obtained quite a long way up the engine speed scale, relatively speaking, the curve is pretty flat, so that you can trickle about in overdrive top at below 20 m.p.h. if you've a mind to, and still find plenty of smooth acceleration from there on up. This low speed performance is such that in normal driving you find yourself using only third and top and their respective overdrive ratios, ignoring second altogether. Second itself is such a poorly chosen ratio that it's all too easy to obtain an acceleration that is actually poorer by using it than by ignoring it, and going straight from first to third. Other faults which are less easily ignored are the extremely heavy, stiff and

Above: You have to provide your own rear end optional extra.

awkward action of the gearlever, and the very noisy noise made by bottom gear.

Like the best vintage cars, the Healey gives you a very firm ride: unlike the best of them, it has very low ground clearance indeed, and even on main roads it is still pretty easy to scrape the silencers on the ground—to their lasting detriment, if you're unlucky. Again unlike the best vintage cars, there is a deal of scuttle shake, and the worse the surface the worse it gets. But the car does hold the road well, despite a rather evil reputation it seems to have developed, and so long as you bear in mind the fact that it is a big powerful car which, in all likelihood, is going like a bat out of hell you shouldn't come to much harm. The stiff suspension allows the wheels—all four of them at times—to dance about if the surface leaves anything to be desired, but the steering, which is precise if heavy, allows you to keep the thing going the way its pointed. Too much power under these conditions, or in the wet, will have you sideways, but that merely serves you right. The big Healey is a fire-eating monster, alright, and as such deserves to be treated with respect. In fact, it demands to be, and we have driven a lot of cars which we could truthfully call more forgiving!

With a top whack of over 120 m.p.h. the Healey, which is no lightweight at 22 cwt., deserves a big fat set of anchors, and it has all that is necessary. At the front there are 11¼ in. discs, with 11 in. drums at the back, and nowadays there is a vacuum servo which still doesn't seem to stop the pedal pressure from being pretty high. Stopping the Healey from high speed in a hurry needs a real bootful, and the car also developes an unnerving tendency to snake, even although the wheels remain unlocked, when braking hard like this. The car continues to run true, and one feels that the snake is in the suspension rather than on the road, if you follow—at all events, it never feels that it's getting out of hand, so it probably doesn't matter all that much. It's just that it frightened us!

With the passing of time the inside of the Healey has been tarted up a good deal, and nowadays you get imitation tree-wood dashboards and rather superior instruments. The speedometer is now calibrated up to 140 m.p.h., although it wasn't so long ago that the figures on the dial hadn't kept up with the performance of the car, and you could go a lot faster than the speedo said you could. The rev-counter is also smarter and more distinct than it used to be, while they give you oil pressure, water temperature and fuel gauges as well. This last item has one of those wildly-dancing needles, so that you never have any idea how much juice you've got left unless the car is stationary and level, the screen-wipers are only single-speed and the steering wheel can be adjusted to bring it nearer to you when, for most people, it would be better if you could get further away from it. The driving position is extremely vintage—you sit right on top of everything, and with two people on board it is all a bit crowded. Visibility completes the dated feel: you peer out through a little slot of a windscreen over a high bonnet, while astern solid quarters to the hood cut off vision rather more than we are used to nowadays. The seats are small and a bit on the hard side, but neither so small nor so hard as the "occasional" seats behind them, which have a folding-down squab so that you can use the space for luggage. As most of the room in the boot is taken up by the spare wheels, this is probably just as well. The boot also contains a master-switch which cuts off all the electricity, and you can turn this off, lock the boot (the only part of the car you *can* lock) and feel reasonably secure that it will be hard to pinch the car. Inevitably, however, cutting off all the electricity means that you can't even switch the lights on, so that if you take this precaution you automatically have to park without lights. Not a matter of importance if you always lock your car in the garage, of course, but then if you do that the master-switch isn't so important either!

Performance? This is what makes it all worthwhile. At just over a thousand pounds, including purchase tax, the big Healey probably offers more urge per pound sterling than nearly any other motor. Top whack, the mean of runs in opposite directions, is 121 m.p.h., and from rest it will reach 60 m.p.h. in exactly ten seconds, eighty in exactly fifteen and the ton in exactly 25. It doesn't hang about, you see: in overdrive top, 100 m.p.h. is only around 4,000 r.p.m., so that the car goes galloping along like this all day, or at least for as long as the motorway lasts. A discreet sort of understeer makes the car and the driver full of the joys of spring at those long, fast open bends, while on the sharper ones you can prod the tail round on the loud pedal provided no-one's looking. Fast getaways will obviously leave a good deal of rubber on the road if you're not careful, but you don't have to drive it like that to get places pretty rapidly.

That's the big 'un. The Sprite isn't a bit like that. The Mark 3 version, which for those who can't keep track of all these numbers of which the motor industry is so fond is the current one, is a first-class car for the sports-car apprentice, whereas to get the best out of the big Healey it's a good plan to know what you're doing. In the Sprite, you can find out what's going on without running much risk of breaking anything—not even your neck—while for those who are a bit out of the apprenticeship stage it is more than immense fun. It is lively, fast enough and handles really well, which add up to a car which anyone, novice or expert, can thoroughly enjoy living with.

The introduction of the Mark 3 meant a revised version of the 1,100.c.c. engine. Bore and stroke remain unchanged at 64·58 mm x 83·72 mm, but the cylinder head is modified, has larger inlet valves and reshaped inlet tracts, there is a higher compression ratio (8·9 to 1), a new exhaust manifold and a stouter crankshaft, with main journals of two-inch diameter instead of the former 1·87 in. The power increase is in fact quite small, going up from 56 to 59 b.h.p. net at 5,750 r.p.m., with no increase in torque (62 lb. ft. at 3,250) but maximum speed has gone up to over ninety and something like four seconds is knocked off the 0-60 acceleration time. Acceleration is better throughout the range, in fact, and if the Mark 3 Sprite had been available when they were making M.G.A.s they wouldn't have sold nearly so many of the latter! Such is progress.

The power starts coming in at about two-five, and from then on it's got clean, brisk acceleration all the way up to around 5,500 if you happen to have the hood down, and fully to six thousand if you are running "closed". The revs go up so easily and smoothly that you need to keep a sharp eye on the rev-counter in the lower ratios, while at the bottom end it is completely tractable—in traffic you can potter along at about fifteen hundred revs in top without fuss or judder. The power unit is mechanically quiet, with a nice sporting sort of exhaust note.

On the road, there's enough urge to make it possible to cruise at about 5,500 r.p.m., which is about 85 m.p.h., but more than a few miles of this makes the oil pressure fall quite sharply, probably due to frothing. So far as motorways are concerned, they become acceptably short at a sustained 4,500 r.p.m., which is a steady seventy as near as makes no odds, and which lets the oil pressure stay where it ought to be. For shorter bursts you can, with the car "closed", get the full six thousand on any decent straight, and this represents about 92 m.p.h., which is the car's top speed in safety. During our performance testing we got a speed of 93 m.p.h. in one direction, which is "into the red" on the tachometer and therefore, presumably, not advisable.

The car's four-speed gearbox, although it hasn't got any synchromesh on bottom gear, has quite unusually well-spaced ratios. Maximum speeds in the gears are 30, 50 and 70, in first, second and third respectively, which is a lot better than you usually get. The gearlever is light, precise and has a nice short movement, and you can really put 'em through if you feel that way inclined. The clutch has a light pedal, but feels a bit soggy, and fast upward changes catch it by surprise, so that it is slow to take up the drive.

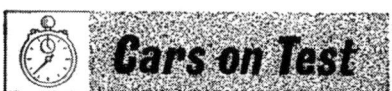

THE AUSTIN-HEALEY 3000

Engine: Six cylinders, 83·34 mm. × 88·9 mm.; 2,912 c.c.; compression ratio 9 to 1; pushrod-operated overhead valves; two S.U. HD8 carburettors; 148 b.h.p. at 5,250 r.p.m.

Transmission: Diaphragm-spring clutch; four-speed and reverse gearbox with synchromesh on upper three ratios; overdrive on third and top on test car; floor-mounted gear-lever.

Suspension: Front, independent with coil springs, wishbones and lever-type shock absorbers. Rear, live axle with semi-elliptic leaf springs and panhard rod. Tyres: 5·90 × 15.

Brakes: Front, 11¼ in. discs; rear, 11 in. drums; vacuum servo assistance.

Dimensions: Overall length, 13 ft. 1½ ins; overall width, 5 ft. 0½ in.; overall height, 4 ft. 1 in.; turning circle, 35 ft. 7 ins.; ground clearance, 4 ins.; kerb weight, 22 cwt.

PERFORMANCE

	m.p.h.			secs.
MAXIMUM SPEED	—122·0	ACCELERATION	0— 30—	2·8
Mean of two ways	—121·0		0— 40—	5·1
SPEEDS IN GEARS	First— 41		0— 50—	7·4
	Second— 52		0— 60—	10·0
	Third— 90		0— 70—	12·0
	overdrive third—109		0— 80—	15·0
	Top—112		0— 90—	17·8
			0—100—	25·0
Fuel consumption	20 m.p.g.	Standing quarter-mile	0—110—	31·2
			—16·8	

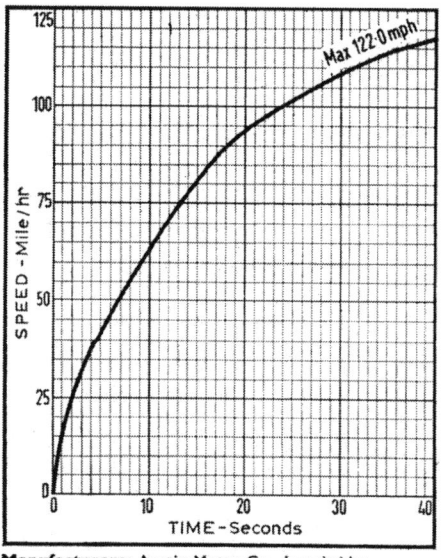

Manufacturers: Austin Motor Co., Longbridge, Birmingham.
Price: £1,045 including purchase tax.

So far as the suspension is concerned, the quarter-elliptic springs at the back which everyone made such a fuss about years ago have been replaced by semi-elliptics, to the cars' enormous benefit, while there is, of course, coil springs i.f.s. This gives a good ride, with excellent roadholding—there's a nice safe feel about the car pretty well wherever it happens to be doing, and it is extremely difficult to spin the back wheels. In the dry the handling characteristics are just about neutral, although in the wet or on loose surfaces the tail goes first. Any sort of slide is very easily held and corrected, however, and under the majority of circumstances the car goes round on rails (albeit with bags of tyre squeal) or else it slides all of a piece. The steering is light and high-geared, needing only 2¼ turns from lock to lock, and the seats are comfortable.

The whole of the driving compartment is well laid-out, even down to angling of the speedometer and rev-counter so that they can be easily and accurately read. There is plenty of room, even for the big fellows among us, all the controls are handily placed, instrumentation is complete and visibility all round is good, even with the hood up: this last item, which often presents a problem, is relatively easy to stow and erect, and when up it stays that way, without flapping or flying off even at maximum speed.

You can't expect everything on a car that only costs just over six hundred quid, of course, but the Sprite seems to have most things. You have to pay extra for a heater and a headlamp flasher, but otherwise there isn't a lot that is lacking. It's a jolly nice litttle car.

THE AUSTIN-HEALEY SPRITE

Engine: Four cylinders, 64·58 mm. × 83·72 mm.; 1,098 c.c.; pushrod-operated overhead valves; compression ratio 8·9 to 1; twin S.U. HS2 carburettors; 59 b.h.p. at 5,750 r.p.m.

Transmission: Diaphragm-spring clutch; four-speed and reverse gearbox with synchromesh on upper three ratios; floor-mounted gearlever.

Suspension: Front, independent, with coil springs and wishbones; rear, semi-elliptic leaf springs. Tyres: 5·20 × 13.

Brakes: Front, 8¼ in. disc; rear, 7 in. two-leading shoe drums.

Dimensions: Overall length, 11 ft. 5½ ins.; overall width, 4 ft. 5 ins.; overall height, 4 ft. 1¾ ins.; turning circle, 32 ft.; ground clearance 5 ins.; kerb weight 14 cwt.

PERFORMANCE

	m.p.h.			secs.
MAXIMUM SPEED	93	ACCELERATION	0–30—	4·1
Mean of two ways	92·2		0–40—	7·0
SPEEDS IN GEARS	First—30		0–50—	9·7
	Second—50		0–60—	14·4
	Third—70		0–70—	19·8
			0–80—	32·0
Fuel consumption:	28 m.p.g.	Standing quarter-mile	—19·4	

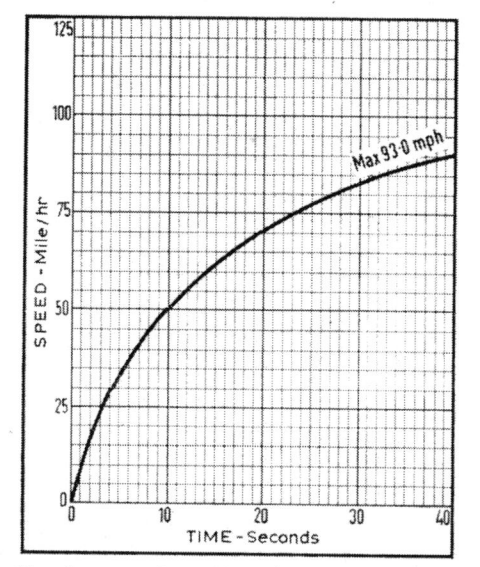

Manufacturers: Austin Motor Co., Longbridge, Birmingham.
Price: £611, including purchase tax.

From the rear the works Healey 3000 could be picked by the enormous filler top, and white circle. Tank itself carried more than 30 gallons.

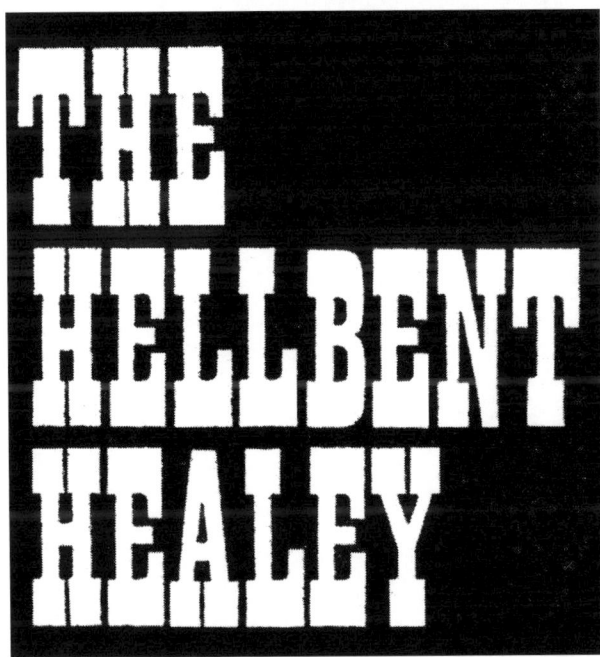

THE HELLBENT HEALEY

In which SCW columnist Eoin Young goes for the British driving test in a full house sports racer, fresh from the Targo Florio — and fails.

APART from the pair of open exhausts poking under the passenger's door, the side vents in the wings, the giant fuel filler in the middle of the boot lid, the strapped-down bonnet, and the white circle on the tail, the red Austin Healey 3000 appeared quite standard — straight from the showroom floor, as it were!

It isn't every day that scribes are allowed to borrow factory racing cars, but the Healey was 'between races' and competition manager, Stuart Turner, kindly made it available for a weekend.

This was the actual car that Paul Hawkins and

SCW BRIEF ROAD TEST

Timo Makinen had been using to towel the GTO Ferraris down at the Targa Florio a few weeks earlier. Hawkins was really pressing on in the best approved hairy Aussie fashion well ahead of the red cars, but the big Healey was wearing out rubber a bit quickly at this pace and they were pitting every couple of laps for tyres. Even so, the best Healey lap for the mountain circuit was 45 min 31 sec compared with the best GTO lap at 44 min 46 sec. Two miles from the pits on the eighth lap a broken distributor arm parked the Healey on the edge of the road, and Hawkins, having diagnosed the trouble, sprinted back to the pits. Was he mad when he learned that there was a spare distributor in the boot all the time!

Counting the Hawkins footwork as well as his general hurry-along on the road, the Healey finished an undisgraced 20th in a race where just being able to finish counts for a lot.

Three Webers, an aluminium head, over-bored 40 thou, a six-branch exhaust manifold, a race camshaft 10½ to 1 compression ratio and a weight of 19½ cwt which brought it lower than the rally Healeys, made my "racer" quite a potent piece of machinery.

A broken speedo for the test made acceleration figures impossible, but BMC Competitions people quote speeds at 6000 rpm in third 71 mph, o/d third 87 mph, top 102 mph, and o/d top 125 mph.

The mods brought the engine power up to 195 bhp and turned what is a hairy and perhaps a little clumsy road car into a Ferrari-beating racer. Indoors the furnishings were definitely turned out with racing in mind. Trim was nil, and everything was matt black to cut down glare. The boot was full of petrol tank, so the spare wire wheel with its knobbly SP tyre, plus jack and tools were strapped behind the seats. The seats themselves were hip-hugging special racing jobs designed to keep the driver firmly at his place during the twisty bits.

THE HELLBENT HEALEY

Instrumentation was kept to a minimum, with a combined oil pressure/water temperature gauge in the centre of the facia above a row of labelled switches for wipers, lights, windscreen washers, panel light, and the key-starter. The defunct speedometer read in kilometres while the rev counter was set at an angle to give the driver the benefit of the red sector at 6000 between the wheel spokes. The wheel was a heavily padded sprung affair of smallish diameter that felt keen after the glut of baked plastic tillers on normal production machinery. This one felt like a four wheel drift just grabbing hold of it!

The body showed signs of 'road rash' at the front where a few walls had no doubt creased its aluminium lines, and side-windows were perspex. The hardtop was securely bolted down, with rounded pieces of wood protecting occupants' heads from skull creasing on the forward bolts.

Tweaking the starter gave rise to a tremendous clattering roar from somewhere on the other side of the car. This was a real head-spinner. The gearbox was delightful to use, being smoother to slot than the standard model. The gear lever was

ARX 91 B.

Cooling ducts were let into the side panel to admit more air to the engine compartment. Hardtop was securely bolted down but leaked a little.

a fist-sized lump of wood which also housed the overdrive (on third and fourth) switch.

The axle ratio had been stepped up in the interests of a longer loping stride on the open road, and also gave the intermediate gears a better burst. The shame of it all was having the speedo out of action, so no speeds could be accurately checked. We tried changing the head, but found that the standard part numbers had been scratched out and other super special ones painted in — it just didn't seem worth while going to our friendly Austin agent and trying his patience!

In gear the big Healey really started to growl, indeed on acceleration the box made as much if not more noise than the blaring exhaust.

As mentioned, the gearchange was smooth and using the two o/d ratios on the way up a fair old steady surge of pace could be wound on. A DB5 Aston Martin (definitely a 007 car) arrived in the mirror with lights flashing while I was tooling along the A3 on a semi-motorway three-lane stretch at around 80 mph. Down to third remembering that the synchromesh wasn't quite as handy on the way down, red line, switch to overdrive 111, red line, IV, red line. No Aston. Damn your eyes, James Bond.

The petrol consumption of the Healey was rather intimidating as the three Webers crowded in under the bonnet kept gulping from the tank that must have held at least 30 gallons. When I collected the car the attendant was rather embarrassed at the fact that the fuel gauge registered only ⅛, so we barked and bellowed round the BMC pump to top up.

Snapping open the big filler cap one could hear subterranean gurglings from deep inside. The little man turned on the pump and began one of those conversations that don't start anywhere in particular, don't go anywhere, and when you finish you can't remember what it was about. This idle reverie was broken abruptly when the bowser snapped itself off, having delivered 14 gallons — and it still wasn't full!

Chugging out into the traffic which was moving at a London traffic crawl, was rather nerve racking as I imagined fouling the plugs well

Correspondent Young opens the door to the business department. Here lurk three Webers atop an aluminium 10½ to 1 head, with six-branch exhaust and racing cam.

before home. I hadn't taken into consideration the placid truck-type qualities of the big six even in racing tune.

The best part of the weekend was the startled gapes from proud owners of other Healeys.

Once you became accustomed to the din, and mastered the art of the shouted conversation, life was easier. Top gear was quieter than the other three but the trees and walls were usually coming up fairly quick at that stage and idle chat was given over in favor of staying between the bits of grass and out of Mini boots.

Brakes were a satisfying part of the Healey performance. Four wheel discs with a servo still took a fair amount of pedal pushing but the anchors were definitely and reassuringly there.

I suppose I came to accept the Healey rather in the same way as those doggy people come to grow fond of a ginormous Alsation that barks a threatened hand amputation at anyone brave or silly enough to approach too close. My state of blissful acceptance of my growling, starkly rather indecent pet reached the stage where I decided to use it for my driving test! I had decided, as pure formality, to try (try being the operative word in this case) for my English driver's licence in addition to my perfectly valid (and un-endorsed) New Zealand licence. The English test is really rather a farce, as despite the fact that you can carry out all the test manoeuvres in an able and polished manner (let's face it: *anyone* can start on a hill, and do a three point turn in a narrow street without puncturing someone's wall) you have to do these things the *official* way. This includes ramming on the handbrake with every pause, and shuffling

Three Webers only just fitted in — must have been mechanics nightmare to tune. They swallowed fuel at a diabolical rate. BHP delivered is 195.

the wheel through your hands rather than any approach at cross-arms work. This is simply dangerous whichever way you look at it. Still, that's what the book says, and that's the way you've got to do it.

To continue: My examiner was, unfortunately, lanking around 6 ft something, and although his blank look didn't become any blanker on spotting the competition appendage of the Healey, his mood obviously didn't improve as he started to curl up into the beast, both seats of which seemed to have been designed for someone about the size of Paul Hawkins who is broad of shoulders, but not very high off the road.

All attempts at conversation were obviously going to be wasted effort, as my rather uncomfortable looking instructor delivered instructions in a sing-song up and down voice. "Now at the end of the road there is a turn to the left and I want you to turn left." Much exaggerated looking in the mirror, down changing, winkers flashing, arms waving. Full marks. "At the intersection I want you to turn right up the hill and stop in your own time at the side of the road." Repeated down changing, mirror craning, arm waving, handbrake on-off-on-off, looking every which-way, venturing bravely across the deserted intersection (failed for cutting the corner!) and then stopped on the hill with handbrake dutifully and officially on. Actually the handbrake didn't work at all, and the cranking on with each stop, and especially the hill start, was performed with great flourish while my right foot was heel-and-toeing on foot-brake and accelerator.

The classic part came when my learned friend tapped his notebook on the dash "like this." I was to make an emergency stop "as though a child was crossing the road." It wasn't hard to judge exactly when the pad was going to alight on the dash, and my foot must have clumped the brake at the same instant. The Healey stopped in a few feet, and I glanced across to see officialdom peering through a cloud of rubber smoke.

When all the hoo-hah and kindergarten questions were over and successfully answered, I was liltingly informed, "I am sorry but you haven't passed the test. Here is a book which might help you with your next attempt." Phooey!

The Healey and I went on a few social excursions over the weekend, and while it didn't ex-

Cockpit is harshly spartan, but equipped with all necessary instruments, comfortable seats and finished in matt black to stop glare.

actly charm any delicate female hearts, it certainly emptied the bars of any pubs we stopped at, and even earned a few beers while 'wottleshedo' questions were pumped. Referring, of course, to the car.

We parted company (referring again to the Healey) on the Monday as the fuel gauge was sinking slowly to the E, and the weekend of tiger-taming was over.

Lots of fun. Thank you BMC. Sorry our speedo didn't work. Oh, and the hardtop leaks when it rains! Still, I don't suppose racing overalls are as sensitive as nylons to little things like a steady drip, drip, drip, from where the window and roof supposedly meet.

But as a proven racer and a crumpet catcher, it was ideal. Hawkins and Makinen proved it was a racer in the Targa!   #

Spoked wheels give a glimpse of the massive four wheel discs which helped to bring the car down from 125 mph to rest in shortest possible time.

132

Austin-Healey 3000

Remember the gutsy old hard-
riding Healey of 10 years ago?
It hasn't changed, thank heavens

IMPORTER British Motor Corporation
734 Grand Avenue
Ridgefield, New Jersey

ENGINE
Type Water-cooled six-in-line, cast iron block,
5 main bearings, pushrod-operated overhead
valves
Bore & Stroke.................................3.28 x 3.50 in.
Displacement....................................178 cu. in.
Compression ratio.............................9.0 to one
Power (SAE)................150 bhp @ 5250 rpm
Torque.........................173 lbs-ft @ 3000 rpm

TRANSMISSION
4-speed manual, non-synchro first

WHEELBASE ....91.75 in.

TRACK....................F: 48.75 in. R: 48.75 in.

CURB WEIGHT................................2425 lbs.

ACCELERATION	Seconds
0-40	4.4
0-60	9.8
0-80	17.9

TOP SPEED....................................110 mph

SUSPENSION
F: Ind., unequal-length wishbones, coil springs,
anti-sway bar
R: Rigid axle, semi-elliptic leaf springs

BRAKES 11.25-in discs front, 11-in drums rear

The British say that the Austin-Healey is "well-proved." This is certainly a fact; all the bugs have been ironed out and the buyer knows exactly what he's getting. It's also a fact that the Austin-Healey is an old car, a vestige of the older British methods of car construction.

The six cylinder engine is heavy and antiquated, putting out some 150 horse-power from 3 liters. Still, it's enough to push the 2500-pound car to 60 mph in less than 10 seconds.

The live rear axle is located by leaf springs attached to a chassis that is sadly lacking in torsional stiffness. The result is that the Austin-Healey needs smooth roads to behave itself without having the rear wheels disporting themselves like a herd of kangaroos. The handling is not quick but is virtually roll-free and the brakes (discs front, drums rear) bring the speed down swiftly and surely.

The overdrive-equipped transmission has no synchro on first, and fast up-and-down shifts can't be made without grating noises from within. The seating position is not very comfortable especially for large people, and luggage space is notably lacking although the two so-called occasional seats in the back seem to have been designed more with luggage than people in mind.

The Austin-Healey comes equipped with adjustable steering wheel, heater, windshield washers, seat belt mountings, overdrive, front disc brakes, Dunlop RS tires and wire wheels all included in the base price. This may sound like a bargain but you have to remember that the Healey's base price is close enough to more exciting merchandise such as a Lotus Elan or Alfa Giulia Sprint GT to make a prospective buyer take a longer look.

HAVE SPRITE WILL TRAVEL

To Le Mans with an Austin-Healey 3000 and Sprite Countryman

Story: Peter Browning

Pictures: Stuart Seager

WE wanted a caravan for Le Mans. Something not too large but not too small. Big enough to seat a fair-sized party for meals, offer comfortable sleeping accommodation, and we *had* to have a roomy and well-equipped kitchen. All this from a caravan which must not be too much of a handful on the steeply cambered, bumpy French roads and not too extravagant lengthwise on the Channel ferry.

As the Austin-Healey team were entering a pair of Sprites, and the towing vehicle for the caravan was to be a 3000, obviously we could not do better than try one of the larger caravans in the popular Sprite range. Earlier this year fellow-staffman Richard Shepherd had enjoyed a splendid holiday with a Midget and a little Sprite 400 caravan, so a trip with a 3000 with one of the bigger Sprite models in tow would be an appropriate follow-up.

A phone call to John Sparrow, the ever-obliging Sales Manager of Sprites, was all that was necessary to procure the use of a demonstration Countryman, the largest touring caravan in the Sprite range. On paper the specification looked to be just the job; length 20 ft. (well it does not look *too* long in the picture in the brochure), width 7 ft. 3 in. (that's not *much* wider than the 3000), weight 18 cwt. (after all that's only the weight of another car). Should go like a bomb!

So far all my caravanning had been on paper. When I was actually confronted with the Countryman I must admit I thought that Sprites had made a mistake and sent down one of their Mobile Homes! The big caravan dwarfed the Healey and I was very glad that I'd had a low rear axle ratio fitted in the car to give us a little more steam.

Sprite caravans are renowned for their good handling—a world record of 102 m.p.h. is held by the little Sprite 400, while the larger Musketeer and Alpine models always do well in the annual Caravan Rally. So I was very surprised (and frightened stiff!) when I hitched up the Countryman for a brisk trial run up the road and at anything over about 30 m.p.h. found that the whole outfit had a distinct tendency to leap over the nearest hedge!

The cause of the trouble was finally traced to the height of the tow hitch which was far too high, thus causing the caravan to ride bows up and start the dreaded 'sways'. (For correct towing the caravan should always ride nose-heavy.) Unfortunately, as no one makes off-the-shelf tow hitches for the big-Healey and there was no way of modifying our hitch in the time available, we had to be content with things as they were.

However, by juggling with tyre pressures on the Healey and adding lots of luggage in the nose of the caravan we found that a steady towing speed of 35 to 40 m.p.h. could be maintained. As 40 m.p.h. is the legal limit in this country, and the bumpy roads kept our speed down once we crossed the Channel, we were quite happy to dawdle along at this pace. Anyway it was quite pleasant to motor slowly for a change—it's surprising how much of the scenery you miss when you're pressing on. (Yes, they do have mini-skirts in France!)

As this was my first experience of towing anything bigger than a very small trailer caravan I must admit that I set off with some trepidation, ever conscious of the towering shape which filled the rear view mirrors. It did not take long to learn that smooth acceleration, gear changing, and braking was the key to keeping the outfit bowling merrily along. But how easy it could have been to sweep through a narrow gap in traffic and forget about the extra 2 feet of width at the back! Or turn sharp left at traffic lights and either chop the corner off with the near-side wheel of the caravan or, more embarrassing, wipe the caravan down a line of traffic as the rear of the caravan swings out to the right as you turn left!

Certainly the outfit raised a few eyebrows, and it was strange how more than one experienced caravanner remarked that we must be mad to tow a great big caravan like that with a sports car. I argued that on the contrary I reckoned a sports car like the 3000 was an ideal towing wagon. Bags of low-down, smooth pulling power, ideal for silky get-aways and for top gear touring. Third gear was only really necessary for maintaining pace on the hills and for overtaking. Second gear took care of the slow-speed traffic manœuvers. Good brakes are essential for caravanning and the Healey's servo-assisted system, coupled with the excellent automatic over-run brakes on the caravan, never caused us alarm. With the hood down, the splendid rear view vision meant that we could out-perform all the saloon car caravanners when it came to delicate reversing manœuvers. And, of course, caravanning with a sports car solves all your luggage-carrying problems; you just chuck it all in the caravan.

The Countryman proved to be absolutely ideal for the job in hand at Le Mans, and although I cannot claim experience of competitive designs, everyone in the party agreed that it would be hard to find a caravan so well designed or well appointed. The forward section has a well-upholstered 'U'-shaped seat

Although the Countryman weighs 18 cwt. it is nicely balanced and can quite easily be manœuvred by hand

which converts to a double berth. A second fully sprung double berth folds down from the centre partition. The main saloon really is roomy and we seated eight people for a meal without too much elbowing. The kitchen has a small sink and draining board, a twin-ring gas cooker with grill, and a gas refrigerator. There are ample cupboards, drawers, and shelves; we stacked away crockery and food supplies for some 20 people on the Le Mans trip and there was still room for more. There's a full sized seat or sleeping berth in the galley and a removable hammock-type bunk can be slung above this, bringing the total sleeping capacity to six (two doubles and two singles). Both the two doubles in the saloon and the singles in the galley can be curtained-off for mixed parties. Ample wardrobe space, cupboards, and drawers are provided. Next to the galley

is a small toilet compartment with provision for mounting a small plastic hand-basin. Bottled gas is used for cooking and the refrigerator; there are gas lights and even a gas fire. The caravan is very well made throughout and we found that the double-skinned construction keeps it warm at night and comfortably cool in the heat of the day. We could make only two criticisms: there was no spare wheel (or provision for carrying one), and there was no water tank (it was a bit of a bind having to hump heavy carriers about every time you wanted some water).

Summing up, the Countryman offers very good value for money at £412 and, although a smaller two-berth caravan is more likely to satisfy the needs of the sports-car owner, certainly we found that the big Healey plus big Sprite was the ideal combination for our purpose. ●

A sports car with the hood down gives excellent visibility and makes easy going of caravan reversing manœuvres

driving Abingdon's musclecar

ERIC DYMOCK describes a dramatic week-end with one of the fiercest road cars ever to come out of Abingdon—a fully modified, works rally team Austin-Healey 3000

STANDING in the middle of Salisbury Plain a year or so ago you might have heard an excited, braying noise in the distance. It would not have remained far off for long because the approaching thunder belonged to Timo Makinen's Healey 3000 and it would have burst on you out of the gathering dusk; the first car to pass in the 1965 R.A.C. Rally of Great Britain; The last time its like was ever to be seen driven 'in anger' in an international rally. This was one of the most exciting road cars in the world.

Until 1966, the big Healeys were the survivors of the sports cars that had fought out the Alpines and Lièges 10 years ago. Saloons do it now and although the other two-seaters nearly all dropped out, giving way to newer designs, the big Healey seemed to go on for ever. The new Appendix J regulations caused their retirement, at least in the tremendously powerful form they reached near the end of their career. How very nearly they went out in a blaze of glory then, when Timo Makinen almost won the R.A.C. Rally at the end of the European Championship season! Icy roads on the very last night snatched victory away after an epic drive in which he led most of the way. Team mate Rauno Aaltonen's win was small

consolation. The Healey had already been second in the R.A.C. four times and if studded tyres had not been prohibited its day would surely have come.

But studs had been banned to try and preserve the surfaces of roads and special stages, so although the book records another second place, most people will remember a stirring drive, and the car's decisive wins including two firsts in the Liège (Pat Moss and Rauno Aaltonen) and two firsts in the Alpine (the Morleys).

The Rally Healey is not much like a standard one to drive. It is faster, heavier, and much noisier. Sound-deadening material has been removed and the inside is filled with heavy mechanical noises coming through the undamped bulkhead, and the deep boom of the exhaust resonates round inside the bare hard top. The racket at speed is like an explosion that goes on happening.

Three fat 45 DCOE Webers are shoe-horned under the narrow bonnet on the inlet side of the engine, and underneath there is a six-branch exhaust manifold which leads out under the passenger's door. The engine has an aluminium cylinder head, a high-lift camshaft, and an 11 : 1 compression

ratio. There is an oil cooler and the bores are enlarged to raise the capacity from 2912 c.c. to 2982 c.c. Undershielding protects the full length of the car and ground clearance, often criticized on Austin-Healeys, is improved from about 5 inches to 7½ inches, by raising the suspension. Heavier springs and dampers are fitted, with close-ratio gears and a final drive of 4·3 : 1.

Inside, the wood fascia has been discarded for a simpler one in black crackle on which there is a speedometer, tachometer, a combined oil pressure and water temperature gauge, and a fuel gauge. Most of the remaining space is used by a switchgear, and there is a miniature sub-station with great banks of fuses immediately in front of the passenger's legs. Seats are improved and there are very comprehensive safety harnesses. The standard steering-wheel is replaced with a very smart Springall soft leather-rimmed one which has padded loops over the aluminium spokes for resting your thumbs on. The heater comes from a Mark I Mini and the lidded vent in the hard top from a Mini-Van. Attention to detail is obvious; there are *two* spare ignition keys screwed to the bulkhead under the bonnet. A spare fan belt is taped to the bonnet strut. There is a spare throttle up by an extra wheel and a 20-gallon fuel tank. Inside the car there is a large padded roll-over cage. The wheels are 70-spoke competition pattern with Dunlop SP44 Weathermasters to grip the loose surfaces of forest roads.

The 20-gallon tank empties at an alarming rate. On rallies it will get down to 8 m.p.g., but 14½ m.p.g. on roads with a 70-m.p.h. speed limit was spring beside the carburetters. The familiar spare-wheel-shaped bulge in the boot lid represents the space taken

Just to prove that you don't need to be all muscle and six feet tall to handle a rally Healey, Frances Dymock drove it, too. Below is the comprehensive dash panel, all clearly labelled, even to the cigar-lighter. Over-drive switch is in the gear lever knob

In its natural habitat—a rough-surfaced special stage, up in the hills. The bulge in the boot lid is necessary to accommodate the 20-gallon fuel tank and two spare wheels shod with Dunlop SP44 radial-ply Weathermasters

expensive enough. Despite a weight increase over the Mark II Healey 3000 of 2½ cwt., and over the Mark III of 1¼ cwt., the acceleration is better. The rally Healey produces 175 b.h.p. at 5,600 r.p.m. *at the wheels* and a lot more torque than the standard engine, so the increase in weight is more than compensated. The close-ratio gearbox and the altered overall gearing help acceleration, but the top speed of the car is not very much different from a good Mark III. With a lot more space than was often available, the engine would wind itself up quite smoothly to well over 120 m.p.h. in overdrive top.

As well as increasing the weight, the undershielding and extra equipment have also altered its distribution. Measured with an insignificant amount of fuel in the tank, it worked out at 51/49 front/rear compared with the standard Mark III's 48/52. Increased understeer was as noticeable as it was understandable in these conditions, especially in the wet when, on a trailing throttle, the car seriously threatened to drive off the outside of sharp bends. Road tyres instead of the special-stage knobblies would probably have improved matters; as it was, the throttle had to be used to help the car round, making driving in the rain a more exciting business than most people enjoy.

You don't really drive the Healey fast in the normal way. It has to be tamed first. It is probably the most highly developed, and the last of the conventional sports cars whose philosophy included big, slow-revving engines firm suspension, and for the driver's part, a certain amount of courage and muscle. On the question of courage, a drive in the rally Healey puts Timo Makinen's beyond doubt.

Not that the Healey is a very heavy car to drive. The clutch is a diaphragm-spring one, extremely light and completely untemperamental. You can use it in traffic without it snatching or getting hot. Likewise the four-wheel disc brakes with servo are light, and almost impossible to fade although they never seem to work properly until they are really hot and then they squeal a little. The pads are DS11 competition material

which resists fade, and who cares if it squeaks a bit? There's so much noise already that a little extra makes no difference. The steering is also fairly light and the standard car's 32-foot turning circle is unimpaired.

By the time the gearbox had covered the R.A.C. and some subsequent, less strenuous running, the synchromesh had pretty well vanished from second and third gears although there is one similar ex-works car which has managed to retain its synchro after about 30,000 miles. On EJB 806 C however, it was essential to double-declutch changing down, and desirable when changing up, but with a little practice gear changes were crisp although the lever has to be moved with a certain amount of decision. A switch on the wooden gear lever knob operates the overdrive which engages and disengages in third and top instantly and smoothly.

Anticipating temperament in traffic proved unnecessary. Not many people would want this car for shopping, but it *will* idle at 800 r.p.m. without difficulty; it does not overheat or oil plugs in long traffic holdups. Use of oil is not excessive and although there were a few minor body rattles the rally Healey is still a road car, unlike its cardboard cousins, the stripped-bare saloon-car racers. Timo's car had carpet and comforts, although weight-saving had received attention, with alloy body panels and Perspex windows in the doors and hard top. The hard top and roll cage seemed to have the effect of stiffening-up the frame for there was virtually no scuttle shake, even on quite rough roads at speed.

A Healey like this would not find a home in *every* enthusiast's garage. The ride would put a lot of people off: the springing is so stiff you get joggled up and down even on roads other cars find smooth, and on rough 'special stages' you need the seat belts to hold you in place. But if you think the days of cars that make you gulp on fast bends, or take your breath away with noise and excitement and acceleration are gone, take one Austin-Healey 3000 Mark III, three 45 DCOE Weber carburetters, remove the padding, sound-deadening, and excess weight . . . ●

Performance figures

Acceleration through the gears: (maximum r.p.m., 6.000)

0–30 m.p.h.	2·9 sec.
0–40	5·0
0–50	6·3
0–60	8·3
0–70	10·2
0–80	12·8
0–90	15·9
0–100	19·1

Standing start ¼-mile: 15·8 sec.

Maximum speed (mean of four runs in opposite directions): 123·3 m.p.h.

Overall fuel consumption for 250 miles: 14·4 m.p.g.

Note: With all the synchromesh operative, the acceleration figures could doubtless be improved upon. The speedometer was reasonably accurate up to 60 m.p.h., then read progressively fast until at 100 m.p.h. it was optimistic by approximately 5 per cent. Oil consumption was roughly one pint of XL 30 for every 125 miles. The weight and weight distribution quoted was certified on a public weighbridge.

LAST OF THE LINE?

JOHN STANLEY rides shotgun on the works rally Healey

I RUN my hand along the wing. The smooth aluminium is warm from the heat of the day. White, distorted clouds chase across the familiar scarlet shell. We wait silently. He sits rugged, dignified, wearing the full battle dress of lamps and trimmings, not unlike a virile Chelsea pensioner. Indeed, the simile is well chosen for in the words of its loving owner, Peter Browning, " The age of the ralliest hairy sports car is passing, yet the incredible Healey won't die." Old soldiers never die, goes the saying, and the fortunate few who have tried to master the beast will know just why it has survived.

I have no intentions of setting before you a complex, clinical data report, linked with superior remarks comparing the thing with a Cobra or what-have-you. It would take a very insensitive enthusiast to do that. A handful of skilled, dedicated men in the BMC Competitions department have created a legend with the " Works " Healey. These cars are not titivated production-line models but competition masterpieces hand built from the start. The Healey history is one of great character, the present line starting with the 100 model in 1952 and developing into the present Mark III 3000. Many great names have been associated with the marque like those of the Morleys, who chalked up two outright wins in the Alpine; Pat Moss and Rauno Aaltonen, with respective first in the Liège, and Timo Makinen, who so nearly brought home the bacon in the '66 RAC Rally which marked the last works entry for this thoroughbred, due to the new Appendix J regulations.

The unit itself is bored out from 2912 cc to 2982 cc and is fitted with a gas-flowed aluminium head raising the compression ratio to 11.1. There is a nitrided crankshaft; nimonic valves and a six-branch exhaust manifold linked to a modified system to improve ground clearance. A bank of triple 45DCOE Weber carburettors complete the cocktail which induces 173 bhp at the wheels! Standard transmission is one of the weaker aspects of the basic Healey 3000 and naturally much work has gone into providing the strength and urge to cope with all those horses. The box is full of straight cut gears, which coupled with overdrive on third and top, provides six evenly spaced ratios right through the box. The overdrive switch is installed on the gear knob itself and takes effect very quickly.

The suspension is raised and toughened at the front, and at the rear, 14 leaf springs and shockers are installed. The combined effect is to raise the ground clearance from 5 in to 7½ in. Braking is a twin system with tandem master cylinders and twin servos together with DS 11 padded discs all round. The steering too, has not been missed by the improving hand of the mechanic. Standard gearing provides a full-time job when driving in anger so a smaller, leather wheel has been provided together with a lower ratio resulting in much the same handling as that of a Mini.

Drop all this powerful equipment in an aluminium body, bolt on steel guards for the sump, gearbox and 20-gallon fuel tank. Dress the eager beast with instruments, furniture and seven powerful driving lights and on paper, you have something approaching a works mount.

An interesting fact is that all the extra bits have made this lightweight-bodied machine 1¼ cwt heavier than the standard steel Mark III. In actual terms of speed, top is 135 mph with a standing quarter in some 15.5 seconds working on about eight miles to the gallon! Ordinary road work achieves around 15 mpg and with the useful overdrive it produces a surprisingly well behaved town car getting down to a mere 800 revs without complaining. The temperature rises to 160 and just sits there. 5.6 is being used as peak revs because that's where the power is and also as there are no more gearboxes!

At last Peter arrives with some trade plates and gets into the driving seat. "We'll go somewhere private, then you squirt it about as you want," he offers, tightening his belt. I climb in. The door needs a firm pull, thank God, at least that's steel! He turns the ignition and the unit bursts into life. The tiny cockpit fills with the lumpy sound of heavy machinery warming up. " I'm afraid this is where conversation has to end." mouths Peter, intent on the gauges. Into first gear and we arc round the forecourt to his competitions department and burble away towards the gate where the uniformed gentleman salutes. Tribute indeed. " We'll take it quietly (if ever there was a wrong word) until things warm up," shouts Peter, nosing his brooding machine through light traffic. The hard top seems a tight fit and before long the cockpit reeks with that warm, musty smell from heavy machinery, worn carpets and memories of forest thrashes. Power plant thunder apart, the constant chattering of the coachwork protesting

at the near solid suspension, is strangely reminiscent of a fine vintage Bentley I once knew.

The long road ahead flaunts itself at the Healey. Peter reflects upon the vision and in a flurry of feet and wrist movements, we drop into low gear. There is a roar quite beyond description, the long powerful bonnet lifts and takes sights on the stretching tarmac. The tail snakes, the wheel kicks, the body pitches. Peter's face is gaunt, intent. His hands twitch around the steering wheel and flash momentarily to the gears to satisfy the beast's insatiable hunger for tarmac. There's little doubt he's in control and no question of the position being assumed permanent. The Healey's heading due north by mutual agreement, any small slip and he'll go his own sweet way. Does that ring true as I watch driver and car arguing and deciding on a line round the fleeting bend. Discs whistle; revs climb.

We straighten out and surge towards infinity. There is small point in description. Perhaps the nearest thing is that famous BBC film which shows a railway engine's view of the London–Brighton run covered in a mere three minutes. Remember the sensation of piling through the darkness of a tunnel towards the advancing daylight. Well, you're back against your seat, being thrown about by the cart-like springing and peering through the narrow screen at advancing Britain, in much the same way.

A local newspaper van appears in our path and we drop two ratios.

The big beast moves out, lifts his dignified nose and stretches out gnashing his teeth. We advance at an unpublished speed with the most incredible sound, rush the modest Mini van, air horns screaming a fanfare to this, surely the last Real sports car. A psychologist could induce endless parallels but very simply, this beast is wild. It was never intended for domesticity. To sit and experience this car's urge for long, intimate forest tracks or twisting Alpine passes, is like watching a lion pacing his zoo cage pining for the plains of central Africa.

Skilled men created this breed; brave men fought with them; let us hope blind men don't write its epitaph.

PERFORMANCE FIGURES
0-60 mph in 8 secs.
0-100 mph in 19 secs.
Top speed 135 mph.
Standing quarter mile 15.5 secs.
Fuel 8 mpg rally work/hard driving
    15 mpg careful roadwork.

Reduce speed now! says the sign as James Ewing storms up to a roundabout in 838 ENX *Photo: Gullachsen*

Hail! *and farewell!*

It's coincidence of course, but the coming of the 70 limit and the passing of the Austin-Healey 3000 could between them mark the end of an era. At least that's how it seems to JAMES EWING, now on his third 'Big Healey'

THIS is going to be rather sentimental. For years they've been telling me that the Big Healey is out of date. 'You're running a vintage job there, old boy,' they'd say, and when I bought my third in a line they wrote me off as bonkers.

Well that's all right with me. The Healey has always had a vintage feel about it and that's why I bought another. I like the ruddy things, and now that they are out of production my affection is all the greater. They are a link with the heroic days of motor-cars. The 3000 looks what I have always considered a sports car should look like. And they have got better and better. My first (2838 UE) took to the road in 1960, and compared with later models, was a comparatively sedate method of transport. This still had the odd gear change coming out of the side of the

tunnel and I made some quite appalling changes at first. But we soon came to terms and I would not have parted with it had some nit in a garage not squirted brake fluid all over the bonnet. I managed to make a satisfactory exchange for a Mk. II (838 ENX) which, as it happens lives near by and is kept in splendid trim. This car was a snorter. It was tweaked a little and had competition rear suspension with works exhaust system. It was very fast indeed and when the rumours hardened about the end of the Healey, I thought long and painfully about the whole business. To carry on with the Mk. II or go out with flying colours with a brand new Mk. III—the last of the line.

I bought a new one. Colorado red it is and this is the best of the lot (LNX 628 E). Better torque, better balance from the new rear axle location, and vastly

better trim. And a deal more poke even than the Mk. II.

Whether there is going to be any point in really fast cars in the future remains to be seen. This may be my last, and I will have no regrets if I end my sports car career with a Healey. They have served me well and faithfully. I will never forget the feeling of exhilaration when I first sat behind that huge wheel and looked away down the long, sleek bonnet; nor the nose lifting under power, the rev.-counter swinging up, the roar of the wind and the scream of tyres. There seemed to be such a hell of a lot going on.

All my cars have been bought from and admirably maintained by that nice bunch of blokes at the Donald Healey outfit at Warwick where their knowledge and enthusiasm has added greatly to the pleasures of Healey motoring.

So it's hail and farewell to a great sports car. The competition records and statistics are there for posterity. Soon, the Healey will be a collector's piece. But no one who has sat behind the wheel of a Big Healey will forget the enduring excitement of it all—the huge surge of power, the tumultuous exhaust, and the rest of the pack shrinking to dots in the mirror. Great days . . . .

THE ABINGDON HEALEY 3000s

LES NEEDHAM traces the history of the works Austin-Healey 3000s, once the pride of the BMC Competitions Department at Abingdon and the most successful rallying sports car in the World—a tribute to these great cars (now out of production) and the brave men and women who tamed them to take them to victory

IN the February 1964 issue of *Safety Fast*, Peter Browning in his series 'From Perranporth to Abingdon' described the development of the Austin-Healey 3000. At that time the works rally cars were at the peak of their success, and so it was not politic to go into too much detail. In 1965, the C.S.I. (the controlling body of motor sport) brought out revised regulations for cars taking part in rallies, one of the results of which was that the works Healey ceased to be eligible for the majority of international rallies, and thus in 1966 the emphasis of the BMC Competitions department shifted to the Mini-Cooper 'S'.

Over a period of seven years, the power output of the 2912-c.c., six-cylinder, BMC 'C'-type engine used in the works Healeys was nearly doubled. Despite this tremendous in-crease in power, the engine has been fantastically reliable, there being virtually no record of failure of this component. Initially, gearboxes had difficulty in handling the extra torque, but straight-cut gears of a special material, with stronger layshafts, soon cured this trouble.

Altogether there were 23 works 3000's plus one 100/6 which was converted to 3000 specification (PMO 203), and between them they were entered in some 70 major international events. Fifteen of the cars were eventually sold to private owners (often the works driver who had been driving it—Pat Moss, John Gott, Don Morley, Rauno Aaltonen, Tony Ambrose) and several of them continue to give a good account of themselves in Club races and sprints.

Competition history

The 3000 competition story starts with the 1959 Alpine Rally, when three works cars were entered for John Gott/Chris Tooley, Bill Shepherd/John Williamson, and Jack Sears/Sam Moore. The first-named came second in class after delays to repair a punctured radiator, but the other two cars both suffered from the rough going and had to retire. Obviously sump guards were going to be necessary for future outings. Following this

Heading picture: The last of the line and the most powerful of all the rally Healeys, PWB 57, owned by BMC Competitions Manager Peter Browning, was prepared for Rauno Aaltonen to drive on the cancelled 1967 R.A.C. Rally. Right: Full house. The engine compartment

140

URX 727, driven to an outright win in the 1960 Liège–Rome–Liège Rally by Pat Moss and Ann Wisdom, with the fruits of victory. Four out of the first 10 places in the Liège were taken by the big Healeys. After its outstanding career with the works team this car was sold to Pat Moss

came the Liège–Rome–Liège, in which the three SMO cars were joined by the 100/6 (PMO 203) which had been fitted with a 3000 engine. Navigational errors eliminated two of the cars, PMO crashed, but Peter (Bear) Riley and Rupert Jones came first in their class and gave the new car its first international award.

Pat Moss and Ann Wisdom tried out the new car in the German Rally, and with fastest times on all but one of the tests she won the Coupe des Dames and came second overall to her future husband Erik Carlsson. The last major event of that year was the R.A.C. Rally, which has gone down in history as the 'Snow Rally'. Part of the route near Tomintoul was blocked by snow, and because of various alternative routes attempted by competitors the final results had to await the outcome of numerous protests and counter-protests. Eventually it was confirmed that the 3000's had taken first and second places in their class with the Morley twins (Don and Erle) taking fourth overall in their first drive for the marque.

The first outing in 1960 was to the 12-hour race at Sebring, where three cars prepared by Donald Healey Motors at Warwick (UJB 141/2/3) were entered. Two of the cars came second and third in class behind a Ferrari; the third car unfortunately crashed. Subsequently UJB 143 ran at Le Mans and in the Tourist Trophy at Goodwood, before

being transferred to Abingdon for rally use.

The year started disastrously for the rally cars, with gearbox trouble on the Circuit of Ireland, and a spectacular crash on the Solitude circuit in Germany on the Lyon–Charbonnières Rally. In both the Geneva and Tulip rallies, however, Pat Moss collected the Ladies award and won her class, with the Morley brothers finishing third in class on the Tulip.

As always, a major effort was devoted to the Alpine, which together with the Liège has always been a favourite with the big Healey crews. Four cars were entered; Pat and Ann came second overall, winning their class, a Coupe des Alpes for a penalty-free run, and the Coupe des Dames. John Gott/Bill Shepherd came second in class, missing their Alpine Cup by less than 20 seconds after a spin on the infamous Les Quatre Chemins stage, and the Morley twins came third in class despite having only top gear left. The Adams/Williamson car retired quite early on, also with gearbox problems. The Healeys between them collected all five team awards, were second, fourth and sixth in General classification, and made Best British Performance, a truly wonderful record.

For the Liège, four cars were again entered, and this proved to be probably one of the best outings ever for the 3000. Out of 13 finishers that returned to Liège (81 starters), three were Healeys—Pat Moss and Ann Wisdom won the rally outright, the first time an all-ladies crew had ever won a

Championship rally, and Dave Seigle-Morris/Vic Elford, and John Gott/Rupert Jones once again made it 1, 2, 3, in class.

Pat and Ann had their troubles, including having a gearbox drain plug knocked off by the rough going; but a service crew were able to replace it with one 'borrowed' from one of the service vehicles. The gearbox suffered from its oil-less run over the Stelvio however, and at a later stage in the rally it was removed to have an oil seal replaced, a job which took the Abingdon mechanics under an hour! Seigle-Morris had his front hub bearings changed, but the Gott car was in good trim, except for damage caused when the bonnet had sprung open. Before leaving the 1960 Liège, it would be wrong not to record the fabulous drive of John Sprinzel and John Patten, who managed to get the 3000's baby brother, the Sprite, into a magnificent third place overall.

In the German Rally, the name of a future BMC Competition Manager, Stuart Turner, appears in the results for the first time, when he partnered Dave Seigle-Morris to a class win, with Don Morley and Pat Moss backing up as second and third in class. The Morleys rounded off the year with a third overall in the R.A.C. Rally, and once again the works cars took the team prize. As a result of their Liège win, Pat and Ann were elected 'Drivers of the Year' by the Guild of Motoring Writers, and in addition won the Ladies European Rally Championship. In the 19 months since the 3000 had been

The Record . . .

A tabulated history of all the works Austin-Healey 3000s, with individual success

The 'works' Austin-Healey 3000s

Reg. No.	Date	Chassis No. Engine No.	History		
PMO 201	1958	BN6–1136 26D/R/63599H (100/6)	1958	Alpine Liège	Pat Moss *Coupe des Dames* Pat Moss *Coupe des Dames, 4th overall* Sold to J. Mahles
PMO 202	1958	BN6–1137 26D/R/63818H (100/6)	1958	Alpine Liège	Bill Shepherd *Coupe des Alpes, 7th overall* Gerry Burgess *9th overall* Sold to Bill Shepherd
PMO 203	1958	BN6–1138 26D/R/62823H (100/6) converted to 3000 spec 1959	1958 1959 1959	Alpine Liège Tulip Liège	Jack Sears *11th overall* Joan Johns *Retired* Jack Sears *8th overall* Gerry Burgess *Crashed* Sold to Small and Parkes
SMO 744	1959	HBN7–1343 XSP/18131/8HC	1959 1960	Alpine Liège	Bill Shepherd *Retired* Peter Riley *7th G.T. category* Siestriere Peter Riley *Event cancelled* **Circuit of Ireland** Pat Moss *Retired* **Acropolis** Peter Riley *Crashed* Liège Dave Seigle-Morris *5th overall* German Morley bros. *12th overall* R.A.C. Ronnie Adams *39th overall* Sold to Mr. Candler
SMO 745	1959	HBN7–1344 XSP/18131/6	1959 1960	Alpine R.A.C. Liège German Geneva Acropolis Alpine German R.A.C.	John Gott *5th G.T. category* Morley bros. *4th overall* John Gott *Retired* Pat Moss *2nd overall* Pat Moss *Coupe des Dames* Pat Moss *Retired* John Williamson *Retired* Dave Seigle-Morris *8th overall* Peter Riley *10th overall* Sold to Dave Grimshaw
SMO 746	1959	HBN7–1342 XSP/18131/9HC	1959 1960	Alpine Liège	Jack Sears *Retired* Jack Sears *Retired* Siestriere Pat Moss *Event cancelled* Lyon–Charbonnieres Pat Moss *Crashed* Alpine John Gott *8th overall* Liège John Gott *10th overall* Sold to John Gott
SJB 471	1959	HBT7–101 26/DR/UH/113	1960	Tulip Alpine Liège R.A.C.	Morley bros. *21st overall* Morley bros. *14th overall* Peter Riley *Retired* Morley bros. *3rd overall* Sold to Derek Astle
UJB 143		BN7–6685 29D/U/H7326	1960 1961	Sebring 12 hrs. Le Mans 24 hrs. Midnight Sun Tour of Corsica	Peter Riley/Jack Sears *3rd in class* Peter Riley/Jack Sears *Retired* Peter Riley *Retired* Pat Moss *1st Sports Car* Sold to George Humble
URX 727	1960	HBN7–8446 29D/HU/12161	1960 1961	Tulip Alpine Liège German Mille Miglia	Pat Moss *8th overall* Pat Moss *2nd overall* Pat Moss *1st overall* Pat Moss *16th overall* Pat Moss *Non-starter* Sold to Pat Moss
XJB 870	1961	HBN7–13709 29D/RU/H25635	1961 1962	Alpine Liège R.A.C. Monte	Dave Seigle-Morris *Crashed* Dave Seigle-Morris *6th overall* Dave Seigle-Morris *12th overall* Dave Seigle-Morris *18th overall* Sold to Rudi Metzger Written off 1966
XJB 871	1961	HBN7–13708 29D/RU/H25616	1961	Acropolis Alpine	Peter Riley *3rd overall* Peter Riley *Crashed* Sold to Rauno Aaltonen

Footnote: PMO 201, PMO 202, and PMO 203, in its original form, were **100/6s**, but are included in this table because with them the big Healey was introduced to International rally success, a foretaste of what was to come

continued opposite

introduced, it had won 10 class wins in 14 international rallies.

1961/2: continuing successes

As usual, the 1961 Tulip rally was run on a class improvement basis, so despite a brilliant drive by Pat and Ann, a relatively low overall position was obtained. Peter Riley and Tony Ambrose took lone works entries on the Acropolis and Midnight Sun rallies, coming third overall in the Greek event. The Alpine saw five works cars on the start line, all the new XJB series cars. The Morley brothers had the sole unpenalized run out of 64 starters, thus winning the event outright and also winning one of the coveted Coupes des Alpes. John Gott/Bill Shepherd were the only other Healey to finish, Pat Moss and Seigle-Morris both crashing in the early stages, whilst Peter Riley had brake troubles on the Stelvio.

The Liège (or *Marathon de la Route*), going to Sofia in Bulgaria for the first time, was probably the toughest yet, with only 8 finishers out of 85 starters. Dave Seigle-Morris/Tony Ambrose were the only Healey crew to finish, Pat and Ann retiring with a broken chassis whilst running in fourth place in Yugoslavia, the other two Healeys also succumbing to the battering they received in Yugoslavia, where one 24-hour stretch saw 55 retirements! In the R.A.C., Pat again came second to Erik Carlsson, winning her class, with Dave Seigle-Morris and Tony Ambrose second in class.

In 1962, the 3000 had one of its rare outings in the Monte Carlo Rally, where despite an embarrassing surplus of power it managed to finished 18th overall in the hands of Seigle-Morris/Ambrose. The Tulip rally still clung to its class improvement basis of marking, so the Morley brothers and Peter Riley/David Astle had to be content with first and second in class, despite the former putting up the aggregate fastest time overall in the eliminating tests. Ann Wisdom had by now married Peter Riley, and so retired from the rally scene, her place with Pat Moss in the Acropolis being taken by Pauline Mayman. This singleton works entry finished eighth overall, collecting their class and, inevitably, the Coupes des Dames.

The Alpine was again a Healey benefit, the Morleys winning the event outright for the second year running. Pat and Pauline came third overall, with Dave and Tony collecting eighth place (despite a puncture on the Vivione), completing the team for the team prize.

The 1962 Liège was not quite as tough as 1961 (18 cars out of 104

Reg. No.	Date	Chassis No. Engine No.	History		
XJB 872	1961	HBN7–13706 29D/RU/H25660	1961	Alpine	John Gott *15th overall*
				Liège	John Gott *Retired*
					Sold to Derek Astle
XJB 876	1961	HBN7–13707 29D/RU/H25633	1961	Tulip	Morley bros. *14th overall*
				Alpine	Morley bros. *1st overall*
				Liège	Dave Grimshaw *Crashed*
				R.A.C.	Morley bros. *Retired*
					Sold to Don Morley
XJB 877	1961	HBN7–13710 29D/RU/H25626	1961	Tulip	Pat Moss *Coupe des Dames*
				Alpine	Pat Moss *Crashed*
				Liège	Pat Moss *Retired*
				R.A.C.	Pat Moss *2nd overall*
			1962	Acropolis	Pat Moss *8th overall*
				Liège	Rauno Aaltonen *Retired*
				R.A.C.	Peter Riley *Crashed*
			1963	Alpine	Paddy Hopkirk *Crashed*
				Liège	Paddy Hopkirk *6th overall*
					Written off 1964
37 ARX	1962	HBN7–18701 29E/RU/H5090	1962	Tulip	Morley bros. *14th overall*
				Solitude race	Bohringer *3rd in class*
			1963	Tulip	Morley bros. *2nd G.T. category*
				Alpine	Morley bros. *Retired*
					Written off 1963
47 ARX	1962	HBN7–18702 29E/RU/H4971	1962	Tulip	Peter Riley *18th overall*
				Alpine	Peter Riley *Retired*
				Liège	Logan Morrison *5th overall*
			1963	Tulip	Logan Morrison *Retired*
				Alpine	Logan Morrison *Crashed*
				R.A.C.	Timo Makinen *5th overall*
					Written off 1964
57 ARX	1962	HBN7–18703 29E/RU/H5225	1962	Alpine	Morley bros. *1st overall*
				Liège	Paddy Hopkirk *Retired*
				R.A.C.	Morley bros. *Crashed*
			1963	Alpine	Timo Makinen *Retired*
				Liège	Timo Makinen *crashed*
					Written off 1963
67 ARX	1962	HBN7–18704 29E/RU/H5220	1962	Alpine	Dave Seigle Morris *8th overall*
				Liège	Dave Seigle Morris *8th overall*
				R.A.C.	Paddy Hopkirk *2nd overall*
			1963	Midnight Sun	Timo Makinen *Disqualified*
				Liège	Logan Morrison *Retired*
				R.A.C.	Morley bros. *9th overall*
					Sold to Tony Ambrose
77 ARX	1962	HBN7–18705 29E/RU/H5454	1962	Alpine	Pat Moss *3rd overall*
				Polish	Pat Moss *2nd overall*
				R.A.C.	Pat Moss *3rd overall*
			1963	Monte	Timo Makinen *13th overall*
				Liège	Rauno Aaltonen *Crashed*
					Written off 1963
ARX 91B	1963	HBJ8–26754 29K/RU/H1502	1964	Austrian Alpine.	Paddy Hopkirk *1st overall*
			1965	Targa Florio.	Hawkins/Makinen *2nd in class*
					Sold to David Hiam
ARX 92B	1964	HBJ8–26753 29K/RU/H1501	1964	Tulip	Morley bros. *1st in G.T. category*
				Alpine	Morley bros. *2nd in G.T. category*
				Liège	Timo Makinen *Retired*
					Sold to Peter Browning
BMO 93B	1964	HBJ8–27537 29K/RU/H3160	1964	Liège	Rauno Aaltonen *1st overall*
				R.A.C.	Morley bros. *21st overall*
					Sold to Pauline Mayman
BRX 852B	1964	HBJ8–28477 29K/RU/H3160	1964	Liège	Paddy Hopkirk *Retired*
				R.A.C.	Timo Makinen *2nd overall*
					Sold to Tony Ambrose
DRX 257C	1965	HBJ8–31336 29K/RU/5899	1965	Tulip	Morley bros. *4th overall*
				Scottish	Timo Makinen *Retired*
					Written off 1965
DRX 258C	1965	HBJ8–31337 29K/RU/H5900	1965	Geneva	Morley bros. *7th overall*
				Alpine	Morley bros. *2nd overall*
				R.A.C.	Morley bros. *Crashed*
					Sold to Pauline Mayman
EJB 806C	1965	HBJ8/31655 29K/RU/H6162	1965	R.A.C.	Timo Makinen *2nd overall*
					Sold to Ted Worswick
PWB 57		(ex ARX 92B)	1967	R.A.C.	Rauno Aaltonen *Event cancelled*

finishing) and two Healeys finished. Dave Seigle-Morris had a six-minute lead over Bohringer (Mercedes) at the start of the last stage in Yugoslavia, but during this stage a rear spring mounting broke. Dave drove the car like this, with the bodywork rubbing on the tyre, for 180 kilometres, dropping $1\frac{1}{2}$ hours in the process. This dropped them to their final placing of eighth.

At Coriza, Dougie Watts, chief BMC mechanic, took the fuel tank out of the car, welded the chassis, and fitted a new spring and replaced the tank in just over the hour, so that Dave was able to achieve a personal ambition and finish three Lièges in a row, and thus qualify for a special Gold Cup (an ambition which had previously been achieved by John Gott as well).

Rauno Aaltonen/Tony Ambrose had to retire for the very unusual reason that their road book 'disappeared' whilst at the Zagreb Control. This automatically caused them to be excluded. Logan Morrison/Rupert (the Rev.) Jones got a second Healey home in a creditable fifth place, despite it being Logan's first Liège and first outing in a 3000. The fourth member of the team, Paddy Hopkirk/Jack Scott, the former at the start of his long association with BMC, retired with suspension failure in the depths of Yugoslavia.

They made up for this in the R.A.C., however, by coming second overall, with Pat and Pauline taking third place and adding another Coupes des Dames to their collection. Pat (with Pauline) once again won the Ladies European Rally Championship, this actually being the third time Pat had achieved this honour.

1963—a disappointing year

1963 was an unlucky year for the Abingdon team, with two outright victories being snatched away literally at the last moment, and an abnormally large number of non-finishers being recorded.

Timo Makinen was teamed with Mini driver Christabel Carlisle for the Monte and after a magnificent drive in typical Monte conditions they won the G.T. category and came 13th overall, this despite the fact that neither could speak the other's language, (other than Chris shouting 'Faster, faster'). Despite once again returning fastest overall times in the Tulip, the Morleys had to be content with second place in the G.T. Category, the class improvement system favouring a Porsche 1600. Gloom was cast over the results by the tragic death of Derek Astle, whose ex-works 3000 left the road on the Trois Epis hill-climb. Although the

Alpine rally 1962, and the outright winners, Don and Erle Morley, round the hairpin on Mont Ventoux timed climb. 57 ARX was eventually written off

car wasn't badly damaged, and the co-driver (Dave Grimshaw) was un-injured, Derek was killed instantly with a broken neck. This is probably the only serious crash ever to happen to one of the works cars.

Tension was high at the start of the Alpine, with the Morleys anxious at least to follow their outright wins of the two previous years with an un-penalized run, and thus win one of the very rare Coupes d'Or, awarded for three consecutive penalty-free runs. Only two crews had previously won one of these Gold Cups (Ian Appleyard in an XK 120 and Stirling Moss in the old-type Sunbeam Alpine), but the popular twins were fated not to join this illustrious company, as on the final night, whilst firmly in the lead, an experimental axle assembly broke, and despite heroic efforts by a BMC service crew, who changed the assembly in 67 minutes, the Morleys were out of the hunt. The Alpine set an all-time low for the big Healeys, not one of the four cars finishing, Paddy Hopkirk and Logan Morrison both running out of road, and Timo Makinen, paired with Mike Wood, smashing a wheel on a road-side kilometre stone.

The team's luck was still against them on the Liège—Rauno Aaltonen/Tony Ambrose crashing on the Vivione whilst two minutes ahead of the ultimate winner Bohringer, and Makinen/Mabbs being hit by a lorry near Titograd. Paddy Hopkirk/Henry Liddon stopped on the Vivione to see if they could help their team-mates, but their efforts were to no avail.

They continued themselves, however, to finish sixth overall, with a total loss of some 48 minutes.

As usual, the year ended with the R.A.C., where Makinen and the Morleys finished first and second in their class respectively. Aaltonen, how-ever, shortened the chassis of his car when he went exploring in the forest of Bin. Timo had a moment on the slippery Tulloch stage and took 12 minutes to regain the road, and Don Morley on a later stage spent some four or five minutes persuading his electrics to operate again after a part-icularly deep mud-splash. So ended a relatively disappointing year, although another five class wins were added to the records, bringing the tally in international events to 29.

1964/5—the final years

By 1964, the major effort of the Competition department had swung over to the ubiquitous Mini, which

proceeded to pile up a fantastic record of competition successes. The 3000 was not completely ignored, however, and during its two-year swan song, the odd singleton entries continued to uphold the Austin-Healey honour.

To start the season, Donald Healey Motors entered a car in the annual 12-hour race at Sebring, to be driven by Paddy Hopkirk and Grant Clark, the Canadian champion driver. Quite early on, Paddy ran over a piece of metal wreckage, bursting a tyre and having to limp back to the pits on the rim. The damage was soon repaired and the car resumed, well down the field. After some 30 laps, the Healey was back into 33rd place, but shortly after Clark took over, he lost it in a big way just after the pits, somer-saulting onto his roof.

The Morleys, in the first competition appearance of the Mk III, once again put up best overall performance in the Tulip rally, but as usual had to be content with a class award, the winner being Makinen/Ambrose in a Cooper 'S', which was also making its competi-tion debut. Paddy Hopkirk/Henry Liddon had a go at the Austrian Alpine (an event which claims to be the *original* Alpine Rally, though since overshadowed by the French event of the same name), and put up fastest times on all the tests to win outright, although hard pushed by a little Steyr-Puch of all things!

The French Alpine followed, and the Morleys had a trouble-free run, col-lecting their class, and a Coupe de Argent for three non-consecutive penalty-free trips, some small consola-tion for missing their Gold Cup the previous year.

'Battered but unbowed'. On one of the finest drives in his career, Timo Makinen fights to hold on to first place in the 1965 R.A.C. Rally. After leading for most of the rally he was pushed into second place by Aaltonen's Cooper 'S'

Pat Moss and Ann Wisdom on their way to second place in the 1960 Alpine with URX 727 in which they later won the Liège carrying the same competition number (76)

Three works cars were entered for the Liège, which was to be the last of this series of 94-hour rallies, its place in 1965 being taken by a marathon regularity run at the Nürburgring. This time Rauno and Tony Ambrose made no mistake, and finished an easy (although that is the wrong adjective) winner, losing some 57 minutes, whilst the second-placed car of Erik Carlsson was 28 minutes further adrift. Paddy retired in Yugoslavia, with only second gear left, and Timo ran out of tyres when a series of seven punctures plagued him. This was a common complaint in the Yugoslavian sections, where the proportion of horse-drawn traffic is still high!

The R.A.C. saw two cars entered for the Morleys, for Timo and Don Barrow; the former lost a lot of time after running out of road on one of the Welsh stages, but Timo and Don drove the big car into second place overall, and best G.T. car. At one stage they were leading the rally, but slippery conditions in Scotland favoured the smaller cars, and they were unable to maintain their early lead.

The final appearances of the works cars came in 1965, with the Morleys collecting class awards in the Tulip, Geneva, and Alpine. This latter event was particularly tough on the G.T. cars, not one of which was able to

1962 Liège–Sofia–Liège. David Seigle Morris (eighth overall) books out of a control in Yugoslavia. Note cooling vent on top of bonnet, slats in wings and hump on boot to take extra spare wheel

win one of the coveted Coupes. Timo had a go at the Scottish and R.A.C., failing to finish in the former, but coming second overall again on the latter. This was an unlucky event for him, as, with Paul Easter as his co-driver, he led for most of the rally only to be literally overtaken on an icy Welsh Hill by Rauno (Mini) who went on to the outright win! Timo reckons that this was his best-ever effort in a 3000.

Timo had an outing of a different type early in the year, when he was paired with Paul Hawkins for the rally-type Targa Florio race in Sicily. Despite using tyres and wheels at a phenomenal rate (it required a tyre change every two laps—approximately 88 miles), the big Healey was leading its class when a rotor arm broke at the start of the eighth lap (10-lap race).

Paul Hawkins walked back to the pits for a replacement, and the gallant pair went on to finish second in class to a Ferrari GTO. Paul Hawkins also drove the 3000 at Sebring, this time with Warwick Banks as his partner, and came 17th overall, winning the class.

In 1966, no works 3000s were entered in international events, but several ex-works cars continued to show that the eight-year-old design was still a force to be reckoned with. At the end of 1967, the International R.A.C. rally included a class for Group 6 sports cars, and it was decided to enter a single works 3000. No new cars were available, but BMC's competition manager, Peter Browning, owned the ex-Morley Alpine car ARX 92B, although this had since been re-registered as PWB 57. It was decided to rebuild this car for Rauno Aaltonen to drive, the result being probably the most powerful road-going 3000 ever built. An all-aluminium engine was fitted, bored out to 2968 c.c., with three 45 DCOE Weber carburetters, giving a power output of nearly 200 b.h.p. *at the wheels!* Despite extensive lightening the additional load of rally gear, sump and underside guards, etc., brought the weight up to just 24 cwt., which was carried on four sturdy Minilite mag.-alloy wheels shod with Dunlop 185—15 SP44 radial Weathermaster tyres.

Alas, all the preparation was in vain. At the very last moment the rally had to be cancelled because of the disastrous outbreak of foot and mouth disease which threatened to cripple the farming community, and so we were unable to have a final look at the big Healey in its natural forest habitat.

AUSTIN-HEALEYS, 1953–1967

Marvelous cars that changed the sports car world

BY THOS L. BRYANT
PHOTOS BY WM. A. MOTTA

ONE COULD WRITE reams about the history, charm and charisma of the Austin-Healey cars and their impact on the motoring enthusiast world. The Big Healeys (to distinguish them from the Sprite) were produced for some 15 years and carved out a niche for themselves as the best selling medium-size sports cars of their day. The Healey was something of a natural progression for the American sports car driver of the Fifties, who had started with an MG TC or TD and wanted to move up to a more powerful car. I remember this was the case with one of my brothers who owned a bright red 1952 MG TD, which he rather generously shared with me and in which I received my first traffic citation. Eventually the red TD gave way to a jet black Austin-Healey 100-4, which seemed to our youthful eyes ever so much more rakish and befitting our dashing self images. Unfortunately, we weren't wise enough to keep both cars and the Healey later went away in favor of something else. A DKW, I think.

The point is, the Austin-Healey was an important factor in the development of the sports car movement in America as well as in other parts of the world, and it's a car that still has a surprising number of devotees eight years after its demise. R&T Contributing Editor Cyril Posthumus wrote about the Big Healeys in April 1972. "Incredibly rough and solid, yet handsome and amazingly cheap. In short, it was a lovable bastard." Posthumus was referring to the fact that the original Healeys had humble origins, using the Austin A90 4-cylinder engine mated to a 4-speed gearbox that had such a low 1st gear it was blocked off in the earliest cars.

The Austin-Healey 100 made its debut at the London Automobile Show in 1952 and was an immediate hit. Donald Healey and his son, Geoffrey, designed the car to be a lightweight, well shaped automobile, using as many stock Austin components as possible to keep the cost down. The original A90 Austin engine was a 2660-cc overhead-valve affair which produced 90 bhp at 4000 rpm. Coupled with the A90 4-speed gearbox which had been slightly modified so that it could be floor-mounted rather than column shift, the combination gave the Healey an excellent power-to-weight relationship. The final drive ratio was 4.10:1 which further aided the acceleration but did little for high-speed cruising. Thus, a Laycock de Normanville overdrive unit was fitted.

The chassis was a relatively simple one with two main 3-in. square box-section frame rails with crossmembers that carried steel floor pressings. The front suspension consisted of coil springs and A-arms with lever-type shock absorbers. The rear suspension consisted of a live axle suspended and located by leaf springs and lever shocks.

The 100-4 went into production at Longbridge in May 1953 and continued little changed until June 1955. In August of that year, improvements were made to the brakes and front springs, and the 4-speed BMC C-type gearbox was installed. Almost 15,000 100-4s were built between the startup and November 1956, including the relatively rare 100M (for Le Mans) and very rare 100S (for Sebring) competition models.

The Sixes

IN THE late summer of 1956, the Austin-Healey 100-6 was born with the BMC C-series 2639-cc engine. This new powerplant produced 102 bhp at 4600 rpm, but this improvement in horsepower was pretty well eaten up by the increased weight of the new Healey. The cockpit had been enlarged at the expense of the trunk and two very small seats had been placed behind the front seats. There were minor revisions to the body, the wheelbase was slightly longer and the original fold-down windshield was replaced with a fixed one. The gearbox remained unchanged from the late 100-4s.

In 1957, modifications were made to the 6-cylinder engine in the form of a new 6-port head, aluminum alloy intake manifold, modified distributor and twin 1.75-in. SU HD6 carburetors. These changes brought the compression ratio up to 8.5:1 and the horsepower rose to 117 at 5000 rpm, giving the 100-6 a slightly quicker elapsed time for the quarter-mile run (18.1 vs 18.8 sec) and improved the top speed in overdrive from 103 to 111 mph.

While the bulk of 100-6 Healeys were of the new 4-seat configuration, the demand for a 2-seater was so strong that in June 1958 the factory began turning out 100-6s with only two seats. Again, almost 15,000 100-6 cars were produced, with more than 10,000 of them being 4-seaters. Production of the 100-6 ended in March 1959 and three months later the first of the 3000s emerged from the factory, which had by now been moved to Abingdon.

The Healey 3000

MORE THAN 42,000 Austin-Healey 3000s were built during the period from June 1959 to December 1967 when the famed marque came to an end. The 6-cylinder C-series engine was bored and stroked to 2912 cc, compression was raised to 9.0:1 and power went up to 124 bhp at 4600 rpm. The 3000 also featured a larger-diameter clutch, stronger cluster gears and the addition of Girling disc brakes. In appearance, the early 3000 was little changed from the 100-6, except for the

fully convertible top (as opposed to a roadster with removable top), a wrap-around windshield, wind-up side windows in place of curtains and other refinements that moved the Healey away from its traditional sporty image and toward a more comfortable touring car position. Performance did not deteriorate with the loss of the third carburetor and, in fact, the convertible became the fastest production Healey ever with a top speed of 117 mph and a quarter-mile time of 17.1 sec.

Over the next five years, until the end of production in December 1967, the Big Healeys were marked by modifications designed to make them well fitted, pleasant GT cars. The horsepower climbed to 150 at 5250 rpm, servo assist was added to the brake system and the interior was groomed with a wood veneer facia and lockable glovebox. The Austin-Healey was still marked by an abundance of smooth power and torque, along with a heavy feel to the handling that inspired confidence in the car's durability. The styling was timeless, one of the cleanest and best-looking sports cars ever. But the U.S. federal safety regulations were announced for January 1, 1968 and the factory decided that too many modifications would have to be made to meet them. After 15 years and more than 70,000 cars, Austin-Healey became a marque of the past.

Buying a Used Healey

THE PURPOSE of the R&T Used Car Classic series is to give the reader sufficient information to make a decision about

flash on the grille and the 3000 insignia.

The 3000 Mark II was introduced in May 1961 and had three SU carburetors, a new camshaft and stronger valve springs, bringing the bhp figure up to 132 at 4750 rpm. The new triple-carb arrangement provided more power, mostly in the top end, and slightly better fuel economy when properly tuned, and those last three words are important. Difficulties in maintaining the proper state of tune were so widespread that the 3-carburetor setup lasted less than a year, and in March 1962 a return was made to twin carburetors.

Several changes were made to the body. These included a

purchasing the subject car. To many of us, buying a new sports or GT car may be financially difficult (if not impossible) or we may simply be caught up in a euphoria of nostalgia that tells us they just don't build them like they used to. Whatever the reason, great joy and exhilaration can result from owning a car such as the Austin-Healey, or the other marques we have covered in this series. It's also prudent to point out that equally great frustration and despair can arise if the buyer makes an unfortunate choice.

For this portion of the report, we solicited the advice of David Ramstad of Everett, Washington, a Healey owner and active member of the Austin-Healey Club, Pacific Centre. Dave writes:

Thinking about adding an Austin-Healey to your stable? But hesitating because well meaning though ignorant friends have done their best to divert you from the heartbreak of cranky old English sports cars? Did they hit you with dire warnings about those devilishly complicated SU carburetors or could it have been hideous word pictures of wire wheels flying off worn splines at speed? While some British sports cars may have earned such reputations (I love them all, regardless), I don't mind shouting that the Austin-Healey is not among them! Now, let's get into the pleasant task of making a wise purchase. All the standard guidelines for choosing any used car apply and will not be dealt with at length here. Our main concern is things peculiar to the Austin-Healey.

Mechanical

THE POWERPLANT, be it A90 4-cylinder or C-series 6, is a rugged, low-stressed, heavy cast-iron unit producing a considerable amount of torque at low speeds. These engines are noted for their reliability and long lives, quite lacking in major trauma. Unlike the highly tuned engines found in Alfas, Porsches, etc., the Healey's engine almost never breaks, but simply increases its clearances with a corresponding increase in oil consumption over a comparatively long period of time. The engine is very easy to live with because of its ample power and infrequent mechanical needs and, happily, pollution control devices are absent because all Healeys were produced prior to 1968.

The prospective buyer should perform a compression check and if possible a full leak down test to see if copious amounts of oil are coming from the lower rear of the engine. If so, this indicates either a failure in the rear plate gasket or a crack in the rear main bearing area, among other less likely possibilities. If you are not planning to tear down the engine in your restoration process, you should avoid a car with this problem. The average, reasonably well cared for engine usually requires little more than a careful valve grind, piston ring replacement and complete tune-up to put it back in the pink. With good lubrication practices, the lower ends of these engines seem to last forever.

The BMC C-type 4-speed gearbox fitted to all Big Healeys from August 1955 on can be a problem if found in a car once owned by an insensitive (read brutal) gear changer. First and 2nd gears normally produce a distinct but not excessive whine, but the mauled gearbox will make obviously expensive noises (most often in 1st and reverse) and will usually exhibit slow or nonexistent synchromesh action. Because of the Healey's ample torque, synchromesh was never felt to be necessary in bottom gear.

The Laycock de Normanville overdrive unit seldom suffers failure in its internals. Poor or no overdrive function is often cured by careful troubleshooting of the unit's electrical control system or by adjustments to the hydraulics. If questions remain after a test drive, consult local Healey enthusiasts, British car repair shops or the nearest Leyland dealer, in that order.

The Big Healey's rear axle is very strong and trouble free, seldom needing more than a seal replacement to cure a leak. This axle is often called upon to handle the torque of an American V-8 and apparently suffices.

Body and Chassis

ENEMY NUMBER one to the A-H semi-unit, aluminum and steel construction is rust. The buyer should carefully examine the lower 12 in. all around the car to determine the extent of deterioration. Lower fender to chassis joints (front and rear), rear fender lower cavity, lower door area and sills and lower flange of the trunk lid are the most common areas for rust. Cars in the north central and eastern U.S. and eastern Canada, where salt is used on winter roads, have usually suffered the most. Many Healeys show some minor, non-structural rust which can be easily repaired, but those cars with major rust in the inner body sills, outrigger beams and floor sections are to be avoided.

I should stress the Big Healey can be kept free of rust with some precautions. The car has few totally closed areas and if water drains in doors, sills and convertible top channels (1963–1967 cars) are kept open, and if accumulations of road dirt and salt are frequently flushed out of wheel wells and lower body areas, the Healey can be preserved intact for many years. Speaking of rust problems, a fast-moving item in the Healey world is the replacement fuel tank. The tank is in the trunk cavity and will occasionally have deteriorated to the point of seepage. Fortunately, replacements are available for approximately $110.

The substantial box-section chassis appears to be indestructible. This is not an illusion—terribly bent Healeys have been reconstructed because of the strength of the frame. However, carefully examine the forward and aft crossmembers. Lack of care when jacking up the car at these points (Healeys are never raised by their bumpers!) has led to serious bending or holes punched through the welded seam by a small but lethal jack pad. Using jacks with wide flat pads or a block of wood will prevent damage of this sort.

Healey front suspension and steering may exhibit considerable looseness. The cure here is to overhaul and re-bush the lower A-arm pivot points and swivel pins, replace the tie rod ends and adjust or overhaul the steering box. You should recognize that the Healey's cam-and-peg steering lacks the taut feel of rack and pinion, and Healeys always display a certain amount of play in the steering wheel.

Rear leaf springs occasionally turn up with broken leaves, in which case the car's attitude will take on a marked list. The four Armstrong lever-type shock absorbers will need to be replaced if leaking badly. Americans haven't seen a car in years that requires refilling the shocks; often a neglected Healey may simply be in need of shock fluid to restore its proper ride and handling. The price of replacement lever shocks has risen to the point where the cost of converting to tube-type shocks is justified. This requires the addition of mounting brackets to the chassis, and these are available along with the proper shocks from major Koni suppliers.

The Achilles heel of most wire wheel-equipped sports cars is the splined hub on which the rear wheels are mounted and, of course, the wire wheels themselves. If you test drive a car that exhibits a momentary lag followed by a clunk from the rear when you engage the clutch, you face a large cash outlay

Six-cylinder engine in early 3000 (foreground) displaced 2912 cc while the original 4-cyl engine (rear) was a 2660-cc affair with 90 bhp.

to replace or re-machine the splined rear hubs. There has been a love-hate relationship with wire wheels forever and their periodic maintenance is costly. This is not helped by the fact that the noble profession of wheelwright is disappearing, and many owners do convert to stamped steel discs or cast alloy wheels. Few owners of traditional British sports cars can tolerate the accompanying character alteration, however. Replacement Dunlop wire wheels have increased drastically in price and you should plan on paying $70–$80 each for new wire wheels—possibly half that for rebuilding your existing wheels. Talk around before committing your wobbly rims to the local wheel wizard because quality varies considerably.

Parts and Prices

WHAT'S THE story concerning parts? Initially, as established dealer spares inventories shifted away from the Healey when it was discontinued, the situation looked quite bleak. Fortunately, circumstances began to turn around just a few years ago and today there is no need to fear any serious shortage of general spare parts. With the Big Healey's emergence as a collectible car there has been a rise in small, specialized businesses in North America and Great Britain dealing in used, new-old stock or newly manufactured copies of obsolete parts. Simply combing the "Market Place" section of *Road & Track* will yield several firms offering extensive lists of spares. You must remember though, that Healeys are not Beetles or Impalas so you may have to do a certain amount of legwork. Considering the car has been out of production for eight years and compared to other sporting cars of recent decades, parts are surprisingly reasonable and not terribly expensive.

How much is that solid, well maintained old Healey going to cost? While wild price fluctuations aren't uncommon in a car of this sort, some approximations can be made. There are very few original or acceptably restored 4-cylinder 100s (1953–1956) below $2000. I believe the same can be said for the 100-6 series (1957–1959) and the early 3000, unofficially known as the Mark I (1960–1961). The 3000 Mark II, the triple-carburetor equipped 1962 roadster and rollup window 1963 convertible, is most often found in the $2000–3000 range. And the final Big Healey, the 3000 Mark III (late 1964–1967), loaded with 150-bhp engine, vacuum-boosted disc brakes, and walnut facia is a bargain between $3000–4000, with figures of $4500–5000 not unusual. Extremes range from badly rusted machines going for a few hundred bucks in eastern Canada to pristine, low-mileage Mark IIIs listed at more than $6000 here in the Seattle area.

Conclusion

UNDAUNTED BY those who consider seekers of old British sports cars completely mad and equipped with the basic data necessary to distinguish a good prospect from a dog, the search for that fine old Austin-Healey can begin. At this point, a mighty plug for Healey clubs is in order. Far from being simply mutual admiration societies, these groups of true believers diligently pursue sources of spare parts, offer discounts to their members on various Healey-related merchandise and publish priceless technical and historical information. And that only accounts for half of their efforts. The number of club tours, regional meets and other happenings increases by the year.

The Austin-Healey is one of the few vintage sports cars still economically available to the average enthusiast. If this big, fast and good-looking machine fits your requirements, you would do well to not hesitate much longer. As the existing supply of cars shrinks, prices of the better examples are definitely on the rise, with no foreseeable end in sight. Good luck and happy Healeying!—*Dave Ramstad*

TYPICAL ASKING PRICES	
Year & Type	Price Range
1953–1956 100-4	$1800–3000
1957–1959 100-6	$1600–3000
1960–1961 3000	$1600–3000
1962–1963 3000 Mk II	$2000–3000
1964–1967 3000 Mk III	$2800–4000

Prices generally lower in the southwest (southern California) because of greater availability. Cars in the north central and northeast portions of the U.S. and in Canada have often suffered damage from salt used on winter roads.

Dash of 100-4 is clean and simple.

Wood veneer facia set later 3000s apart.

BRIEF SPECIFICATIONS					
	100-4	100-6	3000	Mk II	Mk III
Curb weight, lb	2150	2480	2520	2530	2650
Wheelbase, in.	90.0	92.0	92.0	92.0	92.0
Track, f/r	48.8/	48.8/	48.8/	48.8/	48.8/
	50.0	50.0	50.0	50.0	50.0
Length	151.5	158.0	158.0	158.0	158.0
Width	60.0	60.5	60.5	60.5	60.5
Height	49.0	49.0	49.0	50.0	50.0
Fuel capacity, gal.	14.4	14.4	14.4	14.4	14.4
Engine type	ohv 4-cyl	ohv 6-cyl	ohv 6-cyl	ohv 6-cyl	ohv 6-cyl
Bore x stroke, in.	3.44 x 4.38	3.12 x 3.50	3.28 x 3.50	3.28 x 3.50	3.28 x 3.50
Displacement, cc	2660	2639	2912	2912	2912

PERFORMANCE DATA From Contemporary Tires					
	1954 100-4	1957 100-6	1959 3000	1963 Mk II	1965 Mk III
0–60 mph, sec	11.7	12.2	9.8	11.2	9.8
Standing ¼ mi, sec	17.9	18.2	17.1	17.6	17.4
Avg fuel consumption, mpg	23.5	20.0	20.0	18.5	18.5
Road test date	7-54	1-57	1-59	11-62	2-65

It's a dream car to many enthusiasts but a daunting proposition for some.
Mark Dixon sifts fact and fiction about BMC's muscle car

Austin Healey
100 & 3000

STUDIO PHOTOS BY MICHAEL BAILIE, OTHER PHOTOS BY MARK DIXON, ARTWORK BY JAMES RUPPERT

FIRST-TIME BUYERS are often wary of the Big Healey. They imagine it must be a handful to drive, and, while there's a tempting simplicity to the oily bits, the bodywork is a mass of compound curves that suggest large bills to anyone even vaguely acquainted with the costs of restoration.

Yet the 'Healey's macho characteristics are irresistibly appealing. Big engine, simple chassis, rear-wheel-drive — how can you go wrong? It's the poor man's AC Cobra, but it's as British as roast beef, whereas the Ford V8-powered Cobra has more the flavour of pastrami. And despite what the bar-room pundits may tell you, it's not difficult or heavy to drive. The Big Healey is not, in fact, a particularly big car.

'Healeys, of course, were fitted with Austin engines. They came in two guises: the early, four-cylinder 100 model, and the six-cylinder 100-6 and 3000 that superseded it. Engines apart, the cars are pretty similar, although there was a variety of body configurations including two- and four-seater (actually two-plus-two) roadsters, and so-called convertibles (wind-up windows and a sensible hood).

In this article, cars are differentiated by the usual system of Mark numbers, but 'Healey enthusiasts often refer to them by Austin's own code. Under that system, an early 100 is a BN1, and a 3000 Mk III is a BJ8. You'll find the Austin codes on chassis plates, but for most purposes, the Mark labels are easier to grasp, at least until you're thoroughly indoctrinated.

Today, Big Healeys are hugely popular with British enthusiasts, but it's often forgotten that us Brits never got to drive them much when they were new. Some 95% of Big Healeys were exported, mostly to North America. Over the last 20 years, there's been a steady trickle of cars coming back, but they aren't the easiest sports cars to restore so it's crucial to ensure you don't end up with a lemon.

One man who knows a lot about the pitfalls of Healey restoration is Jonathan Everard, proprietor of JME Healeys. His company is literally just down the road from the site of the Healey works, where Jonathan

himself was an apprentice during the Sixties.

'Bear in mind how much a cheap car will need spending on it,' he warns. 'And if you want to take on a project, buy the most complete car you can find, because even small missing parts can be expensive to replace.'

Whichever route you take to 'Healey ownership, a few minutes spent following Jonathan's advice could save you a lot of pain.

BODY AND CHASSIS

ASK ANY mechanically-minded child to design a sports car, and the 'Healey is what they'd come up with. The bodywork, which you can see, is curvy and swoopy looking. The chassis, which you can't, is basically two parallel lengths of metal that hold it together.

It's obviously more complicated than that, but not much. The chassis consists of two box-section rails held apart by crossmembers and braced by a central cruciform. These chassis rails should appear quite straight when viewed along their length from the front of the car. Any waviness or kinks indicate accident damage. That's bad news, for while it is quite possible to straighten the rails or even to fit a replacement chassis, the damage is going to be transferred right into your bank account.

Rustproofing was an alien concept when these cars were new, so there's also the risk, if not the guarantee, of corrosion. As Jonathan points out, the first owners of Big Healeys were mostly affluent types who used them every day and gave up cleaning them within a month.

It's the chassis outriggers that are most likely to have suffered. They support long sills, effectively creating a perimeter chassis, which are themselves vulnerable to rot, as is the whole bottom half of the bodywork.

The vast majority of 'Healeys were exported when new — a fair proportion of them to sunnier places than Warwickshire. While that's helped the survival rate, it's quite common to find cars that are from generally dry environments but which also have rusty floorpans or even chassis top surfaces. That's because owners rarely needed to put the top up, so got caught out when it rained. Repairs are complicated by the fact that floorpans and bulkheads are welded to the chassis, rather than bolted on.

Much more awkward to sort out is damage to the so-called front shroud — the metalwork around the grille and bonnet. This, and the corresponding rear shroud behind the cockpit, are made from several sections of alloy, all butt-welded and planished together. As with many sports cars, front and rear are prone to parking knocks or minor shunts, so

'Rustproofing was an alien concept when these cars were new, so there's the risk, if not the guarantee, of corrosion'

SPOT THE ROT

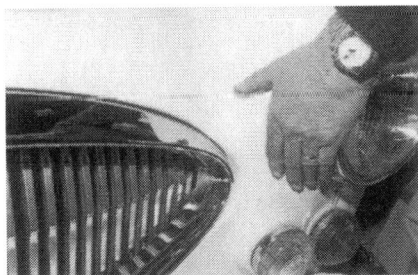

Jonathan runs a practised hand over the aluminium front shroud: it's often bodged.

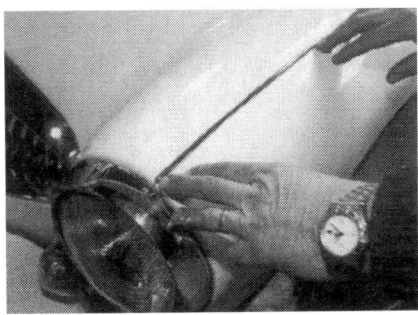

With steel wings, electrolytic action may cause corrosion along the joint with shroud.

You'll find rust just about anywhere in the lower nine inches, including the front wings.

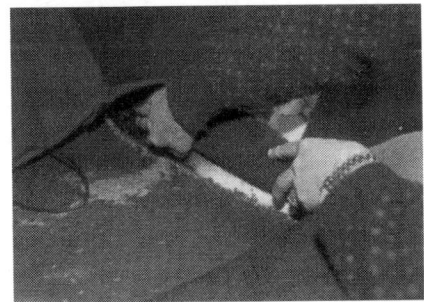

Inner sills are structural and hard to repair. Difficult to see with carpets stuck on them.

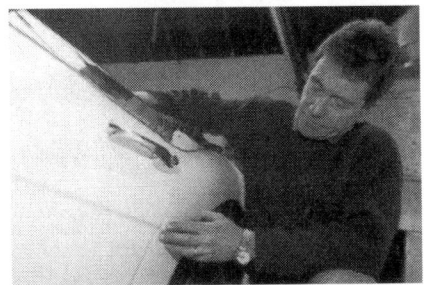

Door fit is an instant guide to condition: check both panel gap and swage line.

OUR EXPERT

JONATHAN EVERARD, proprietor of JME Healeys in Leamington Spa, has been driving since he was six years old. He learned in an old Ford Y-type, in the fields around his home.

More significantly, Jonathan joined the Healey Motor Co after leaving school in 1962. 'It was a very exciting time. Not many people know that 'Healeys also made boats, so we often had film stars visiting.'

After serving his apprenticeship at the factory, Jonathan left in 1968 to join his father at the Wise Terrace premises where he's been working with 'Healeys ever since.

1953-56

❖ **100 BN1**: Austin A90 engine and 'box fitted to box section chassis. Four-cylinder 2660cc engine produced 94bhp, gearbox was three-speed with overdrive.

❖ **100 BN2** with four speeds, 110bhp, anti-roll bar on front suspension in 1955.

❖ **100M**: Healey company modified BN2s with louvered bonnet, leather strap and two-tone paint.

1954-56

❖ **100S** alloy cylinder head, 132bhp aluminium body panels, louvered bonnet with leather straps.

1956-59

❖ **100-6** BN4 2639cc six-cylinder producing 101bhp. Body chassis lengthened by 2in. Fixed 'screen with revised suspension, bonnet scoop and elliptical radiator grille. In 1957, revised six-port cylinder head produced 117bhp. BN6 two-seater from 1958.

1959-61

❖ **3000** 2912cc, 124bhp with disc brakes. BN7s 2 doors, 2+2 BT7.

1961-67

❖ **3000 Mk II** triple SU carbs, twin SU from '62, 132bhp, revised gearbox.

❖ **3000 Mk III** in '64. 148bhp. Servo-assisted brakes, revised rear suspension.

they're prime candidates for bodging with filler. Even careless mechanics or onlookers can dent the alloy by leaning too hard while, for example, peering into an engine bay. The same holds true for cars which have been fitted with replacement alloy wings. Steel wings were standard, but both types are now available; even stones thrown up by the wheels can put dings in the alloy versions.

Good-quality remanufactured panels, such as those sold by A-H Spares, can be made to fit extremely well — but they require a lot of skill because the cars are so individual. It was common practice for the Longbridge or Abingdon line-worker to choose from a number of pressings until he achieved the best fit. At the end of the day, says Jonathan, the least usable panels would be farmed out to dealers, which is why new-old-stock panels aren't automatically a good buy. You could be paying through the nose for factory rejects!

The swage line that imparts a sense of movement to a 'Healey's flank (and which divides the colours on two-tone cars) is crucial to the car's looks, and a good clue to the quality of any previous restoration. Any misalignment where it crosses from door skin to wing will be immediately obvious, which is why experienced restorers will often repair a door rather than reskin it, so as to preserve the swage.

Check the profile of the swage is consistent: Jonathan reckons it's often sharper on repro panels, possibly because the originals were stamped out several at a time.

ENGINES

COMPARED with the grief that bodywork can give you, this is a relatively troublefree zone. The Austin engines are all modified saloon lumps — the design started life as a truck motor — so they're solidly built and mechanically simple. Given proper maintenance, they'll last forever.

The 100 used the 2.6-litre, four-cylinder engine from the A90 Atlantic, while the 100-6 gained the C-series 2.6-litre straight six designed for the BMC big saloons, later bored out to 2912cc for the Healey 3000. Both the four and the six had side-mounted single camshafts, driven by short chains from the crankshaft.

These are Fifties engines, so you can expect Fifties behaviour — which means relatively high oil consumption (up to a pint per 250 miles) and a good chance of minor oil leaks, unless the engine has been recently rebuilt. Oil pressure on the open road should be somewhere around the 50psi mark (usually just below), dropping to 10-15psi at idle. Fully synthetic oils aren't best suited to these engines, which were designed to use relatively heavy monograde oil.

Old age can lead the block to silt up

> 'Exhausts are a constant Healey irritant, because the cars sit so low to the ground'

saloons, although the Cambridge/Westminster Club won't thank us for saying so.

Exhausts are a constant 'Healey irritant as the cars sit so low to the ground. 'The Mk III system is a nightmare to fit, because it passes through two outriggers and runs close over the rear axle,' says Jonathan. 'On the other hand, the Mk III has a little more ground clearance. Earlier cars have simpler systems but they get knocked off more frequently.'

TRANSMISSION

LIKE THE engines, 'Healey transmissions were sourced from contemporary Austin saloons. For the 100, this meant adapting the four-speed gearbox from the A70/90. The problem of an excessively low saloon-type first gear was brilliantly solved by leaving the first gear selector out of 'Healey gearboxes and effectively turning them into three-speeders, where second gear was now first, and so on. To compensate, Laycock overdrive was fitted as standard to give a higher top gear.

Because the A70/90 'box had a column gearchange, it had side-mounted selectors and consequently, the 100 ended up with a floor 'change sprouting from the left of the transmission tunnel. This offset gearchange persisted until the 3000 Mk II, which gained a conventional centre-tunnel 'change. By then, the three-speed gearbox had long been superseded by the Westminster's four-speed unit, which was introduced on the 100 in August 1955 — again, plus overdrive.

Thankfully, the transmissions themselves are less complicated than their production history. Jonathan reckons that first and reverse gears, which have no synchromesh, tend to suffer most wear. The trick with engaging first is often to slip the lever into second beforehand. 'You may notice some gear whine, but there's so much else going on in a 'Healey that it's not obtrusive,' he adds.

You should of course check that overdrive works smoothly — it operates on the upper two ratios — but any problems are more likely to be electrical than hydraulic, unless the unit has been badly neglected. It takes regular engine oil, which JME Healeys prefer to change every 3000-mile service.

Rear axles are generally strong but may leak oil, usually from the end of the axle casing, which could result in contaminated brake linings. However, it only takes an hour to change the seal. Jonathan says he has never had a halfshaft break, even in his 260bhp rally car, so failures are more likely to be due to poor assembly than inherent weakness.

internally, although Jonathan says overheating is more usually due to owners being excessively tightfisted when it comes to replacing radiators. Incorrect ignition timing can also cause hot running, in severe cases leading to piston meltdown. An engine which is in good order and correctly tuned shouldn't overheat, but an electric fan will provide peace of mind for that inevitable summertime traffic jam.

Should the worst happen, at least parts are readily available. Replacement C-series blocks can often be sourced from derelict BMC

Bottom section of rear wing is susceptible to road dirt and stones, promoting rust.

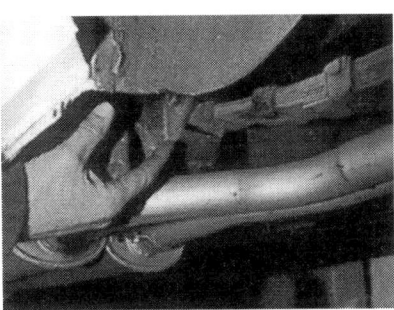

Jack the car up to check vital chassis points such as the rear spring hangers.

Rear bumper suffers from exhaust-accelerated corrosion; new ones don't last well.

With car jacked up, rock front wheel top and bottom to feel for wear in kingpins.

SPECS

	100	100-6	3000 Mk III
ENGINE	2660cc/4-cyl	2639cc/6-cyl	2912cc/6-cyl
POWER (bhp@rpm)	90/4000	102/4600	148/4750
TORQUE (lb ft@rpm)	144/2000	142/2400	165/3000
GEARBOX	3-spd man o/d	4-spd man o/d	4-spd man o/d
TOP SPEED	106mph	102mph	116mph
0-60MPH	10.3sec	11.7sec	9.8sec
CONSUMPTION	23mpg	23mpg	23mpg
LENGTH	12ft 7in (3.8m)	13ft 0.5in (4m)	13ft 0.5in (4m)
WIDTH	5ft 0.5in (1.5m)	5ft 0.5in (1.5m)	5ft 0.5in (1.5m)
WEIGHT	2150lb (975kg)	2422lb (1098kg)	2390lb (1084kg)

WHAT'S A 'HEALEY LIKE TO DRIVE? Old-fashioned, which is hardly surprising given that the car was first shown in 1952. Provided you adopt the classic slow-in, fast-out approach to corners, there's nothing difficult about it. Steering is a little heavy at parking speed but lightens up pleasantly on the move, while the ride is relatively soft. Limited ground clearance has always been a Healey bugbear — watch the speed humps.

WILL I FIT BEHIND THE WHEEL? No problem, once you've got your legs under it.

WHAT BODGES SHOULD I LOOK FOR? Filled and blown-over front shrouds, dodgy panel alignment either end of the doors, hidden corrosion in the body tub behind a glossy external paint job.

WHAT SHOULD I PAY? Anything from £10,000 upwards for a usable car, preferably £14-16,000 for a decent one. Really nice 'Healeys are in the £20-£30,000 bracket, and concours examples can fetch more. Project imports, landed with duties paid, cost from £5000. Be wary of apparent bargains, since restoration costs can be astronomic.

WHAT WILL INSURANCE COST? £794 for a 25yo, 2yrs NCB, clean licence, unlimited miles, only car, kept on drive, club member. £106 for a 42yo, full NCB, clean licence, club member, 3000 miles, second car, garaged. Quotes from Firebond (07000 347326) for a 3000 Mk III, value £16,000, based in P'boro.

WHICH ARE THE OWNERS CLUBS?
❖ Austin-Healey Club: £30pa plus £5 joining fee, 2200 members (all models inc Frogeyes), monthly A4 glossy colour/b&w magazine plus Midland and Southern region newsletters.

WHO ARE THE SPECIALISTS?
Service, restoration, competition preparation
❖ JME Healeys, Leamington Spa (01926 425038)
❖ Orchard Restorations, E Sussex (01435 812374)
❖ Rawles Engineering, Hants (01420 23212)

Parts, service, restoration
❖ John Chatham Cars, Bristol (0117 942 4154)
❖ Murray Scott-Nelson, N Yorks (01723 361227)
❖ Stevenson's Garage, Leics (01509 412469)
❖ Denis Welch, Staffs (01543 472214)

Service, restoration
❖ Ellis Restorations, Northants (01604 755413)

New parts
❖ AH Spares, Warks (01926 817181)
❖ SC Parts Group, W Sussex (01293 547841)

New and used parts
❖ Austin-Healey Associates, W Sussex (0208 393 8831)

Engines
❖ Engine Machining Services, Notts (01909 482649)

WHAT ABOUT SPARES' PRICES?
Where two figures are separated by a forward slash, the first is for a 100-4 model, the next for a 3000.

DIY engine rebuild: £700 (4-cyl)/£1000 (6-cyl)
Front wing, steel: £370/£287
Rear wing, steel: £241-£276/ £241
Wire wheel, 48 or 60 spoke: £91
Windscreen: £81/£80-£87
Instruments, recon exch, each: £64-£80
New hood, vynide: £117/£117-£141
Exhaust system, stainless: £177/£270-£399
Exhaust system, mild steel: £88/£117-£158
Pair of shocks, recon exch, front: £82
Pair of shocks, recon exch, rear: £65

CHEAP
Oil filter: £4
Lower door skin: £32
Carpet set: £88/£105

STEEP
Clutch kit: £140-£150/£152-£156
Retrim kit, seats and doors: £646/£916
Rear wing, aluminium: £317-£350/£317
Prices from AH Spares, rounded to the nearest £, include VAT.

ARE THERE ANY PARTS YOU JUST CAN'T GET? New windscreen frames for all models, and door handles for Mk IIIs.

WILL THEY RUN ON UNLEADED FUEL? Not without fitting hardened valve seats or using an FBHVC-approved additive. With either option, Jonathan Everard recommends Super rather than regular Unleaded. No ignition timing change is necessary.

WHERE ARE THE IDENTIFYING MARKS? Very early 100s had a white plastic plate in the footwell just ahead of the door, giving the car or chassis number. This number was also stamped on a plate fixed to a chassis rail alongside the engine. The engine had its own number stamped on an alloy plate on top of the block.

From August 1954, Austin changed to using a single number for both chassis and engine, which now appeared on a plate fixed to the bulkhead. The 100-6 followed this system, but since the engine block was different, its identity plate moved to a ledge under the exhaust manifold. When the 3000 was introduced, the identity plates stayed in roughly the same locations, but engines reverted to having their own numbering system.

WHICH IS THE BEST BOOK?
Austin-Healey 100/100-6/3000 Restoration Guide by Gary Anderson and Roger Moment, MBI, ISBN 0 7603 0673 7.

RUNNING GEAR

LIKE THE engine and drivetrain, the 'Healey's suspension is based on that of contemporary Austin saloons. Up front are double wishbones and coil springs, plus an anti-roll bar; to the rear is a live axle suspended on leaf springs, with a Panhard rod to control side sway. The system was basically unchanged throughout production, except for the 3000 Mk III Phase II, on which the Panhard rod was deleted in favour of twin radius arms. The bushes in these can produce creaking noises.

Talking of bushes, Jonathan feels that standard rubber suspension bushes are fine for road use, and he'd only recommend urethane types for competition. Likewise, standard springs and shock absorbers are perfectly satisfactory, although stiffer front shocks will help sharpen the handling. Jonathan has noticed a problem with new rear springs, which make the back of the car sit excessively high. 'The makers claim they are to original specification, but I feel something has been lost along the way.'

All cars had durable cam-and-peg steering boxes. If the steering feels excessively loose on the move, try jacking the front of the car up and rocking each wheel top and bottom; it could be that the kingpins are worn. They need greasing at every service.

Brakes were all-drum on the 100, with front discs introduced for the 3000. A servo became standard for the 3000 Mk III — it had been optional for the Mk II — but the non-assisted system should work perfectly well, with good 'feel' through the pedal. Indeed, Jonathan reckons that it can pay to fit a slightly smaller brake master cylinder if converting a car to servo assistance, to prevent the servo masking all feedback.

It's rare to see a 'Healey with disc wheels, although they were supposedly standard fittings. In practice, most owners paid the extra for wires. These should be painted, not chromed, and not just for aesthetic reasons: the chrome plating adds weight to each wheel, which has an effect on handling, especially if wider-than-standard tyres are fitted. Anything wider than 185 section will

> **'Wire wheels should be painted, not chromed, and not just for aesthetic reasons: chrome plating adds considerable weight'**

affect the car's stability in a straight line.

'Some Indian-sourced wires during the Eighties were not properly round, but recent British-made wheels shouldn't give any problems,' says Jonathan. 'However, many tyre-fitting depots don't have appropriate balancing gear, so out-of-balance wheels are the most likely source of vibration on the move. Check, though, that the wheel spinners are done up tightly. People don't like to hit them hard because it damages the chrome!'

TRIM & BRIGHTWORK

'HEALEY soft trim was a mixture of leather, Vynide, carpet and Armacord — the last-named being a kind of ribbed, jute-backed vinyl typically used to cover boot floors. Leather was restricted to the seat facings and was changed to Ambla for the Mk III, although today's owners usually go for all-leather if a retrim is required.

You can buy trim kits and seat covers, but Jonathan doesn't like them much. You'll get better results by having a professional make trim from scratch, he says. That's partly because cars tend to vary slightly from each other, so, for example, standardised door panels won't always fit properly. Similarly, new seat cushions can feel over-stuffed, 'like sitting on a brick,' as Jonathan puts it.

Both two- and four-seater 'Healeys had detachable hoodframes and hoods, which stowed behind the seats. The convertible 3000, however — introduced during Mk II production, and becoming the Mk III — had a much more convenient hood, which could be raised and lowered from inside the car. Originally these hoods were made from Everflex vinyl, but misguided owners sometimes specify fancy mohair or double-duck material instead. Being thicker, it makes the hood harder to fold away.

Only the 3000 Mk III had a full-width wood-veneered dash; earlier cars had sculpted binnacles that were painted (100) or covered in Vynide (100-6 and 3000). New instruments mostly aren't available but can be bought secondhand and reconditioned.

WHICH MODEL TO BUY?

'HEALEYS may be simple cars but they're not cheap. That could explain why the majority of buyers prefer the 3000 Mk III, which at least gives the illusion of luxury. After all, if you're spending E-type money on something that has Austin in its name, you want as much bang for your buck as you can get. The Mk III has wind-up windows, a decent hood and more power than its predecessors.

At the other end of the scale is the 100 — only four cylinders, slightly shorter wheelbase, not much in the way of trim, but a good power-to-weight ratio. Its exhaust note may not be quite as stirring as the BJ8's, but you could argue it's the purer car.

In between lie the many and various six-cylinder models. The weight of the earlier sixes tended to offset their extra power, but none will disappoint. Your best bet is to forget about the badge on the nose and place condition above everything else. Buying a sound car in the first place is the most reliable way there is of curing Big 'Healey phobia.

THANKS TO

CHRIS CLACK, who owns the superb 3000 Mk III shown in our photos. The car was restored by JME Healeys 17 years ago. **(STOP)**

HOTLINKS
■ website: austinhealey.com

SPOT THE ROT

Four- and six-cyl engines are robust, but check electrical wiring while bonnet's up.

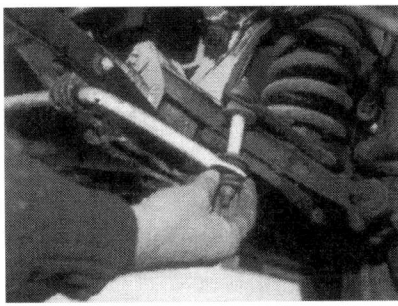

Examine bushes for perishing, but urethane replacements aren't necessary for road use.

It's vital that chassis legs are sound and straight: kinks suggest accident damage.

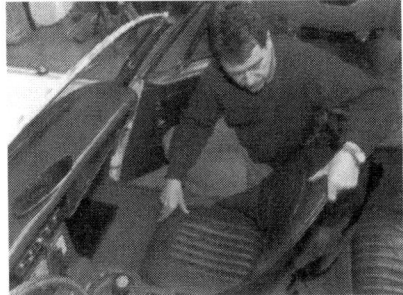

Patinated original seats are a plus point; new ones tend to be hard and unyielding.

With wire wheels, if there is a clonk when you're reversing, inspect the hub splines.

£15-20k trad classic Austin-Healey 3000

From top: badge promises big-hearted character and lusty performance; gorgeous shape set off by two-tone scheme; charismatic 'six'; 2+2 offers more space and lower prices; hood is a pain to erect; smart wires

FACTFILE

Sold/number built 1956-'68/ 57,362 **Construction** steel chassis, steel/aluminium body **Engine** all-iron, pushrod 2912cc 'six', with triple SUs **Max power** 130bhp @ 4750rpm **Max torque** 225lb ft @ 4500rpm **Transmission** four-speed manual, overdrive on third and top, driving rear wheels **Suspension: front** wishbones, coils, a/r bar **rear** live axle, leaf springs, Panhard rod; lever arm dampers f/r **Steering** cam and peg **Brakes** discs front, drums rear, with servo **0-60mph** 11.9 secs **Top speed** 113mph **Mpg** 17 **Price new** £1403 **Now** from £18,000

TROUBLE SPOTS

1 Check for excessive venting and oil leaks on high-mileage engines; hot oil pressure should be at least 30psi. An unleaded head is £1350
2 Front shroud and rear deck are aluminium: check for dents, plus corrosion at join with steel wings
3 Chassis can twist in an accident. A new chassis is £4230 from Denis Welch (www.bighealey.co.uk)

OWNER'S VIEW

Mike and Mel Ward have had their '58 100/6 for more than 30 years. "I fell in love with Healeys when I was 11," says Mike. "I saw one in a neighbour's drive and longed for it – they're just so typically British!" He rebuilt the car 23 years ago, doing all the mechanics himself, and says the simple design makes them easy to maintain: "The big commitment is the time it takes."

THE RIVALS

SUNBEAM TIGER
Sold/no built 1964-'68/7066
0-60mph 9.5 secs **Top speed** 117mph **Mpg** 17
Price new £1471
Now from £17k
Ultimate 'poor man's Cobra', with stonking pace but a bit less balance.

TRIUMPH TR5
Sold/no built 1967-'68/2947
0-60mph 8.8 secs **Top speed** 120mph **Mpg** 20
Price new £1268
Now from £18k
Straight-six pace in pretty Michelotti body: rarest and most desired TR.

ALFA ROMEO GIULIETTA
Sold/no built 1956-'62/2796
0-60mph 14.1 secs **Top speed** 112 **Mpg** 26
Price new £2619
Now from £18k
Twin-cam and Pinin Farina styling make Giulietta the typical Italian sports car.

The sound of a brawny 'six' and that eye-catching oval grille can only mean one thing: a Big Healey. Austin-Healeys are many a petrolhead's archetypical image of what a true British sports car is all about. And it's easy to see why: Healeys are no-nonsense cars, boasting simple mechanicals, attractive styling and plenty of performance, thanks to their big four- or six-cylinder engines.

What's more, they sound fantastic: a deep, throaty timbre that's more akin to the noise of a WW2 fighter than a car. I learnt to drive in my late Dad's 100/6, so I guess I'm biased, but I'll never forget the noise it made nor the attention it got at the school gates.

Drawbacks? Early models (pre-'62) don't have much in the way of creature comforts, and any serious rain will have you soaked as you struggle to bolt on the clumsy side-screens and erect the primitive top. And if it doesn't rain, you'll soon discover why Healeys have a reputation for chronic cockpit heat-soak, thanks to an exhaust that passes a few millimetres below the floor. The steering can be heavy, too – as can the gearchange – while ground clearance is all but non-existent.

But that's all part of what makes them so utterly characterful – even addictive – when you slip behind the big wheel, legs outstretched and buttocks just inches off the road.

Another great thing about Healeys is that, thanks to a 12-year production run, there's a model to suit most tastes and wallets today. Early 100/6s (1956-'58) are the most affordable: £15-17k should land you a decent example privately. With Austin's 2.6-litre 'six' in place of the 100's 'four', the 100/6 was the first of the 2+2 Healeys. With just 102bhp (117bhp from 1957), performance isn't scintillating but it'll still top the ton. Find another £3k or so and you might bag its replacement, the 3000 MkI, which boasted disc brakes and 124bhp.

The later the car, the more comfort it will offer – but you'll have to pay for it. A 1962-on MkIIa (£20-25k) will have wind-up windows, a curved 'screen and a walnut-veneered dashboard, while the most desirable are MkIIIs – in particular the post-'64 'Phase 2' cars, with their improved ground clearance and revised rear suspension. One of the latter will set you back £30-35k, but its 148bhp means it has performance to match.

This MkII combines the later vertical grille with the prettier lines of non-wind-up-window models. With just three owners from new, it's been extensively rebuilt and could be yours for £21,950 from Oakfields (01256 760256; www.oakfields.com). Just add a plough-man's lunch for a truly British experience this summer. **GH**

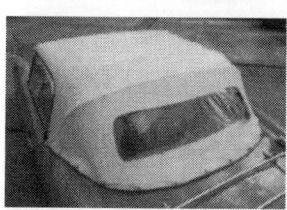

Austin Healey 3000

The quintessential British sports car makes for raucous, primitive fun — or does it?
A rain-soaked weekend in a MkI provides the answer

WORDS SAM DAWSON PHOTOGRAPHY MICHAEL BAILIE

Driving an Austin-Healey 3000, we're told, is like scrumming down in rugby: macho, brutal, uncivilised – and that's just the steering. All in all it's a tough experience to be approached with trepidation... if the clichés are true.

I'm pondering all this as I guide a 1960 3000 MkI down Hampshire lanes on half-throttle, gearbox in fourth, the fingers of my right hand loosely gripping the wood-rimmed Moto-Lita wheel. Far from the set-in-concrete feel, the unassisted cam-and-peg steering is actually light and faithful, a world away from the elbow-dislocating medieval torture implement of legend.

The glove-soft leather seats lack belts or support above my lower back, but they're at just the right angle for relaxation and there's plenty of legroom. The live rear axle, far from being suspended hard enough to shatter your teeth over speed bumps, is acceptably taut on its semi-elliptic leaf springs; you do feel the bumps – it is a sports car after all – but its springing and damping rates stop just short of harshness.

Then there's the windscreen. Most British roadsters have low-cut screens, filling your hair and eyes with flies and grit, but the 3000's is tall enough to deflect the wind over your head, leaving a pleasant breeze flicking in around your fingers.

The Italians have a word for a car like this: *barchetta*, meaning little boat. Elegant, tapered body lines mimic a speedboat's, as do the bicep-high scuttle and minimalist dashboard. They can be quick or sluggish, extravagant or affordable, but they're all pretty, curvy and delicate. As sunlight flashes on chrome, I feel on the edge of a revelation: despite its macho reputation, is the Austin-Healey 3000 in touch with its feminine side? Does it have cosmopolitan, Continental tastes?

It's only fleeting. As a roundabout approaches, I push the gym-workout clutch, blip the throttle, and reach for the Brunel ironwork gearlever. It feels as though the selector forks originated in a Victorian railway points mechanism. It's no Alfa Spider.

Heavier-duty engineering emerges with higher revs. The throttle pedal has a distinct two-stage operation, as the Austin Westminster-derived three-litre pushrod straight-six disgorges a sudden dollop of torque beyond 3000rpm. Coaxed into its power band, the entire car erupts in a very mechanical, very British cacophony of clattering rockers, uncouth exhaust blare and the kind of breezy transmission whine you hear from lorries in Fifties Ealing films. It keeps up with modern traffic too, sitting at 70mph without straining.

And then the rain starts. I pull into a supermarket car park and begin the hood-erecting ritual. It's odd that Italian roadsters designed for sunny markets have such efficient hood designs, while in wet Britain we prefer rather more arcane arrangements. To extract the hood irons I have to remove the backrests from the tiny rear seats (in this BT7 – the BN7 had only front seats), wrestle the frame from its cramped cove and bolt it into the B-posts. Then you scrabble around in the boot for the hood, unfurl it over the top and hurry round the car fastening eight press-studs and clamps.

You're wet through by the time the car is covered and the first thing to greet you back in the driver's seat is a dribble of rainwater down your right leg from the side of the hood. The boot seal isn't very effective either, and luggage space is dominated by the spare wheel and tool roll, so all your chattels have to squeeze into the edges underneath the bootlid flange. If it rains, they get wet.

Ignition is satisfyingly ritualistic. Turn the key and before hitting the starter button savour the fuel pump's eager tapping and the hum of the live electrics, accompanied by a dull glow from dashboard bulbs.

Progress isn't quite as smooth in the rain. Tyre availability has improved now that Avon 185/70 R15s are back in production, but they still slide on wet roads. It's entertaining if no-one else is around, with rear-end breakaway happening at a controllably progressive rate and counter-steering channelling your inner Pat Moss.

However, on the M3, battling spray with a combination of single-speed wipers and candle-like headlights, the front end tramlining

Quintessential British
sports car looks and
macho image make the Big
'Healey one of the most
popular of all classics

Cockpit offers plenty of
front legroom plus comfy
seats and unrivalled
visibility – just sit back and
enjoy the experience

Tall windscreen gives reasonable protection. Extracting and erecting the hood and frame takes time

Spare wheel and tools don't leave much luggage space in the boot

2912cc BMC C-series straight-six is robust and has excellent parts availability

and wandering as the tyres snag patches of standing water, it feels potentially lethal. Staying in the inside lane at 60mph is no solution either, with face-level deluges flying off truck wheels. The power produced by the sudden jerk of acceleration on the long-travel throttle can overwhelm the rear tyres in corners, making crowded wet roundabouts a liability.

Other drivers don't spot the little indicator lights flashing at the base of the tail, so I change lanes like a motorcyclist, throwing lifesaver glances over my shoulder to make sure the lane is clear.

Mercifully, the rain abates as I stop on the outskirts of Basingstoke to pick a friend up for lunch. She doesn't know much about cars, but she does appreciate classic style and is dazzled by the 'Healey. At first she laughs at the notion that something so primitive is still road-legal, but once the car's in top gear and heading down an open A-road towards a coffee shop she says: 'I get the appeal now – it's just about having fun, isn't it?'

And that's the whole point of a car like the Austin-Healey 3000 – early ones especially, before the MkIIa gained a plush luxury interior and wind-up windows. Everyday life with it is full of minor hardships, especially in bad weather when it will soak and freeze you, but you put up with that because the blustery exhaust note, unapologetically trucklike 124bhp straight-six and entertaining handling combine to spread a big lingering grin across your face.

You could say the same of so many hardy British pastimes. Rugby, camping and sailing spring to mind. Rival cars may be easier to live with, but their charisma suffers. The 'Healey, on the other hand, is all about character – that of the car and the one it builds in you. You're a better person for driving one. **CC**

Thanks to: Rawles Motorsport, Hampshire (01420 23212, www. rawlesmotorsport.co.uk); Orchard Restorations, East Sussex (01435 812374, www.orchardrestorations.co.uk)

NEED TO KNOW

- **What to pay**
Sound but scruffy MkIs are sold privately for as little as £20k, with mint examples coming in at £30k-40k.
Triple-carburettor MkIIs and plusher MkIIIs start at £25k, with restored or excellent original cars fetching as much as £50k at specialist dealerships.
- **Running costs**
'Healeys are fundamentally strong and uncomplicated: expect to pay around £400 for annual servicing and maintenance, but keep a contingency fund of £1000 to fight corrosion.
- **Top deal-breakers**
Rust in sills and doors.
Paint blistering by the chrome beading on top of a front wing is a sign of corrosion between the steel wing and aluminium shroud.
Overheating caused by a blocked radiator and damaged exhaust muffler.
- **Will it fit in your garage?**
It should do: a Big 'Healey is 4 metres x 1.5 metres.
- **Availability**
Pretty good: this is one of the world's most popular classics, frequently for sale both privately and at general classic and specialist dealerships.
- **Useful improvements**
185/70 R15 tyres are best for grip; halogen headlights improve visibility.
- **Parts availability**
Everything is readily available and easy to find.

1959-68 AUSTIN-HEALEY 3000

- **Engine** 2912cc, in-line six-cylinder, ohv, two SU HS6 (MkI), three SU HS6 (MkII) or two SU HD8 (MkIII) carburettors • **Power and torque** 124bhp @ 4600rpm – 148bhp @ 5250rpm; 175lb ft @ 3000rpm – 165lb ft @ 3500rpm • **Transmission** Four-speed manual, rear-wheel drive, optional overdrive • **Suspension** Front: independent, coil springs, wishbones, lever-arm dampers, anti-roll bar. Rear: live axle, semi-elliptic leaf springs, lever-arm dampers, Panhard rod • **Brakes** Discs front, drums rear • **Weight** 1139-1180kg (2513-2604lb) • **Performance** Top speed 106-111mph; 0-60mph: 11.5-10sec • **Fuel consumption** 21-35mpg

OFFICIAL TECHNICAL BOOKS

Brooklands Technical Books has been formed to supply owners, restorers and professional repairers with official factory literature.

Model	Original Part No.	ISBN
Workshop Manuals		
Austin-Healey 100 BN1 & BN2	97H997D	9780907073925
Austin-Healey 100/6 & 3000	AKD1179	9780948207471
(100/6 - BN4, BN6, 3000 MK. 1, 2, 3 - BN7, BT7, BJ7 & BJ8)		
Austin-Healey Sprite Mk. 1 Frogeye	AKD4884	9781855201262
Austin-Healey Sprite Mk. 2, Mk. 3 & Mk. 4 and	AKD4021	9781855201255
MG Midget Mk. 1, Mk. 2 & Mk. 3		
Parts Catalogues / Service Parts Lists		
Austin-Healey 100 BN1 & BN2	1050 Edition 3	9781783180363
Austin-Healey 100/6 BN4	AKD1423	9781783180493
Austin-Healey 100/6 BN6	AKD855 Ed.2	9781783180486
Austin-Healey 3000 Mk. 1 and Mk. 2 (BN7 & BT7)	AKD1151 Ed.5	9781783180370
Mk. 1 BN7 & BT7 Car no. 101 to 13750,		
Mk. 2 BN7 Car no. 13751 to 18888,		
Mk. 2 BT7 Car no. 13751 to 19853		
Austin-Healey 3000 Mk. 2 and Mk. 3 (BJ7 & BJ8)	AKD 3523 & AKD 3524	9781783180387
BJ7 Mk. 2 Car no. 17551 to 25314 and		
BJ8 Mk. 3 Car no. 25315 to 43026		
Austin-Healey Sprite Mk. 1 & Mk. 2 and	AKD 3566 & AKD 3567	9781783180509
MG Midget Mk. 1		
Austin-Healey Sprite Mk. 3 & Mk. 4 and	AKD 3513 & AKD 3514	9781783180554
MG Midget Mk. 2 & Mk. 3 (Mechanical & Body Edition 1969)		
Austin-Healey Sprite Mk. 3 & Mk. 4 and	AKM 0036	9780948207419
MG Midget Mk. 2 & Mk. 3 (Feb 1977 Edition)		
Handbooks		
Austin-Healey 100	97H996E	9781869826352
Austin-Healey 100/6	97H996H	9781870642903
Austin-Healey 3000 Mk 1 & 2	AKD3915A	9781869826369
Austin-Healey 3000 Mk 3	AKD4094B	9781869826376
Austin-Healey Sprite Mk 1 'Frogeye'	97H1583A	9780948207945

Also Available

Austin-Healey 100/6 & 3000 Mk. 1, 2 & 3 Owners Workshop Manual	9781783180455
Austin-Healey Sprite Mk. 1, 2, 3 & 4	9781855201255
MG Midget 1, 2, 3 & 1500 1958-1980 Owners Workshop Manual Glovebox Edition	
Austin-Healey Sprite Mk. 1, 2, 3 & 4	9781783180332
MG Midget 1, 2, 3 & 1500 1958-1980 Owners Workshop Manual	

Carburetters

SU Carburetters Tuning Tips & Techniques	9781855202559

Restoration Guide

Restoring Sprite & Midgets	9781855205987

Road Test Series

Austin-Healey 100 & 100/6 Gold Portfolio 1952-1959	9781855200487
Austin-Healey 3000 Road Test Portfolio	9791783180394
Austin-Healey Frogeye Sprite Road Test Portfolio 1958-1961	9781783180530
Austin-Healey Sprite Gold Portfolio 1958-1971	9781855203716

From Austin-Healey specialists, Amazon or, in case of difficulty, from the distributor.

Brooklands Books Ltd., P.O. Box 146, Cobham, Surrey,
KT11 1LG, England, UK
Phone: +44 (0) 1932 865051   info@brooklands-books.com
www.brooklands-books.com

www.brooklandsbooks.com

27360626R00090

Printed in Great Britain
by Amazon